Martha Stone Hubbell

The Shady Side; Or, Life in a Country Parsonage

Vol. I

Martha Stone Hubbell

The Shady Side; Or, Life in a Country Parsonage
Vol. I

ISBN/EAN: 9783337054731

Printed in Europe, USA, Canada, Australia, Japan

Cover: Foto ©ninafisch / pixelio.de

More available books at **www.hansebooks.com**

MEMOIRS

OF THE

LIFE AND WRITINGS

OF

SIR RICHARD STEELE,

SOLDIER, DRAMATIST, ESSAYIST, AND PATRIOT,

WITH

HIS CORRESPONDENCE, AND NOTICES OF HIS CONTEMPORARIES,
THE WITS AND STATESMEN OF QUEEN ANNE'S TIME.

BY

HENRY R. MONTGOMERY,

AUTHOR OF "THOMAS MOORE: HIS LIFE, WRITINGS, AND CONTEMPORARIES,"
"ISAAC BICKERSTAFF," ETC.

TWO VOLUMES.

VOL. I.

EDINBURGH:
WILLIAM P. NIMMO.
1865.

[*All rights reserved.*]

TO

THE LORD DUFFERIN AND CLANDEBOYE,

ONE OF H.M. SECRETARIES OF STATE FOR INDIA, LORD-LIEUTENANT OF DOWN, ETC.,

WHO,

AS A DESCENDANT OF

SHERIDAN'S

(A NAME IN WHICH, WITH RARE GOOD FORTUNE, GENIUS HAS BEEN HEREDITARY,)

AND ONE

WHO HAS HIMSELF ACQUIRED APPLAUSE AS A MEMBER OF THE REPUBLIC OF LETTERS,

IS A FITTING SPONSOR OF A

WORK ILLUSTRATIVE OF THE LIFE AND AGE OF

STEELE,

These Volumes are Inscribed,

WITH ONLY THE FEAR THAT THEY MAY NOT BE FOUND WORTHY OF

THE FAVOUR SO KINDLY ACCORDED,

BY HIS LORDSHIP'S

OBLIGED AND VERY OBEDIENT HUMBLE SERVANT,

THE AUTHOR.

PREFACE.

> "See nations slowly wise, and meanly just,
> To buried merit raise the tardy bust."
> —JOHNSON.

THE present work is something of an experiment. It is an attempt to reproduce in some form, however slight and imperfect, the age of Queen Anne through the medium of a life of Steele, who was perhaps more variously mixed up with the men and the times than any other person of that era. Two or three names—Prior, St John, Atterbury, Arbuthnot, and Defoe—have necessarily been omitted, as no fair opportunity occurred, without going out of the way, of noticing them, except in incidental allusions. How far the plan or execution may be deserving of approval must be left to readers and critics to determine.

Our age is honourably distinguished by the elaborate tributes it has paid—in the shape of biographies—to literary reputations which, to the discredit of their own times, were passed over with trifling or unworthy notice. The number of such which some of these have received may be taken as among the most unequivocal evidences of permanent excellence. The biography of Goldsmith has, in our own times, been written again and again—most elaborately by Prior, most eloquently by Forster,[*] and lastly by the charming and graceful pen of Washington Irving, though perhaps not in his happiest style. The lives of Pope and Swift have also been often written. Various memorials had previously existed of Addison; but his biography has only recently been written for the first time by Miss Aiken, on any extensive scale commensurate with his reputation, and was followed by the masterly review of Macaulay. Recently we have had elaborate lives of Sterne and Bolingbroke, besides others of inferior reputation, the most inconsiderable of whom are, to say the least, as fair a subject of two volumes as the hero of a sensation novel. Steele's biography is now for the first time attempted on a similar scale. The writer would willingly have left the task to others who might have done more justice to the subject; but finding none disposed to undertake it, and

---

[*] This, as well as a great portion of the present work, was written previous to the appearance of the "Essay on Steele" by this distinguished writer, the allusions to which were subsequently added.

wishing to see such a work, which he considered a desideratum in our literature, he was obliged, as Mr Leigh Hunt said on a similar occasion, to undertake it himself. This surely ought not to have been so with one who was the founder of a new and brilliant era in our literature, and whose luminous wake has been followed by many of the most classic names of succeeding times—by Johnson, Goldsmith, Coleman, Canning, Hawkesworth, Chesterfield, Moore, Walpole, Cumberland, Mackenzie, Franklin, Irving, and others.

The reputation of Steele has long been obscured in a great degree by that of his eminent friend and coadjutor Addison.* Many reasons might be assigned for the superior place which Addison has held in popular estimation. Steele himself, perhaps, in his own generous nature and his characteristic self-depreciation, may be considered to have laid the first stone of the superstructure by which he has been overshadowed—in the so oft-repeated graceful and grateful compliment he paid his illustrious friend, when, in allusion to his timely and invaluable literary co-operation, he compares himself to a distressed prince who calls in the aid of a powerful

* Chalmers, in the annotated edition of the Essayists, speaks justly of the "envy which appears in some degree to have pursued him (Steele) to the grave, and of the little that has been attempted in justice to the memory of a man to whom the world is so eminently indebted."

neighbour, and finds himself undone by his ally. In this pleasantry, so creditable to his humility and gratitude, he has been taken rather too literally at his word, as is often the fate of the over-candid with matter-of-fact people; and though the remark has been so often repeated, ostensibly to his credit, it has come to lose half its grace by the evidently covert design it has been made to serve, in making him the victim of his own generous spirit, and wounding him with a shaft drawn from his own quiver, like the unhappy eagle that perceived the arrow rankling in its side to have been feathered from its own wing. Coleridge, however, has expressed his opinion emphatically against the justice to himself of Steele's remark.

The contributions of Steele, too, in the literary partnership which so happily subsisted between these distinguished friends, were less elaborately planned and systematic than those of Addison, and not unfrequently their finish of style overlooked. There was in fact more of the gipsy about the genius of Steele; but if his contributions lack the traces of the midnight oil in the same degree, they claim at least the superiority in freshness and fervour.

The personal habits, also, of Steele were devoid of the fastidiousness which characterised those of his friend, and

Preface. xi

exhibited, indeed, like his writings, a careless irregularity, which has tended to his disadvantage in the general estimate. Addison was of a serene, cool, phlegmatic temperament; and though subject to one of Steele's worst weaknesses, prudently managed to keep the indications of it in the background; whilst in the other, who was all softness, warmth, and impulse, from a more excitable temperament, and a censurable disregard to appearances, it became more a subject of scandal. But with defects thus on the surface, he had eminently what Byron has celebrated as that

> "Something so warm, so sublime in the core
> Of an Irishman's heart." *

Another cause, perhaps, has been the coterie reputation of Addison, which has adhered to him as a tradition. It is sometimes said that a man's reputation in private and among his intimates is the true test of his merit. But this appears very questionable, at least as a universal rule. How much has *prestige* of some kind or other to do with the estimate we all unconsciously form of men.† How seldom is it the man himself as he

---

* "The Irish Avatar."

† A particular instance may be referred to. Sidney Smith, who may be presumed to be at least as good a judge of humour as even the highest of the depreciators of Steele, selected as an illustration of that faculty in his "Lectures on Moral Philosophy," a passage from one of Steele's early comedies, of which he was a great admirer, but was inclined to suspect that Addison, though then abroad, had had a hand in it.

really is, and not rather something connected with him, on which we commonly form our judgment. How would Goldsmith do, for example, to be judged by the general estimate of those who met him in society? He was little regarded by those who listened (and justly so) to Johnson as an oracle. The latter had a great club reputation, yet how few comparatively now read his works, whilst Goldsmith has been increasing in reputation ever since, and is now recognised as the better and more original writer.

The aim of these remarks is not to depreciate either Addison or Johnson, but by the statement of some general considerations of a suggestive nature, and without forcing any dictum on the reader, to endeavour to free his judgment from the bias of prejudice and prepossession.

How often, too, does it happen that some men are gifted with adventitious qualities which give them greatly the advantage over others of equal if not greater merit, and which get mixed up in the general estimate of them. This good fortune Addison joined to his great merits. In addition to his reputation as a writer of Latin verse, he had great personal advantages, great dignity of demeanour, and had attained to an elevated official and social position. These advantages, with immeasurably less merit than his, would have done wonders. As long as the world lasts there will always be many, if not *the* many, who will estimate art above nature, as we often see acting have an effect on the spectator that the reality would fail to produce. Others are wholly deficient in such adventitious qualities, and their merits show to proportionable disadvantage. With regard to the particular case of Addison, when not among strangers, but surrounded by his intimates, he had the most charming flow of converse, and of that delicate, quiet, subtle humour in which his writings abound.

The last circumstance, though not the least, that may be referred to as contributing to the depreciation of Steele was the unparalleled scurrility to which he unfortunately exposed himself by the ardour of his politics. When we find the treatment he experienced from Swift, after his estrangement from him,—when, as Johnson says, he thought him "no longer entitled to decency,"—we need be the less surprised at any foul abuse from any "under spur-leather," "scrub instrument of mischief," or "hang-dog instrument," as Swift described those whom he employed, after he had found that the character of the literary bravo was not without its disadvantages. These, in addition to personal abuse, directly attempted to assign the merits of their joint publications to Addison, who, with greater prudence, avoided exposing himself to their malignity, but for some of whose papers Steele had been exposed to their attacks. It is indeed much to be regretted that he should by his rash political zeal have sacrificed the enviable literary reputation he had previously enjoyed by rushing into troubled waters, and having exhausted upon him all the resources of literary ruffianism.

The question as to the relative merits of Steele and Addison was a very unnecessary and illiberal one ever to have raised, considering that it was to Steele the world owed Addison, and that nothing ever exceeded the unbounded expression of admiration and freedom from envy which he displayed towards his friend. But since it has been unwisely and ungenerously raised, and is not to be evaded, it becomes a question of authority. It is with the greatest diffidence that the writer finds himself forced into opposition, on the ground either of the personal or literary depreciation of Steele, to two such distinguished writers as Lord Macaulay and Mr Thackeray, in his admiration of whom he yields to none, and this feeling of reluctance is enhanced by the consideration that they are two on whose graves the turf is scarcely yet green—but neither can he forget that it is in vindication of one whose memory he considers has been cruelly and unjustly used. In some cases an attempt has been made not only to assert the precedence of Addison, but entirely to sacrifice the claims of Steele to his superior merit. How, then, stand the authorities? We have such men as Coleridge, Hazlitt, Leigh Hunt, and Charles Lamb, in spite of the traditional *prestige* of Addison, giving their independent judgments emphatically in favour of Steele. We have not included Mr Forster, because he has taken the invidious element out of the question, and narrowed it to an assertion of the positive merits of Steele—the others had asserted his precedence. In opposition to these we have the oblique inuendoes of Tickell, to which Steele himself administered a sufficient refutation, the "braying" of a Hurd, and the dictum of a Macaulay. We cannot but think, therefore, that the balance of authority continues to rest on the side of Steele.

With regard to Mr Thackeray, he is by no means to be considered as a positive opponent—but it is to be regretted that in some of his writings, particularly his "Esmond," he should have lent himself, probably without deliberately intending it, to what certainly tends to the depreciation of Steele. Though in his "Humourists" expressing strong personal good feeling towards him, calling him his "favourite," (and indeed he has treated him in a way not unfrequently the fate of favourites,) yet for the sake of being graphic and dramatic, he has, in the former work, drawn rather a caricature than a portrait, which would give the general reader the impression of his being a sort of Captain Costigan, being, at best, but a small part of the truth, and almost all that was objectionable. In this instance, Mr Thackeray has reversed the plan by which the artist who painted Hannibal gained so much credit, and has given us a profile indeed, but with the blind side alone conspicuously displayed. Though Addison was open to the very same reflection, with the difference previously referred to, yet with what different consideration is he treated? In his "Humourists," again, after dwelling on some peculiarities of the times, by way of excuse for his favourite Steele, he gives a comic description, very entertaining and good-natured, no doubt, of all Steele's shortcomings. He then gives Dennis's vulgar and wanton abuse, or "portrait," as he is pleased to term it, picked out of literary dustholes, in the large type of his text, telling us that though it was the work of a cross-grained old critic, who was no man's friend, it bore "a dreadful resemblance," and then thrusts Steele's reply, which he acknowledges "discovers a great deal of humour," which is certainly more than could justly be said of the provocation, into the small letter of a footnote, and concludes by bidding us think kindly of Steele. Well might he say, "Alas for poor Dick Steele," when his friends can find no better way of recommending their "favourite" than by holding up as a portrait of "dreadful resemblance" a farrago of low and vulgar nonsense, and recommending him to our kindly remembrance by a comic sketch of his failings, which, if not buried with him, or covered with a veil, might at least be touched with a delicate hand, and cast into the background of the picture. Steele's services surely deserve some better return than this.

Both he and Lord Macaulay have thought proper, moreover, (the former in his "Virginians,") to represent Steele in the light of a hanger-on of Addison's. This would be much more applicable to Tickell or Budgell, and is wounding him through his best feelings, and degrading the warmth of his affectionate attachment to his friend. But notwithstanding the greatness of his regard for Addison, nothing could be more independent than the bearing he always maintained towards him in the main, even in cases where we may fairly think he would have derived advantage from the counsel of his more prudent friend. He started from college, we may well believe, without consulting him; he set up and discontinued the *Tatler* without making him privy to it, and even incurred the

b

censure of Swift for so doing. He opposed him in public controversy, even after he knew that Addison was his opponent, and carried the day against the unconstitutional Peerage Bill which his friend was unfortunately induced to support. That he took goodnaturedly Addison's playing upon him a little, as Pope stated to Spence, may be quite true, but we see in the passage of arms between them in the discussion above referred to, that he would *not* take anything derogatory, even from him, without resenting it.

With regard to the strictures of Lord Macaulay, unjust, unwarrantable, and uncalled for, as the writer conceives them to be, and illustrative of the occasional recklessness of assertion and undue strength of language of that distinguished writer, if anything could mitigate our regret, it would be their having called forth the masterly vindication of Steele by Mr Forster. Nor are they the first examples we have had, to prove that even the highest ability and character are not always to be implicitly relied on as invariable guarantees of critical discretion, as in the case of Johnson's depreciation of Milton and Gray and his elevation of Savage. We also know that Voltaire in writing, and Byron in conversation, used the most depreciating expressions towards Shakespeare. But Milton and Gray and Shakespeare remain much as

Preface. xix

before, and so we believe will Steele. Brilliant and ardent writers are apt sometimes to be carried away and misled by these very qualities, and when under the influence of prejudice and prepossession are sometimes guilty of injustice that hurts themselves even more than their victims.

Unfortunately in such cases the influence of writers like Thackeray and Macaulay does not end with themselves; but the jeering tone of the one and the invidious spirit of the other are adopted and exaggerated by inferior scribes, who, wanting their finely-tempered weapons and skilful hands, mangle their subjects in their critical dissection. The remarks of at least one pretentious writer, whose tone has beyond a doubt been so taken, are subsequently noticed.*

The life and character of Steele unite much of the dash, wit, and brilliancy of Sheridan—with the adventure, the simplicity, the artless impulsive recklessness of Goldsmith—with all the dross upon the surface and the fine gold at the heart. Steele's sympathies and feelings were all in favour of virtue and religion; and though, under the influence of temptation, he yielded to imprudent excesses, yet no error or vice ever found in him an advocate, under any specious or alluring form. He

* See Note, p. 9.

maintained the spring pure, though the stream might occasionally be muddied in its course.

With regard to the letters of Steele, they were first published from the originals in the British Museum by Nichols, and, with the addition of the whole mass of his epistles dedicatory, and with extensive notes and the aid of typography, expanded into two volumes. The shorter notes have generally been retained, and marked with inverted commas. Some of these letters are to Pope, Swift, Hughes, and other literary friends, but the bulk of them are to his wife. The chief value of them is biographical; and it is believed that their interest will be immensely enhanced by being incorporated with his life, which they tend so much to illustrate. In fact, a mass of such hastily-penned notes, without any intervening commentary, could scarcely be deemed very interesting; but, scattered over a biography, like a spice they tend to give it a flavour. Details in themselves commonplace are deemed essential to the interest and reality of fiction, but in matters of reality none are so satisfactory as those which are documentary. These letters are wholly unlike those of Pope and many other literary men, written for display. They are artless, unpremeditated effusions of the moment, and serve in some degree to supply the absence of anything in the shape of a diary.

or journal. It is indeed to be regretted that he did not leave us something of that kind. But his life was too bustling for that. Swift's Journal to Stella is one of the most interesting things he has left behind him. What would we not give for a Boswell of those men and those times!

In the absence of this, it is sought in the following pages to make Steele, in his combined character as a man of letters and a politician, the centre figure in a group of portraits or sketches, however slight and imperfect, of the leading spirits, both in literary and political life, of an era which, in both points, must ever be regarded as one of the most important and interesting in British annals.

CONTENTS.

VOL. I.

CHAPTER I.

THE YOUTH, THE COLLEGIAN, AND THE SOLDIER—1671–1700.

Value and interest of biography—Birth and parentage of Steele—His account of his mother, and of his father's death—Is sent to the Charter-House School in London, where he makes the acquaintance of Addison—Notice of the Chartreuse—Enters Christ-Church, Oxford — Cultivates dramatic literature, and writes a comedy, which, being disapproved by a college friend, he destroys — Lines on the death of Queen Mary—Fancy for a military life, which, being disapproved by friends, he enters the Guards as a volunteer, and is, in consequence, disinherited by a wealthy relative—Remarkable parallel instances, Cervantes and Coleridge—Acts as secretary to Lord Cutts, his colonel, and receives a commission from him—Notice of that officer—Is led into undue convivial habits by the attractions of his wit and social qualities among his military associates, opposed to his better feelings—His resolve to break with these habits, and the effects of that resolution, ... 1

CHAPTER II.

THE MORALIST AND DRAMATIC WRITER—1701-1704.

Steele writes "The Christian Hero," a moral essay, to fix him in his good resolves—Finds it ineffectual—Resolves to publish it—Dedicates it to Lord Cutts, the colonel of his regiment—Account of the work—Note on Professor Schlosser's criticism—Steele, forced into a duel, seriously wounds his antagonist, though unintentionally—His sufferings on that account—Becomes a decided opponent of the practice—Ridicule suffered by Steele for his efforts at self-reformation—Turns his attention to dramatic literature—Notice of the drama and dramatic predecessors of Steele: Wycherley, Vanbrugh, Farquhar, and Congreve—Jeremy Collier's attack on the stage—His comedy of "The Funeral; or, Grief à-la-Mode"—Its success—Scene from the play—Produces "The Tender Husband"—The prologue written by Addison—Specimen scene—"The Lying Lovers," his next comedy, not equally successful, though one of his best productions—Its unmerited fate induces him for some years to relinquish dramatic pursuits—Specimen scene—Produces "The Conscious Lovers" after a long interval—Remark of Horace Walpole on the writing of comedy—Thackeray's remarks on Steele's plays, ... 16

CHAPTER III.
THE PLACEMAN AND THE LOVER—1707-1708.

Steele's hopes of preferment dashed by the death of the King—Notice of William—Revived early in Queen Anne's reign—Is introduced to Lord Halifax, an eminent patron of literary men, and other leading Whig statesmen—State of parties and of public events—The War—Union with Scotland—Defoe—Receives the appointment of Gazetteer—Strength of friendship among the literary men of this period—Notice of the Kit-Cat Club—Steele's beautiful allusion to the loss of his first wife—Reference to his first love—Mrs Bovey, who has been the supposed object of an early attachment, thought to have been also the original of the "perverse widow" of Sir Roger de Coverley in the *Spectator*—Steele's correspondence with Mrs Mary Scurlock, his second wife, previous to marriage, 64

CHAPTER IV.
THE HUSBAND—1707-1708.

Correspondence after marriage with his wife and her mother—

Prayer on his marriage—A fit of gout—Mrs Scurlock arrives from Wales—Beginning of difficulties—Imprudent establishment—Mrs Steele's amiability to his daughter—Addison's election—Residence at Hampton Court—Repays Addison's debt—Addison drives him in a coach and four to his sister's—Two invoices of walnuts—Addison appointed Secretary for Ireland—Supper on the occasion—Steele fails in his hopes of succeeding to his vacancy—Projects a fresh literary campaign—Reference to public events and characters, Harley and St John, Duchess of Marlborough, Mrs Masham, and Gregg, . 91

CHAPTER V.
THE PERIODICAL ESSAYIST AND DELINEATOR OF CHARACTER—1709-1710.

Steele projects the *Tatler*, forming a new literary era—State of society at the period—A glance at preceding kindred writings—Origin of the assumed name of Isaac Bickerstaff—Adopted from a recent pamphlet in which Swift had foretold the death of Partridge, an almanac-maker and pretender in physic and astrology—The *jeu d'esprit*, which had been joined in by the other wits of the time, taken up by Steele in the *Tatler*—Partridge publishes a disclaimer—Extraordinary success of the *Tatler*—Swift one of its earliest contributors—Notice of the other contributors, Addison, Congreve, &c.—Dedications of the different volumes, and the subjects of them — Its close—General regret caused by its discontinuance—The good it accomplished, ... 131

CHAPTER VI.

Letters of Steele during the publication of the *Tatler*—To his wife, to Mrs Manley, Dennis, and Swift—Steele appointed a Commissioner of Stamps—Notices of Steele in Swift's Journal to Stella—Notice of Public Events—Change of Ministry—Harley and St John — Steele's diversion in favour of his friends in *Tatler*—Loses his Gazetteership in consequence, . 209

CHAPTER VII.
THE PERIODICAL ESSAYIST—"SPECTATOR"—1711-1712.

Steele starts the *Spectator* on a similar plan with the *Tatler*, but

xxvi   *Contents.*

PAGE

with a new set of characters, in conjunction with Addison
—Its unprecedented success—The *Spectator* Club—The De
Coverley series of papers—Notice of the contributors, Philips,
Budgell, Tickell, Hughes, Grove, &c.—The dedications, and
the subjects of them—Close of the original series—An ad-
ditional volume subsequently added, chiefly by Addison, . 232

CHAPTER VIII.

Correspondence during publication of *Spectator*—Reference to his
mother's family—Poetical correspondence with Hughes and
Pope—Anecdote of the *Censorium*, or private theatre of Steele
—Criticism on Pope's "Messiah"—Addison disclaims Pope's
satire on Dennis—Pope's "Dying Christian"—Newcomb's encomium on Steele — Lady Montagu desires Steele's correspondence, ... 301

CHAPTER IX.
THE PERIODICAL ESSAYIST AND DELINEATOR OF CHARACTER.

Steele starts the *Guardian* as a sequel to the *Spectator*—Its plan—
Nestor Ironside, guardian to the Lizard family—Its members
—Notice of the contributors, Bishop Berkeley, Pope, Gay,
Addison, &c.—Subjects of dedications—Controversy with the
Examiner—It diverges into politics, and is discontinued, . 322

CHAPTER X.

Correspondence during the publication of the *Guardian*—Steele's
quarrel with Swift—His letter to Addison complaining of
Steele, in reference to the *Guardian*—Steele's reply—Swift's
farewell letter, and partial reconciliation—His confession of
Whiggism—Notice of the Dean—Steele resigns his Commissionership, and enters Parliament, ... 374

LIST OF ILLUSTRATIONS.

PORTRAIT OF STEELE, ... *Frontispiece.*

			PAGE
,,	,,	ADDISON,	160
,,	,,	CONGREVE,	178
,,	,,	POPE,	338
,,	,,	GAY,	356
,,	,,	SWIFT,	384

SIR RICHARD STEELE,

AND

HIS CONTEMPORARIES.

CHAPTER I.

THE YOUTH, THE COLLEGIAN, AND THE SOLDIER—1671-1700.

Value and interest of biography—Birth and parentage of Steele—His account of his mother, and of his father's death—Is sent to the Charter-House School in London, where he makes the acquaintance of Addison—Notice of the Chartreuse—Enters Merton College, Oxford—Cultivates dramatic literature, and writes a comedy, which, being disapproved by a college friend, he destroys—Lines on the death of Queen Mary—Fancy for a military life, which, being disapproved by friends, he enters the Guards as a volunteer, and is, in consequence, disinherited by a wealthy relative—Remarkable parallel instances, Cervantes and Coleridge—Acts as secretary to Lord Cutts, his colonel, and receives a commission from him—Notice of that officer—Is led into undue convivial habits by the attractions of his wit and social qualities among his military associates, opposed to his better feelings—His resolve to break with these habits, and the effects of that resolution.

THE celebrated sentiment of the old dramatist, which never failed to draw forth the plaudits of a Roman audience, " Nihil humani a me alienum puto," may be considered to embody some of the most important of the various claims

A

of biography upon our interest and attention, and is peculiarly applicable in reference to that of one who was so distinguished by his fine humanity, and the catholic range of his sympathies.

This fascinating field of literature, which unites much of the personal charm of fiction with the utility of history, abounds more than any other in human interest. It appeals to our curiosity, our sympathy, and our self-love. We are curious to know how men who have left their impress on their time, and influenced not merely their own, but, it may be, many a subsequent age, attained to this enviable pre-eminence; we feel a pride in bearing a common nature with such spirits, and are consoled, too, for the mortifying sense of our own mediocrity, in exemption from the envy, care, and disappointment which too often, if not invariably, attend upon superior merit;* and in feeling our weaknesses and shortcomings kept in countenance by finding that, with all their great qualities, the subjects of the historian were men of like passions with ourselves.

Biography brings us acquainted with the best company in the world. The wisest, the wittiest, the bravest, the best, of all ages become our contemporaries,—they converse with us at our firesides, not in pomp and state, but without ceremony or constraint.

From what other source do we derive so much of the spirit of antiquity as from the lives of Plutarch?—one of

---

* This remarkable fact of the large number of "unsuccessful great men" who were distanced in the race by mediocrity, is, according to Swift's theory, explained by their attaching too little importance to the "little helps and little hindrances" to which smaller men look more carefully. This is even applicable to the sons of great men, who though, with few exceptions, excelling like their fathers, have been generally more successful socially.

those productions which, it has been said, we would desire to rescue from destruction if all other books were to suffer annihilation, or which we would choose for our companion if cast upon a desolate island.

Richard Steele was born in Dublin in the year 1671.* He was descended of a good family, one branch of which possessed considerable landed property in Wexford county, of part of which Steele was disinherited, owing to his imprudent wilfulness in entering the army in the way he did, and against the wish of his friends.†

His father, who was a counsellor-at-law, had been private secretary to James, first Duke of Ormond, when Lord-Lieutenant of Ireland, and died when Steele (his only son) was very young. It is a prevalent notion, justified by many striking examples, that the shining qualities of eminent men are most commonly inherited from the mother. Of Steele's mother (whose maiden name was Gascoigne) little is known; but, from a passage in one of his descriptive sketches, which has always been justly admired for its beautiful simplicity, tenderness, and pathos, it appears that she was a very superior woman, and that her

* On the authority of his baptismal register, dated March 12. The inaccuracy of the early authorities in giving the year 1675 or '76 has been followed by a writer generally so careful and painstaking as Dr Drake, in common with the writers of almost every other sketch of his life, except Miss Aikin.

† By a curious coincidence there was a Sir Richard Steele high sheriff of county Dublin in 1821, who was made the subject of one of his squibs by Moore, referred to in his Memoirs, vol. iii., p. 190, where he says,—" Sent a copy of them [lines of Byron to himself] to Perry, [of *Morn. Chron.*,] and added some nonsense of my own about Sir Richard Steele, the high sheriff, who has just dispersed a meeting in Dublin by the military, beginning,—

' Though sprung from the clever Sir Richard this man be,
He 's as different a *sort* of Sir Richard as can be.' "

The genealogical allusion is probably only apparent.

memory was cherished with fond affection by her son. Speaking of the impression of a first grief, "The first sorrow I ever knew," he says, "was upon the death of my father, at which time I was not quite five years of age; but was rather amazed at what all the house meant, than possessed with a real understanding why nobody was willing to play with me. I remember, I went into the room where the body lay, and my mother sat weeping alone by it. I had my battledore in my hand, and fell a-beating the coffin, and calling, 'Papa;' for, I know not how, I had some slight idea that he was locked up there. My mother catched me in her arms, and, transported beyond all patience of the silent grief she was before in, she almost smothered me in her embraces; and told me, in a flood of tears, 'Papa could not hear me, and would play with me no more, for they were going to put him under ground, whence he could never come to us again.' She was a very beautiful woman, of a noble spirit; and there was a dignity in her grief, amidst all the wildness of her transport, which, methought, struck me with an instinct of sorrow that, before I was sensible what it was to grieve, seized my very soul, and has made pity the weakness of my heart ever since."*

Young Steele, at twelve years of age, (1684,) had the good fortune to be sent for his education to a noble institution in London. Some distance in the rear of Christ's Hospital and Little Britain, in the city, stands the Chartreuse, or, as it has been corrupted, Charter-House, founded by Sir Thomas Sutton, in 1611, on the site of a Carthusian priory, and of a terrible charnel-house, caused by the visitation of the plague in 1348, where fifty thousand victims are

* *Tatler*, No. 181.

said to have been interred in one year, to commemorate which a church and religious house called *The Salutation* were established. Many are the celebrated names which it boasts among its *alumni;* and, among other ornaments of recent times, claims the pen of Thackeray, which was employed in its illustration, and the pencil of Leech. The Duke of Ormond being one of the governors of the house, used his interest in placing the son of his former secretary upon the foundation, — not the least considerable advantage of which was the formation of his friendship with Joseph Addison, who, one year his junior, was then pursuing his studies there as a private pupil. Of the life-intimacy thus formed, it is difficult to overestimate the beneficial effect on the happiness and fame of both.

In 1689, Steele was matriculated at Christ Church, Oxford ; and his name stood at the head of the Postmasters* of Merton College in 1691. Of his academic career, in which he was probably assisted by the liberality of his uncle Gascoigne, little is known; but as he began there the cultivation of the dramatic literature to which he afterwards successfully devoted himself, it is not unreasonable to conclude that such pursuits were scarcely compatible with any very ardent devotion to his scholastic studies; nor is it improbable that, like many men of lively parts, and some of the most shining names in literature, including that of Swift, he may have felt the drudgery of the college

---

* A corruption of *Portionistæ*, signifying those having an interest in the emoluments of the house, in other words, scholarships. The date of his entrance, erroneously given in the previous notices of his life, has been authenticated by the kindness of the Rev. J. Griffiths, M.A., keeper of the University archives at Oxford.

course an irksome task, beyond the moderate application necessary to go through the routine without discredit. Thus much, at least, he is believed to have done. He left the university without taking his degree,* but not, however, without leaving the most kindly feelings behind him. During his residence there he completed a comedy, which he submitted to the inspection of one of his particular friends, Mr Parker, afterwards one of the Fellows of Merton, who, either from his high opinion of his friend's powers, or the intrinsic demerit of the performance in his estimate, pronounced unfavourably upon it; and Steele, with that docility which he united to high spirit in a remarkable degree, never called the decision in question, but submitted to it with a humility truly exemplary in a budding author. Of his college tutor, the Rev. Dr Ellis, he afterwards makes grateful mention in the preface to the "Christian Hero," for his valuable services.

Whether Steele afterwards recast the rejected comedy, or in any shape dragged it from the oblivion to which the voice of friendly criticism had consigned it, would be interesting to know, as a somewhat similar fate attended the first production of the author of "Waverley." The first occasion on which he indemnified himself for this miscarriage was in some verses on the death of Queen Mary in 1695. The poem is entitled, "The Procession," and gives a pleasing picture of the mourners of all classes for the loss of their royal mistress, that portion which

* We understand that, in those times, this was not what Miss Aikin, in her Life of Addison, has naturally enough termed it, "a significant circumstance," but might arise from various causes, in no way affecting his scholarship, and that little importance was then attached to it. We state this on the authority of Dr Haig Brown, the present head-master of the Charter-House.

refers to the objects of her bounty being the most striking :—

> "A mourning world attends her to the tomb:
> The poor her first and deepest mourners are,
> First in her thoughts, and earliest in her care;
> All hand in hand, in common friendly woe,
> In poverty, our native state, they go.
> Some, whom unstable errors did engage,
> By luxury in youth, to need in age;
> Some, who had virgin vows to wedlock broke,
> And, where they help expected, found a yoke;
> Others, who in their want feel double weight
> From the remembrance of a wealthier state.
> There mothers walk who oft despairing stood,
> Pierced with their infants' eager sobs for food.
> These modest wants had ne'er been understood
> But by Maria's cunning to be good."

Among the courtly portion of the train, Ormond and Somers alone are brought into relief, in high eulogistic strains. The poem concludes with a picture of the living queen, pathetically contrasted with the cold remains carried in stately pomp to their last resting-place :—

> "I see her yet, nature and fortune's pride:
> A sceptre graced her hand, a king her side;
> Celestial youth and beauty did impart
> Ecstatic vision to the coldest heart." *

These verses cannot be said to indicate any extraordinary aptitude for the higher walks of poetry, though this is only saying what might equally be asserted of the first efforts of many who have subsequently shone in them, which was not Steele's fortune. But the early productions of genius, however trifling, are always interesting.

* Steele's Poetic Miscellanies, 1714.

Having imbibed an ardent passion for a military life, he left the university without taking his degree, as previously stated, but leaving behind him the most kindly recollections, and resolutely bent upon realising his wishes, despite the warm remonstrances of his friends, who were desirous of using their influence for his promotion in some walk of civil life. Finding no other means of accomplishing his purpose, he entered himself, as it has been smoothly phrased by some writers, as a " gentleman volunteer" in the Horse Guards; and we are not aware whether there was any difference in such a distinction from what we would term in plain English a private. We are not in possession of sufficient knowledge of his early history to form an accurate judgment of all the inducements he may have had to take such an apparently imprudent step. We only know, in addition to his strong feeling in favour of a military life, that he had lost his parents. But whether he felt the unkindness of friends, or his high spirit revolted at their dictation, or from being subject to their bounty, we are without the means of judging. But there is reason to believe that his great admiration of the character of King William had something to do with it. There are, however, some curious parallel instances in the case of some of the highest names in literature. Cervantes, the immortal author of "Don Quixote," though his family belonged to the rank of Spanish grandees, proverbial for their pride, served as a private in the war against the Turks, and lost an arm at the battle of Lepanto; and at this very period, or a little earlier, numbers of young noblemen and persons of family went as volunteers, without commissions, in the navy, and were present at some engagements in the times of the Restoration. But we may feel still less surprise at such a step in one of Steele's gay and dashing disposition, when we find that his example was followed by one of the most original thinkers and profound inquirers in the grave pursuits of philosophic speculation that modern times can boast. "I sometimes," said Coleridge to a friend, "compare my own life with that of Steele, (yet, oh! how unlike,) from having myself also, for a brief time, borne arms, and written 'private' after my name, or rather another name; for being at a loss when suddenly asked my name, I answered *Cumberback;* and, verily, my habits were so little equestrian, that my horse, I doubt not, was of that opinion."*

* "Letters, Conversations, and Recollections of S. T. Coleridge," vol. i., p. 189. In connexion with this subject, there is a rare specimen of the kind of invidious, illiberal criticism by which Steele has all along been victimised to the popularity of his friend Addison, in the case of the writer of an introduction to a late handsome edition of the *Spectator*, (T. Bosworth, 1853,) one of those referred to in the preface to this work, who appears evidently to have been influenced by the tone of Mr Thackeray in reference to Steele, and follows suit so awkwardly that he reminds one (without meaning offence) of the fable of the donkey who followed the example of the dog in fawning on his master. This writer, after telling us that "Addison," in contrast with Steele, "never threw a chance away," goes on to state that "Steele was a native of Ireland; and though his parents were English, he had all an Irishman's eccentricities and *absurdities.*" This is modest and liberal for a book intended to circulate through the three kingdoms. But though the writer condescends to claim Steele, with all his eccentricities and absurdities, it may be mentioned, merely as a matter of accuracy, that there is no authority for the statement that his parents were English. His mother was unquestionably an Irish lady. The year of his birth is in like manner given in accordance with the stereotyped inaccuracy of previous writers. We trust no literary young Irelander may be induced to carry the national absurdity to a pitch to which we scarcely think it has yet reached, by retorting, and tracing the eccentricities of Bacon, Defoe, Coleridge, Chatterton, Richard Savage, Addison's cousin, Budgell, and innumerable others, including Byron, thus summarily to their birthplace. This writer goes on to add, in the following coarse strain:—"Nature had intended 'poor Dick' (as Addison often called him) for a vagabond. He had that common symptom of vagabondism, a passion for a military life." The service

The feelings which doubtless led Steele in a great measure to enter the army, the same as those entertained by many inexperienced youths of spirit, are so well expressed

will no doubt feel highly honoured by the compliment; but in France, at least, its members are so sensitive to reflections of the press, that only a few years since a public writer was called out on that account, and lost his life.

From the "passion for a military life," so prevalent at present, as exemplified in the volunteer movement, we seem likely to become a nation of vagabonds. Moreover, the Guards, in which Steele entered, are not marching regiments, we believe, but stationary, which takes away the point of the "vagabond" application. With regard to the invidious part of the comparison, it may be conceded to the writer that Addison excelled Steele in the quality of prudence and a careful regard to No. 1; and he has reaped the benefit in not having had, like Steele, the seamy side of his life turned out. Indeed, Professor Schlosser, a German writer, who does even-handed justice to both, (of the style this writer awards to Steele alone,) thinks Addison had this quality in such perfection, that he speaks of him in these terms:—"The vain, cold, prosaic, *all-calculating*, Addison, who was prudent in pondering on the minutest things, and who, on this very account, was so much the more admired by the egotistical, exclusive circles," &c.—(" History of the Eighteenth Century," vol. i., p. 100.) This may serve to shew the writer of the introduction that there are two sides to every question, and that invidious comparisons seldom end in raising those they are meant to elevate. But was there no mercy to temper the justice of the critic due to Steele, in consideration of his parents being dead, and his being subject to the dictation and bounty of friends? Addison, on the other hand, had his father and his college fellowship to look to; yet, in opposition to his friends, he deferred for years taking orders, though so eminently fitted for the Church, and accepted of a pension of £300 from a minister of the Crown, without having done any service, or any, so far as is known, being stipulated for it, on the ostensible ground of enabling him to "vagabondise," by seeing the world.

With regard to Steele's great weakness, his excessive conviviality, for which he has been so unmercifully rated, Dr J. Hoadley, son of the Bishop of Bangor, who was the friend of both, speaking of Addison, says,—" Whose phlegmatic constitution was hardly warmed for society, by that time Steele was not fit for it." So, that what upset the one was a mere fillip to the other. The present writer disclaims the most distant desire to depreciate Addison, for whose character and writings he has ever entertained the most sincere admiration; and it is only the folly,—he would almost say the ingratitude,—of those senseless admirers who will not be satisfied to let him stand on his own merits, without depreciating, both as a man and a writer, the friend who was the means of bringing him before the world in his most popular aspect, in as deliberate a manner as any lawyer could do if he held a brief on the subject, that leads him to indulge in any remark that may have such an appearance. Does it not occur to such advocates, that if

in his comedy of the "Lying Lover," that it is surprising it should not have been in his first:—
"*Young Book-wit, (just come from Oxford.)*—'But my sword,—does it hang careless? Do I look bold, negligent, and erect?—that is, do I look as if I could kill a man without being out of humour? I horribly mistrust myself. Am I military enough in my air? I fancy people see I understand Greek. Don't I pore a little in my visage? Ha'n't I a down, bookish lour,—a wise sadness? I don't look gay and unthinking enough, I fancy.'"

The immediate effect of this headlong plunge into life was very disastrous to his interest, as, by the displeasure which he thereby gave to a wealthy relative, he forfeited the reversion of an estate in Ireland, to which he would otherwise have succeeded. To this circumstance he alludes when, in after life, attacked with coarse virulence and malignity by Dennis, who reflected upon him as if he had risen from the ranks, without any previous higher standing. "It may, perhaps," said Steele, writing under an assumed name, "fall in my way to give an abstract of the life of

his merits are so transcendently superior to those of his friend, they can afford to speak for themselves, and that it is ungenerous in the highest degree, besides being a needless expenditure of their critical powers, to insist on what to their minds is so self-evident, in order to crush one of the greatest benefactors to our literature, because he may not rise to what, in their view, is supremely excellent? If Steele had ever shewn any envy of Addison, or been niggardly, instead of most generous, in awarding him applause, the case would be quite altered. The folly of such critics is evident; and, besides, all injustice has a reactionary effect.

Before taking leave of the preface alluded to, the writer cannot avoid noticing one other criticism therein,—" Few English versions of *Latin* (!) poems," it is stated, (Pref., p. 26,) " are more estimable than Philips's translations of Sappho." This is the more remarkable, coming from a person of such great pretension, and who is stated to have collated the classical quotations.

this man, whom it is thought thus necessary to undo and disparage. When I do, it will appear that when he mounted a war-horse, with a great sword in his hand, and planted himself behind King William III. against Louis XIV., he lost the succession to a very good estate in the county of Wexford, in Ireland, from the same humour, which he has preserved ever since, of preferring the state of his mind to that of his fortune. When he cocked his hat, put on a broadsword, jack-boots, and shoulder-belt, under the command of the unfortunate Duke of Ormond, he was not acquainted with his own parts, and did not then know he should ever have been able (as has since appeared to be, in the case of Dunkirk) to demolish a fortified town with a goose-quill."*

In this defence there appears something of a tone of triumph at the sacrifice of his interest to his inclination and independence of mind; and though he enters into no particulars, the reference to the state of his mind will warrant the conjecture previously made, of his being at least partly actuated by the desire to free himself from the dictation of friends, which, to one of his high spirit, may have been irksome or intolerable. But, in any case, whether this conjecture be well-founded or otherwise, whatever we might think of such a plea, if gratuitously made, in the coolness of experience and mature reflection, it must be borne in mind that he was repelling the attack of a wanton and malignant calumniator. To whatever extent he may have felt his loss, few men could have been fitted to bear up under it with a better grace. He was blessed with a sanguine temperament, with a frank and open bearing,

* *Theatre*, No. xi.

and a fund of vivacity and sparkling wit, which adapted him peculiarly to the position he had chosen for himself, and made him the life and soul of the mess-room. It may, moreover, be readily believed that there must be something peculiarly gratifying to the universal sentiment of self-love in the feeling of one who, either voluntarily or of necessity, casting aside the vantage-ground of position and birth, usually so highly esteemed, starts in the race of competition with the most lowly, and wins the prize, without any other favour or interest than such as his own personal merit and exertions procure for him. This being precisely Steele's case, he must have enjoyed this consolation under his loss of fortune; for his talents and social qualities, which had made him the delight of his humbler companions in arms, were not long in recommending him to the notice of those who had both the power and the will to serve him. Lord Cutts, an officer of great gallantry, who is mentioned by Addison in his Latin poem on the peace of Ryswick, for the distinguished part he acted at the taking of Buda in 1686, was then Colonel of the Coldstream, or second regiment of Guards, to which Steele belonged; and through him he obtained, first an ensign's commission, and afterwards command of a company in Lord Lucas's regiment of Fusileers. He was also appointed secretary to Lord Cutts, who himself added to his distinguished qualities as a soldier the accomplishment of a wit and a writer of verses, which had something of the grace and sparkling gaiety of Suckling; and in this character is noticed by Horace Walpole in his "Catalogue of Royal and Noble Authors." Some of these are quoted by Steele in the fifth *Tatler*. The verses from which they are taken are here given as a specimen of the noble warrior's graceful talents in this way:—

"Only tell her that I love,
   Leave the rest to her and fate ;
Some kind planet from above
May perhaps her pity move ;
   Lovers on their stars must wait ;
Only tell her that I love.

"Why, oh, why should I despair ?
   Mercy's pictured in her eye ;
If she once vouchsafe to hear,
Welcome hope and welcome fear.
   She's too good to let me die ;
Why, oh, why should I despair ?" *

He particularly distinguished himself at the attack on the Castle of Namur in 1695, and the siege of Venloo in 1702. He was afterwards appointed commander-in-chief of the forces in Ireland, and one of the lords-justices, it was thought with the view of keeping him out of action, which is said to have broken his heart. His besetting infirmity was vanity; and Swift, in a M.S. note on Mackay, a topographical writer of the period by whom he was mentioned, says, with characteristic curt severity, "The vainest old fool alive." He died in Dublin, January 26, 1707, and was interred in Christ's Church Cathedral.

If Steele was now in the way of promotion, he was also in the way of temptation, to which his soft and easy disposition made him but too yielding a victim. The charms of his conversation and the poignancy of his wit were unfortunately the cause of his being led by his brother officers into a course of the most reckless levity and dissipation,

* See Nichols's Select Collection.

which neither the strength of his resolution, nor the force of the religious impressions with which his mind was strongly imbued, enabled him to resist. The conflict in his mind, however, when free from the solicitations of his gay companions, was very sharp and bitter; but, unhappily, the still small voice that whispered to him his folly and weakness, and told him of the misapplication of talents given for higher and nobler purposes, was drowned in the roar of the next convivial meeting, of which his wit was the chief attraction. In this way did he go on for some time, sinning and repenting, and at war with his own better nature. The result of such a struggle, we may well conceive, must have been great unhappiness of mind.

"His, in fact," it has been well remarked by Miss Aikin, "was one of those characters which often inspire the stronger interest from their very infirmities, through the alternate hopes and fears, praises and reproofs, which they call forth, as now the good, now the evil, genius seems about to gain the ascendancy."*

* Life of Addison, vol. i., p. 19.

CHAPTER II.

THE MORALIST AND DRAMATIC WRITER—1701-1704.

Steele writes "The Christian Hero," a moral essay, to fix him in his good resolves—Finds it ineffectual—Resolves to publish it—Dedicates it to Lord Cutts, the colonel of his regiment—Account of the work—Note on Professor Schlosser's criticism—Steele, forced into a duel, seriously wounds his antagonist, though unintentionally—His sufferings on that account—Becomes a decided opponent of the practice—Ridicule suffered by Steele for his efforts at self-reformation—Turns his attention to dramatic literature—Notice of the drama and dramatic predecessors of Steele: Wycherley, Vanbrugh, Farquhar, and Congreve—Jeremy Collier's attack on the stage—His comedy of "The Funeral; or, Grief à-la-Mode"—Its success—Scene from the play—Produces "The Tender Husband"—The prologue written by Addison—Specimen scene—"The Lying Lovers," his next comedy, not equally successful, though one of his best productions—Its unmerited fate induces him for some years to relinquish dramatic pursuits—Specimen scene—Produces "The Conscious Lovers" after a considerable interval—Remark of Horace Walpole on the writing of comedy—Thackeray's remarks on Steele's plays.

UNDER the circumstances referred to at the close of the preceding chapter, Steele bethought himself of drawing up a little treatise intended as a homily for his own private perusal and edification solely. Of his original design in writing this curious and interesting little treatise, he states, at a subsequent period, "When he was an ensign in the Guards, being thoroughly convinced of many things of which he often repented, and as often repeated, he wrote, for his own private use, a little book called 'The Christian

Hero,' with a design principally to fix upon his mind a strong impression of virtue and religion, in opposition to a stronger propensity to unwarrantable pleasures."*

This he still found of little avail, so long as its perusal was merely confined to the privacy of his own closet, and his gay companions unaware of his good resolutions and the painful struggle going on in his mind. With the despair of a man conscious of the weakness of his own resolves, and as a testimony against himself that would be certain to expose him to the ridicule of inconsistency if he yielded to the solicitations of his companions, or his own inclinations, to a course which his own better judgment disapproved, he resolved to publish the Essay, and so commit himself before the world to the principles it inculcated. Accordingly, in 1701, the work appeared under the title of "The Christian Hero," with a dedication to Lord Cutts. The leading aim of the book was to prove that "no principles but those of religion are sufficient to make a great man." The publication produced all the mortifying part of the effect he had anticipated, with little or none of the good results. His gay and thoughtless companions, who had none of his compunctious visitings after their scenes of midnight revelry, saw only the glaring contradiction between the precepts of the writer and the practice of the man, which became a source of much mirth and raillery. They were little disposed to allow of any place of repentance, quite as much in a selfish point of view as from any want of charitable feeling; and the taunt and sneer were not wanting to recall the delightful companion from the prospect of making himself a disagreeable fellow. Thus it

---

* His " Apology for Himself and Writings."

ever will be with the man of right principle, but of too easy a disposition, when he attempts to beat a retreat from the dangerous ground of indulgence, to which a lively and social disposition, and a too ready compliance, may have led.

The attempt to reason himself into the right with his pen had been found equally futile against the attractions of gambling by the poet Denham, because his reason did not want convincing—his error arose from too great facility of disposition and weakness of the will. It is obviously very simple, removed from temptation and in the cool retirement of the closet, to lay down rules for ourselves or others, in accordance with the dictates of the better judgment; and the very attempt voluntarily to do so is proof of the vitality of right in any one; but just as the compass, that all-important guide of the mariner through the trackless deep, led him astray until he learned to make allowance for its deviations; or as the same mariner, should he make his calculations only for fair weather and smooth seas, without taking into account the action of storms and currents; so the man of easy disposition and deficient power of will, who lays his account to be guided by the abstract rules of right, by the mere force of reasoning alone, without considering the active operation of the passions and of circumstances, will often find himself drifted far wide of his mark. The true wisdom is not either in ignoring the passions, or calculating vainly on our own strength to oppose them, but in directing and employing them, as they were designed to be, at least innocently, if not usefully. Steele's excesses arose from abuse of the social feelings, joined to weakness of self-control. These social feelings are among the most powerful and amiable principles of our nature, but their undue indulgence, sometimes, where their legitimate exercise is denied, will be found to be at the bottom of half the follies and vices in the world. Were it not for the prominence that has been given to the excesses of Steele, it would be unnecessary to add that his was no solitary or vulgar toping—that it was associated with conviviality and with wit and intellectual enjoyment. It would be curious to enumerate the great men who have indulged in this vice. Not to speak of Anacreon and his characteristic death; Philip of Macedon, and his greater son Alexander; Addison (especially, it is said, after his marriage), Burns, Sheridan, and Pitt at once occur to the memory. More recently, Coleridge and De Quincey indulged in stimulants in another form. There may be another cause for this indulgence in men of genius besides that social one already referred to—in the greater waste of the animal spirits in their case, by the active operations of the mind, leaving them in an exhausted condition, that causes a craving for artificial stimulants; to which, in many cases, may be added, if not actual disappointment, that arising in imaginative minds from the discrepancy between the ideal and the real in life.

As this little work,* though several times republished, is rather rare, some short notice and specimens of it may not be unacceptable. In the preface the writer dwells upon the fascinating influence of men of wit, and the bad

* In the "History of the Eighteenth Century," by Professor Schlosser of Heidelberg, a work which seems bigotedly wedded to particular systems, in the interest of which it appears to have been written; and which, so far at least as some of the most distinguished English authors are concerned, displays an illiberality of spirit which might have characterised the notice of a living writer

purpose to which, in that age, they had turned it. He then proposes "to search into the reasons why we are so willing to arm ourselves against the assaults of delight and

in a violent partisan review some half century ago, rather than that of the calm and dignified historian of the past, the writer shews the intimate knowledge he possesses of what he treats so confidently by speaking of this historical essay of Steele's thus :—" Steele began his career as a writer with a poem, his 'Christian Hero,' which justified no great expectations. This poem could have little soul or nature in it," he adds, " because the contents stood in a most surprising contradiction with Steele's scandalous and dissolute course of life," &c., vol. i. p. 102. This, from a writer who talks so volubly of superficial attainments, is tolerably well. Not content with converting a prose essay into a poem, he summarily condemns it without a hearing, because of its surprising contradiction to its author's mode of life at the time. He was either not aware, or disingenuously concealed, that it was expressly written as a homily for its author's private use, and afterwards published in order to commit him in the eye of the world to a different course. But the logic is as bad as the spirit of this writer's remarks. Shall we say that the eloquence of Demosthenes could have had little soul in it because it was in surprising contradiction to his failure of nerve in the day of battle? Besides, the strong language used is calculated to mislead general readers, very few of whom, if not aware of the facts, would believe that the "scandalous and dissolute course of life" merely meant the undue indulgence at the festive board of a gay and witty young officer, induced thereto by the importunities of his military companions and his own great social attractions. Steele never was a vulgar or notorious sot. His excesses were among his private friends, not in public. It appears that the learned and charitable Professor was as little disposed to admit of any place of repentance as those who participated in his follies. The same writer had, a few pages previously, in an equally liberal and philosophical spirit, spoken of Addison as, " by God's grace, for some time Secretary of State, since he could neither speak in Parliament, nor, when it was his duty to draw up public documents, was he able to prepare despatches *in a good style* and *with beauty of language*." Though it was obviously a drawback to Addison, in his official capacity, not to have been a speaker, yet it is difficult to avoid smiling, or to decide which is the more monstrous absurdity—of referring to "beauty of style" in public documents, or of supposing Addison deficient in it. It is merely a most illiberal and false construction of a story which Lord Macaulay, in his biographical essay on Addison, has unanswerably disposed of, by shewing, with his characteristic affluence of illustration and as the result of his own experience, what might have appeared obvious enough, that there are technicalities connected with official duties which cannot be arrived at by intuition, and which subordinates, who remain permanently in office, must naturally be most familiar with. But, though this plea be amply satisfactory, yet even if it had been certain that Addison had betrayed some awkwardness in a small matter which to a thoroughly

sorrow rather with the dictates of morality than those of religion; and how it has obtained, that when we say a thing was done like an old Roman, we have a generous and

practical and efficient clerk would have presented no difficulty, are there not abundance of stories of the awkwardness and absence of mind of scholars and men of genius which may create a smile without any serious reflection on their ability, and might not a learned Professor (whose own order have come in for their full share of such) have been expected in such a case to extend his sympathy to a trifling weakness, if it had been such, and if not to extenuate, at least to "set down naught in malice," or indulge in sneers about holding places "by the grace of God?" Hercules was not the less Hercules because he made sad work at the distaff. There appears something almost vulgar, and certainly unworthy of a respectable writer, in the tone of such remarks. If such offices are to be held by persons of acknowledged ability and character, and if Addison did not possess them, where are they to be found?

The attempt to depreciate the periodical papers of Addison and Steele was a natural sequel to their personal depreciation, and rests upon about as good foundation as that just noticed. They were not, of course, learned and loaden treatises on German metaphysics or other abstruse subjects, which might be interesting to a few *savans*, but were eminently calculated, on the contrary, to remove this very reproach of literature, that it was altogether removed from the sphere of general sympathy, and unconnected with the living interests of life and society; and in accomplishing this they happily avoided another reflection upon letters, and, instead of adopting a German mannerism or anything equivalent, steered clear of all pedantry or pretension. They opened up a source of the most delightful entertainment and instruction, in a style replete with elegance, and intelligible to all, by which, in the words of Johnson, "An emulation of intellectual elegance was excited, and, from that time to our own, life has been gradually exalted, and conversation purified and enlarged." Whether they were greater public benefactors than if they had twaddled German metaphysics or any such subjects, the benefit of which to society has yet to be discovered, or instead of a style of elegant simplicity had adopted a German jargon, as if language was given to conceal our thoughts, it is not difficult to determine. Coleridge, whose splendid mind was equally spoilt by his addiction to opium and German metaphysics, confesses that this mannerism induces those who do not know what it is worth to confer the title of *thinkers* upon those who employ it. Mr Jenkinson, in the "Vicar of Wakefield," of cosmogony memory, was a philosopher of this class. But if there be anything more than another characteristic of true greatness, it is simplicity; and to render difficult things easy is alone worthy of greatness, as it is equally characteristic of pretentious mediocrity to render things simple difficult and obscure.

It may perhaps afford some clue to the principle of the Professor's vituperation of such writers as Addison and Steele, to find that it is such as Hume that he

sublime idea that warms and kindles in us, together with
a certain self-disdain and desire of imitation ; when, on
the other side, to say it was like a primitive Christian,
chills ambition, and seldoms rises to more than the cold ap--
probation of a duty, that perhaps a man wishes he were not
obliged to. Or, in a word, why is it that the heathen struts,
and the Christian sneaks, in our imagination ?" In order,
therefore, to satisfy the judgment "whether they or we are
better appointed for the hard and weary march of human
life," he selects some of the most remarkable among the
great characters of antiquity—Cæsar, Cato, Marcus Brutus,
and Cassius—draws minute portraits of them, and, by the
example of two men like Cato and Brutus, so conspicuous
for their wisdom and integrity, yet terminating their lives
by their own hand, demonstrates how utterly insufficient
was the boasted philosophy which could not bear up against
adversity. He quotes the remarkable reply of Brutus to
the inquiry of Cassius on the night preceding the fatal
battle at Philippi, as to his intentions in case of defeat :—
"When I was young, Cassius, and unskilled in affairs, I

delights to honour, who as a historian was the ill-concealed apologist of arbitrary
authority, the almost sole merit of whose work is its incomparable style, and
who, with reference to his other writings, was a man of too sagacious a mind to
have been himself misled by the self-refuting sophistry of his own philosophy.

Perhaps Steele's share of the vituperation of the learned Professor may have
resulted from spleen at the remarks, if he had seen them, in the *Tatler*, No.
197, elicited by the honour conferred on Isaac Bickerstaff by some German writers
in a Latin dedication of a collection of Latin letters:—" It seems this is a collection of letters which some profound blockheads who lived before our times
have written in honour of each other, and for their mutual information in each
other's absurdities. They are mostly of the German nation, whence, from time to
time, inundations of writers have flowed, more pernicious to the learned world
than the swarms of Goths and Vandals to the politic. It is, methinks, wonderful
that fellows could be awake and utter such incoherent conceptions, and converse
with great gravity, without the least taste of knowledge or good sense," &c.

was engaged, I know not how, into an opinion of philosophy which made me accuse Cato for killing himself, as thinking it an irreligious act against the gods, nor any way valiant amongst men, not to submit to divine Providence nor be able fearlessly to receive and undergo whatever shall happen, but to fly from it. But now, in the midst of dangers, I am quite of another mind; for if Providence shall not dispose what I now undertake according to our wishes, I resolve to try no further hopes, nor make any more preparations for war, but will die contented with my fortune, for I already have given up my life to the service of my country on the ides of March, and all the time that I have lived since has been with liberty and honour."

"However gallant," says Steele, "this speech may seem at first sight, it is upon reflection a very mean one; for he urges no manner of reason for his desertion of the noble principle of resignation to the Divine will, but his dangers and distresses; which, indeed, is no more than if he had plainly confessed, that all the schemes we can propose to ourselves in a composed and prosperous condition, when we come to be oppressed with calamities, vanish from us, and are but the effects of luxuriant ease and good humour, and languish and die away with them."

He then notices some of the most remarkable events of what he terms "a certain neglected book, which is called, and for its genuine excellence above all other books, deservedly called, *the Scriptures*," dwelling particularly on the life and actions of St Paul. In contrast with his doctrines and precepts, he quotes Seneca: "A gallant man is Fortune's match; his courage provokes and despises those terrible appearances that would enslave us: a wise man is out of the reach of Fortune, but not free from the malice of it, and all attempts upon him are no more than Xerxes' arrows; they may darken the day, but they cannot strike the sun." "This," says Steele, "is Seneca's very spirit, opinion, and genius; but, alas, what absurdity is here! After the panegyric of a brave or honest man, as the disciple and imitator of God, this is instanced in the basest action a man could be guilty of, a general despatching himself in an extreme difficulty, and deserting his men and his honour : and what is this but doing a mean action with a great countenance? What could this imitator of God, out of the power of Fortune, do more in obedience to what they call so, than sacrificing his life to it? But this is bombast got into the very soul,—fustian in thinking!"

As a contrast, and commentary on the history of Paul, he says that "his one constant motive for living was a confidence in God ; for had he breathed on any other cause, instead of application to the Almighty, he must (on many occasions we have mentioned) have run to the dagger or the bowl of poison ; for the heathen virtue prescribes death before stripes and imprisonment; but whatever pompous look elegant pens may have given to the illustrious distressed, (as they would have us think the persons are who, to evade miseries, have profused their lives, and rushed to death for relief,) if we look to the bottom of things we shall easily observe that it is not a generous scorn of chains, or a delicate distaste of an impertinent being, (which two pretences include all the varnish that is put upon self-murder,) but it ever was, and ever will be, pride or cowardice that makes life insupportable ; for, since accidents are not in our power, but will, in spite of all our care and vigilance, befall us, what remains but that we accommodate ourselves so far as to bear them with the greatest decency and handsomest patience we are able? And, indeed, resistance to what we cannot avoid is not the effect of a valiant heart, but of a stubborn stomach."*

Having thus brought the heathen philosophy to this test, he next enters upon a consideration of the motives and springs of human actions, and asserts that "true greatness of mind is to be maintained only on Christian principles." But we have, perhaps, dwelt at too great length on this elegant little Essay,† and shall only add, that it concludes with a contrast between Louis XIV. and the illustrious William, and a high panegyric on the latter, whom he seems to have had in his eye as the model of a Christian hero.

As Steele justly objected to the recognition of suicide among the ancients, it is highly to his credit that, though a military man, he also opposed the practice of duelling among the moderns, which he attacked in the *Tatler* with all the force of wit, and reason, and ridicule on various occasions. Yet he was about this time, greatly against his will, dragged into a duel, which had nearly proved fatal to his antagonist, whose life for a considerable time hung in the balance. Yet, strange to say, this duel was actually forced upon him in consequence of his endeavours to prevent another. A brother officer in the Coldstream regiment having communicated to Steele an affront, as he imagined, that had been put upon him, and his intention of forthwith calling out the author of it, he used every means to dis-

* ." Christian Hero," pp. 108–9.

† It was so successful, that in the course of the year a new edition, with additions, was brought out, and by the year 1712 it had reached the extent of six editions.

suade him from his design. To his surprise, however, when he fancied he had succeeded, he found that the companions of the young officer had wrought him into a belief that the advice had been given in the interest of his antagonist, to the compromise of his own honour. His resentment was, in consequence, transferred to his pacific adviser, whom he ridiculously challenged in turn. Steele was just recovering from a severe attack of fever, and, feeling the folly and absurdity of the affair, exhausted every source of argument and raillery to avoid the issue. Failing in these, he had no alternative, as a military man in those days, but reluctantly to accept the challenge. Conscious, however, of skill in the use of his weapon, he did not doubt of humbling his hot-headed opponent, without any serious results. They met accordingly, and Steele, after standing on the defensive for some time, and merely warding off the thrusts of his antagonist, at length attempted to disarm him; but in doing so, the other hastily turning to parry the stroke, he unfortunately ran him through. Though he ultimately recovered, his life long hung in uncertainty; and the grief and care with which Steele was harassed during the period of suspense, added depth to the feeling of reprobation with which he ever regarded this barbarous practice, on which he subsequently brought to bear all the force of wit and invective. Whether this young man was made a tool of, and this was one of those occasions to which Steele alludes, when he says that, after the publication of the "Christian Hero," some of his acquaintance thought fit to try their valour upon him, is not certain, though highly probable.

The simplicity with which Steele implies surprise that he should have met with so little encouragement as a self-reformer is certainly rather amusing. However, finding the task an ungrateful one, and wearied with the constant rebuffs that he met with, he felt the necessity, he tells us,* of enlivening his character, with which view he set about exercising that dramatic talent which had first shown itself, though in an unsuccessful essay, during his residence at Oxford.

Before entering on this subject, however, it may be desirable to glance cursorily at the then state of the drama, and the immediate predecessors of Steele in its cultivation. At the period when he commenced his career as a dramatic writer, Congreve, perhaps the most brilliant of the group who flourished at this time, had just retired, having laid down his pen the previous year, in disgust at the want of success of his last production, and also at another circumstance presently to be noticed.

The brilliant comic drama of this period was a faithful reflection of that terrible saturnalia of libertinism into which the nation had rushed at the Restoration, influenced in a great part by the example of the Court, but under an impulse also to indemnify itself for the enforced restraint of the Puritan times. The earliest of its cultivators, and, indeed, of the English prose comic drama generally, with the exception of Etherege, who was little more than a mere flashy ephemeral sketcher, was WILLIAM WYCHERLEY, the son of a country gentleman of ancient family and moderate estate at Clive, in Shropshire, where he was born about the year 1640. The family were loyalists, and Puritanism being then in the ascendant in the colleges as well as elsewhere, young Wycherley, after receiving the rudiments of

* In his " Apology."

education at home, was sent to France, where being made free of the brilliant circle of the Duke of Montausier and his accomplished Duchess, the celebrated Mademoiselle Rambouillet, in return for the advantages he acquired, he was induced to relinquish his religion, which, considering the facility he afterwards shewed in this respect, was probably a small loss.

At the Restoration (1660) he returned, and was entered a student of Queen's College, Oxford, where he left without taking his degree, but not until he had been reconverted to Protestantism by Dr (afterwards Bishop) Barlow. He then entered at the Temple, though he made the gay world much more of his study than the law. In his old age Wycherley gave Pope a chronology of his plays, which represented "Love in a Wood" to have been written when he was only nineteen, "The Gentleman Dancing-Master" at twenty-one, "The Plain-dealer" at twenty-five, and "The Country Wife" at one or two and thirty; but his memory was at the time little to be depended on, and the internal evidence is opposed to these dates.

If even partially true, however, (that is, if sketched and afterwards filled up), he displayed an amount of patience very unusual with young authors, since he must have produced his whole stock before he made any of them public. "Love in a Wood" was successfully brought upon the stage in 1672, and was the occasion of a remarkable episode, which tinged his whole future life. It brought him acquainted with the notorious Duchess of Cleveland. The manner of this event has been variously stated. She is represented to have put her head out of the window of her carriage, and reviled him in passing. This led Wycherley to call the following day, and very demurely inquire in what way he had been so unfortunate as to offend her Grace. This led to an explanation, involving a reference to his play, and so the affair was amicably settled, and the acquaintance made. Wycherley was subsequently introduced by her to her cousin Buckingham, then Master of the Horse, who made him one of his equerries, gave him a commission in his regiment, and brought him acquainted with the King. Charles does not appear to have displayed any jealousy of his handsome rival, (as he was regarded in popular estimation,) but, being pleased with his company, took much notice of him, and is even said to have befriended him in a way that might least have been expected from the chronic infirmity of his finances; for when Wycherley was recovering from a fever, the good-natured monarch called at his lodging in Bow Street, and sat by his bedside, recommended a change of air, and furnished him with L.500 to defray his expenses to Montpelier. He also fixed upon him as tutor to his natural son, the young Duke of Richmond.

Before referring, however, to the sequel of this piece of good fortune, it should be stated that Wycherley had now brought upon the stage and published his three other plays, "The Gentleman Dancing-Master" in 1673, " The Country Wife" in 1675, and " The Plain-dealer" in 1677. The incident that follows may be supposed to have occurred some short time after the latter date. As his first play, " Love in a Wood," was the means of introducing him to the Duchess of Cleveland, so his last, " The Plain-dealer," led to another fashionable but more creditable acquaintance.

Elated with the royal proposal respecting the young duke, Wycherley went for a day's variety to Tunbridge Wells, in company with a Mr Fairbeard of Gray's-Inn. There the two friends dropped in at a bookseller's shop, just as a young widow lady, handsome, and, as it proved, rich, inquired for the recently-published "Plain-dealer." Wycherley's friend, with ready tact and wit, told the lady, if she was for the Plain-dealer, there (giving him a gentle push) he was for her. Wycherley, then, as readily taking his cue, paid the lady the courtly commonplace, that she might well bear plain-dealing, since what would be compliment to others would be plain-dealing to her. The lady condescended to make a modest reply, deprecating flattery and disclaiming exemption from the faults of her sex. Thus was an acquaintance begun which did not end there. The lady turned out to be the Countess of Drogheda. She was captivated with the conversation and appearance of Wycherley, and without any long probation they were privately married. This has been attributed to the dread of Wycherley that the step might interfere with the plans of Charles. But while that supposition seems difficult to account for, the clandestine plan had the very effect he feared. When the secret came out, the king is said to have been offended at what he regarded as want of candour and respect, and the breach was widened by the extravagantly jealous temper of the lady, who kept him away from Court, the temptations of which she well knew, from having been one of the maids of honour—one of the Mdlle Robartes of Grammont's "Memoirs."

But the real cause of the permanent loss of favour at

Court, and one that can hardly create much surprise, was probably the very decided part he took in favour of Buckingham, in his quarrels with the Court—even when he was in the Tower for his opposition, addressing some lines to him which, in no equivocal terms, branded the Court with the blame. This may have been very creditable to him as a man, but was certainly very imprudent as a courtier. The favour he had enjoyed was withdrawn in consequence—not, perhaps, of the lines, which may never have been seen, though some candid friend is seldom wanting in such cases,—but of the feeling they indicated manifesting itself in other ways. The consolation which he should have derived from a helpmeet, if other things had met in her with beauty and riches, he found instead to be a thorn in the flesh. The lady had a temper and will of her own, in addition to a jealousy that was inordinate. The string that she allowed him was a short one. Within eyeshot on the opposite side there was a tavern, and there he was permitted to meet his acquaintance; only the meeting was to be an open one, that is, with open windows for inspection. But all things have an end; the chain was snapped; and the lady left him only a legacy of litigation. The will was disputed, and the property successfully claimed by her family.

In proper sequence it should have been stated previously that Wycherley, probably in the early days of his favour at Court, when noblemen and gentlemen were volunteering their presence at least in the navy, whatever their services may have been, following the prevailing fashion, had put on his sea legs, and been present at an engagement with the Dutch—either that with Opdam in 1665, or that with De Ruyter in 1773, but probably the latter.* The single experiment quite satisfied him with scenes of glory. This we find from some verses he wrote on the occasion, for, like Cicero, it was his weakness to indulge in versification, for which he had no vocation. It might have been all very well for him to have followed the prevailing fashion, which made the writing of copies of verses the necessary accomplishment of a gentleman about town, if he had had no character to maintain, or had even remembered the *litera scripta manet*, and forborne to publish.

The fortune of the dramatist now sunk from bad to worse, till it culminated in a seven years' residence in the Fleet, with an utter obliviousness of his existence, apparently, on the part of those summer friends who had fluttered with him in the sunbeams of fortune. Even in quarters connected with the ties of business, where romance is sometimes found to linger when she has forsaken more congenial regions, all resource failed him. The publisher who had realised largely by his writings is even said to have denied him a loan of L.20. But fortune at length relented. The loves and the hates of Charles were now no more, and his brother, James, Duke of York, reigned in his stead. The works of Wycherley, with a fortune better than that of their author, were not banished from the stage, and the "Plain-dealer" chanced to be performed one evening when the king was present. Admiration of the piece, and commiseration for the misfortunes of its

* Mr Leigh Hunt, "Works of Wycherley, Congreve, Vanbrugh, and Farquhar, with Biographical Notices," inclines to the former; Lord Macaulay to the latter : "Essay on Dramatists of the Restoration."

author, seem to have moved him to an act of unwonted liberality, an almost solitary instance on behalf of men of letters, and he gave directions not only for the payment of Wycherley's debts, but settled on him a pension of L.200 a year. It is impossible to connect this with any certainty with the casting again of his theological coat; but as the event did occur, it must be regarded as suspicious. Nothing is known of any conditions on the subject. One, indeed, there was which was only less illiberal than the other would have been. It was made dependent on his residence in England.

Somewhere about the same time, or a little later, he fell into the property by the death of his father; but even this failed to remove his still existing embarrassments; for, singular as it may seem, he is said, from a feeling of modesty, to have understated his liabilities to the noble friend deputed by the king to wait upon him, and to have stated only those necessary to relieve him from present difficulties. His extravagant habits may probably have added to the unliquidated claims, and the property (like that of many other loyalists) may have been encumbered, as his father had been previously either unable or unwilling to assist him. He was not then a young man; the property was strictly entailed; and as he was on bad terms with the next heir, all these circumstances were unfavourable to his raising any considerable sum of ready money. Time and care had told on both mind and body. His appearance was so altered that Pope, who spoke of him as having the true nobleman look, says it mortified his vanity so deeply that he would sigh over the early portrait of him by Lely, and repeat, *Quantum mutatus ab illo.* Nor was the change confined to his outward appearance. An illness had affected his memory in a most singular way. What he had heard or read over night would return to his waking thoughts with singular freshness and tenacity, though he was not aware of the source, nor suspected that it did not originate in his own mind. He was still haunted with a morbid desire, in which judgment by no means entered, of extending his literary fame. In pursuance of this feeling, he had published in the year 1704 a volume of wretched verses, amatory and satirical, which were an anachronism in every way. He was then in his sixty-fourth year, neither was the taste of the times by any means so depraved as formerly, and this improvement was indicated in the practice of most of the recent writers.

Among these, a youth destined to take a foremost place among the wits of the time, and then residing in the shades of Windsor Forest, had just published a volume of pastorals, and this had led to a friendship which was strikingly antithetical in all its parts. This youth had an intense reverence for the veterans and chiefs of letters. He had sought with eagerness at his club a sight of Dryden, in his declining years, and the same feeling induced him to seek the acquaintance of Wycherley, and to frequent his company like his shadow. The contrast between the two persons thus brought together was very striking. The youth was sixteen, diminutive, weakly, and deformed, but with eyes that told of the brightness within; the other sixty-four, but with the remains of a commanding presence, and a countenance from which beauty had not perhaps quite departed. Nor were the two volumes thus simultaneously given to the world less dissimilar than the persons. The one, feeble, hobbling, and careless in manner, and in matter obscene; while the other, breathing of the freshness and purity of rural life, was nervous, epigrammatic, and marked with carefulness. Wycherley had still another volume similar to the last, yet unpublished. This, in an evil hour, he committed to his young friend for revision, and a correspondence ensued. Pope,—for of course it was he,—with his fastidious taste and vigorous style, in order to make anything of the worthless mass, was obliged to score out, and interline, and mangle in a sad way. In the correspondence, the confession of his diffidence in taking too great but necessary liberties being made with more candour than delicacy, naturally grated upon the feelings of the foolish old man, and the intercourse came to an abrupt conclusion.

The close of Wycherley's life was marked by a strange episode. At the age of seventy-five, with the double purpose of inflicting an injury on the next heir to the family property, whom he disliked, and of contributing to his own comfort, he married a young wife, under the supposition of her having considerable property. He survived the event little more than a week. Shortly before his decease, having obtained her consent to a parting request, he told her "it was only that she should never marry an old man again." His death occurred at the close of 1715.

The young widow did not make any unnecessary mourning for him, but very shortly after married a man with whom it was suspected she was in collusion in her designs upon the old man. She, of course, became possessed of the manuscript volume of verse, which, though almost illegible with erasures and interlineations, and utterly worthless but for the touches of Pope visible throughout, was, on the strength of these and the reputation of Wycherley, ultimately made public.

Wycherley had the reputation of having been personally modest and gentle, good-natured and sincere. He afforded an evidence of the first in having declined to join with Dryden in writing a comedy, which he has recorded in some verses. The title of Manly applied to himself from his character of that name in "The Plain-dealer," is supposed to have been given from its applicability; but his comedies, though abounding in wit, would not give a favourable idea of his morality. Indeed, in them especially, it may be said, in the words of an eminent writer in his ingenious plea for the comic dramatists of this period, "that there no cold moral reigns."* Even in the wit of the dialogue, though abundant and in some respects in excess, since the fools come in for their full share, the effort is not always concealed. Wycherley's writings, on the whole, cannot be said to belong to the first order. Hints are taken freely both from the French and Spanish comedy, as well as from Shakespeare; and what he takes he by no means improves, especially in a moral point of view. His style, though deficient in airiness, is clear and forcible, unaffected and pure.

The next of these writers to be noticed is SIR JOHN VANBRUGH, soldier, dramatist, and architect, descended from a Flemish family, according to the most probable of the confused and contradictory accounts respecting him, and born

* See Lamb's essay "On the Artificial Comedy of the Last Century," in which he has ingeniously expressed his predilection for these entertaining productions, and endeavoured to prove their immorality innocuous by removing them from all connexion with actual life into the category of mere conventional fiction. The argument is certainly equivocal and singular, coming from so pure a writer.

in 1666 or 1672. After spending some part of his youth in France, he returned to England, entered the army, and was styled captain for some time. He must also have studied architecture at some time, though nothing is definitely known on the subject. In 1695, we find him appointed, through the interest of the famous John Evelyn, secretary to the commission for endowing Greenwich Hospital. About two years subsequently appeared his first piece, "The Relapse," on the boards of Drury Lane, and was succeeded in the following year by "The Provoked Wife." Both of these are said to have been sketched while he was in the army, and to have been brought out in the inverse order of their production. At the instance of Montague, afterwards Lord Halifax, this second piece was brought out at the theatre in Lincoln's-Inn-Fields. It had been intended for Drury Lane, of which his friend Sir Thomas Skipwith (one of the first to encourage his dramatic talents, and to whom he was under other obligations) was one of the shareholders. To supply its place, therefore, he produced, in the course of the same year, an adaptation from the French of Boursault, entitled "Æsop," with the addition of a more lively second part of his own. The experiment shewed, however, that though the public cordially accepted such entertainment as his former pieces afforded, they were not prepared to accept a moral lecture at his hands.

Two other adaptations for the same house followed in close succession. These were Fletcher's comedy of the "Pilgrim," and a Spanish love-story, "The False Friend," in 1700 and 1702. The proceeds of one night of the former were appropriated to the benefit of the great luminary of letters, Dryden, now hastening to his setting. Some of his very latest effusions in a line in which he stood unapproached,—namely, in epilogues and prologues,—were contributed on this occasion.

In the year last mentioned, Vanbrugh began to distinguish himself in his rather incongruous double capacity of architect by his design of Castle Howard, the seat of Earl Carlisle, who being then Deputy Earl Marshal, as a mark of approbation conferred on Vanbrugh, in default of something better, the office of Clarencieux King-at-Arms. This gave occasion to Swift, who indulged his raillery at his expense, not merely as a consistent Whig, but that he did not always respect the cloth, to say that "now indeed he might pretend to build houses." Vanbrugh, however, professed only to laugh at heraldry.

A few years later, Congreve and Betterton having procured a patent for the erection of a new theatre, Vanbrugh united with them, and having obtained the co-operation of about thirty persons of fortune who contributed L.100 each, resolved to give his fancy full scope in stone and lime. The monster edifice was duly erected in the Haymarket on the site of the Opera-house. He also wrote for it "The Confederacy," one of the wittiest but most licentious of his productions, thus displaying his various talents side by side. But some great mistake or oversight, in reference to the purpose of the magnificent pile, caused the whole scheme to collapse; for when the experiment came to be tried, the dialogue of the actors was little more than dumb show, with an accompaniment of resounding echoes.

Though Vanbrugh's family had taken a high social position previously, his good nature and other amiable and agreeable qualities made him personally very popular. In

1706 the queen paid him the compliment of selecting him as the bearer of the insignia of the order of the Garter to the Elector of Hanover. In the course of the same year he built a residence for himself at Whitehall, the diminutiveness and peculiar structure of which, especially in comparison with the grandeur of his public designs, occasioned the raillery of Swift on the subject. He also built two other similar playthings of his fancy at Greenwich, one of which was called, either by himself or some one else, the "Mince-pie House." Swift says in his journal that the Duchess of Marlborough used to tease him with his lines referring to the house in Whitehall. They represented inquirers vainly searching for it, but

> "At length they in the rubbish spy
> A thing resembling a goose-pie."

With regard to the Duchess of Marlborough's teasing, Vanbrugh would no doubt have gladly compounded for his vexation on that subject, if her grace had spared him any from other sources; but his having been appointed architect of the magnificent mansion of Blenheim, voted by Parliament to Marlborough, proved a source of endless trouble to him. No supply had been voted for the work in anticipation. The queen had at first supplied the funds; and afterwards the duke, notwithstanding his fondness for money, had furnished driblets, but after his death the duchess endeavoured to throw the burden upon him. This led to an extended correspondence, and ultimately to a Chancery suit. From some notices of her in his letters to other correspondents, it appears evident that his good-nature was taxed to speak of her with any forbearance.

After much vexation, he succeeded in obtaining through Sir Robert Walpole the liquidation of his claims.

Vanbrugh was married to a daughter of Colonel Yarborough of Haslington, near York, about the year 1710, and on the accession of George I. in 1714, he received the honour of knighthood. In the year following he was appointed comptroller of the royal works, and in that succeeding, surveyor of the works at Greenwich Hospital. He was nominated to the office of Garter King-at-Arms, but had to yield to prior claims.

He died of a quinsy, at his house in Whitehall, March 26, 1726. Dr Evans, a wit of the time, made an epitaph on him in reference to the attributed heaviness of his architectural structures:—

> "Lie heavy on him, earth, for he
> Laid many a heavy load on thee."

Though this was a subject of pleasantry with the wits of the time, yet posterity has recognised the grandeur of his designs, as indeed the public of his own day probably did as well. Even from a painter, and that Sir Joshua Reynolds, his architectural works have received a high tribute of praise. "In them," he says, "there is a greater display of imagination than we shall find perhaps in any other. To speak of him," he adds, "in the language of a painter, he had originality of invention, he understood light and shadow, and had great skill in composition.... This is a tribute which a painter owes to an architect who composed like a painter, and was defrauded of the due reward of his merit by the wits of the time."

Besides his great works of Blenheim and Castle Howard, Vanbrugh built numerous other mansions.

As a dramatist, it is to be regretted that while he excelled in invention, variety of character, and a natural and manly style, his animal spirits and the licence of the times should have led him to indulge in the excessive licentiousness with which he is chargeable.

Personally, all the accounts of Vanbrugh concur in being highly laudatory. Rowe, in an imitation of Horace, makes Tonson the publisher, who was a country neighbour of his at one time, describe Captain Vanbrugh as

> " A most sweet-natured gentleman, and pleasant ;
> He writes your comedies, draws schemes and models,
> And builds dukes' houses upon very odd hills."

It was perhaps after having met him personally, and experienced his amiable and agreeable qualities, that both Pope and Swift expressed their compunction for the raillery in which they had indulged at his expense.

The last of this very entertaining group of writers to be noticed is GEORGE FARQUHAR, son (according to the most probable of the varying accounts respecting him) of a clergyman of small means, at Londonderry, where he was born in 1678. After receiving his elementary education at home, he entered the University of Dublin as a sizar; and to the mortifying effect, to a youth of spirit, of the unworthy degradation entailed at the period on those entering in that humble capacity, may have been owing a paralysing mental influence and a recklessness of disposition which he is said to have displayed during his college career. Owing either to certain acts of levity and indiscipline which have been attributed to him, or some other cause, he took an abrupt leave of college. Whether this was compulsory or voluntary is uncertain, but its result could scarcely have been unacceptable to such a disposition in introducing him to the larger and more congenial school of the world. He immediately tendered his services to a theatrical manager. But his love of the histrionic art was not destined to run smooth. He was possessed of average qualifications, except in deficiency of voice and nerve; but an accident which acutely affected his sensitive nature soon caused him to relinquish this first love, before he had overcome the great difficulty of young actors, the terror of facing an audience. In a hostile encounter in one of his performances, the disposition to give reality to the mimic scene caused him to overlook the fact that it was a real sword he wore, and he wounded his antagonist so severely as almost to prove fatal.

Wilks, an actor of established reputation, to whose intimacy congenial education and tastes had recommended him, being about to proceed to London, Farquhar was induced to join him, and by his advice to turn his attention to dramatic composition. An event soon after occurred which influenced his future life, but of which no particulars are known, nor whether his friend contributed to it. An introduction to Lord Orrery procured him the favourable notice of that nobleman, who presented him with a commission in his regiment. In 1700 we find him doing duty in Holland. His profession was no doubt of service to him in his dramatic pursuits, not only by relieving his mind of anxiety, but by enlarging the sphere of his observation and increasing his facilities for the study of character.

The favourable reception of his first venture, "Love and a Bottle," which made its appearance at Drury Lane in 1698, at once gave him assurance of success, and opened his way to the favour of the town. His encouragement and influence at the same time were the means of opening the way to the brilliant career of the celebrated Mrs Oldfield. With success, rapidity of production followed as a natural consequence, and his works appeared in quick succession. A little volume, published anonymously under the title of " The Adventures of Covent Garden," in imitation of Scarron's city romance, from which he is known to have taken some hints, has been traced to him by his latest biographer, Mr Leigh Hunt.* In the following year (1700) appeared with success on the same boards as the former, " The Constant Couple."

Of the funeral of Dryden, which occurred at this time, he was a spectator, and has written an account, from which the ceremonial appears to have been a very ill-managed affair. The latter part of the year found Farquhar in Holland, from which he appears to have returned in the train of the illustrious William.

" Sir Harry Wildair," a sequel to the preceding comedy, appeared in the following year, which, though well received, was not equally successful with the former. This was followed by his " Miscellanies," including an " Essay on Comedy." In 1703 appeared " The Inconstant; or, the Way to Win Him," founded on Fletcher's " Wild-goose Chase."

About the same time, probably, a lady who was enamoured of the young officer found a " Way to Win *Him*." She pretended to be possessed of a fortune, and as he was too gallant to baulk her fancy, he took her without inquiry on the subject. When she confessed the deception, he

* Biographical Notices to Works of Farquhar, &c., p. lxv.

never reproached or ill-treated her, though both suffered for it.

In 1704 he produced "The Stage-coach" from the French, which was followed in each succeeding year by "The Twin Rivals," "The Recruiting Officer," and his latest masterpiece, "The Beaux Stratagem," in 1707. These, with the exception of the last, were produced in the intervals of his military duties, and with the stimulus to meet the claims of a growing family.

Poor Farquhar had been the dupe of a second deception. Some one had filled him with false hopes of patronage, and cruelly induced him to sell his commission. The disappointment, with other causes perhaps, led to a fatal termination. He sickened, and in the flush of his final success expired, short of his thirtieth year.

A benefit was got up for his widow and two daughters, and some friend procured for them a trifling pension; but they appear ultimately to have sunk into a state of extreme indigence, a sad response to the brief and touching deathbed note in which he had commended them to the care of his friend Wilks, who was in good circumstances.

Farquhar united high animal spirits to sensitiveness and a tendency to melancholy. And the reflection of this thrown into his plays, was combined with the happiest invention, great variety of character and a more natural tone than is to be found in most others of the same school. His plots, with the two exceptions of "The Inconstant" and "The Stage-coach," which were professed adaptations, were all his own. Owing to his experience and his models, he was, like most of his contemporaries, too conventional; and from the same cause, perhaps, his moral tone is, like that of the others of the period, though not certainly in the same degree, to be condemned. The objection to the moral tone of these writers does not, of course, rest on the ground of mere coarseness and want of delicacy of expression, as in Swift; but that they endeavoured, in accordance with the manners of the time, to render what was vicious attractive, and *vice versa*. But the evil becomes more diluted as we recede from the fountain-head of this inspiration. There is also a greater tone of sentiment and humanity in Farquhar, his wit is less artificial and more spontaneous and hearty, and he has in consequence, no doubt, retained possession of the stage far beyond any of his contemporaries.

Congreve, though perhaps the most brilliant of the list, is reserved for a more convenient opportunity of noticing him, where his name again occurs.

But while these writers were revelling in the display of the fireworks of their wit, an event occurred that had an effect among them, like the falling of a bomb into a camp. This was a fierce onslaught made upon the stage by JEREMY COLLIER, a High-Church parson of considerable ability and much learning, with the bigotry of a Laud, and the spirit of a martyr. This fanatical priest had previously displayed, in the maintenance of his theological, but especially his political, principles, a heroism worthy of a better cause. He had strenuously defended the exiled monarch, had been arrested in 1692 on suspicion of complicity in a treasonable plot, and could with difficulty be prevailed on to accept of bail. He had previously relinquished his position rather than take the oaths to William, against whom he attempted to stir up, by the fierceness of his pen, an opposition that had failed with the sword. He even gave public absolution to Friend and Parkins previous to their execution for an attempted assassination of the king. It is true that when he had to confront the tempest of obloquy, which the terrible scandal of his daring act had raised in the general public opinion, and the censure of the dignitaries of the Church, he inconsistently disclaimed the imputed inference of not regarding the act as a crime. But it was not pretended that the culprits had made any confessions of penitence, which could alone have given any colour of propriety to his act. Yet by a strange example of human inconsistency, the man who had blasphemously dared to grant absolution to two assassins in intention, soon after set himself up as the censor of the immorality of words. Murder might be absolved, though unrecanted, but *double entendres* were without the pale.

The "Short View of the Profaneness and Immorality of the English Stage," in which this member of the church militant brought his heavy artillery to bear against his opponents, made its appearance in 1698, as if to complete, in a social view, the revolution recently accomplished in the state. It was unquestionably in itself a well-timed public service; and though full of the most absurd crotchets, it produced a wonderful effect, and claimed for its author the title of a master of controversial art. There was no opponent that could stand before him; he routed the whole dramatic phalanx. The one that would have been most a match for him at his own weapons—Dryden—became a convert. Congreve was unwise enough to enter the lists, and came to grief. Not only did all the brilliancy of his wit seem to forsake him, but his characteristic affectation, that had disgusted Voltaire, which he retained, laid him open to the most palpable hits. His pieces were trifles written for his own amusement, begun in the levity of youth, and to beguile the time in his recovery from a fit of sickness. "What his disease was I am not to inquire," was Collier's retort; "but it must be a very ill one, to be worse than the remedy." The case was hopeless, indeed, when the unrivalled wit of Congreve paled its ineffectual fires.

Such was the state of dramatic affairs when Steele now produced his first comedy, "The Funeral; or, Grief à-la-Mode," which appeared early the year after "The Christian Hero." The author displays a wonderful knowledge of life and character, as indeed he does in all his writings, and brings his wit and humour to bear especially upon the incredible enormities of the undertakers, and the chicanery and absurd technical phraseology of the lawyers. With reference to the former, he says, "It is not in the power of any pen to paint them better than they do themselves. As, for example, on a door I just now passed by, a great artist thus informs us of his cures upon the dead:—

"'W. W., known and approved for his art of embalming, having preserved the corpse of a gentleman sweet and entire thirteen years without embowelling, and has reduced the bodies of several persons of quality to sweetness, in Flanders and Ireland, after nine months' putrefaction in the ground, and they were known by their friends in England. No man performeth the like.'

"He must," adds Steele, "needs be strangely in love with his life who is not touched with this kind invitation to be pickled; and the noble operator must be allowed to be a very useful person for bringing old friends together; nor would it be unworthy his labour to give us an account at large of the sweet conversation that arose upon meeting such an entire friend as he mentions." In speaking of the part aimed at the lawyers, he says, "Nor could there be a reward high enough assigned for a great genius, if such may be found, who has capacity sufficient to glance through the false colours that are put upon us, and propose to the English world a method of making justice flow in an uninterrupted stream; there is so clear a mind in being," he concludes, in a strain of high compliment to Lord Somers, then out of office, "whom we will name in words that, of all men breathing, can only be said of him: 'Tis he that is excellent.

"'Seu linguam causis acuit, seu Civica Jura,
Responsare parat, seu condit amabile carmen.'"*

The liveliness, humour, and variety of incident in this comedy, made it received as it deserved, and the measure of its success also received some addition from the author's military connexion. The manner of my Lord Brompton cheating his wife into a belief of his death, on which the plot turns, though, perhaps, rather obscure and improbable, is worked out with much comic effect. The rehearsal of Sable the undertaker, with his hired mourners, and his being scandalised by one hearty-looking fellow, whose countenance appeared to have no indication of sadness, is admirable. "Look yonder at that hale, well-looking puppy. You ungrateful scoundrel, did not I give you ten, then sixteen, now twenty shillings a week to be sor-

* Preface to "The Funeral."

rowful? and the more I give you, I think the gladder you are." As a specimen of the dialogue, we give the scene between the two sisters, Lady Sharlot and Lady Harriot, to whom Lord Hardy, son of Lord Brompton, and Mr Campley, his friend, are paying their respective addresses:—

LADY SHARLOT *reading,* LADY HARRIOT *admiring herself in a mirror.*

Lady H. Nay, good sage sister, you may as well talk to me as sit staring at a book which I know you cannot attend to. Good Dr Lucas may have writ there what he pleases, but there's no putting Francis, Lord Hardy, now Earl of Brompton, out of your head, or making him absent from your eyes. Do look at me now, and deny it if you can!

Lady S. You are the maddest girl—— [*Smiling.*

Lady H. Look ye, I knew you couldn't say it, and forbear laughing. [*Looking over* SHARLOT.] Oh, I see his name as plain as you do—F-r-a-n, Fran, c-i-s, cis, Francis—'tis in every line of the book.

Lady S. [*Rising.*] 'Tis in vain, I see, to mind anything in such impertinent company. But granting 'twere as you say as to my Lord Hardy, 'tis more excusable to admire another than one's self.

Lady H. No, I think not. Yes, I grant you, than really to be vain of one's person; but I don't admire myself. Pish! I don't believe my eyes have that softness. [*Looking in the glass.*] They ain't so piercing: no, 'tis only stuff—the men will be talking. Some people are such admirers of teeth. Lord, what signifies teeth? [*Shewing her teeth.*] A very blackamoor has as white teeth as I. No, sister, I don't admire myself, but I've a spirit of contradiction in me: I don't know I'm in love with myself, only to rival the men.

Lady S. Ay, but Mr Campley will gain ground even of that rival of his, your dear self.

Lady H. Oh! what have I done to you, that you should name that insolent intruder—a confident, opinionative fop. No, indeed, if I am, as a poetical lover of mine sigh'd and sung, of both sexes,

"The public envy and the public care,"

I shan't be so easily catched—I thank him. I want but to be sure, I should heartily torment him by banishing him, and then consider whether he should depart this life or not.

Lady S. Indeed, sister, to be serious with you, this vanity in your humour does not at all become you.

Lady H. Vanity! All the matter is, we gay people are more sincere than you wise folks: All your life's an art—Speak your soul—Look you

D

there. [*Haling her to the glass.*] Are you not struck with a secret pleasure when you view that bloom in your looks, that harmony in your shape, that promptitude of your mien?

Lady S. Well, simpleton, if I am at first so silly as to be taken with myself, I know it is a fault, and take pains to correct it.

Lady H. Pshaw! Pshaw! Talk this musty tale to old Mrs Fardingale, 'tis too soon for me to think at that rate.

Lady S. They that think it too soon to understand themselves, will very soon find it too late. But tell me, honestly, don't you like Campley?

Lady H. The fellow is not to be abhorred; if the forward thing did not think of getting me so easily. Oh, I hate a heart I can't break when I please! What makes the value of dear china, but that 'tis so brittle? Were it not for that, you might as well have stone mugs in your closet.

As the incidents of Steele's life are so various, and his publications so numerous, it may be desirable, for the sake of perspicuity, to notice his dramatic productions in one view. The talents displayed in his first comedy, and its excellent moral tone, had made him popular with the public, and had also brought him under the favourable notice of King William, who, had he lived, designed to have conferred upon him some substantial mark of his approbation. We have this on the author's own authority. "Nothing," he says, in his "Apology," "ever makes the town so fond of a man as a successful play; and this, with some particulars enlarged upon to his advantage, (for princes never hear good or evil in the manner others do,) obtained for him the notice of the king. And his name, &c., to be provided for, was in the last table-book ever worn by the glorious and immortal King William III." This success was so stimulating to his energies that he set himself about the production of a second piece, entitled, "The Tender Husband; or, The Accomplished Fools," which he dedicated to Addison, as a "memorial of an inviolable friendship," and adds, "I should not offer it to you as such, had I not been careful to avoid everything ill-natured, immoral, or prejudicial to what the better part of mankind hold sacred and honourable." His distinguished friend kindly gave this play the benefit of his revision, and some touches from his hand, and aided in promoting its success. He also contributed the prologue to it; and, after his death, Steele, with that generous warmth of affection, and utter freedom from envy which did him so much honour, refers to his obligations to his lost friend. "I remember," he says, "when I finished "The Tender Husband," I told him (Addison) there was nothing I so tenderly wished as that we might, some time or other, publish a work written by us both, which should bear the name of "The Monument," in memory of our friendship. When the play above mentioned was last acted, there were so many applauded strokes in it which I had from the same hand that I thought very meanly of myself that I had never publicly acknowledged them."* In this second performance, which was presented to the public in 1703, the author appears to have made considerable advances in his art. It is an improvement on the "Funeral" in all respects. Sir Harry Gubbins brings his son Humphrey, a booby young squire, a sort of Tony Lumpkin, without his shrewdness and cunning, totally innocent of letters or any knowledge of the world, up to town to effect a match with his cousin, the niece of Hezekiah Tipkin, a city banker. The young lady is an heiress, with her head turned with reading romances. She consequently scorns her booby cousin. Meantime, Captain Clerimont manages to get introduced to the young lady, by bribing Mr Pounce, the lawyer who is engaged in drawing up the

* Preface to the "Drummer."

settlements. By means of a prepossessing person, and humouring her romantic notions, he wins the lady's good graces at their first interview; and at the second, disguised as an artist engaged by Mr Pounce to paint the lady's portrait, he reveals himself, and carries her off in triumph. This is the main plot; but there is an under one, which (though not immoral) would scarcely suit the fastidiousness of the present day to repeat. As a specimen of the dialogue, the painting scene is here given:—

Humphrey. Your servant, ladies.—So, my dear—
Niece. So, my savage—
Aunt. O fye, no more of that to your intended husband, Biddy.
Hump. No matter, I like it as well as duck or love ; I know my cousin loves me as well as I do her.
Aunt. I'll leave you together ; I must go and get ready an entertainment for you when you come home. [*Exit.*
Hump. Well, cousin, are you constant?—Do you hate me still?
Niece. As much as ever.
Hump. What a happiness it is where people's inclinations jump! I wish I knew what to do with you: can you get nobody, d'ye think, to marry you?
Niece. O *Clerimont, Clerimont!* where art thou? [*Aside.*

Enter AUNT, *and* Captain CLERIMONT, *disguised.*

Aunt. This, sir, is the lady you are to draw.—You see, sir, as good flesh and blood as a man could desire to put in colours.
Cler. Madam, I'm generally forced to new-mould every feature, and mend nature's handiwork ; but here she has made so finished an original that I despair of my copy's coming up to it.
Aunt. Do you hear that, niece?
Niece. I don't desire you to make graces where you find none.
Cler. To see the difference of the fair sex! I protest to you, madam, my fancy is utterly exhausted with inventing faces for those that sit to me. The first entertainment I generally meet are complaints for want of sleep; they never look'd so pale in their lives as when they sit for their pictures. Then so many touches and re-touches when the face is finished. That wrinkle ought not to have been—these eyes are too languid, that colour's too weak, that side-look hides the mole on the left cheek. In

short, the whole likeness is struck out. But in you, madam, the highest I can come up to will be but rigid justice.

Hump. A comical dog this!

Aunt. Truly, the gentleman seems to understand his business.

Niece. Sir, if your pencil flatter like your tongue, you are going to draw a picture that won't be at all like me. Sure I have heard that voice somewhere.   *[Aside.*

Cler. Madam, be pleased to place yourself near me, nearer still, madam—here falls the best light. You must know, madam, there are three kinds of airs which the ladies most delight in. There is your haughty, your mild, and your pensive air. The haughty may be expressed with the hand a little more erect than ordinary, and the countenance with a certain disdain in it, so as she may appear almost, but not quite inexorable. This kind of air is generally heightened with a little knitting of the brows. I gave my *Lady Scornwell* the choice of a dozen frowns before she found one to her liking.

Niece. But what's the mild air?

Cler. The mild air is composed of a languish and a smile. But if I might advise I'd rather be a pensive beauty. The pensive usually feels her pulse, leans on one arm, or sits ruminating with a book in her hand, which conversation she is supposed to choose, rather than the endless importunities of lovers.

Hump. A comical dog.

Aunt. Upon my word, he understands his business well. I'll tell you, niece, how your mother was drawn. She had an orange in her hand, and a nosegay in her bosom; but a look so pure and fresh-coloured, you'd have taken her for one of the Seasons.

Niece. I leave these particulars to your own fancy.

Cler. Please, madam, to uncover your neck a little, a little lower still—a little, little lower.

Niece. I'll be drawn thus, if you please, sir.

Cler. Ladies, have you heard the news of a late marriage between a young lady of great fortune, and a younger brother of a good family.

Aunt. Pray, sir, how is it?

Cler. This young gentleman is a particular acquaintance of mine, and much about my age and stature. (Look me full in the face, madam.) He accidentally met the young lady, who had in her all the perfections of her sex. (Hold up your hand, madam,—that's right.) She let him know that his person and discourse were not altogether disagreeable to her. The difficulty was to gain a second interview—(your eyes full upon mine, madam)—for never was there such a sigher in all the valleys of Arcadia as that unfortunate youth during the absence of her he loved.

Aunt. A-lack-a-day!—poor young gentleman!

Niece. It must be he—what a charming amour is this! [*Aside.*

Cler. At length, ladies, he bethought himself of an expedient; he dressed himself, just as I am now, and came to draw her picture. (Your eyes full upon mine, pray, madam.)

Hump. A subtle dog, I warrant him.

Cler. And by that means found an opportunity of carrying her off, and marrying her.

Aunt. Indeed, your friend was a very vicious young man.

Niece. Yet, perhaps, the young lady was not displeased at what he had done.

Cler. But, madam, what were the transports of the lover when she made him that confession?

Niece. I daresay she thought herself very happy when she got out of her guardian's hands.

Aunt. 'Tis very true, niece, there are abundance of those headstrong young baggages about town.

Cler. The gentleman has often told me he was strangely struck at first sight; but when she sat to him for her picture, and assumed all those graces that are proper for the occasion, his torment was so exquisite, his passion so violent, that he could not have lived a day had he not found means to make the charmer of his heart his own.

Hump. 'Tis certainly the foolishest thing in the world to stand shilly-shallying about a woman when one has a mind to marry her.

Cler. The young painter turned poet on the subject. I believe I have the words by heart.

Niece. A sonnet! pray repeat it!

[After hearing it, and expressing her approval, the Aunt exits, when an explanation ensues, and Mr Pounce enters.]

Hump. Well, cousin, the coach is at the door. If you please, I'll lead you.

Niece. I put myself into your hands, good savage; but you promise to leave me.

Hump. I tell you plainly you must not think of having me.

Pounce [*to Cler.*] You'll have opportunity enough to carry her off; the old fellows will be busy with me. I'll gain all the time I can, but be bold and prosper.

Niece. Clerimont, you follow us.

Cler. Upon the wings of love.

Again, he set to work, and in the following year produced "The Lying Lover; or, Ladies' Friendship." The author tells us that he wrote this comedy in conformity with the severity required by that dramatic censor, Jeremy Collier. The result is stated by himself in his defence in the House of Commons, many years after, against the factious charge of sedition, and of being an enemy to Church and State :—" I acknowledge that I cannot tell, sir, what they would have me do to prove myself a churchman ; but I think I have appeared one even in so trifling a thing as a comedy. And considering me as a comic poet, I have been a martyr and confessor for the Church, for this play was damned for its piety."* Some of the scenes were regarded as too serious and pathetic for comedy, and an invasion of the domain of the tragic Muse. The hero of the piece is made to leave his antagonist for dead in a duel, and is committed to prison on the charge of murder. " The anguish he there expresses," as the preface states, " and the mutual sorrow between an only child and a tender parent in that distress, are perhaps an injury to the rules of comedy, but I am sure they are a justice to those of morality." They are, moreover, a proof of the versatility of their author's talents, being very powerful and natural pictures of the effects of remorse, and indicate a capability to have shone in the walks of tragedy also, which Horace Walpole thought demanded less ability than those of her gayer sister. " The critics," that writer ingeniously, and perhaps truly, remarks, " generally consider a tragedy as the next effort of the mind to an epic poem. For my part, I estimate the difficulty of writing a good comedy to be greater than that of composing a good tragedy. Not only is equal genius required, but a comedy demands a more uncommon assemblage of qualities—knowledge of the world, wit, good sense,

* "Apology," &c., p. 48, ed. 1714.

&c., and the qualities superadded to those requisite for tragical composition."*

The hero of the "Lying Lover," Young Book-wit, on leaving Oxford, casts lots with a college friend, Latine, which should be the other's footman in entering on their adventures in the gay world. He sinks his academic character, and affects that of the dashing soldier who has seen service, distinguished himself at sieges, and so forth. He becomes enamoured of a lady whose acquaintance he casually makes, drives a previous admirer into a frenzy of jealousy by pretending to have been favoured with her company on a festive excursion, which leads to a challenge; excuses himself from paying his addresses to a lady proposed to him by his father, who turns out to be no other than his inamorata, on the ground of a pretended clandestine marriage at Oxford. His military pretensions are discovered by the young lady and her friend to be without foundation, when he blunders in paying his addresses to the friend of the one he affects instead of herself, and they consent to an appointment, at which they rally him with his impudent assumption of the martial character. The scene is given as a specimen:—

YOUNG BOOK-WIT *and* LATINE *waiting the arrival of the ladies.*

Y. Book. [*After a song of his own.*] There's for you, Jack; is this not like a fine gentleman that writes for his own diversion?

Lat. And nobody's else.

Y. Book. Now I warrant one of your common sparks would have stamped, fretted, and cried, What the d——l! fooled, jilted, abused! while I, in metre, to shew you how well nothing at all may be made to run—

"The savages about me throng,
Moved with the passion of my song,
And think Victoria stays too long."

---

* "Walpoliana." The candour of these remarks must be admitted, as Walpole was himself the author of a tragedy, "The Mysterious Mother."

Lat. I begin to be one of those savages.

Enter VICTORIA, PENELOPE, LETTICE, *and* BETTY.

Vict. We had better have stayed where we were, and listened to the charming echo, than have come in search of that l——r.

Lat. Do you see yonder?

Y. Book. [*Gives the sign, and sings himself.*] Thus, madam, have I spent my time ever since I saw you, repeated your name to the woods, the dales, and the echoing groves.

Pen. Pr'ythee, observe him. How he begins.

Y. Book. I had not time to carve your name on every tree; but that's a melancholy employment, not for those lovers who are favoured with assignation.

Vict. Pr'ythee, cousin, do you talk to him in my name. I'll be silent till I see further.

Pen. The spring is now so forward, that it must indeed be attributed to your passion that you are not in the field [of war.]

Y. Book. You do me justice, madam, in that thought, for I am strangely pestered to be there. Well, the French are the most industrious people in the world. I had a letter from one of their generals that shall be nameless, (it came over by the way of Holland,) with an offer of very great terms if I would but barely send my opinion in the use of pikes, about which, he tells me, their prince and generals have lately held a grand court-martial.

Both Ladies. Ha! ha! ha!

Lat. These cunning things keep still together to puzzle us. I'll alarm him. Sir, one word—

Vict. Come, come, we'll have no whispering, no messages at present. Some other ladies have sent, but they sha'n't have you from us.

Both. Ha! ha! ha!

Y. Book. I hold myself obliged to be of the same humour ladies are in—Ha! ha! ha! Now, pray, do me the favour to tell me what I laughed at!

Pen. Why, you must know. Your talking of the French and war put us in mind of a young coxcomb that came last night from *Oxford*, calls himself soldier, treats ladies, fights battles, raises jealousies with downright lies of his own inventing—ha! ha! ha!

Y. Book. That must be an impudent young rascal, certainly—ha! ha! ha!

Vict. Nay, this is beyond comparison.

Y. Book. I can't conceive how one of these sneaking academics could personate such a character; for we, tried in camps, have a behaviour that shews we are used to act before crowds.

Pen. 'Tis certainly so; nay, he has been confronted with it, as plainly as I speak to you, and yet not blush'd for it; but carried it as if he knew not the man.

Y. Book. That may be ; 'tis want of knowing themselves makes these coxcombs so confident.

Pen. The faithless, shameless ——. Well, then, to see if it is possible such a one may be brought to that sense, I tell you this worthy hero two days ago was in hanging sleeves at Oxford, and is called Mr Bookwit. Ha ! ha !

Y. Book. Well, was it not well enough carried ? Pho, I knew you well enough, and you knew me before you writ to me for Mr Bookwit's son. But I fell into that way of talking purely to divert you. I knew you a woman of wit and spirit, and that acting that part would at least shew I had fire in me, and wished myself what I would be half an age to serve and please you—suffer in camps all the vicissitudes of burning heats and sharp afflicting colds.

Vict. Look you, sir, I shall tell *Mrs Matilda Newton*, your spouse at Oxford, what you are saying to another lady.

Y. Book. Ha ! ha ! ha ! Why, madam, have they told you of the marriage too ? Well, I was hard put to it there. I had like to have been gravelled, faith. You were more beholden to me for that than anything. Had it not been for that, they had married me to Mrs Penelope . . . the great fortune. But I refused her for you, who are a greater. [*Aside.*

Lat. Sir, sir, pray one word.

Pen. and Vict. Stand off, sirrah.

Vict. You sha'n't come near him—none of your dumb signs.

Pen. Then you refused, Penelope, though a greater fortune. What could you dislike in her ?

Y. Book. The whole woman. Her person nor carriage please me.

Pen. This is not to be endured. I do assure you, sir, Mrs Penelope has refused your betters.

Y. Book. I don't much value my betters in her judgment, but am sorry to see you are concerned for her. In short, I don't like the woman, and would go to *Tunis* or *Aleppo* for a wife before I'd take her.

Vict. I cannot bear this of my friend ; if you go on, sir, at this rate, *Tunis* or *Aleppo* are the properest places for you to shew your gallantry in ; 'twill never be received by any here. I hope she believes me. [*Aside.*

Pen. The lady's in the right on 't ; who can confide in a known common impostor ?

Y. Book. Ah, madam ! how can you use a man that loves you so unjustly ? But call me what you will, . . . do but add your servant, and I am satisfied. I have, indeed, madam, run through many shifts in hopes to gain you, and could be content to run through all the shapes in Ovid's "Metamorphoses," could I but return to this on my bended knees of my fair one's humble servant.

Vict. Pr'ythee let us leave him ; as you told me, I wonder you can suffer him to entertain you so long. Leave him, and let him kneel to the trees, and call to the woods if he will. How ugly he looks kneeling to her. [*Aside*.

Pen. No, I'll stay to plague him more. But what opinion can I have of this sudden passion? You hardly know me, I believe, or my circumstances.

Y. Book. No, no, not I; I don't know you; your mother was not Alderman Stirling's daughter; your father, Mr Philips of *Gray's-Inn*, who had an estate, and never practised? You had not a brother killed at *Linden*? your sister Diana is not dead? nor you are not co-heiress with Miss Molly? No, madam, I don't know you, no, nor love you.

Pen. I wish I had taken her advice in going. He means her all this while. Pshaw, this is downright fooling. Let's go, my dear, and leave him to the woods, as you say. I wish 'twas full of bears. [*Aside*.

Vict. No, now I'll stay to plague him.

Pen. No, you sha'n't stay. Sir, we have given ourselves the diversion to see you and confront you in your falsehoods, in which you have entangled yourself to that degree, you know not even the woman you pretend to; and therefore, sir, I do so far despise you, that if you should come after me, I have a porter—ready to let you in. [*Aside*.

Vict. I don't know how to threaten a gentleman in that manner; but I'm sure I shall never entertain any man that has disobliged my friend, while my name's *Victoria!* [*Exeunt arm in arm.*

The unfavourable, and, as he considered, unmerited fate of this play had such an effect upon the author that he relinquished his dramatic efforts for a long period, and only after a lapse of eighteen years produced "The Conscious Lovers," which is considered his master-piece; and indeed for tenderness, purity of sentiment, and moral tone, it stands almost unrivalled among the productions of the comic Muse. Parson Adams considered it the only play fit for a Christian to see, and as good as a sermon. This indeed has been made a charge against the plays of Steele by one who, though given to striking and extreme opinions, was both a very acute critic and a great admirer of the other writings at least of their author. This writer (strange to say, if he had ever read them, and was not rather giving expression to an impression arising from the statement of their origin,) thinks them rather homilies in dialogue than comedies.* His *beau-idéal* of perfection in comedy, Congreve, is on the other hand considered by Walpole to possess no characteristic of the comic dramatist but wit ; so strangely do doctors differ. This graceful adieu of Steele to the dramatic art was founded on the " Andria " of Terence, though with great alterations both in incidents and the working up. It was brought out at Drury Lane in 1722, with immense success, so that between the profits of the performance, the sale of the copy, and a purse of five hundred guineas presented to him by the king, to whom the play was inscribed, it must have remunerated him handsomely.

On the whole, the plots of Steele's comedies are laid with skill and care, the characters are well drawn and sustained, and they abound in humour ; but in the dialogue there is perhaps a shortcoming, especially from the comparison with his predecessor Congreve, whose plays are remarkable for sustained liveliness, quickness of repartee, and a prodigal and indiscriminate expenditure of wit, which from keeping the mind continually on the stretch, becomes wearying ; while, in common with the other eminent predecessors of Steele, Wycherley and Vanbrugh, he abused and misapplied his remarkable powers by pandering to the corrupt taste of the age. It is the glory of Steele that he did not stoop to this, but sought to make mirth not inconsistent with wisdom, and amusement with innocence, if not improvement. " All men of true taste," he himself says, speaking on this subject, " would call a man of wit who should turn his ambition this way, a friend and benefactor to his country ; but I am at a loss what name they

* Hazlitt's Comic Writers of the Last Century.

would give him who makes use of his capacity for contrary purposes."*

The misfortune, as well as the fault of the comic dramatists previous to Steele was, what indeed has been adduced in their praise by the very able critic already alluded to, that they drew from existing life and manners; or, more properly, that writing at the time they did, when manners were so excessively corrupt, they did not use discrimination, if not for the sake of morality, at least as a matter of taste, so that when the state of manners changed for the better, their pictures of them ceased to be true to nature, and were offensive from their grossness, combined with what was highly artificial. "The comedies of Steele," remarks the writer referred to, "were the first that were written expressly with a view not to imitate the manners, but to reform the morals of the age. . . . It is almost a misnomer," he adds, "to call them comedies, they are rather homilies in dialogue, in which a number of very pretty ladies and gentlemen discuss the fashionable topics of gaming, of duelling," &c.† Surely any one after reading these plays, or even such an analysis of them as has been given in these pages, can scarcely think this other than a caricature, and suppose that the writer, without having read them, hazarded an opinion from his knowledge of the circumstances under which they were written. It surely cannot be considered as adding to the dignity of genius to represent as its highest function the mere passive copying of manners, especially when they are both corrupt and artificial. High art is not an indiscriminate copying even

---

* *Spectator*, No. 51.
† Hazlitt's Lectures on the Comic Writers, pp. 341-2.

of nature itself, but the instinctive seizing and combining of what is permanently agreeable or elevating by its beauty. Nor is it small praise to a writer that, in an age suffering from the excessive viciousness of the one preceding, he should have had the courage to exert his talents by introducing virtue in company with the graces, and in endeavouring to stem the current of licentiousness that had flowed down from the times of the Second Charles. There seems no reason why the dramatic writer should not be a moralist in the same manner that a novelist may, not ostensibly or obtrusively, without in any degree trenching on the province of the pulpit. Indeed, the writer who is not so, in some degree, fails in the highest dignity of his office. The lessons of the author differ widely from those of the pulpit in more than their embodiment in action and examples, as they do also in their result. They owe all their effect to their truthfulness to nature, and the force with which they are drawn, and they may influence many who, if they listened to the sermon at all, might be apt to overlook the lesson because it was a sermon; but it can scarcely be denied that it is at least as legitimate to adopt a moral tone as one positively the reverse, as in the predecessors of Steele; nor is it easy to see why the comic Muse among a Christian people should be less moral than that of the ancient heathen, among whom it was not alone the tragic Muse (as witness Terence) that sought

> " To wake the soul by tender strokes of art ;
> To raise the genius, and to mend the heart."

Mr Thackeray's remarks on Steele's comedies being "so pleasant, and their heroes such fine gentlemen," with the circumstances to which he alludes as contributing to that effect, will be referred to on another occasion.

It should have been stated previously, that Steele's first play, "The Funeral; or, Grief à-la-Mode," was dedicated to the Countess of Albemarle, to whose husband, then colonel of the first troop of Horse Guards, it has been supposed he owed the favourable notice of King William. Of the humour of that piece, Sydney Smith, himself the prince of humorists, was so great an admirer that he took the rehearsal of Sable, the undertaker, as an illustration in his lectures.

The "Lying Lover" was dedicated, "out of gratitude to the memorable and illustrious patron of his infancy," to the Duke of Ormond, his grandson, who was then captain of Steele's regiment, the second troop of Guards. He, also, was afterwards Lord-Lieutenant of Ireland in Queen Anne's reign, and being dismissed from his places, and attainted, on the accession of George I., retired to the Continent, where he joined the Pretender, and died at Madrid in 1745, at the advanced age of eighty-one.

The collected edition of Steele's comedies was dedicated to the Duchess of Hamilton, with a handsome acknowledgment of the obligation they owed to her Grace's partiality for them after they had had their run with the general public.

CHAPTER III.

THE PLACEMAN AND THE LOVER—1707, 1708.

Steele's hopes of preferment dashed by the death of the King—Notice of William—Revived early in Queen Anne's reign—Is introduced to Lord Halifax, an eminent patron of literary men, and other leading Whig statesmen—State of parties and of public events—The War—Union with Scotland—Defoe—Receives the appointment of Gazetteer—Strength of friendship among the literary men of this period—Notice of the Kit-Cat Club—Steele's beautiful allusion to the loss of his first wife—Reference to his first love—Mrs Bovey, who has been the supposed object of an early attachment, thought to have been also the original of the "perverse widow" of Sir Roger de Coverley in the *Spectator*—Steele's correspondence with Mrs Mary Scurlock, his second wife, previous to marriage.

QUEEN ANNE had now succeeded to the crown,—the premature demise of her illustrious predecessor and kinsman, William, (Steele's model of a Christian hero,) having resulted from an accident in hunting, which fractured his collar-bone, and proved fatal on the 2d of March 1702. He was taken from a world of trouble, for he met with a degree of factious opposition which must have been very galling to his spirit, and was an ungrateful return for his eminent services. This probably tended to aggravate the natural coldness and reserve of his disposition, which was adduced so much to his disadvantage, as was also his natural attachment to his own countrymen and to foreign politics. Indeed, he was too liberal-minded for his time; and by a singular turn of events, the representatives of the very party which so opposed and thwarted him in life, who tried to break his heart, and gave occasion to Defoe's trenchant satire of "The True-born Englishman," now pretend peculiar claim to him, and veneration for his memory. But while thus opposed by the Tories, he was also disappointed at times in the implicit attachment which he naturally expected from the Whigs, so much so, that he had been induced to listen to the representations of their opponents—that the state machinery would work more smoothly under their direction. But the trial proved to him that, whatever occasional ground of complaint he might have with his tried friends, the Whigs, he could gain nothing by trusting to their opponents; and he never repeated the experiment.

If such a valuable life was an irreparable loss to the state, it was no less so to the private interests of Steele, towards whom the illustrious monarch had manifested the most favourable disposition, his name, we are told,* having been noted down in the last tablets worn by William. He was not distinguished for his homage to letters; but the dramatic author has peculiar advantages over others in this, that his productions come before the world in the shape of entertainment in their hours of social recreation, and do not require, in order to appreciate them, any abstract regard for letters; and in this way Steele may have attracted the notice of William. But we are not informed of the circumstances; we only know the result. And the fact of his giving pleasure being endorsed by his military character would have been greatly in his favour, for the bent of William's mind was altogether military. He seemed to regard as the mission of his life the curbing

* Steele's "Apology," for his life and writings, p. 81, ed. 1714.

of the inordinate ambition of Louis the XIV., whose career of conquest and aggrandisement seemed to aim at little short of universal monarchy, and whose recent usurpation of the crown of Spain for his grandson, contrary to treaty, seemed to threaten destruction to the balance of power in Europe. The war which on that ground he had just declared against France, in conjunction with the States-General and Austria, he left as a legacy to his successor.

On the accession of Queen Anne it was anticipated that the continental policy of her predecessor would be reversed. Her strong leaning (imbibed from Compton, Bishop of London) towards the Tory party, who were unfavourable to the war, her personal distaste for it, naturally assumed, and the fact that the struggle was one in which this country apparently was little concerned, all pointed in that direction. Yet there was a concurrence of circumstances which tended to confirm her adherence to the engagements of William with the Allies. Commercial considerations made the mercantile interest, to which the Spanish trade was important, favourable to the war. The old hereditary feeling of jealousy towards the French, and considerations of public interest for the preservation of the balance of power in Europe, which the exorbitant ambition of Louis seemed seriously to threaten, as well as his open recognition of the claims of the Pretender to the British crown,—all these circumstances, added to the all-prevailing influence of the Marlborough family with the Queen, caused the scale to turn in favour of a war in which this country, at first sight, would appear to have had so little concern; and of which, though it led to many "a famous victory," its results were so stultified by the Tory

treaty of Utrecht that we might perhaps ask, in the words of the ballad,
"But what good came of 't at last ?"

In addition to the glory of the war, there was another event of a domestic nature, (which had long been a favourite measure with William,) the consummation of which shed lustre upon the reign of Queen Anne. This was the completion of what had been partially effected in the merging of the crowns of Scotland and England by the union of the legislatures of the two kingdoms. This measure passed the English Parliament in July 1706, was ratified by the Parliament of Scotland in January 1707, and became law the 1st of May following. On the 23d of October following, was opened the first imperial Parliament of Great Britain. The Duke of Queensberry, who had been the first Scotsman to give in his adhesion to the Revolution of 1688, and hence called by the Jacobites the "proto-rebel," was the principal agent in bringing about the Union. The celebrated Daniel Defoe (who has written its history) was also very instrumental in promoting it, being employed in making the calculations on the subject of trade and taxes; and his replies to the adverse publications on the subject tended materially to the removal of prejudice in candid and enlightened minds. But though the terms were considered highly favourable to the less opulent country, it was succeeded by a long period of gloomy popular dissatisfaction, before the people began to reap the benefits in trade and material prosperity to compensate for what they regarded as the surrender of their ancient nationality.

The bells that rang in Queen Anne must have sounded to Steele as the knell of his hopes. It was not merely that one had arisen, in place of the king, who knew not Steele, but who would not know his friends either. She was not long in manifesting her known sympathies. She made an immediate and clean sweep of the Whigs from office, and erased with her own hand the names of some of their leading men—that of Lord Halifax, at least—from the list of the Privy Council.

But the overweening confidence and assumption of her favourites, when they supposed they had disgraced their opponents, and had the field entirely to themselves, led to results that tended to cool the ardour of the sovereign on their behalf. Other causes operated in the same direction. Marlborough, on being appointed commander-in-chief of the English forces, and those in English pay in the war, had stipulated for the appointment of Lord Godolphin at the head of the Treasury. Godolphin's son was married to a daughter of Marlborough's, but, independent of that consideration, he was an admirable finance minister, and one on whom Marlborough knew he could rely. Both had belonged to the Tory party. But, apart from the influence of the Duchess upon his mind, who, whatever her faults otherwise, had been the stanch supporter of a liberal policy through good and ill report, Marlborough soon discovered that his interest—that magnet to which he turned with scarcely the deviations of the needle—lay in the direction of the Whigs, whose policy led them to support the war. That discovery was indicative of changes in a Cabinet where he reigned supreme, though Godolphin was its nominal chief. Gradually the doors were opened to Whigs of moderate views, and who would be least objectionable to the other party. But from the unbounded expectations of the Tories from the known feelings of the Queen in their favour, they were little disposed to submit to a divided reign. The result was that they began to range themselves in opposition; and members of the Cabinet—one after another—either retiring or being dismissed, finally left the field entirely to their opponents, so that the Whig influence was becoming once more in the ascendant.

Such was the process which was now in progress at the period at which we have arrived—when in May 1707 Steele received the appointment of Gazetteer, and somewhere about the same time was made one of the gentlemen-ushers to the Prince-Consort, George of Denmark. The former of these appointments at least he probably received through the interest, not of Addison, by whom he was introduced to the notice of Lord Halifax, (as has usually been stated,) but of Arthur Maynwaring, to whom he dedicated the first volume of the *Tatler*. He himself calls this the lowest minister of state, and assures us that he discharged the duties of the office with fidelity according to order, without erring against the rule observed by all ministers, to keep that paper very innocent, and very insipid. "It is believed," he adds, "that it was to the reproaches he heard every *Gazette* day against the writer of it, that he owed the fortitude of being remarkably negligent of what people say that he does not deserve."* This post he is usually said to have owed to the recommendation of Addison, who, having himself been introduced by Congreve to the notice of Halifax, Somers, and Sunderland, now used his influence

* His "Apology" for himself and his writings, p. 81, ed. 1714.

it is supposed, with these ministers in favour of his friend and fellow-student.* Sunderland had come into office the previous December.

Steele, no longer the gay guardsman or captain of fusileers, now stood among the foremost wits of the time, frequenting Wills's, the headquarters of wit, where Congreve had succeeded to the chair of Dryden, and the St James's Coffeehouse, where the Whig politicians assembled, and that more select society, the Kit-Cat Club, into which Addison had been recently welcomed on his return from his continental sojourn, and where he found his friend probably already installed. As the mention of this famous club occurs frequently in these pages, a few words may be necessary to give the reader some definite idea respecting it. It is remarkable that though so notable in its day, and formed chiefly of the cream of the Whig aristocracy and wits, there is little contemporary record of it but what is casual and incidental.

It appears to have originated about the beginning of the century, or to have sprung out of one previously in existence under the title of the "Knights of the Toast," in the meeting of the principal noblemen and gentlemen who had been instrumental in bringing about the Revolution, in order to watch over the interests of the Protestant succession in the House of Hanover. Ostensibly, however, their aim was to promote conviviality, and advance the interests of literature and the arts. Their first place of meeting was at the house of a pastry-cook, named Christopher

* Though it remains doubtful whether he received it originally through Lord Halifax, or by the influence of Maynwaring with Harley, it is at least certain that it was the latter who made it of any considerable value to him, and raised the salary from a mere nominal amount to £300 a year.

Cat, then residing in the obscure locality of Shire Lane, and famous for the manufacture of mutton-pies. These came in time to be called, after the maker, Kit-Cats, and, forming the favourite part of the entertainment of his distinguished guests, gave in turn the designation to this famous club. Their patronage led to the removal of the establishment to the more commodious premises of the Fountain Tavern in the Strand. The original members numbered thirty-nine, but subsequent accessions increased them to forty-eight, whose portraits by Sir Godfrey Kneller were suspended to the walls of their room. Jacob Tonson, the eminent publisher, was the secretary. In the summer season the club migrated into the country, sometimes to the country-house of their secretary, at Barn Elms, in Surrey, where he added a room to be appropriated to their use. Hampstead was also another favourite place of resort with them; and the Upper Flask Inn, a very popular place of entertainment, on the edge of the Heath, was the house they frequented, when they went

"To feast on Hampstead's airy mead;
Hampstead that now in fame Parnassus shall exceed."*

It appears that each member was required to name a toast, and some produced epigrams on the subjects of their nomination, which were inscribed with a diamond on the writer's wine-glass, and from these a reigning toast was elected for the year. This custom of drinking toasts is referred to by the *Tatler:* "Though this institution had so trivial a beginning, it is now elevated into a formal order; and that happy virgin who is received and drunk to

* "The Kit-Cats," a poem by the Marquis of Normanby, 1709.

at their meetings, has no more to do in this life but to judge and accept of the first good offer. The manner of her inauguration is much like that of the choice of a Doge in Venice; it is performed by ballot; and, when she is so chosen, she reigns indisputably for that ensuing year, but must be elected anew to prolong her reign a minute beyond it. When she is regularly chosen, her name is written with a diamond on one of the drinking-glasses. The hieroglyphic of the diamond is to show her that her value is imaginary; and that of the glass to acquaint her that her condition is frail, and depends on the hand that holds her."*

Epigrams written by most of the literary members are preserved, including those by Lords Dorset, Wharton, and Halifax; Addison, Maynwaring, and Sir Samuel Garth.

The Duke of Somerset first presented Tonson with his portrait in his capacity of secretary, and this was formed into a precedent to all the members. After Tonson's death they came into possession of his nephew, who, in like manner, built a gallery, with a dome-light, for their reception at his residence at Water Oakley, near Windsor.

The club probably died out about the year 1720. Though the origin of the name previously given is the generally received one, there appears to have been a question raised on the subject, which is referred to in an epigram attributed to Arbuthnot:—

> "Whence deathless Kit-Cat took its name
> Few critics can unriddle;
> Some say from pastry-cook it came,
> And some from Cat and Fiddle." †

---

* *Tatler*, No. 24.   † "Memoirs of the Kit-Cat Club."

An anecdote is related of the celebrated Lady Mary W. Montagu, that when only a child she was carried by her father, the Duke of Kingston, to the club, and proposed as a toast.

"As a leader of the fashionable world," (writes Lady Louisa Stuart, the grand-daughter of the celebrated wit and beauty,) "and a strenuous Whig in party, he (Lord Kingston) belonged to the Kit-Cat Club. One day at a meeting to choose toasts for the year, a whim seized him to nominate her, then not eight years old, a candidate, alleging that she was far prettier than any lady on their list. The other members demurred, because the rules of the club forbade them to select a beauty whom they had never seen. 'Then you shall see her,' cried he; and in the gaiety of the moment sent orders to have her finely dressed, and brought to him at the tavern, where she was received with acclamations, her claim unanimously allowed, her health drunk by every one present, and her name engraved in due form upon a drinking-glass. The company consisting of some of the most eminent men in England, she went from the lap of one poet, or patriot, or statesman, to the arms of another, was feasted with sweetmeats, overwhelmed with caresses, and, what perhaps already pleased her better than either, heard her wit and beauty loudly extolled on every side. Pleasure, she said, was too poor a word to express her sensations,—they amounted to ecstasy. Never again throughout her whole future life did she pass so happy a day. Nor indeed could she, for the love of admiration, which this scene was calculated to excite or increase, could never again be so fully gratified. There is always some alloying ingredient in the cup, some drawback upon the triumphs of grown people. Her father carried on the frolic, and, we may conclude, confirmed the taste by having her picture painted for the club-room, that she might be enrolled a regular toast." *

It is a common impression that men of letters are, even among themselves, irritable and envious, of which there may be occasional instances; but if we take the friendships that existed between them at this period—and similar instances might be found both in earlier and later times, as that between Swift, Pope, Bolingbroke, and others, and that between Steele, Addison, Congreve, Halifax, and

---

* Lord Wharncliffe's Life and Writings of Lady Montagu.

others—and see how they spoke of and stood by one another, the common-place friendships of the world will appear trifling in comparison. One of the most memorable of them all was renewed by the return of Addison from his travels. He was now Under-Secretary of State.

Steele having left the army, from the opening of civil advancement, had every prospect of being in easy circumstances, if he had only been blessed with a larger share of prudence; but unfortunately his profusion and generosity were ever apt to run in advance of his means.* From his appointment as *Gazette* writer, the duties of which could not have been very onerous, he had L.300 a year. He also held a place in the household of Prince George of Denmark, consort of Queen Anne; and after the publication of the *Tatler*, he was made a Commissioner of Stamps. The proceeds of his dramatic writings must likewise have been considerable, and he had also a fortune with his wife. This lady, of whom scarcely anything is known, only survived her marriage a few months. Little is recorded of her, except that she was a native of Barbadoes, in the West Indies, and that she became possessed of a plantation in that island on the decease of her brother, who was taken prisoner in the vessel in which he was coming to England, and carried to France, where he died. An allusion to the death of this lady, as there is every reason to believe it is, forms a beautiful illustration of what Dr. Beattie calls " a sublime and interesting moral" in one of the *Tatlers*. It

* The celebrated Lady M. W. Montagu remarks on the great similarity between the characters of Steele and her cousin Henry Fielding:—" They both agreed in wanting money, . . . and would have wanted it if their hereditary lands had been as extensive as their imagination; yet each of them was so formed for happiness, it is a pity he was not immortal."

inculcates by a dream, which has all the appearance of a real one, the important lesson of trust in Providence, shewing that there is no calamity, however apparently irremediable, but may admit of alleviation, and that the anticipation of evil is often, perhaps always, more vivid and harassing than the reality.

"I was once myself," he says, "in agonies of grief that are unutterable, and in so great a distraction of mind, that I thought myself even out of the possibility of receiving comfort. The occasion was as follows :—When I was a youth, in a part of the army which was then quartered at Dover, I fell in love with an agreeable young woman of a good family in those parts, and had the satisfaction of seeing my addresses kindly received, which occasioned the perplexity I am going to relate.

"We were, in a calm evening, diverting ourselves upon the top of the cliff, with the prospect of the sea, and trifling away the time in such little fondnesses as are most ridiculous to people in business, and most agreeable to those in love.

"In the midst of these our innocent endearments, she snatched a paper of verses out of my hand, and ran away with them. I was following her, when, on a sudden, the ground, though at a considerable distance from the verge of the precipice, sunk under her, and threw her down from so prodigious a height upon such a range of rocks as would have dashed her into ten thousand pieces had her body been made of adamant. It is much easier for my reader to imagine my state of mind on such an occasion than for me to express it. I said to myself, it is not in the power of Heaven to relieve me! when I awaked, equally transported and astonished to see myself drawn out of an affliction which, the very moment before, appeared to me altogether inextricable.

"The impressions of grief and horror were so lively on this occasion that, while they lasted, *they made me more miserable than I was at the real death of this beloved person, which happened a few months after, at a time when the match between us was concluded;* inasmuch as the imaginary death was untimely, and I myself, in a sort, an accessary ; whereas, her real decease had at least these alleviations, of being natural and inevitable."*

---

* *Tatler*, No. 117.—Though this paper is usually ascribed to Addison, the respective authorship of the *Tatlers* is not so well ascertained as in the case of the *Spectator ;* yet, notwithstanding the use of initials in the latter, we find some

That Steele had an earlier attachment would appear from a paper in the *Tatler*, which has all the appearance of a biographical reminiscence, and where he records its unhappy termination immediately after the mention of his mother. Speaking on the subject of grieving for the departed, he says, " Here (were there words to express such sentiments with proper tenderness) I should record the beauty, innocence, and untimely death of the first object my eyes ever beheld with love. The beauteous virgin! how ignorantly did she charm, how carelessly excel ! Oh death ! thou hast right to the bold, to the ambitious, to the high, and to the haughty; but why this cruelty to the humble, to the meek, to the undiscerning, to the thoughtless ? Nor age, nor business, nor distress, can erase the dear image from imagination. In the same week I saw her dressed for a ball, and in a shroud."*

How long Steele remained a widower we have no means of ascertaining, as we have no information respecting the date of his first marriage. Regarding his second wife, our information is much more satisfactory. We learn on her own authority that they had been acquainted previous to the decease of the first Mrs Steele, and that she was at her funeral. Miss Mary Scurlock, only daughter and heiress of Jonathan Scurlock, Esq. of Llangunnor, in Caermarthen, was a lady of great personal attractions, and possessed of an estate of about L.400 a year. At the time of her marriage she was about eight or nine and twenty ; and in the correspondence previous to that event, she is styled, accord-

---

of these are still unsettled. The incidents in this paper appear so clearly to refer to Steele's history that, as critics agree, if Addison was the writer, the particulars must have been communicated to him by his friend.

* *Tatler*, No. 181.

ing to the mode of the period, "Mrs," though a single lady, and her mother still surviving, the term "Miss" being deemed derogatory to persons of mature age. Though Steele accuses her of something of prudishness, yet such was his ardour, that, from the time of his beginning to pay his addresses to her to the consummation of their union, only about a month elapsed. She appears to have been possessed of many admirable qualities, which her husband, after they had been united upwards of seven years, celebrated in a dedicatory address in the "Lady's Library," with all the warmth of a lover. He dwells upon her wit and beauty, and the worldly sacrifices she had made in accepting his hand. Yet he often humorously rallies her in his letters for what he seemed to consider her too great regard for money, though that disposition may have been forced upon her, or at least heightened, by the unhappily too habitual extravagance of her husband, whose faults in that way, with the candour and self-criticism for which he was remarkable, no one more readily admitted and regretted than himself.

The mention of the "Lady's Library" recalls the fact that the second volume of that work is dedicated to Mrs Catherine Bovey, a lady who, with an ample fortune, was left a widow in her twenty-second year, and has been supposed to have been the object of Steele's early attachment, as well as the original of the immortal "perverse widow" of the Coverley papers in the *Spectator*. If so, Steele and Addison had both been sufferers from perverse widows, though the latter is suspected to have suffered still more from his ultimate success. With regard to Mrs Bovey, there are many points of similarity to give at least plausibility to the surmise, which will be referred to in speaking of Sir Roger de Coverley.

Of the following letters addressed by Steele to his future second wife, it is interesting to know that they were admired by so good a judge, both as regards the head and heart, as Samuel Taylor Coleridge. We are told that, on one occasion, " He dwelt with much *unction* on the curious and instructive letters of Steele to his wife, and with much approval on the manliness with which, in the first letters, he addressed the lady to whom he was afterwards united. He quoted the following [parts of the second letter] as models of their kind, and worthy of especial admiration :"—*

LETTER I.   *To Mrs Scurlock.*

[*Saturday, Aug.* 9,] 1707.†

MADAM,—Your wit and beauty are suggestions which may easily lead you into the intention of my writing to you. You may be sure that I cannot be cold to so many good qualities, as all that see you must observe in you. You are a woman of a very good understanding, and will not measure my thoughts by any ardour in my expressions, which is the ordinary language on these occasions.

I have reasons for hiding from my nearest relation any purpose I may have resolved upon of waiting on you, if you permit it; and I hope you have confidence from mine as well as your own character, that such a condescension should not be ill used by, madam, your most obedient servant,

R. STEELE.

LETTER II.   *To Mrs Scurlock.*

[*Aug.* 11,] 1707.

MADAM,—I writ you on Saturday, by Mrs Warren, and give you this trouble to urge the same request I made then; which was, that I may be

---

* "Letters, Conversations, and Recollections of S. T. Coleridge," vol. i., pp. 180-181.

† The additions in the dates are made by Nichols in the edition published by him from the originals in the British Museum.

admitted to wait upon you. I should be very far from desiring this if it were a transgression of the most severe rules to allow it. I know you are very much above the little arts which are frequent in your sex, of giving unnecessary torment to their admirers; therefore hope you will do so much justice to the generous passion I have for you, as to let me have an opportunity of acquainting you upon what motives I pretend to your good opinion. I shall not trouble you with my sentiments till I know how they will be received; and as I know no reason why the difference of sex should make our language to each other differ from the ordinary rules of right reason, I shall affect plainness and sincerity in my discourse to you, as much as other lovers do perplexity and rapture. Instead of saying " I shall die for you," I profess I should be glad to lead my life with you. You are as beautiful, as witty, as prudent, and as good-humoured as any woman breathing; but, I must confess to you, I regard all these excellences as you will please to direct them for my happiness or misery. With me, madam, the only lasting motive to love, is the hope of its becoming mutual. I beg of you to let Mrs Warren send me word when I may attend you. I promise you, I will talk of nothing but indifferent things; though, at the same time, I know not how I shall approach you in the tender moment of first seeing you after this declaration which has been made by, madam, your most obedient and most faithful humble servant, RICH. STEELE.

LETTER III.   *To Mrs Scurlock.*

[*Aug.* 14,] 1707.

MADAM,—I came to your house this night to wait on you; but you have commanded me to expect the happiness of seeing you at another time of more leisure. I am now under your own roof while I write; and that imaginary satisfaction of being so near you, though not in your presence, has in it something that touches me with so tender ideas, that it is impossible for me to describe their force. All great passion makes us dumb; and the highest happiness, as well as the highest grief, seizes us too violently to be expressed by our words.

You are so good as to let me know I shall have the honour of seeing you when I next come here. I will live upon that expectation, and meditate on your perfections till that happy hour. The vainest woman upon earth never saw in her glass half the attractions which I view in you. Your air, your shape, your every glance, motion, and gesture have such peculiar graces, that you possess my whole soul, and I know no life, but in the hopes of your approbation: I know not what to say, but that I love you with the sincerest passion that ever entered the heart of man. I will make it the business of my life to find out means of convincing you that I prefer you to all that is pleasing upon earth.—I am, madam, your most obedient, most faithful humble servant,

RICH. STEELE.

For a man struck "dumb" by his passion, the gallant captain gets on astonishingly. They have a saying in Ireland, "Beware of a Munsterman's flattery," but a Leinsterman seems not far behind. The citadel must have been in a tottering condition after such a heavy cannonade from the captain, and ready to surrender at discretion. It still, however, maintained a make-believe of holding out for the honours of war.* After he had been admitted to a parley, he thus writes :—

LETTER IV.   *To Mrs Scurlock.*

Friday Morning [*Aug.* 15, 1707.]

MADAM,—Hoping you are in good health, as I am at this present writing, I take the liberty of bidding you good morrow, and thanking you for yesterday's admission. To know so much pleasure with so much innocence is, methinks, a satisfaction beyond the present condition of human life; but the union of minds in pure affection is renewing the first state of man.

You cannot imagine the gratitude with which I meditate on your obliging behaviour to me, and how much improved in generous sentiments I return from your company: at the same time that you give me passion for yourself, you inspire me also with a love of virtue.

Mrs Warren informed me of your intention† on Sunday morning. I forbear indulging myself in a style which my eager wishes prompt me to, out of reverence to that occasion.—I am, madam, your most obliged, most faithful servant,

RICH. STEELE.

---

* It is stated by Nichols that Lady Steele had the weakness to erase the dates in some of her husband's letters, on allowing a friend to see them, that she might not be supposed to have surrendered at the end of a month.

† To receive the Sacrament.

LETTER V.   To Mrs Scurlock.

Aug. 16, 1707.

MADAM,—Before the light this morning dawned upon the earth, I awaked, and lay in expectation of its return; not that it could give any new sense of joy to me, but as I hoped it would bless you with its cheerful face, after a quiet [? rest] which I wished you last night. If my prayers are heard, the day appeared with all the influence of a merciful Creator upon your person and actions. Let others, my lovely charmer, talk of a blind being that disposes their hearts; I contemn their low images of love. I have not a thought which relates to you, that I cannot with confidence beseech the all-seeing Power to bless me in. May He direct you in all your steps, and reward your innocence, your sanctity of manners, your prudent youth, and becoming piety, with the continuance of His grace and protection. This is an unusual language to ladies; but you have a mind elevated above the giddy notions of a sex ensnared by flattery, and misled by a false and short adoration, into a solid and long contempt. Beauty, my fairest creature, palls in the possession; but I love also your mind: your soul is as dear to me as my own; and if the advantages of a liberal education, some knowledge, and as much contempt, of the world, joined with endeavours towards a life of strict virtue and religion, can qualify me to raise new ideas in a breast so well disposed as yours is, our days will pass away with joy, and old age, instead of introducing melancholy prospects of decay, give us hope of eternal youth in a better life. I have but few minutes from the duty of my employment to write in, and without time to read over what I have writ; therefore beseech you to pardon the first hints of my mind, which I have expressed in so little order.—I am, dearest creature, your most obedient, most devoted servant,

RICH. STEELE.

LETTER VI.   To Mrs Scurlock.

[Aug. 17,] 1707.

MADAM,—I could not omit writing to you, though on Sunday morning, when I know I interrupt your meditation on higher subjects;* there is nothing but heaven itself which I prefer to your love, which shall be the pursuit of my life; and I hope there will not a day appear, to our lives' end, wherein there will not appear some instance of affection not to be excelled, but in the mansions of eternity, to which we may recommend ourselves by our behaviour to each other here.—I am, my lovely charmer, your obedient † . . . . .

---

* The Sacrament—see preceding letter.
† The name is wanting in the original.

LETTER VII.   To Mrs Scurlock.
                              Lord Sunderland's Office, 1707.

MADAM,—With what language shall I address my lovely fair to aquaint her with the sentiments of a heart she delights to torture? I have not a minute's quiet out of your sight; and when I am with you, you use me with so much distance, that I am still in a state of absence, heightened with a view of the charms which I am denied to approach. In a word, you must give me either a fan, a mask, or a glove you have worn, or I cannot live; otherwise you must expect that I'll kiss your hand, or, when I next sit by you, steal your handkerchief. You yourself are too great a bounty to be received at once; therefore I must be prepared by degrees, lest the mighty gift distract me with joy. Dear Mrs Scurlock, I am tired with calling you by that name; therefore, say the day in which you will take that of, madam, your most obedient, most devoted humble servant,

                                                  RICH. STEELE.

We have now the fortress regularly summoned to surrender, and the captain begins to doubt, rather, of the freedom of the besieged from "the usual little arts" adopted in such warfare. Let us see how the treaty proceeds:—

LETTER VIII.   *To Mrs Scurlock.*
                              Smith Street, Westminster, 1707.

MADAM,—I take up pen and ink to indulge the sensibility I am under in reflecting upon the agreeable company in which I passed yesterday evening. The day hangs heavily upon me, and the whole business of it is an impertinent, guilty dream, in comparison with a few moment's of real life at your house, which go off in privacy and innocence. Were it possible the concern I have for you were mutual, how tedious would be the moments of each other's absence—how fleeting the hours we should be together—how would my mirth be heightened—how my sorrow banished by the appearance of a smile in that countenance where are so charmingly painted complacency, good sense, innocence, honour, and truth! Since this is the figure you bear in my imagination, you cannot blame my desire of having those good qualities my constant companions, and for ever engaged in my interests. My heart overflows with the pleasing prospects that throng into my mind when I think of you. What shall I say? Pr'ythee, Mrs Scurlock, have pity on, madam, your most obedient, most faithful servant,   RICH. STEELE.

LETTER IX.   To Mrs Scurlock.
                                    Smith Street, Westminster, 1707.

MADAM,—I lay down last night with your image in my thoughts, and have awakened this morning in the same contemplation. The pleasing transport, with which I am delighted, has a sweetness in it attended with a train of ten thousand soft desires, anxieties, and cares. The day arises on my hopes with new brightness; youth, beauty, and innocence are the charming objects that steal me from myself, and give me joys above the reach of ambition, pride, or glory. Believe me, fair one, to throw myself at your feet is giving myself the highest bless I know on earth. Oh, hasten, ye minutes! bring on the happy morning wherein to be ever hers will make me look down on thrones!—Dear Molly, I am passionately, faithfully thine,   RICH. STEELE.

LETTER X.   To Mrs Scurlock.
                                                      Aug. 22, 1707.

MADAM,—If my vigilance, and the ten thousand wishes for your welfare and repose, could have any force, you last night slept in security, and had every good angel in your attendance. To have my thoughts ever fixed on you, and to live in constant fear of every accident to which human nature is liable, and to send up my hourly prayers to avert these from you; I say, madam, thus to think, and thus to suffer, is what I do for her who is in pain at my approach, and calls all my tender sorrow impertinence. You are now before my eyes, my eyes that are ready to flow with tenderness, but cannot give relief to my gushing heart, that dictates what I am now saying, and yearns to tell you all its achings. How art thou, oh my soul, stolen from thyself! How is all thy attention broken! My books are blank paper, and my friends intruders. I have no hope of quiet but from your pity: to grant it would make more for your triumph. To give pain, is tyranny; to make happy, the true empire of beauty. If you would consider aright, you would find an agreeable change in dismissing the attendance of a slave, to receive the complaisance of a companion. I bear the former, in hopes of the latter, condition. As I live in chains without murmuring at the power that inflicts them, so I could enjoy freedom without forgetting the mercy that gave it. Dear Mrs Scurlock, the life which you bestow on me shall be no more my own.—I am your most devoted, most obedient servant,   RICH. STEELE.

LETTER XI.   To Mrs Scurlock.
                                              Chelsea, Aug. 25, 1707.

MADAM,—I am observed, by a friend who is with me, in every motion

and gesture I make. I have stolen a moment, while he is in the next room, to tell the charmer and inspirer of my soul I am her devoted, obedient servant,
RICH. STEELE.

LETTER XII.   *To Mrs Scurlock.*

Thursday, Aug. 27, 1707.

MY DEAREST CREATURE,—I beg the favour of you to let me pass this day in your company, I have contrived my business so that I have till eight at night at my own disposal. I can come in a coach ; and Mrs Warren, being in the way, may let me in without observation. My loved creature, do not deny this request, nor think I am capable of being allowed that liberty without a true sense of your goodness to me in it. Your generous condescension in all your carriage towards me shall always give you a powerful and lasting influence upon the thoughts and actions of him who hopes to be, madam, your most obliged and grateful husband,
RICH. STEELE.

LETTER XIII.   *To Mrs Scurlock.*

Aug. 29, 1707.

MADAM,—I fear it will be an hour later than usual that I wait upon you to-night, for I have an appointment which will detain me, and which concerns both you and, madam, your most obliged, most obedient servant,
RICH. STEELE.

LETTER XIV.   *To Mrs Scurlock.*

Aug. 30, 1707.

MADAM,—I beg pardon that my paper is not finer, but I am forced to write from a coffeehouse, where I am attending about business. There is a dirty crowd of busy faces all around me, talking of money ; while all my ambition, all my wealth is love ! Love, which animates my heart, sweetens my humour, enlarges my soul, and affects every action of my life. It is to my lovely charmer I owe that many noble ideas are continually affixed to my words and actions ; it is the natural effect of that generous passion to create in the admirer some similitude of the object admired. Thus, my dear, am I every day to improve from so sweet a companion. Look up, my fair one, to that heaven which made thee such, and join with me to implore its influence on our tender, innocent hours, and beseech the Author of love to bless the rites He has ordained, and mingle with our happiness a just sense of our transient condition, and a resignation to His will, which only can regulate our minds to a steady endeavour to please Him and each other.—I am, for ever, your faithful servant,
RICH. STEELE.

LETTER XV.   To Mrs Scurlock.

MADAM,—It is the hardest thing in the world to be in love, and yet attend to business. As for me, all who speak to me find me out, and I must lock myself up, or other people will do it for me.

A gentleman asked me this morning, "What news from Lisbon?" and I answered, "She is exquisitely handsome." Another desired to know when I had been last at Hampton Court. I replied, "It will be on Tuesday come se'nnight." Pr'ythee, allow me at least to kiss your hand before that day, that my mind may be in some composure. O love!

> A thousand torments dwell about thee!
> Yet who would live to live without thee?

Methinks I could write a volume to you; but all the language on earth would fail in saying how much, and with what disinterested passion, I am ever yours,   RICH. STEELE.

We find from this, which might have answered for one of the letters of his *Tatler*, that the day of their union was fixed, as indeed appears by a note appended to it in Lady Steele's handwriting.

LETTER XVI.   To Mrs Scurlock.
                          Sept. 7, 1707, between One and Two.

DEAR CREATURE,—Ever since seven this morning, I have been in company; but have stolen a moment to pour out the fulness of my thoughts, and complain to you of the interruption that impertinent amusement called business has given me, amidst my contemplation on the best of women, and the most agreeable object that ever charmed the heart of man.—I am, dearest, loveliest creature, eternally thine,

                                RICH. STEELE.

LETTER XVII.   To Mrs Scurlock.
                          Sept. 3, 1707, Seven in the Morning.

DEAR CREATURE,—Next to the influence of Heaven, I am to thank you that I see the returning day with pleasure. To pass my evenings in so sweet a conversation, and have the esteem of a woman of your merit, has in it a particularity of happiness no more to be expressed than returned. But I am, my lovely creature, contented to be on the obliged side, and employ all my days in new endeavours to convince you and all the world, of the sense I have of your condescension in choosing, madam, your most faithful, most obedient, humble servant,   RICH. STEELE.

The next letter is addressed to Mrs Scurlock, sen., with a statement of his circumstances, and requesting her approval of his union with her daughter. She appears to have been in delicate health, and was then residing at Caermarthen, in South Wales, where her property lay, and where she seems also to have been detained by her affairs:—

LETTER XVIII. *To Mrs Scurlock, sen.*

Lord Sunderland's Office Whitehall,
Sept. 3, 1707.*

MADAM,—The young lady, your daughter, told me she had a letter from you of 22d instant, [? ult.,] wherein you gave her the highest marks of your affection, and anxiety for her welfare in relation to me. The main prospect on these occasions is that of fortune; therefore, I shall very candidly give you an account of myself as to that particular. My late wife had so extreme a value for me, that she, by fine, conveyed to me her whole estate, situate in Barbadoes, which, with the stock and slaves, (proper securities being given for the payment of the rent,) is let for eight hundred and fifty pounds *per annum*, at half-yearly payments; that is to say, £425 each 1st of May, and £425 each 1st of December. This estate came to her encumbered with a debt of £3000 by legacies and debts of her brother, whose executrix she was, as well as heiress. I must confess it has not been in my power to lessen the encumbrance, by reason of chargeable sicknesses, and not having at that time any employment of profit. But at present, and ever since May last, I have been appointed by the Secretaries of State to write the *Gazette*, with a salary of £300 a year, paying a tax of £45. I am a gentleman-waiter to his Royal Highness the Prince, with a salary of £100 a year, not subject to taxes.

Thus my whole income is at present, per annnm,	£1250	0 0
Deduct the interest of £3000,	180	0 0
Taxes for my employment,	45	0 0
	£225	0 0
Remains, after deductions,	£1025	0 0

* Nichols is of opinion that the date of this letter was altered in the original from September 3, to September 30, and that the marriage took place privately about the 7th of that month, in order to frustrate all opposition, and in consequence partly of the inability of the lady's mother to come to town. There must

This is, madam, the present state of my affairs; and though this income is so large, I have not taken any regard to lay up anything further than just what pays the interest above mentioned. If I may be so happy to obtain your favour, so as we may live together with singleness of mind, I shall readily go into such measures as shall be thought most advisable for our mutual interests; and, if it is thought fit, will sell what I have in the plantations.

Your daughter acquaints me there is a demand of £1400 upon your estate, the annual income of which is better than £400 *per annum.* You have now the whole view of both our circumstances before you; and you see there is foundation for our living in a handsome manner, provided we can be of one mind, without which I could not propose to myself any happiness or blessing, were my circumstances ever so plentiful. I am at a present juncture in my affairs, and my friends are in great power, so that it would be highly necessary for us to be in the figure of life which we shall think convenient to appear in, as soon as may be, that I may prosecute my expectations in a busy way while the wind is for me, with just consideration that, about a Court, it will not always blow one way. Your coming to town is mightily to be wished. I promise myself the pleasures of an industrious and virtuous life, in studying to do things agreeable to you. But I will not enlarge into professions, I assure you. I shall always contend with you who shall lay the greater obligations on the other; and I can form to myself no greater satisfaction than having one day permission to subscribe myself, madam, your most obedient son, and most humble servant,   RICH. STEELE.

Writing is painful to me.

If you will enclose your letters to your daughter, they will come free, " To Richard Steele, Esq., at the Secretary's Office, Whitehall."

The next letter, probably written some weeks before the foregoing, is on the same subject, namely, to obtain the consent of the elder Mrs Scurlock to the marriage, and the sentiments it expresses do great credit to the writer :—

---

be some mistake in the letter, as Steele refers to one received by the young lady from her mother on the 22d inst., which must be intended for ult. The date here given must be correct, as in writing again to his wife's mother under date Sept. 7, he alludes to this letter.

LETTER XIX.   *Mrs Mary Scurlock to her Mother.*

[*Undated.*]

DEAR MADAM,—By a letter I had from Cousin Betty Scurlock, I find you are resolved to winter in Wales, which is the cause of this speed in my writing, having kept a secret from you, through fear that a letter might (by the usual impertinent curiosity of people) make a discovery of what is proper for your own ear only, and not to direct any in that tattling place, where that wretched impudence H. O. resorts, who (lest he should think God had not wholly forsaken him) had the boldness to send me a letter, which I had the very last post. I tore it without once reading it, he being beneath my scornful laugh.

But the matter is hand in this :—Your frequent declarations of your earnest wishes that I might happily please you in obliging myself by my choice of a companion for life, has emboldened me, now fate has put it in my power, to give so far encouragement as to promise speedy marriage, upon condition of your consent, which I do not question having, when I tell you, I not only make use of the most weighing considerations I am mistress of, but also hope my inclination is the direction of Providence, whose guidance, in every particular of this nice affair more particularly, I cease not to implore continually. I cannot recommend the person to you as having a great estate, title, &c., which are generally a parent's chief care ; but he has a competency in worldly goods to make easy, with a mind so richly adorned as to exceed an equivalent to the greatest estate in the world, in my opinion : in short, his person is what I like ; his temper is what I am sure will make you, as well as myself, perfectly happy, if the respect of a lover, with the tender fondness of a dutiful son, can make you so, and for his understanding and morals, I refer you to his "Christian Hero," which, I remember, you seemed to approve. By this, I believe, you know his name ; but, lest memory may not befriend me, it is the survivor of the person to whose funeral I went in my illness. Inquiries about him, any further than I have made, are altogether needless, for I am fully satisfied, and do not qestion but you will be so, when business will permit you to be an eye-witness and partaker of my happiness. In the meantime, what I desire is, your consent and blessing to my putting it out of my power to delay, and so perhaps to lose my first and only inclination ; for I shall never meet with a prospect of happiness if this should vanish. You, doubtless, wonder at the assurance of my style, for really I do myself ; but then, if you consider the necessity of it, it will palliate the boldness. For, first, the distance between us is so great, that the speediest answer to a letter terminates an age of days ; then the constant visits, in the form fit for a lover, make a mighty noise in an idle, prying neighbourhood ; so will cause the uneasiness of an endless nine days' wonder, as they call it. But the main matter of all, since Fate, I believe, has ordained him mine, is the neglect of his business, which his coming in the manner he does must cause. These considerations, with several more when known, though now too tedious to write, will, I hope, lessen the censure this incomprehensive letter may at first sight cause.

There is nothing I should more desire than your presence at the giving my hand, with that part of my heart you can spare; but the misfortune of your lameness, if you were here, would deny me that happiness, unless public doings were intended, which is what I abhor; insomuch, if you consent to my changing the name of lover for husband, it shall not be in the power of the town to more than guess there may be such a thing, until your affairs will permit you to come and be a witness to our manner of living and appearing in the world, which God Almighty direct us in the way of, and also * . . . . this letter to your dutiful Molly; . . . . . . there being no room for long consideration . . . . understood.

LETTER XX.   To Mrs Scurlock.
                                        Sept. 4, 1707.

DEAR MISS† MOLLY,—I am loath to interrupt your prayers, or my indispensable business, with a long epistle this morning; therefore forgive me that I only just say I am ever yours.   R. S.

I shall come at night, and make all the despatch here I can not to be wanted.

LETTER XXI.   To Mrs Scurlock.
                                        Sept. 5, 1707.

DEAR MADAM,—The pleasing hope with which my mind is possessed is too delicate a touch of the soul to be explained, but it is founded on so solid and lasting motives that I am sure it will actuate the behaviour of my whole life; for I do not entertain my imagination with those transports only which are raised by beauty, but fix it also on the satisfactions which flow from the reverence due to virtue. Thus, I am not only allured by your person, but convinced by your life, that you are the most amiable of women. Let us go on, my lovely creature, to make our regards to each other mutual and unchangeable, that, whilst the world around us is enchanted with the false satisfactions of vagrant desires, our persons may be shrines to each other, and sacred to conjugal faith, unreserved confidence, and heavenly society. While we live after this manner, angels will

---

* The original, which Nichols thinks was probably written about Aug. 16, 1707, is here accidentally torn.

† *Miss*, says Nichols, seems here used as a term of endearment.

be so far from being our superiors that they will be our attendants. Every good being guard my fairest, and conduct her to that bosom that pants to receive her, and protect her from all the cares and vicissitudes of life with an eternal tenderness.—I am, ever most obligedly yours,

RICH. STEELE.

LETTER XXII.   *To Mrs Scurlock.*

Saturday, Sept. 6, 1707.

MADAM,—I am at a friend's house, where they have given me, as you see, but very ordinary instruments to write with. However, I hope the sincerity of my heart is not to be measured by the dress in which I clothe it. My thoughts hurry upon me, in consideration of the approach of the moment in which those fair lips are to give me, in one monosyllable, more than all the eloquence in the world can express, when you say *yes* to the accepting of, madam, your most obliged, most grateful, most obedient servant,

RICH. STEELE.

LETTER XXIII.   *To Mrs Scurlock, sen.*

Sept. 7, 1707.

MADAM,—In obedience to your commands by your daughter, of hearing every post from this town of her health and welfare, I do myself the honour to inform you of it, and humbly desire you would accept my own duty.

I hope you have, before now, received a letter from me, wherein I laid before you at large the state of my affairs ;* and that when we come to be acquainted, you will not esteem it a disadvantageous accident that I have the honour of being, madam, your most obedient son, and most humble servant,

RICH. STEELE.

---

* Letter XVIII.

CHAPTER IV.

THE HUSBAND—1707, 1708.

Correspondence after marriage with his wife and her mother.

THE next letter appears to have been written after the private marriage, which is conjectured to have taken place some days previously, when Steele seems to have strongly urged upon his wife, though in vain, the open acknowledgment of him as her husband, in anticipation of her mother's consent or presence:—

LETTER XXIV.   *To Mrs Scurlock.*
                                    Sept. 9, 1707.

MADAM,—I hope your denying what I urged with so much passion, and which I complained of in too vehement a manner, has not been a grief to my tender companion; for, upon reflection this morning, I extremely approve your conduct, and take your behaviour to proceed from an inclination to come to my arms hallowed by your parent's blessing. I comply with your measures in bringing that happiness about, and shall behave myself as if only in the beginning of a sacred love made at the altar.

I promise to myself sincere felicity in a woman that sacrifices all desires to her duty; and I assure you, whatever appearance of care and disturbance you may observe now and then in my countenance, it is not the image of spleen, ill-nature, or dissatisfaction, but a strong propensity to make you the happiest of your sex, which I shall endeavour to do, rather by an industrious ambition to promote your fortune, than by a mere dalliance of your person only, to shew a greater regard to the beauty than the wife. I beg of you to shew my letters to no one living, but let us be contented with one another's thoughts upon our words and actions, without the intervention of other people, who cannot judge of so delicate a circumstance as the commerce between man and wife.—I am, eternally yours,   RICH. STEELE.

Pray write me a line.

LETTER XXV.   To Mrs Scurlock.*

Sept. 10, 1707.

MADAM,—Being very uneasy when absent from you, I desire you would give me leave to take coach and come to your house; in order to which, pray let Mrs Warren be in the way to admit your obliged, humble servant,

RICH. STEELE.

LETTER XXVI.   To Mrs Scurlock, sen.
            Lord Sunderland's Office, Whitehall, Sept. 20, 1707.

MADAM,—By Tuesday's post I took the liberty to write to you on the most important occasion, and have been in a thousand anxieties ever since that time, for the reception which that letter is to find. The circumstance is so tender, and my happiness hangs so much upon it, that I could not forbear seconding my first address to you with a second, though I protest to you, I set pen to paper with as much diffidence as if I had the same passion for yourself as for your daughter. I do not entertain you with an account of my fortune, and those particulars which will naturally be inquired into by a parent, because I doubt not you have so good an opinion of Mrs Scurlock's prudence, that you do not believe she would throw herself away. As to your favour to my pretensions, I hope it upon no other foundation than making it appear to you that, as to your own part in the affair, there is not that man breathing that could come into your alliance who should, in all the offices, and peculiar esteem for yourself, exceed the gratitude of, madam, your most obedient, most humble servant,

RICH. STEELE.

LETTER XXVII.   To Mrs Scurlock.

Sept. 21, 1707.

DEAR CREATURE,—Your letter gave me a great deal of satisfaction. I hasten my business to see you early in the evening. In the meantime, I recommend myself to your prayers and kind thoughts, and am ever yours,

RICH. STEELE.

LETTER XXVIII.   To Mrs Scurlock.

Oct. 6, 1707.

DEAR CREATURE,—I write to tell you beforehand that I am not in a very good humour, but all shall vanish at her sight whom Providence has given me for the banishment of care and the improvement of delight to your most obliged husband and most humble servant,

RICH. STEELE.

---

* This and the remaining letters to his wife under her own name, were addressed under cover " To Mrs Warren."

LETTER XXIX. To Mrs Steele.*

Oct. 7, 1707.

MY DEAR,—Cousin Pen is much in the same condition we left her last night. I am going with great cheerfulness and industry about my business to-day, in order to pass my time hereafter without interruption with the most agreeable creature living, which you are to the most obliged man living.—Your obedient husband, RICH. STEELE.

LETTER XXX. To Mrs Steele.

Oct. 7, 1707.

MY LOVED CREATURE,—I write this only to bid you good night, and assure you of my diligence in the matter I told you of.

You may assure yourself I value you according to your merit, which is saying that you have my heart by all the ties of beauty, virtue, good nature, and friendship. I find, by the progress I have made to-night, that I shall do my business effectually in two days' time. Write me word you are in good humour, which will be the highest pleasure to your obliged husband,
RICH. STEELE.

I shall want some linen from your house to-morrow.

---

* From this date Steele persisted in addressing his letters as to his wife, though contrary to her wish; but he was still obliged to yield in the matter of living apart, until her mother's arrival in Swallow Street. The solemn feelings with which Steele entered upon the married state, will be seen by a devotional exercise which he wrote, shortly after the event, in these words:—

"Oh, Almighty Lord God, who hast been pleased, out of Thy righteous mercy and careful providence, to place us two in the state of marriage, according to Thy own institution and guidance of the first mortals; grant, we beseech Thee, that we may live in that state with mutual love, and that we endeavour to accommodate ourselves to each other's just desires and satisfactions; that we may be a mutual help in all the vicissitudes of life through which Thou hast designed us to pass, in such manner as we may contribute to each other's virtue in this world, and salvation in that which is to come. Protect us, O Lord most mighty; bless us, O merciful Father; and redeem us, O holy Saviour! Guard our paths from error, and keep our eyes from introducing wandering desires; but grant such peace and tranquillity of mind, and such a steady course of virtue and piety, that we may be at Thy altar never-failing communicants; and, by a worthy receipt of the elements representing Thy meritorious passion, we may through that be partakers of eternal life; which permit us to beseech Thee in the words which Thou hast taught us:—

"'Our Father, which art heaven,'" &c.

LETTER XXXI.   *To Mrs Steele.*

Oct. 8, 1707.

MY DEAR WIFE,—You were not, I am sure, awake so soon as I was for you, and desired the blessing of God upon you. After that first duty, my next is to let you know I am in health this morning, which I know you are solicitous for. I believe it would not be amiss if, some time this afternoon, you took a coach or chair, and went to see a house next door to Lady Bulkley's, towards St James's Street, which is to be let. I have a solid reason for quickening my diligence in all affairs of the world, which is, that you are my partaker in them, and will make me labour more than any incitation of ambition or wealth could do. After I have implored the help of Providence, I will have no motive to my actions but the love of the best creature living, to whom I am an obedient husband.

RICH. STEELE.

LETTER XXXII.   *To Mrs Steele.*

Oct. 8, 1707.

DEAR MADAM,—I could not forbear letting you know that I have received letters this moment from Barbadoes, which will facilitate my business; so natural is it that all things must grow better by your condescending to be partner to your most obliged husband, and most humble servant,

RICH. STEELE.

LETTER XXXIII.   *To Mrs Steele.*

Monday Morning, Oct. 13, 1707.

DEAR MADAM,—This comes to beg your pardon for *every act of rebellion* I have committed against you, and to subscribe myself in an error for being impatient of your kind concern in interesting yourself with so much affection in all which relates to me. I do not question but your prudence will be a lasting honour and advantage to me in all the occurrences of my life; the chief happiness in it is, that I have the honour of being your most obliged husband, and most humble servant,

RICH. STEELE.

LETTER XXXIV.   *To Mrs Scurlock.*[*]

Oct. 14, 1707.

HONOURED MOTHER,—I am very sorry to find, by Mr Scurlock's letter, that you keep your bed, which makes me almost in despair of seeing you so soon as I had promised myself.

---

[*] Mrs Steele's mother.

I have taken a house in Berry Street, St James's, and beg your leave to remove your goods thither; where I hope we shall live all together in the strictest love and friendship. Whatever better prospects your daughter might well have given herself, from her great merit and good qualities, I'll take care to have it said she could not have married more advantageously with regard to her mother, who shall always find me her most obedient son, and most humble servant,

RICH. STEELE.

Your daughter gives her duty to you.

LETTER XXXV.   To Mrs Steele.
Oct. 16, 1707.

DEAREST BEING ON EARTH,—Pardon me if you do not see me till eleven o'clock, having met a school-fellow from India, by whom I am to be informed in things this night which extremely concern your obedient husband,   RICH. STEELE.

LETTER XXXVI.   To Mrs Steele.
Oct. 16, 1707.

MY DEAR,—Pray send word where your landlord of the house in Swallow Street lives, that my friend Col. Borr may treat with him for the house. —Your obedient husband,   RICH. STEELE.

LETTER XXXVII.   To Mrs Steele.
8 o'Clock, Fountain Tavern, Oct. 22, 1707.

MY DEAR,—I beg of you not to be uneasy, for I have done a great deal of business to-day, very successfully, and wait an hour or two about my Gazette.—Your obliged husband,   RICH. STEELE.

LETTER XXXVIII.   To Mrs Steele.
Charing Cross, almost 3 in the Afternoon.

MY DEAR,—I have been detained all this morning soliciting some business between the Treasury and our office; and, my boy slipping out of the way, I have not had any one to send that you might not stay dinner. Mr Addison does not remove till to-morrow; therefore I cannot think of moving my goods out of his lodgings. I am come to a tavern alone to eat a steak, after which I shall return to the office, whither I desire you to send Will.—I am, with the most tender affection, your obedient husband,   RICH. STEELE.

Send by Will the receipt.*

---

* See Letter XXXIX.

LETTER XXXIX.   *To Mrs Scurlock.*
                    Lord Sunderland's Office, Oct. 28, 1707.

HONOURED MADAM,—I was very glad to find last post that my wife had a letter which informed her of the amendment of your health. She tells me there is at the same time a message sent her that my hand is required for the payment of some money in the country. I accordingly enclose such a direction; and, in anything that it may be necessary to have my concurrence, you have it without reserve; for I sincerely rely upon your prudence and goodness, both in acting for me and in favour to me. If you think it convenient that I do this in a more formal way, be pleased to command, madam, your most obedient son, and most humble servant,

RICH. STEELE.

LETTER XL.   *To Mrs Scurlock.*
                                Nov. 4, 1707.

HONOURED MADAM,—I am sorry your indisposition continues, and keeps you in the country; I have myself been under a very severe illness for some days, but am now almost recovered. This is my wife's birthday, and I am come down stairs to celebrate it with as much good humour as my present health will permit. Your health is not omitted in our cheerful moments, and your company will extremely improve them.—I am, madam, your most obedient son and most humble servant,

RICH. STEELE.

LETTER XLI.   *To Mrs Scurlock.*
                                Nov. 13, 1707.

HONOURED MADAM,—I am very glad to hear by uncle Scurlock's last letters, that you have taken in your horses in order to your journey. Since my last to you, I have had an affliction which was perfectly new to me—a fit of the gout. I am a little awkward at my crutches, and have been not so patient as longer experience of this sort of evil usually makes us. Our new house will be ready for our goods next week; and as soon as it is so, we will remove to it. I am out of pain, though I cannot stir; in the meanwhile, your daughter is dancing at the other end of the room. She gives her duty to you. I am extremely obliged to my uncle Scurlock for his kind present, which will be in town to-morrow night.—I am, madam, your most obedient son, and most humble servant,

RICH. STEELE.

LETTER XLII.   *To Mrs Scurlock.*
                    Lord Sunderland's Office, Nov. 26, 1707.

HONOURED MADAM,—My wife shewed me a letter of the 15th from Mrs Pugh, wherein there are the general complaints under which every body at present is sighing, whose concerns are wholly in land. Cheerful and ingenuous tempers may agree so well, and concert their affairs in such a manner, as to make all things easy. I extremely long to see you, and hope to be on my legs to receive you, when I first do myself the honour of kneeling to you, and telling you how much I am, madam, your most obedient son, and most humble servant, RICH. STEELE.

My absolute governess gives her duty to you.

LETTER XLIII.   To Mrs Steele.
Dec. 8, 1707.

DEAR RULER,—I cannot wait upon you to-day to Hampton Court. I have the West Indian business on my hands,* and find very much to be done before Thursday's post. I shall dine at our table at Court, where the bearer knows how to come to me with any orders for your obedient husband, and most humble servant, RICH. STEELE.

My duty to my mother.

LETTER XLIV.   To Mrs Steele.
Dec. 22, 1707.

MY DEAR, DEAR WIFE,—I write to let you know I do not come home to dinner, being obliged to attend some business abroad, of which I shall give you an account (when I see you in the evening,) as becomes your dutiful and obedient husband, RICH. STEELE.

LETTER XLV.   To Mrs Steele.
Devil Tavern, Temple Bar, Jan. 3, 1708.

DEAR PRUE,—I have partly succeeded in my business to-day, and enclose two guineas as an earnest of more. Dear Prue, I cannot come home to dinner. I languish for your welfare, and will never be a moment careless more.—Your faithful husband, RICH. STEELE.

Send me word you have received this.

LETTER XLVI.   To Mrs Steele.
Eleven at Night, Jan. 5, 1708.

DEAR PRUE,—I was going home two hours ago, but was met by Mr Griffith, who has kept me ever since meeting me, as he came from Mr Lambert's. I will come within a pint of wine. RICH. STEELE.

We drank your health, and Mr Griffith is your servant.

---

* "The Barbadoes plantation left him by his first wife."

LETTER XLVII.   *To Mrs Steele.*
                                            Jan. 14, 1708.
DEAR WIFE,—Mr Edgecombe, Ned Ash, and Mr Lumley have desired me to sit an hour with them at the George in Pall Mall, for which I desire your patience till twelve o'clock, and that you will go to bed.—I am ever thine,   RICH. STEELE.

LETTER XLVIII.   *To Mrs Steele.*
                                      Gray's Inn, Feb. 3, 1708.
DEAR PRUE,—If the man who has my shoemarker's bill calls, let him be answered that I shall call on him as I come home. I stay here in order to get Tonson* to discount a bill for me, and shall dine with him for that end. He is expected at home every minute.—Your most humble, obedient husband,   RICH. STEELE.

LETTER XLIX.   *To Mrs Steele.*
                                            Feb. 11, 1708.
DEAR WIFE,—Having your absolute commands to make an end to-day,† I shall dine with Mr Tryon, in order thereto. I will be at home early, and desire you would make much of yourself, which is the greatest favour you can do your affectionate husband, and dutiful servant,
                                    RICH. STEELE.

LETTER L.   *To Mrs Steele.*
                                            April 9, 1708.
DEAR, DEAR PRUE,—I have sent Dawson thirty pounds, and will not rest till I have enough to discharge her. In the meantime I thought fit to let you know this, that you may see that I cannot forbear making you acquainted with anything that concerns us, without your asking.—Yours ever,   RICH. STEELE.

LETTER LI.   *To Mrs Steele.*‡
                            Tennis Court Coffeehouse, May 5, 1708.
DEAR WIFE,—I hope I have done this day what will be pleasing to you; in the meantime shall lie this night at a barber's, one Leg, over against the Devil's Tavern at Charing Cross. I shall be able to confront the fools

---

* The bookseller, who then lived in Gray's-Inn.
† With reference to the Barbadoes business.
‡ Directed "To Mrs Steele, at her house, the last house but two on the left hand, Bury Street, St James's."

who wish me uneasy, and shall have the satisfation to see thee cheerful and at ease.

If the printer's boy be at home, send him hither; and let Mrs Todd send by the boy my night-gown, slippers, and clean linen.

You shall hear from me early in the morning.   RICH. STEELE.

The meaning of this is obvious, as well as the flurry and anxiety of mind which it indicates. It was the beginning of those unhappy shifts to which his imprudence and carelessness in money matters occasionally reduced him all through life, and appears utterly unaccountable at this early period of his married life, and in circumstances so apparently easy as his. This first difficulty seems to have been tided over. But from a mistaken desire of doing honour to his "capricious beauty," his "absolute governess," as he playfully called her, he appears to have begun his establishment on a scale which he may have thought justified by his expectations, if not by his existing means, which he had no doubt put in the best light they would bear in his representation to his wife's mother. In that letter he thus expressed his views on the subject:—"I am now at a present juncture in my affairs, and my friends are in great power, so that it would be highly necessary for us to be in the figure of life which we shall think convenient to appear in as soon as may be, that I may prosecute my expectations in a busy way while the wind is for me, with just consideration that, about a Court, it will not always blow one way."

No doubt, (to pursue his nautical illustration,) pressing on all sail is the way to make progress, and with a steady hand at the helm may even, in certain circumstances, be the means of weathering the breakers ahead, but it requires an exact knowledge of your ground, that you may not be involved in insidious currents, and care that you do not hoist more canvas than your ship will carry.

He commenced with a house in Bury Street, St James's, to which he soon after added a country house at Hampton Court. They had their chariot and pair, and, on occasions, four horses. Mrs Steele had also a saddle-horse of her own. The establishment of servants was on the same scale. The house at Hampton Court, to which he gave the fanciful name of the *Hovel*, in contrast to the palace against which it stood, was probably the greatest sinking fund of all, being near the residence of his friend Lord Halifax, with whom he was on such terms of intimacy as probably to involve an expenditure that was the beginning of his troubles. On the other hand, his wife's mother had a life-interest in her fortune, his West Indian property was involved, and a failure in it aggravated the affair. The costly furniture of this elegant so-called *Hovel*, with its attendant expenses, involved a loan of a L.1000 from Addison, which was repaid within a year, but a fresh account to a similiar extent was soon after opened, and remained unliquidated for some years, which led to a very painful result, that, like everything connected with Steele, has got distorted to his disadvantage; and the advocates of Addison, in their zeal to exonerate him from blame, have succeeded in putting it in a worse light for both than the original statement of the case, assigning, as it did, motives doing no discredit to either.

LETTER LII.   *To Mrs Steele.*

May 10, 1708.

DEAR PRUE,—I dine at the Gentleman Usher's table at St James's. I have done a great deal of business this morning. Pray, send Richard to me as soon as he has dined.—Yours ever,   RICH. STEELE.

LETTER LIII. To Mrs Steele.
Lord Sunderland's Office, May 19, 1708,
Eleven o'clock.

DEAR PRUE,—I desire you to get the coach and yourself ready as soon as you can conveniently, and call for me here, from whence we will go and spend some time together in the fresh air in free conference. Let my best periwig be put in the coach-box, and my new shoes, for it is a great comfort to be well-dressed in agreeable company. You are vital life to your obliged, affectionate husband, and humble servant,

RICH. STEELE.

From the evident state of pleasurable excitement of Steele's mind when the foregoing was written, and a degree of mystery in it, it appears not improbable that this may have been the occasion of a little episode which occurred soon after his marriage, and which may be introduced here as indicating the perfect confidence of Steele in his wife, and her exceeding amiability. The carriage was ordered, and, without acquainting his wife with his object, they drove to a boarding-school in the suburbs, where a young lady shortly after made her appearance, towards whom Steele manifested so much interest and affection that his wife asked him if the child was his. He confessed she was; "Then," replied the lady, "I beg she may be mine too." From that time she resided with them as a member of their family, and was treated by Mrs Steele as if she had been her own daughter, except that she went by the name of Miss Ousely. Her mother was a connexion of Tonson's the bookseller. Steele was very much attached to her, and intended to give her in marriage, with L.1000 dowry, to the well-known Richard Savage, the early friend of Johnson and the reputed natural son of Lord Rivers. Steele had shewn him great kindness. But the ingratitude, impudence, and viciousness of that unfortunate young man obliged him to alter his intention, and she afterwards married a Mr Aynston, a respectable tradesman and manufacturer at Amely, near Hereford. Though he was a man in good circumstances, yet, as it was not a marriage altogether in accordance with the accomplished education she had received, the manner in which she had been brought up, and the personal merit she appears to have possessed, it is not unnatural that it was promoted in some measure by a feeling of pique on the part of Steele's other children, when they grew up, at finding her enjoy so large a share of their father's affection, and of chagrin on her part arising from this cause.

LETTER LIV.   *To Mrs Steele.*

Two o'clock, May 21, [1708.]

DEAR PRUE,—Mr Addison being chosen for Lestwithiel,* in Cornwall, I am obliged, with some persons concerned, to go to him immediately. —Yours ever,   RICH. STEELE.

LETTER LV.   *To Mrs Steele.*

St James's, Gentleman Usher's Table, May 24, 1708.

MY DEAR PRUE,—I cannot dine at home, but am in haste to speak with one about business of moment. Dear Prue, be cheerful, for I am in pursuit of what will be good news to you.—I am, your most affectionate, obliged husband,   RICH. STEELE.

Think of going with me in the afternoon.

---

* "Mr Addison was at this period returned to Parliament for Lestwithiel, together with James Kendall, Esq., (though they had not the majority of votes,) either by the misunderstanding or the partiality of Alex. Jones, the mayor, who was the returning officer. But they were not permitted to take their seats, their opponents (the Hon. Francis Robartes and the Hon. Russel Robartes) having proved that the right of election had been violated. (See Journals of the House of Commons, vol. xvi., p. 14.) Mr Addison was afterwards chosen for Malmesbury."

LETTER LVI.   To Mrs Steele.
Lord Sunderland's Office, May 24, 1708.

DEAR PRUE,—I beg the favour of you to put my night-gown, slippers, a clean shirt, and cravat, into the coach-box, and make my apology to my mother for staying out to-night. We shall be back to-morrow evening. To-morrow shall be spent in free conference between you and me at Mrs Bradshaw's. Give strict orders to Mrs Watts about her care and attendance on my mother. I am taking pains in removing into my new office—I am, your most obedient husband,   RICH. STEELE.

I love the country most mightily, indeed I do; so you say, so I think. Who are you? I am true. I am . . .*

LETTER LVII.   To Mrs Steele.
Almost one o'clock,
[Lord] Sunderland's Office,
[May 25, 1708.]

DEAR PRUE,—I wish sleeping so long this morning, after I came out to work, may not do you harm. I design to dine at Court, after which I shall return to the office, and shall be glad of a visit there from so agreeable a lady as yourself.—I am, yours unreservedly,
RICH. STEELE.

LETTER LVII. (a)   To Mrs Steele.
June 1, [1708.]

DEAR PRUE,—I shall be at the office exactly at seven, in hopes of seeing the [most] beautiful object that can present itself to my eyes—your fair self. Pray be well dressed.—Your obedient servant and affectionate husband,   RICH. STEELE.

We shall stay in town.

LETTER LVIII.   To Mrs Steele.
June 4, [1708.]

DEAR PRUE,—I have been earnestly about the affairs we talked of last night, and am to meet Mr Foulerton at four in the afternoon again.—Believe me to be, what I really am, your affectionate, tender, obliged husband and lover,   RICH. STEELE.

I shall dine abroad, and cannot go with you to the Park. It would not be amiss if you visited Mrs Tryon in Lime Street. Be in good humour if you go.

---

* So in the original.

LETTER LIX.   *To Mrs Steele.*

June 5, 1708.

DEAR PRUE,—What you would have me do I know not. All that my fortune will compass you shall always enjoy, and have nobody near you that you do not like, except that I am myself disapproved by you for being devotedly your obedient husband,   RICH. STEELE.

LETTER LX.   *To Mrs Steele.*

June 7, 1708.

DEAR PRUE,—I enclose you a guinea for your pocket. I dine with Lord Halifax.

I wish I knew how to court you into good humour, for two or three quarrels more will despatch me quite. If you have any love for me, believe I am always pursuing our mutual good. Pray consider that all my little fortune is to [be] settled this month, and that I have inadvertently made myself liable to impatient people, who take all advantages. If you have [not] patience, I shall transact my business rashly, and lose a very great sum to quicken the time of your being rid of all people you do not like.—Yours ever,   RICH. STEELE.

The meaning of the foregoing, and the character of the "people you do not like," are sufficiently obvious. He was again in straits, and had guests of a troublesome nature, it would appear, in the house, with whom his after experience made him but too familiar. He is even said to have sometimes turned their presence to account, when he had company, and, to save appearances, dressed these disagreeable visitors up in livery.

LETTER LXI.   *To Mrs Steele.*

June 11, 1708.

DEAR PRUE,—I cannot dine with you to-day, but shall, I hope, be able to wait upon you at five o'clock, or a little after.—Your most obedient husband,   RICH. STEELE.

LETTER LXII.   *To Mrs Scurlock.*

June 15, 1708.

MADAM,—After having been with Mr Owen, I choose this way of communicating to you my sense on that occasion, rather than by word of mouth, in a case wherein I am too nearly concerned not to be fearful of letting fall something which might appear too negligent or too careful of my own interests, which are faults I would equally shun.

The sum of the orders you have given your counsel I take to be, that you would settle £160 a year, liable to certain debts, upon us, and the survivor of us, and to our children, and reserve two and forty in yourself, to be given to whom you shall think fit after your decease; adding a very unexpected clause in my behalf, of making the whole estate liable to £2500 after my death, in case I outlive my wife without issue. After I have thanked you in the humblest manner for this very great instance of kindness to me, I beg leave to represent to you that I sincerely have no regards in this world (divested as I am of all relations that might enjoy anything after me) but what have an immediate prospect towards a plentiful maintenance of my wife and children; and, therefore, I can say with the strictest truth, that, in case I shall live to a time when I shall have neither, I should be very far from desiring to turn the current of the estate out of the channel it would have been in had I never come into the family.

Forgive me, then, if I humbly desire that you would take it into your consideration to settle even less, if you think fit, on us during your life, but absolutely fix the whole on your daughter and her posterity, which you will, upon reflection, find to be giving less out of yourself (in case you survive us both) than if at my death, after that of my wife, I should lay upon you such a sum as you are inclined to give me.

I am very confident you have no thoughts of alienating anything from your child; and, however too great a sensibility of spirit may sometimes suspend your kindness to each other, you know nature does revive, and all little bitternesses vanish into tenderness. Now, madam, if you duly weigh this, I believe you will be convinced that there can be no consequence of your reserving a power of alienation in yourself, but laying yourself open to the suggestions of sudden passion, to do what you would in a deliberate temper not have it in your power to recall. But if you keep very plentifully for yourself while living, and bestow the whole after your death, you lay a foundation for your being always above fears of any change in her, or disregard to you; and at the same time secure yourself against the temptations which all mortals are liable to,—that is to say, to other people's designs, or our own infirmities.

I will not trouble you longer at this time, but leave it to your own good nature, and good understanding, to determine your resolutions towards me and mine, which I beseech God to conduct and reward.—I am, madam, your most obedient son, RICH. STEELE.

LETTER LXIII.   *To Mrs Steele.*
Aug. 11, 1708.

DEAR WIFE,—I have ordered Richard to take your directions whether you will have the chariot with two or four horses, to set you and your friend down at your house at Hampton Court. Watts is gone over the water, and says she has your commands to follow in the stage-coach. I shall make it the business of my life to make you easy and happy. Consult your cool thoughts, and you will know that it is the glory of a woman to be her husband's friend and companion, and not his sovereign director.—I am, with truth, sincerity, and tenderness, ever your faithful husband,   RICH. STEELE.

Pray let the gardener put the place in order.

The foregoing contains the first intimation we have of Steele's residence at Hampton, which he afterwards jocosely called the *Hovel*. Here he had his friend Lord Halifax for neighbour; which, as it was probably one inducement in selecting the locality, did not, we may imagine, contribute to the economy of his arrangements. This allusion perhaps explains the enigmatical reference in letter LVI. to his love of the country; and the trip he then took was doubtless thither in order to make arrangements respecting it. Whether the present was a step towards retrenchment may well be questioned. His habitual thoughtlessness and tendency to profusion, as much in what concerned others as himself, had already, as we see, begun to embitter his matrimonial felicity. How far this fruitful element of discord may have entered into the difference referred to in the next letter, it is impossible to say; but we cannot too much admire the tenderness and mildness of his tone, and at the same time the independence of the stand he takes, without an approach to anything sharp or wounding, which appears utterly foreign to his nature, in which there seems not to have mingled a single drop of gall.

LETTER LXIV.   *To Mrs Steele.*
                                                    Aug. 12, 1708.

MADAM,—I have your letter, wherein you let me know that the little dispute we have had is far from being a trouble to you; nevertheless, I assure you any disturbance between us is the greatest affliction to me imaginable. You talk of the judgment of the world; I shall never govern my actions by it, but by the rules of morality and right reason. I love you better than the light of my eyes, or the life-blood in my heart; but when I have let you know that, you are also to understand that neither my sight shall be so far enchanted, nor my affection so much master of me, as to make me forget our common interest. To attend my business as I ought, and improve my fortune, it is necessary that my time and my will should be under no direction but my own. Pray give my most humble service to Mrs Binns. I write all this rather to explain my own thoughts to you, than to answer your letter distinctly. I enclose it to you that, upon second thoughts, you may see the disrespectful manner in which you treat your affectionate, faithful husband,   RICH. STEELE.

LETTER LXV.   *To Mrs Steele.*
                                                    Aug. 13, 1708.

MADAM,—I hope this will find you in good health, as I am at this present writing, thanks be to God for it.

I have not only rebelled against you, but all the rest of my governors, from yourself, whom I acknowledge to have the right of partnership, to the lowest person who had to do with me. I have a very just sense of your merit, and think when I have put you into the proper methods which you ought to follow, I shall be the happiest man living in being your most affectionate husband and humble servant,   RICH. STEELE.

LETTER LXVI.   *To Mrs Steele.*
                                          Monday Morning, Aug. 16, 1708.

DEAR PRUE,—I hope you have composed your mind, and are convinced that the methods I have taken were absolutely necessary for our mutual good. I do assure you, there is not that thing on earth, except mine honour, and that dignity which every man who lives in the world must preserve to himself, which I am not ready to sacrifice to your will and inclination.

I dined yesterday with my Lord Halifax, where the *beauties in the garden* were drunk to. I have settled a great deal of business within these few days, of all which I will give you an account when we meet.—I am, with the most sincere affection, your obliged husband,   RICH. STEELE

I sent you some tea on Friday last. My most humble service to Mrs Binns.

LETTER LXVII.   *To Mrs Steele.*
Aug. 18, 1708.

DEAR PRUE,—I have your letter; and all the great severity you complain of is, that you have a husband who loves you better than his life, who has a great deal of troublesome business, out of the [annoyance] of which he removes the dearest thing alive.—Yours faithfully, in spite of yourself,   RICH. STEELE.

LETTER LXVIII.   *To Mrs Steele.*
Aug. 20, 1708.

DEAR PRUE,—Yours by penny-post came to my hands just now. You extremely mistake me in believing me capable of any cruelty or unkindness to you. I scorn that any man living should have more honour and regard to his wife than myself. You speak with heat to me, but I will not answer you in that style, but make it my utmost aim to make you easy and happy, to which you * [. . . .] nothing but doing me the justice to believe, with all the attention imaginable, your faithful husband,
RICH. STEELE.

I have paid Mr Addison the whole *thousand pound*, and have settled every man's payment, except one, which I hope to perfect to-morrow. Desmaiseaux † is gone to the Bath for his health.

I enclose a guinea and a half, and will send more to-morrow or Monday, if I do not come myself.—I am Mrs Binns's servant.

LETTER LXIX.   *To Mrs Steele.*
Aug. 21, 1708.

DEAR PRUE,—I hope this will find you in good health, as I am at this present writing. I design, when I come down, to let Kerwin ride your little horse to Hampton Court, where I think to leave him at grass, for he costs *five shillings a week* in town. There is no manner of news in town; and I send this without any other business than to repeat to you that I am your affectionate, faithful husband,   RICH. STEELE.

LETTER LXX.   *To Mrs Steele.*
Aug. 23, 1708.

DEAR PRUE,—I have your letter, and will take care to do as you desire

---

* So the original.

† Peter Desmaiseaux, Secretary of the Royal Society, and editor of the English editions of the writings of St Evremond and Bayle, and other works, illustrated with biographical and literary anecdotes.

in every particular of it. I hope in the meantime the cook's husband may go of errands till the servant comes down.—I am, your affectionate and faithful husband, RICH. STEELE.

My most humble service to Mrs Binns.

LETTER LXXI. To Mrs Steele.

Aug. 28, 1708.

DEAR PRUE,—The afternoon coach will bring you £10. Your letter shews you are passionately in love with me. But we must take our portion of life without repining; and I consider that good-nature, added to that beautiful form God has given you, would make our happiness too great for human life.—Your most obliged husband and most humble servant, RICH. STEELE.

LETTER LXXII. To Mrs Steele.

Aug. 28, 1708.

DEAR PRUE,—I send you with this £10, and should come to see you, as ungodly as you are, but that a mail is every moment expected, as you may gather from reading the last *Gazette*, which I enclose; and am, dear, dear Prue, sincerely, your fond husband, RICH. STEELE.

LETTER LXXIII. To Mrs Steele.

Aug. 30, 1708.

DEAR PRUE,—I sent £10 by the afternoon coach of Saturday, and hope you received it safe. The manner in which you write to me might perhaps to another look like neglect and want of love, but I will not understand it so, but take it to be only the uneasiness of a doating fondness, which cannot bear my absence without disdain.

I hope we shall never be so long asunder more, for it is not in your power to make me otherwise than your affectionate, faithful, and tender husband, RICH. STEELE.

LETTER LXXIV. To Mrs Steele.

Whitehall, Sept. 4, 1708.

DEAR PRUE,—You will receive by Watts some wine. I had not the good fortune to see her, because I lay last night at Addison's, and she was in haste, for fear of losing her tide to-day, therefore could not stay till I came to the office out of the city.

I did not receive your letter, writ on Sunday, till Wednesday night. You may think what you please, but I know you have the best husband in the world in your most affectionate, faithful, humble servant, RICH. STEELE.

LETTER LXXV. To Mrs Steele.

Afternoon, Sandy-end,* Sept. 8, 1708.

DEAR PRUE,—Having reached London about eleven, despatched what was further necessary after what papers Mr Addison had before sent to the press, I am just now arrived here to dinner. You desire me to make submissions in my epistles, which I think is not to be insisted upon; but if acknowledgments will satisfy you, I cannot but own to you, what you too well know, that you have a power almost sovereign over your most enamoured husband and humble servant, RICH. STEELE.

Mr Addison is your humble servant.

LETTER LXXVI. To Mrs Steele.

Seven in the morning, Sept. 9, 1708.

DEAR PRUE,—I am going this morning to visit Mr Sartre,† at his country-house, to which place Mr Addison conveys me in coach and four.

Mr Clay,‡ who is now at Thistleworth, will not be in town till to-morrow, and I want to consult him in some despatches I am making for the West Indies.

I am Mrs Binns's humble servant, and your most affectionate, obedient husband, RICH. STEELE.

My service to Ally.

LETTER LXXVII. To Mrs Steele.

Sept. 13, 1708.

DEAR PRUE,—I write to you in obedience to what you ordered me, but there are not words to express the tenderness I have for you. Love is too harsh a word for it; but if you knew how my heart aches when you speak an unkind word to me, and springs with joy when you smile upon me, I

---

* Sandy-end, whence Steele dates, is a hamlet adjoining Fulham, where Addison had either lodgings or a cottage, for the benefit of the air, and of retirement for study.

† "James Sartre, M.A., formerly minister at Montpelier, and Prebendary of Westminster, from May 17, 1688, till his death, Sept. 5, 1713. Swift, in his Journal to Stella, Oct. 25, 1710, says, 'I dined to-day with Mr Addison and Steele, and a sister of Mr Addison's, who is married to one Mons. Sartre, a Frenchman, Prebendary of Westminster, who has a delicious house and gardens; yet I thought it was a sort of monastic life in those cloisters, and I liked Laracor better. Addison's sister is a sort of wit, very like him. I was not fond of her.' This lady was afterwards married to Daniel Combs, Esq."

‡ "Afterwards one of Steele's coadjutors in the *Spectator*."

am sure you would place your glory rather in preserving my happiness, like a good wife, than tormenting me like a peevish beauty. Good Prue, write me word you shall be overjoyed at my return to you, and pity the awkward figure I make when I pretend to resist you, by complying always with the reasonable demands of your enamoured husband,

RICH. STEELE.

P.S.—I am Mrs Binns's servant.

LETTER LXXVIII.   *To Mrs Steele.*
Sept. 14, 1708.

DEAR PRUE,—I fear I shall not be so happy as to see you till Thursday, having some business which keeps me in town. I shall to-day visit my mother, in order to discourse about proper methods for paying off, or laying the debt on your estate into one hand. I hope God will bless my sincere endeavours, so as that we may live without the cares of this life, with a cheerful prospect of a better. It is in no one's power but Prue's to make me constant in such a regular course; therefore will not doubt but you will be very good-humoured, and be a constant feast to your affectionate husband,
RICH. STEELE.

My obedient service to Mrs Binns.

LETTER LXXIX.   *To Mrs Steele.*
Five in the Evening, Sept. 19, 1708.

DEAR PRUE,—I send you seven pennyworth of walnuts, at five a penny, which is the greatest proof I can give you at present of my being, with my whole heart, yours,
RICH. STEELE.

The little horse comes back with the boy, who returns with him for me on Wednesday evening; in the meantime, I believe, it will be well that he runs in the park.

I am Mrs Binns's servant.

Since I writ this, I came to the place where the boy was ordered with the horses; and, not finding him, sent this bearer, lest you should be in fears, the boy not returning.

P.S.—There are 29 walnuts.

The foregoing grave postscript appears to be one of the first of many humorous touches in which he rallies his wife for her minute carefulness in small matters, of which her preservation of this unique marital correspondence has been adduced as an example. For that instance of it at least which proves her estimate of her husband, when she thought every casual scrap from his pen worth preserving, the admirers of Steele have reason to thank her. For though some may be disposed to put an uncandid construction on some of the disclosures here made in a strictly confidential correspondence with his wife, without considering how few there are that would bear such a test, which he is perhaps the first to have had applied to him, yet the effect of the whole is surely highly to his advantage, and it supplies what but for it—from his maintaining little general correspondence, and not keeping anything in the shape of a diary (indeed his *Tatlers* and *Spectators* were his diaries)—would have left a great blank in the details of his life. But while regretting the absence of a diary, which would have taken in a wider range of topics, this correspondence, which is almost as regular as a journal, supplies its place in a more limited circle, it is true, but, so far as it goes, in a more interesting form.

LETTER LXXX.   *To Mrs Steele.*

Sept. 20, 1708.

DEAR PRUE,—If a servant I sent last night got to Hampton Court, you received 29 walnuts and a letter from me. I inclose the *Gazette*, and am, with all my soul, your passionate lover, and faithful husband,

RICH. STEELE.

Since I writ the above, I have found half a hundred more walnuts, which I send herewith.

My service to Mrs Binns.

LETTER LXXXI.   *To Mrs Steele.*

Sept. 21, 1708.

DEAR, DEAR PRUE,—Your pretty letter, with so much good-nature and kindness, which I received yesterday, is a perfect treasure to me. I am at

present very much out of humour upon another account, Tryon having put off payment of my £800, which I ought to have received yesterday, till further time. But I hope when Mr Clay comes to town to-morrow, he will see me justified.—I am, with the tenderest affection, ever yours,
                                                            RICH. STEELE.

LETTER LXXXII.   *To Mrs Steele.*
                                        Sandy End, Sept. 22, 1708.

DEAR PRUE,—After being very busy all this day, I am come hither to dine with Mr Addison and Mr Clay, who are your servants; and I take this time from eating, while others are busy at it at the table.—Yours, yours, ever, ever,   RICH. STEELE.

LETTER LXXXIII.   *To Mrs Steele.*
                                        Monday, seven at night,
                                            Sept. 27, 1708.

DEAR PRUE,—You see you are obeyed in everything, and that I write over-night for the following day. I shall now in earnest, by Mr Clay's good conduct, manage my business with that method as shall make me easy. The news, I am told, you had last night, of the taking of Lille, does not prove true; but I hope we shall have it soon. I shall send by to-morrow's coach.—I am, dear Prue, a little in drink, but at all times your faithful husband,   RICH. STEELE.

LETTER LXXXIV.   *To Mrs Steele.*
                                        Secretary's Office,
             between six and seven at night, Sept. 28, 1708.

DEAR PRUE,—I thought it better to enclose this thus, than to direct so small a sum to you. I have but half as much left in my pocket, but shall be much richer on Thursday morning.

My dear wife, it is not to be imagined by you the tender achings my heart is frequently touched with when I think of you.

Mr Clay has shewn himself a man of address in settling my affairs, in spite of the tricks and artifices of those I have to deal with.

I recommend thee, my heart's desire, to the good God who made thee that amiable creature thou art, to keep thee safe. My service to your companion Binns.—I am, your devoted, affectionate husband, and humble servant,   RICH. STEELE.

LETTER LXXXV.   *To Mrs Steele.*
                                Half-hour after ten, Sept. 28, 1708.

DEAR PRUE,—It being three hours since I writ to you, I send this to assure you I am going very soberly to bed, and that you shall be the last thing in my thoughts to-night, as well as the first to-morrow morning.—I am, with the utmost fondness, your faithful husband,

RICH. STEELE.

LETTER LXXXVI. *To Mrs Steele.*

St James's Coffeehouse,
eight in the morning, Oct. 2, 1708.

DEAR PRUE,—Mr Gervase* going this morning to Hampton Court, I desire him to throw this over our wall. I have much difficulty to accomplish everything necessary to be done here, which makes me fear I cannot come till Tuesday noon. If it pleases God that I can be so happy as to live cheerfully with thee, and in thy favour, it is the utmost good that can arrive to, dear Prue, eternally thine, RICH. STEELE.

LETTER LXXXVII. *To Mrs Steele.*

Berry Street,
seven at night, Oct. 5, 1708.

DEAR WIFE,—I send this to beg pardon for not coming to-night, but I have some good glimpse in my affairs; and, if I do not fail to-morrow, we shall be out of difficulties hereafter. I come into waiting on the Prince† to-morrow, and am, my dear Prue, yours, with the utmost kindness and duty, RICH. STEELE.

I hope to see you before twelve to-morrow.

LETTER LXXXVIII. *To Mrs Steele.*

Secretary's Office,
near ten at night, Oct. 6, 1708.

DEAR PRUE,—I got to town about six, found all things well, and have just despatched the proof‡ for to-morrow. I wish you a good night, and shall always keep myself in a capacity of taking the oaths that I am, with the strictest fidelity and love, your enamoured husband and humble servant, RICH. STEELE.

LETTER LXXXIX. *To Mrs Steele.*

Oct. 7, 1708.

DEAR PRUE,—I send, directed to Watts, a bottle of tint. You must not expect me to-night, but I will write by the penny post.—I am, yours faithfully, RICH. STEELE.

---

* Mr Gervase, probably the famous painter.
† Prince George of Denmark, the Royal Consort, to whom he was gentleman usher. See note to Letter CI.
‡ Of the *Gazette.*

LETTER XC.   *To Mrs Steele.*
                                    Thursday, Oct. 7, 1708.
DEAR PRUE,—I fear I shall not be able to come out of town till Saturday morning.—I am, my dear creature, thine for ever,   RICH. STEELE.

LETTER XCI.   *To Joseph Keally, Esq., Dublin.*
                                            Oct. 7, 1708.
SIR,—I thank you for the kind part you took in my affairs; and understand I am to wish you joy upon the happiness of being a husband, which is at least a snug, if not a rapturous, condition. Harry[*] lives still a knight-errant, by what means it is impossible to tell you. But I now and then meet him, and give him the proper compliment, that I am glad to see him alive. The paragraph you mention was very much censured in the town; but I acted so as to answer it where I am accountable. As to the rest, I take my employment in its very nature to be what is the object of censure, since so many interests are concerned in the matters that I am to relate twice a week: but I am armed *cap-à-pie* with old sentences, among which I prefer that of Horace with £300 per annum[†] salary—

"Populus me sibilat; at mihi plaudo
Ipse domi; simul ac nummos contemplor," &c.

The taste for plays is expired. We are all for operas, performed by eunuchs of every race impotent to please. Lord Manchester is returning from Venice with a singer of great expectation. My way of life should make me capable of entertaining with much politics, but I am not a bit wiser than you knew me.—Yours, &c.,   RICH. STEELE.

LETTER XCII.   *To Mrs Steele.*
                                            Oct. 8, 1708.
DEAR PRUE,—This brings you a quarter of a pound of Bohea and as much of green tea, both which I hope you will find good. To-morrow your favourite Mr Addison and I shall set out for Hampton Court; he to meet some great men there, I to see you, who am but what you make me. —Yours, with the utmost fondness,   RICH. STEELE.

LETTER XCIII.   *To Mrs Steele.*
                                            Oct. 8, 1708.
DEAR PRUE,—I write according to order, and hope, before the receipt of

---

[*] Harry Keally.
[†] This was the salary attached to his office of Gazetteer.

this, you will have had the tea which I sent by the morning coach. I shall be at Hampton Court, God willing, before twelve to-morrow.—Your faithful husband, RICH. STEELE.

LETTER XCIV.   To Mrs Steele.
Hyde Park Corner,
eight in the morning, Wednesday, Oct. 13, 1708.

DEAR PRUE,—The bearer is one I propose to be our footman. He is, as you see, very queer, and fit for what I often heard you call it, *a* thorough servant; besides which, he speaks the Welsh tongue fluently. I believe he will be a proper fellow enough, for he lived a great while with one Dr Price, an acquaintance of mine at Richmond. I hope he will be approved by you; if he is, the livery shall be fitted for his shape against the time that he and I can attend the chariot to bring Mrs Binns and you to town, which shall be done with all suitable ceremony. In the meantime, I am busy about the main chance. I have ordered him to be here again this evening, except you direct otherwise. I hope I shall see you to-morrow. —I am, with every dictate of my affections, and every pulse of my heart, dear Prue, sincerely yours, RICH. STEELE.

LETTER XCV.   To Mrs Steele.
Thursday, Oct. 14, 1708.

DEAR PRUE,—I intended to have certainly gone out to Hampton Court to-day; but the West Indian post going on Saturday, and Mr Clay having leisure but this day, I am forced to prepare my letters for his perusal before night. I am in haste, as you see by this scribble.—I am your faithful and most affectionate husband, RICH. STEELE.

I shall observe what you desire about James, and everything else.

LETTER XCVI.   To Mrs Steele.
Berry Street,
seven at night, Oct. 14, 1708.

DEAR PRUE,—I writ you before this day by the coach, and send this to tell you that Mr Clay has been here since that, and I find I must stay in town this whole week to attend my business, or leave some things undone, which is as bad to do as to neglect the whole. You may be sure, if I find I may be six or seven hours employed where I please, it shall be at Hampton Court. Pray keep yourself warm, be cheerful, and believe me, dear creature, sincerely thine, RICH. STEELE.

LETTER XCVII.   To Mrs Steele.
Oct. 16, 1708.

DEAR PRUE,—I should have rid down to Hampton Court this evening, but that I am to be with my mother about a mortgage to be made for paying off the bonds which stand out, that we may be easy on all hands. We must write this night to Mr Thomas for the title, &c.

The Queen comes next week to Hampton Court, and stays a fortnight. —I am, with my whole heart, your faithful husband, RICH. STEELE.

LETTER XCVIII.   *To Mrs Steele.*
                                                       Oct. 20, 1708.

DEAR PRUE,—I had yours last night, with an enclosed to my mother, which I do not design to deliver. You accuse me of unkindness, for I cannot imagine what. If you want for anything, it is that you will not supply yourself with it, for I very regularly send you wherewithal.

My Lord Chamberlain is expected this night in town, from whom I hope for an order for a very handsome apartment in Whitehall. As soon as I receive it, I will immediately remove into it, where I hope you will be pleased. I am sure it is the utmost of my ambition to make you so.—I am your faithful and affectionate husband,   RICH. STEELE.

P. S.—My mother has altered her mind about the mortgage. I think to come down to-morrow night to give you an account of everything. In the meantime, send by your countryman two guineas.

LETTER XCIX.   *To Mrs Steele.*
                              Seven in the morning, Oct. 26, 1708.

DEAR PRUE,—I desire you would put yourself in a readiness to com away on Thursday, on which day the coach will come, and, if I can, attended by me. Mr Harrison, a gentleman-usher of the privy chamber, is dead; the employment is £200 a year salary, and £100 perquisites: it is a place for life, and I am putting in for it this morning with all the force I have. I shall send down enclosed money by to-morrow morning's post, directed to Watts. You can imagine the difficulties I am put to; but I can go through anything, provided I have the happiness of being esteemed by you as your affectionate husband and humble servant,
                                                       RICH. STEELE.

I am very sick with too much wine last night.

LETTER C.   *To Mrs Steele.*
                                              Kensington,
                                three, afternoon, Oct. 28, 1708.

DEAR WIFE,—I came hither according to my [duty], to attend the Prince

my master,* by whose dead body I sit while I am writing this. He departed this life half an hour after one. I am ordered to wait here, and believe I shall not be relieved till to-morrow morning. As soon as I can get to town I will despatch the coach for you.—I am, my dear wife, your obliged husband, and humble servant,
                                                RICH. STEELE.

LETTER CI.   *To Mrs Steele.*
                                        Kensington, Oct. 29, 1708.

DEAR WIFE,—I enclose all the cash I can well spare, which is four guineas. I writ you word by the penny post last night that I was detained here to sit up with the Prince's body, and must do so every third night till he is interred.† I am still kept bare of money by the men I have to deal with; but as soon as I can get to town, I will send away the coach for you. Please to come to Mrs Hardresse's house in the Square at Kensington, where it will be convenient for you to be till all things are ready for our greater ease in town. More I cannot till we meet.—I am, with the sincerest affection, your obliged husband and humble servant,
                                                RICH. STEELE.

P. S.—Send the bearer back with an account how you do. My service to Mrs Binns.

LETTER CII.   *To Mrs Steele.*
                                    Almost nine at night, Oct. 29, 1708.

DEAR PRUE,—I beg the favour of you to take care to wrap yourself up very warm for your journey to-morrow. The coachman has his orders; and I have agreed with him to bring you to Kensington Square, and carry Mrs Binns home, in hopes she will dispense with your waiting upon her, and returning afterwards to your lodgings.

I shall take care to have your lodgings fit for your reception, and will never omit anything in my power to make your hours agreeable.—Your affectionate husband,   RICH. STEELE.

---

* "His Royal Highness the Prince Consort, George of Denmark, died at the time here mentioned, at Kensington, of an asthma. He was born at Copenhagen in April 1653, married the Princess Anne in July 1683, and was an illustrious instance of conjugal affection among the great. On the 11th of November his corpse was brought from Kensington to Westminster, and, having lain in state in the Painted Chamber till the 13th of that month, was privately interred in Westminster Abbey."

† "After the death of the Prince the Queen bestowed annuities on all his attendants. Of this bounty Steele's portion was £100 a year."

LETTER CIII. *To Mrs Steele, at Mrs Hardresse's, in Kensington Square.*
Bow Street, Covent Garden, Nov. 10, 1708.

MY DEAR WIFE,—I write this to do my duty in complying with your desire of hearing from me this night. I am heartily tired, and go on with hope and perseverance. There is nothing troubles me so much as the consideration that the most amiable and most deserving of her sex is obliged to suffer all the uneasiness that I do. But, my dear life, be of good comfort, and continue to be the only happiness of, dear Prue, your faithful husband, RICH. STEELE.

You know I must come to-morrow evening to Kensington, but you shall hear from me before.

LETTER CIV. *To Mrs Steele.*
House of Lords, Nov. 12, 1708.

DEAR WIFE,—I send this to desire you would think of coming to-morrow to town; there is room at my mother's,* where you may be for a few days. I am to be here till after the funeral. You shall have this bearer to wait on you to town to-morrow, with necessaries for your change of abode.—I am, my dear creature, your most enamoured husband,
RICH. STEELE.

LETTER CV. *To Mrs Steele.*
Nov. 13, 1708.

DEAR PRUE,—I send you all the money I have, which I hope will bring you to town. Since you have an inclination to see the funeral, I have spoken for a place at the housekeeper's of the House of Lords to place you in till I can get a more convenient one for seeing the procession; and I take it that it will be best to be in the Abbey itself, for which end you must come soon. I am ordered to stay here, or should come for you.—Yours, with all my soul, R. STEELE.

The fleet is come in.

LETTER CVI. *To Mrs Steele.*
Garter Tavern, Nov. 16, 1708.

DEAR PRUE,—I am sorry I cannot come to sit an hour with you to-night, being detained by business with Mr Huggins,† which you know of. I have

---

* " Query, Was Steele's own mother alive at this time? and where did she live? or, Does he mean here old Mrs Scurlock, his wife's mother?"

† " An attorney, probably, employed at this time by Mrs Vandeput to recover from Steele some arrears of rent for his house in Berry Street, of which she

to-day been with Mr Tryon, who does not now deny his having effects, but pretends to complain of bad usage in suing him. Within a day or two I doubt not but we shall have our money, which will be the introduction to that life we both pant after with so much earnestness.—Your obliged husband,   RICH. STEELE.

LETTER CVII.   *To Mrs Steele.**

Nov. 17, 1708.

DEAR WIFE,—How can you add to my cares by making so unjust complaints against me as in yours of last night. I take all the pains imaginable to bring you home to ease and satisfaction, and made a great step in it yesternight, which I could not had I spent my time elsewhere than where I did. My dear, be cheerful, and expect a good account of things this evening from, dear wife, your most affectionate and most obliged husband,   RICH. STEELE.

LETTER CVIII.   *To Mrs Steele.*

Nov. 18, 1708.

DEAR WIFE,—I am going this morning into the city, to make my demand of the money long due to me. I shall hasten thence to you; and am, with the tenderest love, ever yours,   RICH. STEELE.

LETTER CIX.   *To Mrs Steele.*

Nov. 26, 1708.

DEAR WIFE,—I am, by applying to my adversary,† prepared for ending my present calamity, but was denied by my friend.‡—I am, dear creature, your constant, faithful lover and obliged husband,   RICH. STEELE.

I am making it my business to find out Mr Huggins, in order to withdraw his officer.

LETTER CX.   *To Mrs Steele.*

Nov. 28, 1708.

DEAR WIFE,—Take confidence in that Being who has promised protec-

---

appears to have been the landlady, and the insufferable brute in Let. May 5, 1709. Steele mentions [Letter CXII.] his going in quest of Mr Huggins in Westminster Hall."

* Directed, " To Mrs Steele, to be left at Mrs Scurlock's lodgings, last house, left hand, in Bromley Street, Holborn." This seems to prove that it was his wife's mother he referred to in Letter CIV.

† " His landlady possibly," [Letter CVI., note.]

‡ Addison has been supposed to be the friend who refused to bail Steele on this occasion, or at least avoided being seen by him; but from the cordial tone of the letters immediately after, probably erroneously. See Letters CXIII., &c.

tion to all the good and virtuous when afflicted. Mr Glover* accommodates me with the money which is to clear this present sorrow this evening. I will come to Mrs Binns's exactly at eight.—I am, your most affectionate husband and obedient servant, RICH. STEELE.

LETTER CXI. *To Mrs Steele.*
Nov. 30, 1708.

DEAR WIFE,—Be of good cheer, for I find friendship among the lowest when disappointed by the highest. I have called at Mr Elderton's † to keep things at a stand till I come to him at ten o'clock.

Dear creature, be cheerful. God be your comfort and your protection. While that is so, and you are safe, nothing can disturb RICH. STEELE.

LETTER CXII. *To Mrs Steele, at her house in Berry Street.*
Ten o'clock, Nov. 30, 1708.

DEAR WIFE,—This is to acquaint you that honest Glover has effectually served me. I am now in search of Mr Huggins in Westminster Hall. Elderton, without my knowledge, has also removed the other storm to some distance, so that we prepare in time to weather. Be of good cheer; God will bless me, and make me a better provider hereafter for my wife and dear child.‡—Yours ever, RICH. STEELE.

LETTER CXIII.—*To Mrs Steele, at Mrs Scurlock's Lodgings, Bromley Street, Holborn.*
Dec. 6, 1708.

MY DEAR WIFE,—I will not defer telling you that there is a thing in agitation that will make me happy at once. Your rival, A———n,§ will be removed; and if I can succeed him in his office, it will answer all purposes. This will be determined before to-morrow at noon. I cannot see Mr Glover till six o'clock.—I am, your faithful, loving husband, RICH. STEELE.

Keep this to yourself. I will come to you as soon as I have dined.

LETTER CXIV. *To Mrs Steele.*
Half-hour after five o'clock,
Dec. 14, 1708.

DEAR PRUE,—Mr Addison is just now gone to Lord Wharton; and I wait his return to know my own next steps.

---

* Who was "honest Glover?"—*Nichols.* See Letter CXII.

† "Steele's attorney."

‡ "Perhaps the child here spoken of was Richard, who died in his infancy."

§ "Mr Addison, at that time Under-Secretary of State, was on the eve of being appointed Secretary to Lord Wharton, the new Lord-Lieutenant of Ireland. See the next letter."

My heart is as much disturbed as yours can be on the same occasion; but this seasonable hope breaking in upon me, will, I hope, cure all, and refresh our spirits. I wish you would come directly to the *garret;* where you can, from time to time, hear from me what passes this evening.

I send this moment to my mother, and am, yours faithfully,

RICH. STEELE.

LETTER CXV.   *To Mrs Steele.*

Dec. 18, 1708.

DEAR PRUE,—Mr Addison has engaged me about extraordinary business all this day. I hope I have engaged him to take Desmaiseaux.*

I am obliged to go to supper where he treats to-night, to help him in doing the honours to his friends.—Yours tenderly,

RICH. STEELE.

LETTER CXVI.   *To Mrs Steele, Berry Street.*

Cockpit, Dec. 22, 1708.

DEAR PRUE,—I desire you to take a coach, and come to this lodgings. I am obliged to wait hereabouts. James will find me at Mr Delafaye's† house in Downing Street, or at the Coffeehouse.—Yours faithfully,

RICH. STEELE.

On the appointment of Addison to the Chief-Secretaryship for Ireland, under Lord Wharton, Steele, as we see, put in his claim, it is said at the instance of his friend, to the Under-Secretaryship which he vacated. The result is thus stated in a letter to a friend in Ireland, who was also a correspondent of Addison's, and perhaps a companion of school days:—

LETTER CXVII.   *To Joseph Keally, Esq., Dublin.*

Jan. 20, 1709.

DEAR SIR,—I have your very kind letter of the 1st inst., and am sorry you had not intelligence sooner of Mr Addison's being Secretary of State for Ireland. The same messenger who carried an account of it to the Lords Justices, had a letter for you in Dublin, wherein I told you the

---

* See Letter LXVIII., p. 108.

† " Charles Delafaye, Esq., one of the clerks in the Secretary of State's Office, and afterwards himself an Under-Secretary of State."

happiness your old acquaintance proposed to himself in your friendship and conversation. I have communicated your friendly design to the Secretary, relating to his being chosen a member. He gives you his hearty thanks, and desires me to tell you that he believed that matter already provided for.

Since he had the honour to be named himself for this post in Ireland, a brother of his has been chosen by the Directors of the East India Company Governor of Fort St George, in the room of Mr Pitt.*

I had hopes of succeeding him in this office; but things are ordered otherwise in favour of the North Britons, one of whom is come into that employment very suddenly. In the meantime, something additional will be given to, dear sir, your most affectionate friend and humble servant,

RICH. STEELE.

LETTER CXVIII.   *To Mrs Steele, Berry Street.*

Jan. 31, 1708-9.

MY DEAR WIFE,—I am with young Mr Tonson, at the Griffin Tavern, where I shall dine on a scrap, and afterwards go to Mr Longueville,† to appoint the meeting of Tryon to-morrow, to make a final end.

I shall come home before eight o'clock, and am, dear creature, eternally yours,   RICH. STEELE.

LETTER CXIX.   *To Mrs Steele.*

Feb. 5, 1708-9.

DEAR PRUE,—I was coming home, but am indispensably obliged to dine at Tonson's, where, after dinner, some papers are to be read, whereof, among others, I am to be a judge. I have the money for you and the other occasions. This absence I hope you will excuse in your affectionate, faithful,

DICK STEELE.

LETTER CXX.   *To Mrs Steele.*

March 2, 1708-9.

MY DEAR WIFE,—I enclose a guinea, lest you should want. I am resolved to do something effectually to-day with Tryon; therefore do not expect me to-day at dinner.

My life is bound up in you. I will be at home before six.

RICH. STEELE.

---

* "Mr Gulston Addison, who was born in August 1673, died at Fort St George in the office of Governor and President."

† Of whom the industrious Nichols was unable to procure any account.

LETTER CXXI. 　　　To Mrs Steele.
　　　　　　　　　　　　　　　　　　　March 11, 1708-9.

DEAR PRUE,—I enclose five guineas, but cannot come to dinner. Dear little woman, take care of thyself, and eat and drink cheerfully.
　　　　　　　　　　　　　　　　　　　　RICH. STEELE.

LETTER CXXII.　　　To Mrs Steele, Berry Street.
　　　　　　　　　　　　　　　　　　　March 21, 1708-9.

DEAR PRUE,—I send you this by the boy I have a mind to take, if you like him. Things go pretty well. I shall dine at court. If there are any letters, let the boy bring them to me thither, at the gentleman-usher's table.—Yours unreservedly and faithfully,　　　　RICH. STEELE.

LETTER CXXIII.　　　To Mrs Steele, Berry Street.
　　　　　　　　　　　　　　　　　　　March 23, 1708-9.

DEAR PRUE,—Having some doubt about Tilden, I dine at court, and will look into all things between this and six o'clock. The bearer is a boy well recommended, whose father has been with me, and whom I approve (as I do all other things) as you like him.—Yours faithfully,
　　　　　　　　　　　　　　　　　　　　RICH. STEELE.

LETTER CXXIV.　　　Mrs Steele to her Husband.
　　　　　　　　　　　　　　　　　　　[*Undated.*]

It is but an addition to our uneasiness to be at variance with each other. I beg your pardon if I have offended you. God forgive you for adding to the sorrow of a heavy heart, that is above all sorrow, but for your sake.*

---

* Another prayer by Steele :—

"Almighty God, who of Thy infinite goodness and mercy didst create, and dost preserve, all things both in heaven and earth; look down with an eye of mercy on us, whom Thy good providence has ordained to live together in holy matrimony. Grant, O God, that no allurement, passion, jealousy, plenty or want, may so far transport us as to make us forget a sacred vow, made to each other, and before Thee. Let us, O Lord, with a lively, cheerful, and habitual sense of such our obligations, check the first motives to anger and distress; and cherish all, and omit none the least instances of tenderness and good-will: so shall we enjoy and pass through this human, transient life, in a daily preparation for one that is celestial and eternal; not regarding posterity so as to forget eternity; yet believing it not displeasing in Thy sight, that in our way to a certain and unchangeable Being, we neglect not a provision for such as Thou mayst make us instruments to introduce into one that is various and uncertain. This, and whatever else Thy omnipresent wisdom sees necessary for us, with relation to ourselves and the whole race of mankind, we beseech Thee, O Father of all things, bestow upon us. All which we beg in Thy name, and through the mediation of Jesus Christ, who hath taught us, in a perfect and an unblameable manner to approach Thee, saying,

"Our Father," &c.

As Steele's interests were intimately connected with the ministerial fluctuations, a glance may here be taken at the chances and changes affecting public events and characters.

The chiefs of the Whigs, including Lord Somers, not being satisfied with the apparent conversion of Marlborough and Godolphin to their principles, had at first stood aloof from the ministry, so far as taking office, at the same time giving their support to its measures. This gave rise to the terms *Old* and *New* Whigs. Latterly, however, they had united with them more cordially, which tended materially to consolidate the power of the Cabinet. But from its composite nature it had elements of weakness within itself, which only required any adverse turn of fortune to make themselves felt.

The vitality of the Queen's prejudice in favour of the Tory party was only suspended, not destroyed, by her chagrin at their conduct on coming into power previously, and causes were now at work to revive her sympathies in that direction.

The ardour of her early attachment to the Duchess of Marlborough, by whose mental vigour her own weaker mind was no doubt captivated, and who had warmly espoused her cause in her differences with the Court in the preceding reign, was destined to realise the proverb on that subject, and the fate of all extremes. She had taken a romantic fancy in former days, in order to avoid the restraints of ceremony, to carry on their correspondence under fictitious names, and gave the Duchess the choice of *Mrs Morley* or *Mrs Freeman*. Alluding to the circumstance, "My frank temper led me," says the Duchess, "to pitch upon *Freeman*, and so the Princess took the other."* But after coming to the throne, as different circumstances and periods of life have different feelings, the display of the naturally imperious disposition of the Duchess, and the advantage she took of her position, joined to a grasping rapacity that was insatiable, at length exhausted the patience of the Queen, and made her long to rid herself of what she regarded as an irksome and intolerable bondage. Before matters had got to an extremity, a Mrs Hill, a lady of fallen fortune, who was related to the Duchess, had applied to her for her interest on behalf of her family. Among other services which she rendered on this occasion, she obtained for one of the ladies a place in the royal household, all but menial, the result of which she could have little foreseen. This *protégée*, Mrs Abigail Hill, being either more humble and amiable, or from being more favourably situated for affecting those qualities, soon gained the confidence of the Queen, who found in her society that repose and freedom from perturbation for which she had so long sighed. Ultimately Mrs Hill, who, with whatever other qualities, does not appear to have been deficient in cunning, succeeded in completely supplanting the Duchess in the dangerous position of royal favourite.

The first unequivocal intimation the Duchess received that her reign was over, and that the object of her patronage was now her rival, was the private marriage of her relative to Mr Masham, without her knowledge, but with the sanction of the Queen, who was the only witness present. These doings within the palace were pregnant with results.

* Conduct of Duchess of Marlborough, p. 14.

Among the rising politicians from the Tory camp that Godolphin and Marlborough had introduced to office in 1704, were Henry St John and Robert Harley,—the former a very young man of shining abilities, as Secretary-at-War; and the latter a man of practical talents, and of such tact that he had been twice chosen Speaker, as Secretary of State. Mr Harley happened to be related in the same degree as the Duchess to the new favourite, Mrs Masham; and though he had not formerly troubled himself much with the connexion, he was not slow to recognise it now, when he met her in the course of his frequent audiences with the Queen in his official capacity. If Mrs Masham was cunning, Mr Harley was no less so. He affected a sort of frank playfulness, and by means of this, and flattering the prejudices of the Queen, he succeeded in insinuating himself into her good graces. His efforts were seconded by Mrs Masham, whom he had made his friend, and both were sanguine of promoting their ambitious views by this union of their interest.

Mr Harley seemed to see his way to rising to power on the ruins of the present administration. There was an increasing peace party in the House. The drain of the war was beginning to be felt in the scarcity of specie; complaints were loudly made of the conduct of the allies, and of their being the only parties benefited. These considerations, with the usual amount of exaggeration, had produced considerable effect. At the same time it was complained that the war was so feebly prosecuted in Spain as to result in failure; whilst in the Low Countries, where Marlborough commanded, it was conducted on a great scale, for his benefit and that of the allies. The Queen, moreover, was becoming ardently desirous of its termination, not merely on these, but, in addition, on higher grounds, from the natural tenderness of her sex, on those of humanity.

Harley was now admitted to frequent clandestine conferences with the Queen, which were arranged by Mrs Masham. At the same time, he was making the most obsequious professions to Marlborough, to whom he was under great obligations.

Whilst the opponents of the ministry were attacking them with vigour, they of course were not without making reprisals. They branded their antagonists with the epithet of the *French faction*, and insinuations were made of their maintaining a correspondence with the exiled court. A rumour now also got afloat of an intended invasion of Scotland by the Pretender. The intrigues of Harley meantime had got wind, and Godolphin and Marlborough demanded his immediate dismissal. The Queen hesitated. In this critical state of affairs, a letter written by one Gregg, a clerk in Mr Harley's office, discovering to the court of France the designs of the ministry in relation to the war, was intercepted by the Duke of Marlborough. Though the most rigid investigation failed in tracing any complicity to the secretary, and Gregg himself exonerated him in the most emphatic manner, yet the affair was so damaging in public estimation that, taken in connexion with his recent duplicity and intrigue, now fully discovered, he found himself called upon to resign, (Feb. 11, 1708.) As he had assiduously cultivated a party to aid in the designs he had been maturing, they had sufficient faith in his prospects to follow his fortunes, leaving the Whigs for the present in undisputed possession of power, and the

Queen to chafe in her bonds, all the more rankling from the triumph obtained over her by those from whose sway she had been seeking to break loose. Nor can it be considered an unfitting termination of a scene of double duplicity, ingratitude, and disloyalty (to their patrons) in the agents she had employed.

Such is an outline bringing the events of public interest up to the period at which we have arrived.

To return to Steele: Since the relinquishment of his dramatic pursuits he had not attempted anything further than a little trifling dalliance with the Muses.* But though his then trivial appointments perhaps occupied him sufficiently to fritter away his time, he had too active a mind and too strong a motive for the exercise of his talents to continue so permanently. He was now, in fact, concerting a fresh literary campaign, destined to be more memorable than any of the preceding. The supper to which he alludes as given by Addison in honour of his new appointment, at which he was to assist in doing the honours, was not a farewell one, as he remained in London for some months after, and it was but two days preceding the appearance of the first result of his new literary labours that

* "In the *Muses' Mercury* for January 1706-7 are some humorous lines by Steele to a young lady who had married an old man; and in that for February is the following lively song by him:"—

"'Me Cupid made a willing slave,
   A merry wretched man;
   I slight the nymphs I cannot have,
   Nor dote on those I can.

"'This constant maxim still I hold,
   To baffle all despair—
   The absent ugly are and old,
   The present young and fair.'"

his friend started for the scene of his new official ones. That he did not communicate his design to Addison we may believe was not from any want of friendship, but doubtless that he might test the success of his experiment previously, and give him an agreeable surprise.

CHAPTER V.

THE PERIODICAL ESSAYIST AND DELINEATOR OF CHARACTER—
1709-1710.

> Steele projects the *Tatler*, forming a new literary era—State of society at the period—A glance at preceding kindred writings—Origin of the assumed name of Isaac Bickerstaff—Adopted from a recent pamphlet in which Swift had foretold the death of Partridge, an almanac-maker and pretender in physic and astrology—The *jeu d'esprit*, which had been joined in by the other wits of the time, taken up by Steele in the *Tatler*—Partridge publishes a disclaimer—Extraordinary success of the *Tatler*—Swift one of its earliest contributors—Notice of the other contributors, Addison, Congreve, &c.—Dedications of the different volumes, and the subjects of them—Its close—General regret caused by its discontinuance—The good it accomplished.

SHORTLY after the date of the last of the foregoing letters, namely, on the 12th of April (o.s.) following, Steele commenced the first of that celebrated series of periodical papers of which the delineation of character, life, and manners, combined with literature and criticism, was the leading characteristic. For this task his previous experience as a dramatic writer rendered him peculiarly well qualified, and on these works his literary fame for the most part rests. They formed a new era, and added an additional department to the national literature, which has commonly been designated by the title of the British Classics, or Essayists. They produced such important effects for good in their own age, have had such a beneficial influence in giving a tone to the tastes and manners of successive generations since, have afforded mingled delight and instruction to such multitudes of readers before we had come to be a nation of merely superficial novel-readers, are still so delightful when recurred to, and have left such an impress upon our language and literature,* that it is difficult to speak justly of their various claims without appearing to exaggerate. Though they long enjoyed a monopoly (which has ceased in consequence of the great multiplicity of new books) of being deemed the most indispensable portion of every family library, and the most delightful and instructive guides to initiate the youthful mind in the charms of elegant letters,—a neglect which they unfortunately share with most of the standard literature, just as on the stage the regular drama has been superseded by trifling *ad-captandum* pieces of the most frivolous description,—yet they can never cease to claim the attention of all readers of taste and discrimination.

The writer may here quote what he has elsewhere said respecting the state of society at the period, previous to entering on an account of these papers:—

"For half a century preceding the appearance of the *Tatlers*, these kingdoms had been the scene of civil strife, the most cruel and distressing of the forms of war, with little intermission. The bright streaks that had appeared upon the horizon, and seemed to herald a halcyon time of repose and prosperity, on the setting of 'that bright occidental star,' Queen

---

* It is easy to trace this influence on the most finished writers of subsequent times down to Washington Irving. Among those who owed the elegant simplicity of their style to a careful and sedulous attention to these models, was Benjamin Franklin, to whom Lord Brougham pays a just compliment ("Sketches of Statesmen") in speaking of the elegant simplicity of his style in comparison with the cumbrous and pedantic manner of Bacon. And critics have also professed to trace in the pages of the *Tatler* the origin of the splendid antithesis of Burke.

Elizabeth, in the settlement of the question of succession, by the union of the two kingdoms, and the consequent elevation of a heartless royal pedant to the throne, proved but a deceitful lull, a flattering and fickle gleam of sunshine, the precursor of a long day of storm and gloom. With much of versatile talent, an evil fatality seemed to cling to that Stuart race, which, like the judgment denounced against some of the old Hebrew kings, pursued them relentlessly till it had left them neither root nor branch.

"That doomed house had only reached its next in descent when an indignant nation, in an age, doubtless, cast in too stern and uncompromising a mould, rose and flung a perfidious and would-be-arbitrary ruler from his seat, and ultimately exacted a retribution of terrible vindictiveness on the scaffold. The royal adherents, on the contrary, prided themselves in a laxity directly the reverse of the stern mannerism of their opponents, (so that the term *cavalier*, by which they were distinguished, has become synonymous with what is free and easy;) and when, after the Restoration, the followers of the exiled court returned, they brought back with them this disposition, aggravated with the frivolities of French manners and the licentiousness of French morals, which impregnated the atmosphere with a moral miasma. Again, with the last of that ill-fated race, following his family traditions with a blind fatuity that seemed to challenge his fate, and was equally reprobated by friends and enemies, another deadly struggle for liberty and right ensued, which, though glorious and successful, was productive of serious, though unavoidable temporary disadvantages.

"Amid this furious strife of parties, the tottering of thrones, and the rise and fall of dynasties, those arts of peace were necessarily retarded, the cultivation of which contributes equally to individual happiness and the prosperity and embellishment of society. The little glimmer of science which appeared under the auspices of the famous Boyle, after a few feeble flickerings, expired, though subsequently revived under the title of the Royal Society. A general ignorance and licentiousness, both in principle and practice, prevailed. The streams of public amusement were polluted at their source, for the writers of the drama pandered shamelessly to the popular taste; and it was customary for ladies who had a regard to reputation to frequent the theatres in masks, and to attend the first performance of any new piece before they could be supposed to be aware of the prurient jest or indecent allusion. All decorum was a jest; the most sacred social institutions considered a subject of polite raillery. Gambling and duelling were the pursuits of those styling themselves men of honour. Amusements of the most brutal and savage description—prize-fighting, bull-baiting, and bear-baiting—were prevalent among the populace, and participated in by many among those of the highest rank. Conversation was at the lowest ebb as regarded rationality, literature was deemed synonymous with pedantry, and religion was a scoff. Life was spent among the populace in ignorance and brutal entertainments; and among the polite in a round of frivolities and trifles, of show and ostentation.

"Such was the state of society at the opening of the eighteenth century, when Isaac Bickerstaff, like a bold knight-errant, appeared upon the scene with his Ithuriel (*Tatler* No. 237) spear." *

"But in addition to the general levity and frivolity in which life was spent among the most refined, the amusements indulged in by some of the very highest rank, as well as the populace, were of the most brutal and savage description. Prize-fighting, bull-baiting, and bear-baiting were prevalent diversions, and were not only attended, we are informed by an annotator of the *Tatler*, (edit. 1797,) by butchers, drovers, and great crowds of all sorts of mob, but likewise by dukes, lords, knights, and squires. 'There were seats particularly set apart for the quality, ornamented with old tapestry hangings,' &c. It was a time when duelling was extensively prevalent; and an officer, (Captain Hill,) in company with Lord Mohun, murdered Mountford the actor, in the open street, in cold blood, and without provocation. Clubs of wild young bucks, under a variety of names, particularly that of Mohocks, infested the streets, and rendered them dangerous after nightfall, by savage and barbarous pranks worthy of the name they adopted, insulting, wounding, and maiming passengers in a variety of ingenious methods, for they professed a sort of wit and drollery in their diabolical pranks. It seems utterly incredible; but, in addition to slashing, maiming, and wounding their victims, we have it on the authority of Gay, that they actually would thrust women into barrels and roll them down Ludgate or Snow Hill. Another and more harmless sort of these bloods went by the name of 'Nickers,' whose delight it was to break windows with showers of ha'pence, to whom Steele wittily alludes in the *Tatler*, No. 77, on finding his floor strewed with coppers, 'I have not yet a full light into this new way, but am apt to think that it is a generous piece of wit that some of my contemporaries make use of, to break windows and leave money to pay for them.'" †

In thus inaugurating what may be termed a new department in literature, it may be desirable to take a hasty glance at what had previously been done of a kindred nature by preceding writers, and see in how far Steele may be considered as having acted upon the suggestions of others in instituting the periodical essay. It is unnecessary

* Introduction to the "History, Opinions, and Lucubrations of Isaac Bickerstaff, Esq.," pp. 2-4. Longmans, 1861.

† *Ibid.*, Notes and Illustrations, p. 291.

to revert to the *Acta Diurna* of the Romans, or even the *Gazetta* of the Venetians, except for the purpose of an unprofitable display of research, unless we were professing to trace an outline of the history of periodical literature, which is wholly beside the present design. Both among the ancients and moderns, works of the nature of disconnected essays on a variety of subjects connected with literature, taste, manners, and character had not been wanting, of which the works of THEOPHRASTUS and AULUS GELLIUS may be referred to among the former. In France and Italy this species of composition had been adopted with distinguished success by various writers of the sixteenth century of classic reputation. *The Courtier* of Castiglione and the *Galateo* of De la Casa were rather books of etiquette than literature, similar to the letters of Chesterfield. The Essays of MICHAEL DE MONTAIGNE, in the same age, take a higher range, and display a knowledge of men and manners with such a peculiar charm of *naïveté* as have rendered them deservedly popular, though the writer is the prince of egotists. At the distance of a century, LA BRUYÈRE produced another similar work of classic reputation, "The Characters or Manners of the Age," which was professedly founded on Theophrastus, but surpassed its model.

In our own country we find some of the highest minds had adopted this style of short dissertations so early as the sixteenth century; and the great Bacon now lives, in popular appreciation at least, almost entirely on the fame of his Essays. At the interval of three-quarters of a century, Temple followed in the same field, and if he fell short of the former in general breadth and solidity, he surpassed him in simplicity and elegance. Still earlier, Cowley had written essays on familiar topics in a style which Dr Johnson, though no very partial critic of his poetry, thinks has never received its due commendation. At the close of the seventeenth century appeared essays on various subjects by Collier, who about the same time made his memorable onslaught on the stage, but, though not without merit, either the coarseness of their style or some other cause has proved fatal to their vitality. The *Review* of De Foe—begun in 1704, during the incarceration to which tyranny and intolerance had consigned him, and published at first twice and afterwards thrice a week for nearly ten years, which was as much superior to anything of a periodical nature that had preceded it in this country, as it was inferior to those which shortly followed it—has been supposed to have formed in some degree a precedent and model for the labours of Steele. The *Review* was devoted almost entirely to the usual topics of the public journals, trade and politics, on which De Foe displayed great sagacity and very enlightened views for those times. But in addition to the ordinary subjects, the writer incorporated the plan of what he called a *Scandal Club*, which was devoted to the discussion of social questions; and so far as this was concerned it may have afforded a hint, but was too inartistic and deficient in design or dramatic interest to have afforded any model to Steele, or anything more than a rough suggestion. We have seen that miscellaneous literary essays were by no means unknown at the time of commencing the *Tatler;* but they wanted the unity of design, the dramatic interest, and the portraiture of the salient points of the social life and manners of the time which characterise the periodical essay. The classic precedents of

Montaigne and La Bruyère were in form the nearest models of Steele. "But," as Dr Johnson has justly remarked, "to say that they united the plans of two or three eminent writers, is to give them but a small part of their due praise; they superadded literature and criticism, and sometimes towered far above their predecessors, and taught with great justness of argument and dignity of language the most important duties and sublime truths. All these topics were happily varied with elegant fictions and refined allegories, as well as illuminated with different changes of style and felicities of invention."*

If it is considered that to the elegance and taste of Montaigne and La Bruyère Steele added a dramatic framework which bound the whole together, and gave it unity of design and a connected interest; that he shot his bolts at "the manners living as they rose," took them upon the wing, and made the whole series a repository of the social aspect of the times—a gallery of etchings done with the lightest and most graceful touch; that with all this there was combined the discussion, from time to time, of every variety of topic connected with literature, art, and taste, as well as the graver subjects of ethics and religion, in a style which makes them to this day, what they must ever continue to be, models of elegance; and that over the whole there is thrown the lambent play of a wit and humour the most charming and genial, alternating with narratives of the most touching pathos, it will afford some faint general notion of the variety of the claims to interest in such a work. But if, in addition to this, it be added, that all this was undertaken by one man, and issued for years,

* Lives of the Poets.

in daily or tri-weekly sheets, with any considerable assistance from only a very few others, we may well stand divided between admiration and amazement at such an unparalleled effort of energy and intellectual resource.

To the arduous task of counteracting the prevailing evils of the times—moral, intellectual, and social—and to plant a flower where he plucked up a weed, Steele, with astonishing confidence in own resources, now set himself as if to the mission of his life. *The Tatler; or, Lucubrations of Isaac Bickerstaff, Esq.*, made its appearance on the 12th of April 1709, and was published thrice a week, on Tuesdays, Thursdays, and Saturdays. The title of the paper was stated to have been adopted out of compliment to the fair sex, though it may appear rather an equivocal one; and the assumed name of Bickerstaff was taken from a humorous pamphlet by Swift, in which, under the character of an adept in astrology, professing to rescue that science out of the hands of ignorant pretenders to it, he applied the force of his peculiar and irresistible irony to those who traded on the credulity of the times, particularly one Partridge, the most noted almanac-maker of his day, who assumed to predict therein the events of the ensuing year. The title of Swift's pamphlet was, " Predictions for the Year 1708, &c.; written to prevent the people of England from being further imposed on by vulgar almanac-makers. By Isaac Bickerstaff, Esq." By predicting the death of Cardinal Portocarero, or of the Cardinal de Noailles, it had the honour of being actually burned by the Inquisition in Portugal, who anathematised it and its readers.* The prediction, however, respecting the great philomath, John

---

* Vindication of Bickerstaff—Swift's Works.

Partridge, professor of astrology and physic, was that on which the chief point of the pamphlet rested, and was thus stated :—

"My first prediction is but a trifle; yet I will mention it to shew how ignorant those sottish pretenders to astrology are in their own concerns: It relates to Partridge the almanac-maker; I have consulted the star of his nativity by my own rules, and find he will infallibly die upon the 29th of March next, about eleven at night, of a raging fever; therefore I advise him to consider of it and settle his affairs in time."* This was followed up by an account of "The accomplishment of the first of Mr Bickerstaff's predictions, being an account of the death of Mr Partridge the almanac-maker upon the 29th inst."

The predictions were a source of great amusement to the public and the wits, who joined in supporting Swift, and of distress and vexation to Partridge, who actually had the folly to insert the following advertisement, which is copied in the *Tatler*, in his next year's almanac :—

"Whereas it has been industriously given out by Isaac Bickerstaff, Esq., and others, to prevent the sale of this year's almanac, that John Partridge is dead: this may inform all his loving countrymen that he is still living, in health, and they are knaves that reported it otherwise."

To this Swift added "A Vindication of Isaac Bickerṣtaff, Esq." A reply, in the character of Partridge, followed, replete with humour, which has been attributed to Nicholas Rowe, the poet, to the Rev. Dr Yalden, and to Congreve,† entitled, "Squire Bickerstaff Detected; or, The Astrological Impostor Convicted, by John Partridge, Student in Physic and Astrology," which may not be unacceptable to the reader :—

"It is hard, my dear countrymen of these united nations—it is very hard, that a Briton born, a Protestant astrologer, a man of revolution prin-

---

* Swift's Works.
† To the latter, by Addison, in a letter to Lord Wharton.

ciples, an assertor of the liberty and property of the people, should cry out in vain for justice against a Frenchman, a Papist, and an illiterate pretender to science; that would blast my reputation, most inhumanly bury me alive, and defraud my native country of those services which, in my double capacity, I daily offer the public.

"What great provocations I have received let the impartial reader judge, and how unwillingly, even in my own defence, I now enter the lists against falsehood, ignorance, and envy; but I am exasperated, at length, to drag out this Cacus from the den of obscurity where he lurks, detect him by the light of those stars he has so impudently traduced, and shew there is not a monster in the skies so pernicious and malevolent to mankind as an ignorant pretender to physic and astrology. I shall not directly fall on the many gross errors, nor expose the notorious absurdities of this prostituted libeller, till I have let the learned world fairly into the controversy depending, and then leave the unprejudiced to judge of the merits and justice of my cause.

"It was towards the conclusion of the year 1707 when an impudent pamphlet crept into the world, entitled, 'Predictions, &c., by Isaac Bickerstaff, Esq.' Among the many arrogant assertions laid down by that lying spirit of divination, he was pleased to pitch on the Cardinal de Noailles and myself, among many other eminent and illustrious persons that were to die within the compass of the ensuing year, and peremptorily fixes the month, day, and hour of our deaths. This, I think, is sporting with great men and public spirits to the scandal of religion and reproach of power; and if sovereign princes and astrologers must make diversion for the vulgar, why then farewell, say I, to all governments, ecclesiastical and civil. But I thank my better stars I am alive to confront this false and audacious predictor, and to make him rue the hour he ever affronted a man of science and resentment. The cardinal may take what measures he pleases with him; as his excellency is a foreigner and a Papist, he has no reason to rely on me for his justification; I shall only assure the world he is alive; but as he was bred to letters, and is master of a pen, let him use it in his own defence. In the meantime, I shall present the public with a faithful narrative of the ungenerous treatment and hard usage I have received from the virulent papers and malicious practices of this pretended astrologer:—

"A true and impartial Account of the Proceedings of Isaac Bickerstaff, Esq., against me, John Partridge, Student in Physic and Astrology.

"The 28th of March, *anno dom.* 1708, being the night this sham prophet had so impudently fixed for my last, which made little impression on myself; but I cannot answer for my whole family; for my wife, with a concern more than usual, prevailed on me to take somewhat to sweat for a cold, and between the hours of eight and nine to go to bed. The maid, as she was warming my bed, with a curiosity natural to young wenches, runs to the window, and asks of one passing the street who the bell tolled for? 'Doctor Partridge,' says he, 'the famous almanac-maker who died suddenly this evening.' The poor girl, provoked, told him he lied like a rascal; the other very sedately replied, the sexton had so informed him, and if false, he was to blame for imposing on a stranger. She asked a second and a third, as they passed, and every one was in the same tone. Now, I do not say these were accomplices to a certain astrological squire, and that one Bickerstaff might be sauntering thereabouts, because I will assert nothing here but what I dare attest for plain matter of fact. My wife, at this, fell into a violent disorder; and, I must own, I was a little discomposed at the oddness of the accident. In the meantime, one knocks at my door; Betty runs down, and opening, finds a sober, grave person, who modestly inquires if this was Dr Partridge's? She, taking him for some cautious city patient that came at that time for privacy, shews him into the dining-room. As soon as I could compose myself, I went to him, and was surprised to find my gentleman mounted on a table, with a two-foot rule in his hand, measuring my walls, and taking the dimensions of the room. 'Pray, sir,' says I, 'not to interrupt you, have you any business with me?' 'Only, sir,' replies he, 'order the girl to bring me a better light, for this is but a very dim one.' 'Sir,' says I, 'my name is Partridge.' 'Oh! the Doctor's brother, belike,' cries he; 'the staircase, I believe, and these two apartments hung in close mourning, will be sufficient, and only a strip of bays round the other rooms. The Doctor must needs be rich, he had great dealings in his way for many years; if he had no family coat, you had as good use the scutcheons of the company; they are as showish, and will look as magnificent as if he was descended from the blood-royal.' With that, I assumed a greater air of authority, and demanded who employed him, or how he came there? 'Why, I was sent, sir, by the company of undertakers,' says he, 'and they were employed by the honest gentleman who is executor to the good Doctor departed, and our rascally porter, I believe, is fallen fast asleep with the black cloth and sconces, or he had been here, and we might have been tacking up by this time.' 'Sir,' says I, 'pray be advised by a friend, and make the best of your speed out of my doors, for I hear my wife's voice, (which, by the by, is pretty distinguishable,) and in the corner of the room stands a good cudgel; if that light in her hands, and she know the business you come about, without consulting the stars, I can assure you it will be employed very much to the detriment of your person.' 'Sir,' cries he, bowing with great civility, 'I perceive extreme grief for the loss of the Doctor disorders you a little at present, but early in the morning I will wait on you with all necessary materials.' Now, I mention no Mr Bickerstaff, nor do I say that a certain star-gazing squire hath been playing my executor before his time; but I leave the world to judge, and if it puts things and things fairly together, it will not be much wide of the mark.

"Well, once more, I got my doors closed, and prepared for bed, in hopes of a little repose after so many ruffling adventures. Just as I was putting out my light in order to it, another bounces as hard as he can knock; I open the window, and ask who is there, and what he wants? 'I am Ned, the sexton,' replies he, 'and come to know whether the Doctor left any orders for a funeral sermon, and where he is to be laid, and whether his grave is to be plain or bricked?' 'Why, sirrah,' says I, 'you know me well enough; you know I am not dead, and how dare you affront me after this manner?' 'Alack-a-day, sir,' replies the fellow, 'why it is in print, and the whole town knows you are dead; why there is Mr White, the joiner, is but fitting screws to your coffin, he will be here in an instant, he was afraid you would have wanted it before this time.' 'Sirrah, sirrah,' says I, 'you shall know to-morrow to your cost that I am alive, and alive like to be.' 'Why, it is strange, sir,' says he, 'you should make such a secret of your death, to us that are your neighbours; it looks as if you had a design to defraud the Church of its dues; and let me tell you for one that has lived so long, by the Heavens, that it is unhandsomely done.' 'Hist, hist,' says another rogue that stood by him, 'away Doctor into your flannel gear as fast as you can, for here is a whole pack of dismals coming to you with their black equipage; and how indecent will it look for you to stand frightening folks at your window, when you should have been in your coffin these three hours?' In short, what with undertakers, embalmers, joiners, sextons, and your damned elegy-hawkers, upon a late practitioner in physic and astrology, I got not one wink of sleep that night, nor scarce a moment's rest ever since. Now, I doubt not but this villainous squire has the impudence to assert that these are entirely strangers to him; he, good man, knows nothing of the matter; and honest Isaac Bickerstaff, I warrant you, is more a man of honour than to be an accomplice with a pack of rascals, that walk the streets o' nights, and disturb good people in their beds. But he is out if he thinks the whole world is blind; and there is one John Partridge can smell a knave as far as Grub Street; although he lies in the most exalted garret, and writes himself squire: but I will keep my temper, and proceed in the narrative.

"I could not stir out of doors for the space of three months after this, but presently one comes up to me in the street—'Mr Partridge, that coffin you was last buried in, I have not yet been paid for.' 'Doctor,' cries another dog, 'how do you think people can live by making of graves for nothing? Next time you die, you may even toll out the bell yourself for Ned.' A third rogue tips me by the elbow, and 'wonders how I have the conscience to sneak abroad without paying my funeral expenses.' 'Lord,' says one, 'I durst have sworn that was honest Dr Partridge, my old friend; but, poor man, he is gone.' 'I beg your pardon,' says another, 'you look so like my old acquaintance that I used to consult, but, alack, he is gone the way of all flesh.' 'Look, look, look,' cries a third, after a competent space of staring at me, 'would not one think our neighbour the almanac-maker was crept out of his grave to take another peep at the stars in this world, and shew how much he is improved in fortune-telling by having taken a journey to the other.'

"Nay, the very reader of our parish, a good, sober, discreet person, has sent two or three times for me to come and be buried decently, or send him sufficient reasons to the contrary; or, if I have been interred in any other parish, to produce my certificate, as the act requires. My poor wife is run almost distracted with being called Widow Partridge, when she knows it is false; and, once a term, she is cited into the court to take out letters of administration. But the greatest grievance is a paltry quack that takes up my calling just under my nose, and, in his printed directions, with N.B., says he lives in the house of the late ingenious Mr John Partridge, an eminent practitioner in leather, physic, and astrology.

"But to shew how far the wicked spirit of envy, malice, and resentment can hurry some men, my nameless old persecutor had provided me a monument at the stone-cutter's, and would have erected it in the parish church; and this piece of notorious and expensive villainy had actually succeeded, if I had not used my utmost interest with the vestry, where it was carried at last but by two voices, that I am alive. That stratagem failing, out comes a long, sable elegy, bedecked with hour-glasses, mattocks, skulls, spades, and skeletons, with an epitaph, as confidently written to abuse me and my profession as if I had been under ground these twenty years.

"And after such barbarous treatment as this, can the world blame me when I ask, what is become of the freedom of an Englishman? And where is the liberty and property that my old glorious friend came over to assert? We have driven Popery out of the nation, and sent slavery to foreign climes. The arts only remain in bondage, when a man of science and character shall be openly insulted in the midst of the many useful services he is daily paying the public. Was it ever heard, even in Turkey or Algiers, that a state astrologer was bantered out of his life by an ignorant impostor, or bawled out of the world by a pack of villainous, deep-mouthed hawkers?. Though I print almanacs, and publish advertisements; though I produce certificates under the minister's and church-wardens' hands, I am alive, and attest the same on oath at the quarter-sessions, out comes a full and true relation of the death and interment of John Partridge; truth is borne down, attestations neglected, the testimony of sober persons despised, and a man is looked upon by his neighbours as if he had been seven years dead, and is buried alive in the midst of his friends and acquaintance.

"Now, can any man of common sense think it consistent with the honour of my profession, and not much beneath the dignity of a philosopher, to stand bawling before his own door, Alive! alive! ho! the famous Dr Partridge! no counterfeit, but all alive?—as if I had the twelve celestial monsters of the zodiac to shew within, or was forced for a livelihood to turn retailer to May and Bartholomew fairs. Therefore, if her Majesty would but graciously be pleased to think a hardship of this nature worthy her royal consideration, and the next Parliament, in their great wisdom, cast but an eye toward the deplorable case of their old philomath that annually bestows his good wishes on them, I am sure there is one Isaac Bickerstaff, Esq., would soon be trussed up for his bloody predictions, and putting good subjects in terror of their lives: and that henceforward, to murder a man by way of prophecy, and bury him in a printed letter either to a lord or commoner, shall as legally entitle him to the present possession of Tyburn, as if he robbed on the highway, or cut your throat in bed.

"I shall demonstrate to the judicious that France and Rome are at the bottom of this horrid conspiracy against me, and that the culprit aforesaid is a Popish emissary, has paid his visits to St Germain's, and is now in the measures of Louis XIV. That, in attempting my reputation, there is a general massacre of learning designed in these realms; and, through my sides, there is a wound given to all the Protestant almanac-makers in the universe."*

In the first number of the *Tatler* the subject is again referred to as "a matter which I at the very first mentioned as a trifle;" and in reference to Partridge's assertion in his almanac for 1709, Bickerstaff says, "I have in another place, and in a paper by itself, sufficiently convinced this man that he is dead, and, if he has any shame, I do not doubt but that by this time he owns it to all his acquaintance: for though the legs and arms and whole body of that man may still appear, and perform their animal functions, *yet since*, as I have elsewhere observed, *his art is gone, the man is gone.*"†

* Swift's Works.
† This Partridge was a native of Mortlake, near Richmond. He was the son of a shoemaker, and must have been possessed of abilites, having taught himself

The design of the *Tatler* was probably first suggested to Steele by his employment as official Gazetteer. In the irksome duty of superintending such a publication, it may not unnaturally have occurred to him that he might produce a periodical sheet of a more interesting and congenial nature, which, instead of the odium that he hints the other frequently drew upon him, might create a salutary interest in the mass of society. Though the character of Bickerstaff was happily chosen, and well sustained, in his qualities of astrologer, philomath, and public censor, yet the original design was rather crude, and it is evident that the author never dreamed of the importance and dignity to which the machinery he had set in motion would ultimately attain.

The censorial character is represented as resulting from the astrological. The reputation of a conjurer having had the effect of excluding him from public employment, he says, he resolved to establish a post for himself, by reviving the ancient Roman office of public censor. " And forasmuch as this globe is not trodden upon by mere drudges of business only, but men of spirit and genius are justly to be esteemed as considerable agents in it," he proposes to treat the reader to passages of what may transpire among such, from time to time, throughout the town, or elsewhere, dividing his labours into various departments,

---

Latin, Greek, and Hebrew. He also applied himself to the study of medicine, while still pursuing his trade as a shoemaker, and procured a medical degree at Leyden. He afterwards had the interest to get himself appointed physician to Charles II., but whether merely honorary or *bond fide*, we cannot say. He was interred in the churchyard of his native place, where there is the following inscription on his tombstone :—

"Johannis Partridge, astrologus et medicinæ doctor, natus est apud East Sheen in comitatu Surrey, 8 die Januarii anno 1644, et mortuus est Londini, 24 die Junii 1715," &c.

extending over the whole field of life,—*Quicquid agunt homines*, (as the motto expressed it,)—and obviating the necessity of any detailed efforts in each. These were dated from the respective head-quarters where the various subjects were usually most fully discussed—the age being essentially one of clubs and coteries. Thus White's Chocolatehouse was the head-quarters of tattle connected with gallantry, pleasure, and entertainment; Will's Coffeehouse, of poetry; the Grecian Coffeehouse, of learning; St James's Coffeehouse, of foreign and domestic news; and Bickerstaff's own apartment, of miscellaneous topics.

Nor did he confine his attention to what transpired in "The Town" alone, which, in the opinion of those constituting what went by the name in those days, was the only thing worth thinking of, but established a rural correspondence, (for he often took the liberty of writing to himself,) in which he says, "Doubtless among friends, bred as we have been to the knowledge of books as well as men, a letter dated from a garden, a wood, a meadow, or the banks of a river, may be more entertaining than one from Tom's, Will's, White's, or St James's. Such a frame of mind," he adds, " raises that sweet enthusiasm which warms the imagination at the sight of every work of nature, and turns all round you into picture and landscape."* Gradually, however, as the importance of the undertaking, judging from its popularity, became apparent, wider views opened, and with the development of his own powers and resources he gradually discarded much of the original framework.

In whatever degree the elevation of its tone may have

* *Tatler*, No. 89.

resulted from the accession of his friend Addison,* as Steele says he aimed at something that he had not designed, there can be little doubt that such would have been the natural result of the great success of the paper, and of greater experience in the hands of its projector. The original design of the paper, as stated by its author, was "to expose the false arts of life, to pull off the disguises of cunning, vanity, and affectation, and to recommend a general simplicity in our dress, our discourses, and our behaviour."† And, again, "to rally all those singularities of life, through the different professions and characters in it, which obstructed anything that was truly good and great."‡ And, once more, where referring to the various characters he assumed, of philosopher, humorist, and censor, he states his design "to allure the reader with the variety of his subjects, and insinuate, if he could, the weight of reason with the agreeableness of wit."§ Steele had commenced the paper entirely on the strength of his own resources, and without the knowledge of his friend, or, so far as is known, of any other party; but he had only proceeded as far as the sixth number when his connexion with it became apparent to Addison, who was then engaged

---

* Steele himself, with that generosity of spirit and freedom from envy which so conspicuously characterised him, in reply to the invidious remarks of Tickell, in his edition of Addison's Works, in reference to his contributions to the *Tatler*, acknowledges, " It was advanced indeed, for it was raised to a greater thing than I intended it; for the elegance, purity, and correctness which appeared in his writings, were not so much to my purpose, as in any intelligible manner I could to rally all those singularities of human life, through the different professions and characters in it, which obstruct anything that was truly good and great.'—*Dedication of the Drummer, addressed to Congreve.*

† Dedication to first volume of *Tatler*.
‡ Letter to Mr Congreve in reply to Tickell.
§ Concluding paper of the *Tatler*.

in the important official capacity of Secretary for Ireland, and had started for the scene of his labours only two days previous to the publication of the first number. The cause of his detecting his friend in Bickerstaff was the insertion of a criticism on a passage in Virgil which, though of no great importance in itself, he recollected having been communicated by him to Steele from the stores of his elegant scholarship. Nor did he long delay in aiding his friend with his pen; for, though then absent in Ireland and engaged in responsible official duties as Secretary of State under Lord Wharton, he communicated the "Distress of News-writers," in No. 18, and became an occasional contributor. His valuable accession is thus gracefully acknowledged by Steele in his preface:—"This good office he performed with such force of genius, humour, wit, and learning, that I fared like a distressed prince who calls in a powerful neighbour to his aid; I was undone by my auxiliary; when I had once called him in, I could not subsist without dependence on him."*

From the time of his accession, Addison became an occasional assistant, at least in hints or suggestions; but it was not until a period of greater leisure, after the appearance of eighty numbers, when the success of the work was established, that he became a frequent contributor, when he came to share, and no doubt in some degree to heighten, the triumph of his friend.† Forty-one papers are ascribed

* Preface to the collected edition.

† Addison's biographer, Miss Aikin, acknowledges as a probable result what was in fact an accomplished one: " It is probable [independent of the communications of Addison] the undertaking would have proved highly successful, since it was at once novel in its plan, and admirably adapted to the circumstances of an age which required above all things to have a mirror held up to it."—*Life of Addison*, vol. ii., p. 4.

to him, and thirty-four to the two friends jointly. The chief labour all along fell upon Steele, of course. Of the occasional contributors, almost the only one of note was SWIFT, who began before Addison, and was the writer of the "Description of the Morning," in No. 9. His contributions were about a dozen altogether. Even in this limited number he displayed the characteristic asperity of his temper by the only two instances of personal attack, (if we except those designed to expose imposture and trading on popular credulity in the case of Partridge,) and those on two ladies of repute and literary accomplishments, and indeed on that very ground, to be found in the pages of the *Tatler*. It must be admitted that there are few persons from whom the ironical proposal for the formation of a Platonic college could have come with a worse grace, since he became the founder of one himself on a small scale at a later date.

Steele acknowledged, with his usual frankness and generosity, the services of Swift, "whose pleasant writings in the name of Bickerstaff," he states in the general preface, "created an inclination in the town towards anything that could appear in the same disguise. I must acknowledge also that, at my first entering upon this work, a certain uncommon way of thinking, and a turn in conversation peculiar to that agreeable gentleman, rendered his company very advantageous to one whose imagination was to be continually employed upon obvious and common subjects, though at the same time obliged to treat them in a new and unbeaten method."* Of Swift some notice will be

* That the treating of obvious and common subjects in a new and unbeaten method was a remarkable characteristic of Swift is apparent in all his writings, but especially in his "Polite Conversation" and "Advice to Servants."

taken on a future more convenient occasion. He afterwards in a great degree cancelled any obligations Steele might have been under by the not very handsome proceeding of lending himself to the starting of a new *Tatler*, after the original work had been dropped, by a *protegé* of Bolingbroke's, and reviving the name of Bickerstaff in connexion with it, which perhaps he may have thought he had some claim of paternity to do. Whether this had any latent influence in the subsequent difference between him and Steele, as it might readily have had with a man of less easy temper, there is no means of ascertaining.*

* The originator of this rival work was a Mr William Harrison, who contributed " Medicine, a Tale," in No. 2 of the original *Tatler*. He had been for some time a fellow of New College, Oxford, and tutor to one of the Duke of Queensbery's sons. Attracting the attention of Swift, who describes him as " a little, pretty fellow, with a great deal of wit, good sense, and good nature," he was by him recommended to the appointment of Secretary to the embassy at the Hague, from which he appears to have derived little emolument and much vexation. He died Feb. 14, 1712-13. He must have possessed some good qualities, since he was " praised, wept, and honoured " by Young in his epistle to Lord Lansdowne. Nevertheless, Swift appears considerably to have altered his opinion of his abilities when he came to assist him in the new or spurious *Tatler*, and speaks somewhat contemptuously of him in his journal to Stella :—" I doubt he will not succeed, for I do not much approve his manner; but the scheme is Mr Secretary St John's and mine, and would have done well enough in good hands." He adds, " I am tired with correcting his trash." Steele closed the *Tatler*, Jan. 2, 1710, and on the 13th of the same month the spurious work commenced, but only proceeded the length of fifty-two papers, of which six are attributed to Swift, and was brought to a close May 19 of the same year. Though it was two or three times reprinted as a supplementary volume of the *Tatler*, it was altogether a work of little merit. Steele had numerous other imitators and rivals, if they may be dignified by the name, among which were the *Female Tatler*, which laboured to work itself into notoriety by virulent abuse of Bickerstaff and his lucubrations. There was even a *Tatler* published at Edinburgh by Donald Macstaff.

Among the other minor contributors to the pages of Bickerstaff were Mr JOHN HUGHES, an intimate friend of Steele's, afterwards to be noticed among the contributors to the *Spectator*, to whom are attributed Nos. 64, 66, 73, 76, 113, and 194; Mr TWISDEN, who wrote the humorous genealogy of the Bickerstaff family in No. 11, and who, as Steele tells us in the general preface, " died at the battle

The *Tatler* was published three days in each week, on Tuesdays, Thursdays, and Saturdays, on a half-sheet folio, originally at a penny, and somewhat resembled the *Gazette*, or one of the larger of the present literary papers, as the *Spectator* or *Saturday Review*, in its form. Unlike its successor, it also combined the purposes of an ordinary journal of the day, containing articles of news, in the priority of which his position of Gazetteer gave him great advantages. Though there is no positive statement of the extent of its circulation, it was regarded as immense at that time; and the emolument derived from it by Steele was greatly increased by the republication in volumes in royal octavo at a guinea each, (the value of money being then of course much higher than now,) in which form they were considered a necessary addition to the library of every person of taste or fashion. Though the paper was conducted with remarkable freedom from personality or scurrility, yet there appears to be little doubt that one cause which contributed originally to its extensive circulation was the love of scandal, and the popular impression, probably from its title, that the fictitious characters drawn and held up to censure or ridicule were real persons. In this error Steele allowed his readers to remain, leaving in undisturbed enjoyment those who busied

of Mons, and has a monument in Westminster Abbey suitable to the respect which is due to his wit and his valour;" a Mr FULLER, a very young man, of whose promise Steele speaks in high terms in No. 26 of the *Theatre*, was the author of the excellent paper on Gluttony, No. 205. Of the writer's subsequent history nothing is known with certainty. Mr JAMES GREENWOOD, teacher of a boarding-school at Woodford, Essex, wrote the letter on Language, Education, &c., in No. 234. He was the author of an "Essay towards a Practical English Grammar;" "The London Vocabulary, English and Latin ;" and published a poetical collection of select pieces under the title of the " Virgin Muse." He held for a considerable time the office of Sur-master of St Paul's School, and died Sept. 12, 1737. Anthony Henley, Charles Dartiquenave, and Mr Asplin also contributed.

themselves in complacently fitting the caps which he made at random to their neighbours' heads. It was sufficient for him if they found instruction and innocent amusement where they had sought the indulgence of ill-nature, and that

"Those who came to scoff, remain'd to *pay*."

In some cases indeed, having reference to the public events of the times, as in the matter of the Bangorian controversy, in which Steele's friendship for Mr Hoadley led him, perhaps unwisely, to interfere, and for which he thought proper to apologise in No. 51, the characters aimed at were real. Such was also the case in the onslaught he made upon the gamblers, but such were exceptions and not the rule. Some of the favourable portraits, he himself admits, were also drawn from life, as that of Aristæus, in No. 176, for Addison; and he adduces it as a plea for his freedom from party prejudice, that the character of Favonius was meant for Dr Smalridge, and that of the Dean, in No. 66, for the learned and amiable Dr Atterbury.

After continuing the paper to 271 numbers, extending over a period of a year and nearly nine months, he suddenly brought it to a close in the very height of its reputation, and to the great regret of his readers. We are told that a general gloom was thrown over the public mind, as if every one had lost some dear friend and companion, whose agreeable and instructive qualities they only fully appreciated when deprived of them.* This step Steele took, as he did in the starting of the paper, without consulting his friend Addison, to which Tickell alludes with

---

* See "The Present State of Wit," attributed to Gay, and reprinted in some editions of Swift's works from a scarce pamphlet in the Lambeth Library.

something like a reflection. In taking leave of his readers, he makes his exit with gracefulness and candour. He disclaims having assumed a mask with the view of hurting any one. "The general purpose of the whole," he states, "has been to recommend truth, innocence, honour, and virtue as the chief ornaments of life; but I considered that severity of manners was absolutely necessary to him who would censure others, and for that reason, and that only, chose to talk in a mask. I shall not carry my humility so far as to call myself a vicious man; but at the same time must confess, my life is at best but pardonable. And, with a greater character than this, a man would make but indifferent progress in attacking prevailing and fashionable vices, which Mr Bickerstaff has done with a freedom of spirit that would have lost both its beauty and efficacy had it been pretended to by Mr Steele."

In the short period of their existence these papers had taken a wide range over the whole field of life, and had left few subjects untouched that concerned the wellbeing of society. They treated of matters of taste, recommended refinement of mind and manners, and touched upon moral subjects in a manner to come home to those who were little likely to be reached by grave and elaborate treatises. The gamblers they attacked with unsparing severity. The regulation of the passions, and the evils arising from their excesses; the duties and obligations of domestic life, in opposition to a sneering libertinism then prevalent; the folly of extravagance, and the superior happiness and wisdom of simple tastes; the qualities of friendship, with the distinctions between what is real and the various disguises it assumes; and, lastly, religion as the foundation on which every system of real goodness and happiness must ultimately rest. These are some of the leading topics of which these papers treated, while over them all it threw a light and grace, a wit and humour, a knowledge of the world, mingled with quaintness and whim in its various assumed characters, and of dramatic illustration, which rendered them highly attractive. Portions of the *Tatler* especially, and of the other papers of its class in a less degree, present us with revelations of past manners and customs among our own countrymen, somewhat akin to what we derive of those of a still earlier date from the unearthing of Herculaneum or Pompeii,—with this difference, that the latter are merely physical, while in the former we have both the life and spirit preserved. In the words of an acute and powerful writer, "London a hundred years ago would be much better worth seeing than Paris at the present moment. I have on this account always preferred the *Tatler* to the *Spectator*. The indications of character and strokes of humour are more true and frequent; the reflections that suggest themselves arise more from the occasion, and are less spun out into regular dissertations. . . . Steele seems to have gone into his closet chiefly to set down what he had observed out of doors. Addison seems to have spent most of his time in his study, and to have spun out and wire-drawn the hints which he borrowed from Steele, or took from nature, to the utmost."*

Such is the point of superiority in the *Tatler* to the numerous other works of the class of which it was the model and the parent. If less regular in its plan, and less elaborate in a literary point of view, than its immediate and more celebrated successor the *Spectator*, it has cer-

* Hazlitt's Comic Writers.

tainly at least a spirit more fresh and racy if less dignified and elaborate. The portrait of Sir Roger de Coverley in the *Spectator*, however exquisite a specimen of painting, is drawn in very faint colours, and is not equal in heartiness to that of Bickerstaff, which is like a vivifying spirit running through the weft and woof of the whole. Though not so fully drawn or sharply defined as Sir Roger, yet it is very much more than the shadowy *Spectator*; and in his varied character of astrologer, philomath, censor morum, and humorist, is depicted with a wit, quaintness, sagacity, and benevolence which is well preserved throughout—presenting characteristics similar in some degree to those which have immortalised the later creation of my Uncle Toby, without any of its objectionable points.

But in addition to Mr Bickerstaff and his own connexions, to whom he introduces us, we have a series of very striking portraits of the characters of his club at the Trumpet, among whom he says it was his usual custom "to relax and unbend in the conversation of such as were rather easy than shining companions." He confesses it probable he was not the less pleased with them that he found himself the greatest wit in this select society, and appealed to as their oracle in all points of learning and difficulty.

Sir Jeoffery Notch, the elder and foreman of the club, is a decayed gentleman of an ancient family, who, having come to a great estate some years before he had discretion, and run it out in hounds, horses, and cock-fighting, looks upon himself as an honest worthy gentleman who has had misfortunes in the world, and calls every thriving man a pitiful upstart.

Major Matchlock, the next senior of the society, served

in the last civil wars, and had all the battles by heart. He didn't think any action in Europe worth talking of since the fight of Marston Moor, and every night told of his having been knocked off his horse at the rising of the London apprentices, for which he was held in great esteem.

Honest old Dick Reptile, the third character of the club by seniority, was a good-natured, indolent creature, who spoke little, but laughed at the jokes of others. He sometimes brought his nephew to give him a taste of the world, to whom he winked to mind what passed, and would sometimes say, "Ay, ay, Jack, you young men think us fools, but we old men know you are."

The greatest wit of the society, next to Mr Bickerstaff, was a bencher of a neighbouring inn, who professed to have been acquainted with the noted Jack Ogle, an associate of Rochester's in his mad pranks, who would shake his head at the dulness of the present age, and relate a story of Ogle. His standing resource was ten distiches of Hudibras which he had without book, which he never failed to apply before leaving the club.

Mr Bickerstaff found their company, he tells us, the best possible preparative for sleep.

What would otherwise have been merely a series of unconnected essays, derived a unity, as well as a personal interest and highly dramatic spirit, from the variety of narratives and illustrations of character which pervaded it. The club, though not so directly connected with the paper as the subsequent one in the *Spectator*, is turned to very good account, and the description of the members and their doings afford a series of incidents and sketches of character very entertaining, and displaying a wonderful knowledge of human nature as well as life. Mr Bickerstaff's own history is so interwoven with the whole work as to give it something of the air of an autobiography, and that of his half-sister, Jenny Distaff, who is introduced as the exponent of the views and interests of her sex, is a sort of *novelette*, forming occasional episodes in his own story. His three nephews are introduced for the purpose of illustrating his views on education and the bringing up of youth, and the *dramatis personæ* is completed with a familiar spirit or good genius named Pacolet, who is the vehicle of conveying a variety of information beyond human ken or experience. "Isaac Bickerstaff, Esq., astrologer," says Lord Macaulay, writing on Addison, "was an imaginary person almost as well known in that age as Mr Paul Pry or Mr Samuel Pickwick is in ours." The notoriety, however, is the chief point of resemblance; for, though Mr Bickerstaff is a humorist of the most delightful description, yet his humour is that of genteel comedy, not farce, combined with the teaching of a philosopher and scholar, which is at the same time imparted with the air of an agreeable friend. Mr Bickerstaff's themes are of the most various description, but such as (to use Bacon's expression) " come home to men's business and bosoms," and are treated with such a charm of manner as would have made any subjects interesting, even though they had been as unpromising as that of Swift when he wrote upon a broomstick. Mr Bickerstaff's sympathy with humanity was unlimited, and he dwelt on topics which are universally interesting. Combining the humorist with the moralist, he brought the most agreeable sort of raillery to bear upon the follies of men, from which he sought to divorce them by getting them to laugh with him at their absurdity. His teaching is never delivered in a dry didactic way, or in an oracular tone, but insinuated in a dramatic form, and illustrated with sketches of character. The pervading aim of the writer cannot be so well or briefly stated as in the words of his concluding paper, "To allure my readers with the variety of my subjects, and insinuate, if I could, the weight of reason with the agreeableness of wit." The writers were the founders of our periodical literature. The novel did not then exist, unless in French translations. Swift, indeed, produced a satirical work of fiction, and De Foe became the founder of the English novel, at a later period of the same age; but Steele inaugurated the classical tale in a style not unlike that which on a larger scale has delighted so many readers in "The Vicar of Wakefield." Of these narratives and sketches an eminent living writer thus speaks:—"All these tales have an artless, unpretending simplicity, and a charm quite unpremeditated, but which is yet combined with a reality and intensity of pathos, *affecting to a degree that the equally brief narrations of any other writer have never, in our judgment, equalled.*"*

* Forster's Biog. Essays, vol. iii., pp. 192, 193.

Mr Thackeray, in his "Humorists," has quoted as a specimen a domestic picture, one of Steele's narrative sketches, with these words of applause:—"He wrote so richly, so gracefully often, so kindly always, with such a gush of good spirits and good humour, that his early papers may be compared to Addison's own, and are to be read with quite an equal pleasure." Indeed, we do not know where we should go to look for such a paper of Addison's as that he has quoted. Though of a more tragic cast, we give the sequel of the same narrative, in order not to repeat that portion already given in a work so well-known:—

"I was walking about my chamber this morning in a very gay humour, when I saw a coach stop at my door, and a youth about fifteen alighting out of it, whom I perceived to be the eldest son of my bosom friend, that I gave some account of in my paper of the 17th of last month. I felt a sensible pleasure rising in me at the sight of him, my acquaintance having begun with his father when

Domestic Picture from "Tatler."

To the good accomplished by the *Tatler* we have the testimony of the poet Gay, a contributor to some of its

he was just such a stripling, and about that very age. When he came up to me, he took me by the hand, and burst out in tears. I was extremely moved, and immediately said, 'Child, how does your father do?' He began to reply, 'My mother'—but could not go on for weeping. I went down with him into the coach, and gathered out of him that his mother was then dying, and that while the holy man was doing the last offices to her, he had taken that time to come and call me to his father, who, he said, would certainly break his heart if I did not go and comfort him. The child's discretion in coming to me of his own head, and the tenderness he shewed for his parents, would have quite overpowered me, had I not resolved to fortify myself for the seasonable performance of those duties which I owed to my friend. As we were going, I could not but reflect upon the character of that excellent woman, and the greatness of his grief for the loss of one who has ever been the support to him under all other afflictions. How (thought I) will he be able to bear the hour of her death, that could not, when I was lately with him, speak of a sickness that was then past without sorrow. We were now got pretty far into Westminster, and arrived at my friend's house. At the door of it I met Favonius, [Rev. Dr Smalridge,] not without a secret satisfaction to find he had been there. I had formerly conversed with him at his house; and as he abounds with that sort of virtue and knowledge that makes religion beautiful, and never leads the conversation into the violence and rage of party disputes, I listened to him with great pleasure. Our discourse chanced to be upon the subject of death, which he treated with such a strength of reason and greatness of soul, that, instead of being terrible, it appeared to a mind altogether to be contemned, or rather, to be desired. As I met him at the door, I saw in his face a certain glowing of grief and humanity, heightened with an air of fortitude and resolution, which, as I afterwards found, had such an irresistible force as to suspend the pains of the dying, and the lamentations of the nearest friends who attended her. I went up directly to the room where she lay, and was met at the entrance by my friend, who, notwithstanding his thoughts had been composed a little before, at the sight of me turned away his face and wept. The little family of children renewed the expressions of their sorrow, according to their several ages and degrees of understanding. The eldest daughter was in tears, busied in attendance upon her mother; others were kneeling about the bedside: and what troubled me most was to see a little boy, who was too young to know the reason, weeping only because his sisters did. The only one in the room who seemed resigned and comforted was the dying person. At my approach to the bedside she told me, with a low, broken voice, 'This is kindly done—take care of your friend—do not go from him.' She had before taken leave of her husband and children, in a manner proper for so solemn a parting, and with a gracefulness peculiar to a woman of her character. My heart was torn in pieces to see the husband on one side suppressing and keeping down the swellings of his grief, for fear of disturbing her in her last moments,

successors, who in a tract published anonymously, but generally attributed to him, says of Bickerstaff—

and the wife even at that time concealing the pain she endured for fear of increasing his affliction. She kept her eyes upon him for some moments after she grew speechless, and soon after closed them for ever. In the moment of her departure, my friend (who had thus far commanded himself) gave a deep groan, and fell into a swoon by her bedside. The distraction of the children, who thought they saw both their parents expiring together, and now lying dead before them, would have melted the hardest heart; but they soon perceived their father recover, whom I helped to remove into another room, with a resolution to accompany him till the first pangs of his affliction were abated. I knew consolation would now be impertinent, and therefore contented myself to sit by him, and condole with him in silence, . . . till made capable of receiving it by those three great remedies—the necessity of submission, length of time, and satiety of grief.

"In the meantime, I cannot but consider with much commiseration the melancholy state of one who has had such a part of himself torn from him, and which he misses in every circumstance of life. His condition is like one who has lately lost his right arm, and is every moment offering to help himself with it. He does not appear to himself the same person in his house, at his table, in company, or in retirement; and loses the relish of all the pleasures and diversions that were before entertaining to him, by her participation of them. The most agreeable objects recall the sorrow for her with whom he used to enjoy them. This additional satisfaction from the taste of pleasures in the society of one we love is admirably described in Milton, who represents Eve, though in Paradise itself, no further pleased with the beautiful around her, than as she sees them in company with Adam, in that passage so inexpressibly charming:—

> ' With thee conversing, I forget all time,
> All seasons, and their change; all please alike.
> Sweet is the breath of morn, her rising sweet
> With charm of earliest birds; pleasant the sun,
> When first on this delightful land he spreads
> His orient beams, on herb, tree, fruit, and flower,
> Glistering with dew; fragrant the fertile earth,
> After soft show'rs, and sweet the coming on
> Of grateful evening mild; the silent night,
> With this her solemn bird, and this fair moon,
> And these the gems of heaven, her starry train.
> But neither breath of morn when she ascends
> With charm of earliest birds, nor rising sun
> In this delightful land, nor herb, fruit, flower,
> Glist'ring with dew, nor fragrance after showers,
> Nor grateful evening mild, nor silent night,
> With this her solemn bird, nor walk by moon,
> Or glittering star-light,—without thee, is sweet.' "

"It is incredible to conceive the effect his writings have had on the town; how many thousand follies they have either quite banished or given a very great check to; how much countenance they have added to virtue and religion; how many people they have rendered happy, by shewing that it was their own fault if they were not so; and, lastly, how entirely they have convinced our fops and young fellows of the value and advantage of learning." *

As the two distinguished friends were now fortunately so situated as to renew an intimacy which was productive of the happiest effects,—not merely to themselves, but towards society at large, by enabling Steele to realise his ardent wish for a joint literary reputation with Addison,—this may be the most appropriate place for some notice of the latter.

Joseph Addison, one of the most honoured names in English literature, (born 1672, died 1719,) was the son of the Rev. Dr Launcelot Addison, a man of learning, amiability, and literary talents, who then held a living at Milston, in Wiltshire, but who had been for some years chaplain at Tangiers, in Barbary, and also at Dunkirk, and subsequently became Dean of Lichfield and Archdeacon of Salisbury; and who left behind him, as Steele acquaints us, in his letter to Congreve, "four children, each of whom, for excellent talents and singular perfections, was as much above the ordinary world as their brother Joseph was above them." The friendship of these two eminent men, as previously stated, began at the Charterhouse School, where they both received the first part of their education. Though there was only the difference of a year in their ages, and that in Steele's favour, Addison may probably have been considerably the more advanced in his studies,

---

* "Present State of Wit."

as he entered Queen's College, Oxford, in 1687, while his friend joined that of Christ Church, in the same university, only in 1689. But this may also be partly accounted for by the fact of Steele being on the Charterhouse foundation, and Addison only a private pupil. Of their college intercourse we have, strange to say, no notice whatever; but Steele mentions the warm approval of their intimacy by Dr Addison, who died in 1703, before the period when they met in after-life. "Were things of this nature," he says, in the letter already quoted, "to be exposed to public view, I could shew, under the Dean's own hand, in the warmest terms, his blessing on the friendship between his son and me; nor had he a child who did not prefer me in the first place of kindness and esteem, as their father loved me like one of them." It is much to be regretted that we should not have some particulars of the beginnings of a friendship commenced under such sanction, and ratified and confirmed so remarkably by the circumstances of after-life. Addison became a fellow of his college; but though destined for orders, long deferred committing himself to that irretrievable step, until circumstances threw him into public life. At five-and-twenty, he remained still "like one waiting upon fortune." His friend and literary executor, Tickell, in the prefatory memoir to his collected works, observes on this subject:—"His remarkable seriousness and modesty, which might have been urged as powerful reasons for his choosing that life, proved the chief obstacles to it. The qualities by which the priesthood is so much adorned, represented the duties of it as too weighty for him, and rendered him still more worthy of that honour which they made him decline." This remark, so very obscurely expressed, must of course be understood as referring to the responsibilities of the office which a very scrupulous and tender mind like his would naturally feel strongly. However, Steele, with the affectionate zeal for the memory of his friend, which did him so much honour, and to which the illiberal and carping spirit of Tickell in reference to himself added naturally a degree of personal indignation, repudiates such an inference. After alluding resentfully to what he terms the "cold, unaffectionate, dry, and barren manner in which this gentleman gives an account of as great a benefactor as any one learned man ever was to another," he adduces, as the true reason of Addison having adopted the path of civil life, "the warm instances that noble Lord [Halifax] made to the head of the college not to insist upon Mr Addison's going into orders,"—that is, to permit him to retain his fellowship on those terms. "The contention," he adds, "for this man, in his early youth, among the people of greatest power, Mr Secretary Tickell, the executor for his fame, is pleased to ascribe to a seriousness of visage and modesty of behaviour." This is more sarcastic and less candid than is usual with Steele. The reason, as stated by Tickell, is good so far as it goes, but cannot be considered as a wholly satisfactory solution of the question. It may well be imagined that, notwithstanding his gravity and strong religious tendencies, a latent feeling of ambition, and a certain consciousness, if not of distaste, at least of disqualification, for the practical and every-day duties of the priesthood, had much to do with his delay in taking the irrevocable step—for delay there was.

He gave early and consistent indications indeed of the

qualities of the courtier, and invoked his Muse as a prudent nymph to his aid. At two and twenty he addressed to Dryden, from his college, some highly complimentary verses on the unquenched fires of his age, in which he ventures the length of making even the translations of the veteran bard, which are usually regarded as bearing the traces of haste, and of being written under the pressure of necessity—

"Outshine the bright original."

When we are told that, in after years, he sat in the midst of his admiring circle indulging in depreciation of the fine old man, let us hope that it is an exaggeration, as it rests on suspicious authority. Meantime, no one was more open to a little flattery than "glorious John," and his young admirer and eulogist was taken to his friendship, and introduced to Congreve, then a man of influence, to whom, in the following year, he also awarded the meed of praise in the verses on the principal English poets, addressed to his friend Sacheverell, who, with mediocrity of talent, managed afterwards to make himself the hero of an hour, and to "ride upon the whirlwind" of faction. By Congreve, Addison was in turn introduced to Charles Montague, Lord Halifax, the Mæcenas of his age, who had wisely relinquished the functions of a mediocre versifier, in which capacity he was not overlooked by Addison in the verses above referred to, for those of a successful statesman and patron of poets. A year or two later, Addison inscribed to him one of his best Latin poems, that on the "Peace of Ryswick." He also, about the same time, addressed complimentary verses in English to Somers, Lord Keeper of the Great Seal, and likewise to the King. Montague, when Addison, in 1697, addressed his Latin poem to him, was Chancellor of the Exchequer, and the next year rose to be First Lord of the Treasury, and his first act of patronage was to obtain for Addison a pension of L.300 a year to enable him to travel, preparatory to his taking office.

Having printed his Latin poems as a passport to the notice of continental scholars, Addison set out in 1699 on a tour comprising parts of France, Switzerland, and Italy, of which, on his return, he published an account, with a dedication to Lord Somers. Though it has been objected to the work that there was little in it that might not have been written in the study, its fate was remarkable, as it rose to five times its original price before it was republished. He occupied about four years on this tour, which is surmised to have been connected with some private political mission. The fall of his friends from power at the death of King William in 1702, obliged him to return to England, where he arrived in the latter end of the following year, rather poor and dejected. By this event he lost his pension, as well as an appointment he had just received as English resident about the Prince Eugene.

Swift said, though the fact is not authenticated, that he now engaged as tutor or travelling companion to a young squire during the next year. Considering, however, that he declined the terms offered for a similar appointment by the Duke of Somerset, it is scarcely probable. He was now in his thirty-third year, without any other provision than the scanty income of his fellowship and the resources of his pen; but with these such a man had no great reason for despondency of his ultimate prospects. The munificent offer of a hundred a year, and his travelling expenses, made him by the Duke of Somerset to accompany his son on his travels, he had properly declined. It is easy, of course, reasoning on after events, to reflect on the niggardliness of such a proposal, as Miss Aikin has done; but it must be remembered that he was then only an accomplished gentleman, and not the Addison of after years. Shortly after his return he was elected a member of the famous Kit-Cat Club, consisting of a number of distinguished noblemen and gentlemen of Whig principles. One of the first duties of a member on his introduction was to propose some beauty as a toast, whose name was inscribed on his glass and her portrait hung up. Addison's toast was Lady Manchester; and, in his lines on the occasion, he would lead us to infer that the fair among our Gallic neighbours appeared ordinarily in blushes not their own ; but for once, at the sight of the Lady Manchester,

> " Confusion in their looks they shew'd,
> And with unborrow'd blushes glow'd."

The turning point of Addison's fortune was consequent on Marlborough's brilliant victory at Blenheim in 1704. He then occupied an humble lodging in the Haymarket. It is said that the Lord-Treasurer, Godolphin, casually meeting Lord Halifax, then out of power, asked him if he knew of one competent to celebrate Marlborough's exploit, to which the other replied that he knew of one eminently qualified ; but while so many dolts were pampered in pride and luxury at the public expense, and men who were an honour to their age and country were suffered to languish in obscurity, he would never urge any gentleman of ability to employ his talents in the service of a ministry which had not the generosity to make it worth his while. The Lord-Treasurer having pledged his word that any gentleman his Lordship should name as capable of the task would not have reason to regret undertaking it, Lord Halifax mentioned Addison. He was accordingly waited upon immediately by Mr Boyle, afterwards Lord Carleton, then Chancellor of the Exchequer, who, after having made his proposals respecting the poem, acquainted him at the same time that the Lord-Treasurer had appointed him one of the Commissioners of Appeal in the Excise, as an earnest of future promotion.* Such is said to have been the history of "The Campaign." Lord Godolphin was as good as his word to Addison. In 1706,

---

* The writer of the introduction to the *Spectator*, already perhaps too amply referred to as having adopted his tone in speaking of Steele from Mr Thackeray, says, in sober seriousness, "The simile of the angel immediately procured the poet a commissionership of £200 a year." It appears that, chronologically, the commissionership might more properly have been said to have produced the angel. Mr Thackeray had made some very witty remarks about angels' visits, and their proverbial rarity, especially to gentlemen occupying second floors, which of course were very well; but when put into plain matter of fact, as in this writer, the case is very different. It is certainly stated that he submitted his poem to the inspection of the Lord-Treasurer when only arrived at the angel simile, and some accounts even represent him as having then received the commissionership, though Miss Aikin, his latest and fullest biographer, gives a different version. But even this would not justify the statement that a simile had procured him a commissionership, unless there had been no *previous pledge* given. The angel riding on the whirlwind appears to have made this writer quite figurative himself at this point, "The dark clouds, &c., were dispelled, and Joseph Addison became a great man." We really thought his patent of greatness dated earlier, and would have existed even if the sun had never shone upon his holding the scals as Secretary of State. Of the tens and hundreds of thousands in successive generations who have acknowledged the greatness of the delightful essayist, not one in a thousand, we believe, connected it in any way with his being either a commissioner or secretary.

having the previous year accompanied Lord Halifax on his mission to Hanover, he was appointed Under Secretary of State, and afterwards became Chief Secretary for Ireland, a post which he held twice.

The following year he produced his English opera of "Rosamond," which, though one of his most pleasing and elegant productions—light, airy, and graceful—failed in the representation, which has been attributed to the music of Clayton. It was published with a dedication to the Duchess of Marlborough. Shortly after the failure of this first dramatic essay, he assisted his friend in his comedy of the "Tender Husband," for which he wrote the prologue, and received in return a complimentary dedication from Steele.

In 1709, Addison went as Chief Secretary to Ireland, on the appointment of Lord Wharton to the Vice-Royalty, when the Queen, as a mark of special favour, augmented his salary, in the additional office he held of Keeper of the Records in Birmingham Tower, to L.300 a year. His departure took place only a few days previous to the commencement of the *Tatler* by Steele; and on learning the secret of his friend's connexion with it, he became a frequent contributor. His contributions were without any signature. He afterwards adopted in the *Spectator* one of the letters in the name of the Muse, "Clio," * and in the *Guardian* a *hand.* To the *Spectator*, commenced in 1711 by the two friends in concert, Addison became a still more regular contributor. The *Guardian* followed, (March 1713,)

---

* Nichols ingeniously conjectures that these may have signified the place where each was written, as Chelsea, London, Islington, Office. This is probably only fanciful, however.

and was the shortest lived of the three, reaching only to 176 numbers, at the cessation of which Addison revived the *Spectator*, which, however, was only published thrice a week, and not daily, as formerly. It extended to eighty numbers, of which twenty-three were by Addison. The revived paper did not equal its former reputation. The extraordinary confidence in their resources, displayed by Addison and Steele in venturing on a daily issue of the *Spectator*, is partly accounted for by the fact that Addison had a large amount of matter on hand previously, and had only to draw upon this stock and remodel it, as far as may have been necessary, piecemeal. Those different series of papers on the Imagination, (which formed the groundwork of Akenside's poem,) on Wit, and on Milton, were of this description; so that there was something literally applicable to himself in the remark made in the person of the *Spectator* of printing himself out.

Addison writes to Mr Wortley Montagu, July 21, 1711, some particulars of his private affairs, the details of which have never been explained. "I have within this twelvemonth lost a place of L.2000 per annum, an estate in the Indies of L.14,000, and, what is worse than all the rest, my mistress. Hear this, and wonder at my philosophy. I find they are going to take away my Irish place from me too; to which I must add, that I have just resigned my fellowship, and that the stocks sink every day."

In 1713, the tragedy of "Cato," which he had planned and partly written during his travels, was finished and exhibited at Drury Lane. Though it was rather a dramatic poem than an acting piece, which Addison himself felt, yet the violence of party at the time contributed to give it extraordinary success, and it was performed thirty-five successive nights. The sentiments in favour of liberty caused it to be vehemently applauded by the Whigs, and the applause was echoed by the Tories, to shew that the application was either unfelt or unheeded. Pope wrote a fine prologue to it, and Garth the epilogue. Among others, Steele contributed his quota of complimentary verses on the occasion, which may here be quoted :—

> "While you the fierce divided Britons awe,
> And Cato with an equal virtue draw,
> While envy is itself in wonder lost,
> And factions strive who shall applaud you most;
> Forgive the fond ambition of a friend,
> Who seeks himself, not you, to recommend,
> And join th' applause which all the learn'd bestow
> On one, to whom a perfect work they owe.
> To my light scenes I once inscribed your name,
> And impotently strove to borrow fame ;
> Soon will that die which adds thy name to mine ;
> Let me then live, join'd to a work of thine!"

It met, however, with more than one assailant; but the attack of Dennis, though he belonged to the Whig party, was marked by peculiar and characteristic asperity; and though some of his remarks have considerable force, it was evident from their spirit that he was actuated by envy and malice. The result shewed that the world did not care to be taught by rule that it ought not to applaud. The play was translated into Italian and Latin. The faults of "Cato," as regards style, must be attributed to his having followed the model of the French tragic dramatists, whose declamatory style it resembles. Having been written in France, he probably read them at the time as a study in acquiring the language. It bears marks also of some of its fire having been kindled from Lucan, who is open to the same fault. But while deficient in dramatic interest, it is undeniable that he has made it the vehicle of very noble sentiments elegantly expressed.

A reply to Dennis, written by Pope, entitled "A Narrative of the Phrenzy of John Dennis," which was a satire on the man rather than a refutation of his criticism, not meeting with Addison's approval, led to a memorable coolness between the two poets; and the breach was still further widened on the appearance of the rival version of "Homer," attributed to Tickell. Various opinions have been entertained and expressed on this passage in the lives of these two eminent men. Some have held that Addison was above the envy of Pope, which has been attributed to him; that he entertained such feeling towards no one else, and is said never to have spoken harshly even of Dennis. The popular opinion that attributed the rival version to Addison is also now commonly regarded as an error. Dryden, whom he had formerly flattered, is the only other towards whom he has been accused, if not of envy, at least of depreciation; but Spence, who makes the charge, was the mouthpiece of Pope. With regard to the rival "Homer," though Pope's proposals had long been published, it is certain that Addison encouraged with all his influence the one of which Tickell was ostensibly the translator. But, on the other hand, it was only the first book, which he published as a specimen to introduce a proposal for a similar complete translation of the "Odyssey," which Pope had not then undertaken. Addison had also made Pope dine with him, to explain to him that having previously looked at Tickell's first book, he must excuse himself looking at his. Pope expressed his satisfaction, and requested that one of the other books of his might have that benefit. He at the same time expressed himself satisfied that there was a fair field for both. As regards Tickell's capability, he was really in many respects a more accomplished master of versification than Addison. To complete the case, on the authority of Miss Aikin, the MS., which still exists in the possession of the Tickell family, is in his handwriting, with interlineations by Addison. Though Pope expressed himself satisfied at the first, his suspicions or feelings seem to have been aggravated by time and some subsequent occurrences, particularly a ridiculous story that he said some one had told him of Addison having bribed Gildon, the author of the "Life of Wycherley," to malign him. He must have forgotten the transaction with reference to Dennis, where Addison had disclaimed his own volunteered services against an envenomed critic. Again, with regard to his imputation against Addison of giving envious counsel in advising him not to risk spoiling his first sketch of his "Rape of the Lock," by the addition which he afterwards so felicitously made of the Rosicrucian machinery of the sylphs, he should have remembered the same imputation exactly was open to his advice to Addison not to venture "Cato" on the stage, where it was so great a success. The *chances* were, that in either case the advice would have been good, and in Addison's case he could not be expected to have been aware of what the other had matured in his mind, or to have anticipated such a happy execution of the design. On the whole, there appears little ground of censure against Addison, whilst there is ground of grave suspicion of the malignity of Pope; and at the least, he was probably actuated by that morbid irritability which he unfortunately so generally displayed, and by which he must have wounded himself, whilst he annihilated enemies of so little mark, that it would have been more consistent with dignity to have passed them by unnoticed. There can be little doubt that a large share of this must in justice be attributed to physical infirmity; but even after a fair allowance on that score, there remains much that must be considered *prepense* and wanton. In the finished portrait of "Atticus," which was the most memorable result of this misunderstanding, he at least tempered the darts of that forked tongue of flame with the tones of expostulation, whilst he made Addison feel what a dangerous antagonist he had to do with.*

> * " Peace to all such ! but were there one whose fires
> True genius kindles, and fair fame inspires ;
> Blest with each talent, and each art to please,
> And born to write, converse, and live with ease;
> Should such a man, too fond to rule alone,
> Bear, like the Turk, no rival near the throne,
> View him with scornful, yet with jealous eyes,
> And hate four arts that caused himself to rise ;
> Damn with faint praise, assent with civil leer,
> And, without sneering, teach the rest to sneer ;
> Willing to wound, and yet afraid to strike,
> Just hint a fault and hesitate dislike ;
> Alike reserved to blame or to commend,
> A timorous foe, and a suspicious friend ;
> Dreading e'en fools, by flatterers besieged,
> And so obliging that he ne'er obliged.
> Like Cato, give his little senate laws,
> And sit attentive to his own applause ;
> While wits and templars every sentence raise,
> And wonder with a foolish face of praise ;
> Who but must laugh if such a man there be ?
> Who would not weep, if Atticus were he ? "

In the same year Addison wrote a few papers, probably without any intention of continuing them, under the title of the *Whig Examiner*, in reply to the Tory one of the same name. These papers displayed a pungency not usual with him, and in them his wit and satire shone so conspicuously as to have preserved them from the usual fate of the mere weapons of ephemeral strife. Swift, who was the leading writer for its antagonist, referring to it, said exultingly that it was, (in the words of an old Tory song,) "down among the dead men;" and such was its merit that even Johnson, with all his prejudices arrayed on the opposite side, added, "That the Dean might well exult in the death of that he could not kill."

On the death of Queen Anne, in 1714, Addison was appointed Secretary to the Regency, with the duty of notifying to the Court of Hanover the fact of the royal demise, and the consequent vacancy of the throne. On the arrival of George I., Addison was proposed as one of the principal Secretaries of State, but declined the office, and accompanied Lord Sunderland as Chief Secretary to Ireland. In the following year, on the removal of Lord Sunderland from the Viceroyalty, Addison was appointed one of the Lords of Trade. At this time, when rebellion was raising its head in the north in favour of the Pretender, Addison published a paper, called the *Freeholder*, in favour of the existing government, which appeared twice a week from December of this year till June 1716. In this work the humour is unsurpassed, especially in the delineation of the Tory fox-hunter. Steele, however, said not untruly that the government had employed a lute when they wanted a trumpet.

In 1716 was consummated his marriage with the Countess-Dowager of Warwick, to whom he had paid long and assiduous court,—an event which affords no favourable precedent for ambitious matches. It is believed not to have added much to his happiness; and, amid the splendours of Holland House, he probably often looked back with envy to the days of his bachelorhood, and the happy social meetings of that time.* In the following year, he became one of the principal Secretaries of State, which office he had previously declined; but indifferent health, and perhaps some degree of disqualification in not being able to speak in the House of Commons, induced him soon to relinquish the office, which, however, he did with a pension of L.1500 a year. Lady M. W. Montagu made a very remarkable prophecy on hearing of his marriage and his promotion to the Secretaryship—that neither such a wife nor such an office were suitable for a man with an asthma, and that he would soon be glad to be rid of both.

In his retirement he partly wrote a work he had designed on Christian Evidence, which has not added to his literary reputation, and planned a tragedy on the death of Socrates, and other works. Unfortunately, he did not confine his attention exclusively to such pursuits, but was tempted once more into the stormy atmosphere of party strife. In 1718-19, he published the " Old Whig," in defence of the Peerage Bill of Lord Sunderland, in which (without mutual knowledge at first) he had Steele for his antagonist in a paper called " The Plebeian." There was a

---

* Button, from whom the famous Coffeehouse took its name, who had been a butler of Lady Warwick's, was set up in business by him, and it is said that after his marriage, he often resorted to it, when vexed with his Countess at home.

sharp passage between the two friends, but that quotation so often made about "Little Dickey whose trade was to write pamphlets," which has so long been supposed, to Addison's disadvantage, to have been unhandsomely applied to his friend, has been quite misunderstood, the reference being to the performer of a character (Gomez) in Dryden's "Spanish Fair." This error, we believe, was first pointed out by Coleridge, as it has also been by Lord Macaulay. Indeed, it might have occurred to some one, in the long time this quotation has floated about, that the diminutive epithet was not likely to have been applicable to one who had been a guardsman, but it is a curious proof of the vitality of error. The result of this controversy was not in Addison's favour.

In his unmarried days, after devoting the morning to study or business, he dined at a tavern, and spent his evenings mostly in a coffeehouse in Covent Garden, (which supplied the place of the modern club,) in converse with his intimate friends, of whom the chief were Steele, Budgell, Philips, Casey, and Davenant. There he often sat to a late hour, charming the circle with his colloquial accomplishments, which, according to the general testimony, were of the most delightful kind.

His death occurred at Holland House in 1719, in his forty-seventh year. He left behind him only one child, a daughter.

If exact similarity of disposition and temperament were the chief bond of friendship, no two men could have been more unequally yoked than Steele and Addison. But if it be an agreement in some of the most material points, and the opposite in others, filling up those voids which every

one feels in himself, and so making of two one perfect character, then did they exactly answer to this ideal of the requirements of friendship. They had the same strong religious sentiments, the same goodness of heart, the same fund of humour, the same exquisite conversational powers. But there the resemblance ceased. The one was frank, gay, impetuous, impulsive, and deficient in self-command; the other was diffident, retiring, and contemplative, with a serene gravity and well-regulated prudence. Steele, however, was always his own most unmerciful censor, and in various sketches has hit off his own shortcomings with the skill of a microscopic observer and the sternness of an inexorable judge. But while thus severe with himself, the tenderness, affection, and utter freedom from envy which he manifested towards his friend are above all praise. " We never had any difference," he says, " but what arose from our different way of pursuing the same thing: the one with patience, foresight, and temperate address, always waited and stemmed the torrent; while the other often plunged himself into it, and was as often taken out by the temper of him who stood weeping on the bank for his safety, whom he could not dissuade from leaping into it."*
Speaking elsewhere of the charms of his conversation, he dwells upon " that smiling mirth, that delicate satire, and genteel raillery in Mr Addison when he was free among his intimates—I say, when he was free from his remarkable bashfulness, which is a cloak that hides and muffles merit. He was above all men in that talent we call humour, and enjoyed it in such perfection that I have often reflected, after a night spent with him, apart from all the world, that

* *Theatre*, No. 12.

I had had the pleasure of conversing with an intimate acquaintance of Terence and Catullus, who had all their wit and nature heightened with humour more exquisite and delightful than any other man ever possessed."* Pope, too, though he belonged to the opposite party, and had been treated with coldness by Addison, says, " Addison's conversation had something in it more charming than I have found in any other man. . . . Before strangers, or perhaps a single stranger, he preserved his dignity by a stiff silence."

It is a general impression that Addison was very slow in the process of composition, but the reverse appears to have been the case. " This," says Steele, " was particular in this writer, that when he had taken his resolution, or made his plan for what he designed to write, he would walk about a room, and dictate it in language with as much freedom and ease as any one could write it down, and attend to the coherence and grammar of what he dictated." And Pope adds, on the same subject, that " he wrote very fluently, but was slow and scrupulous in correcting ; many of his *Spectators* were written very fast, and sent immediately to the press ; and it seemed to be for his advantage not to have time for much revisal. He would alter anything to please his friends before publication, but would not re-touch his pieces afterwards." Dr Johnson has said of the writings of Addison, that he did not wish to be energetic, while Warton refers to his energy ; but with reference at least to manner, Johnson is certainly nearer the mark. The distinctive characteristic of Addison may perhaps be compared to what is said to give the peculiar

* Letter to Congreve.

charm to Circassian beauty—a certain luxurious air of dreamy repose in the half-closed eyelids.

After Swift and Addison, the only other contributor of note to the *Tatler* was Congreve, who, as we have seen, was one of those who took part in Swift's jest about Partridge, and who communicated the character of Aspasia, No. 42 of the *Tatler*, intended to celebrate the virtues of Lady Elizabeth Hastings, daughter of the Earl of Huntingdon. It was greatly to his credit that he should have appreciated so exalted a character. But from the characteristic manner of its execution, it has been surmised by the critics, and Mr Leigh Hunt among others, that Steele's hand is discernible in some of the finest touches.

In an age distinguished for wits, WILLIAM CONGREVE ranked among the foremost in brilliancy. But, unfortunately, he has not more tarnished than abridged his fame by making that wit the vehicle of the lax morality of the age that was then going out. He was the second son of an officer, himself a younger son of one of the old county families of Staffordshire, who for his services in the civil war was one of those nominated for the honour of the intended Order of the Royal Oak. The dramatist was probably born at Bardsey, near Leeds, between 1669 and 1672, both time and place having been subjects of question.

His father having settled in Ireland, as agent for the Burlington property, he received his education there, first at the grammar-school of Kilkenny, where he must have been about the same time as his afterwards intimate friend Swift, and then at Dublin University, where he had the same tutor as Swift, St George Ashe, subsequently Bishop of Clogher and Derry, to whom his attainments are admitted by the most competent authorities to have done the greatest credit.

From thence he removed to the Middle Temple, London. But the study of the law was the least of his cares. His personal and mental graces and gifts marked him as eminently qualified to shine in the more congenial spheres of society and letters, and to them he accordingly devoted himself. In the former, his various advantages in point of family and personal accomplishment gained him easy admission into the best circles, and the first result of his courtship of the latter appeared in the shape of a novel, a species of literary production then only known through the medium of French translations. It was entitled, as if to mark the struggle for precedence in his own pursuits, "Incognita; or, Love and Duty Reconciled," of which Johnson, with a curious confession of critical pliancy, says he would rather praise it than read it; and Mr Leigh Hunt, his latest considerable biographer, having read it, professes himself unwilling to be so complaisant as the former. This appears certainly rather remarkable, as an evidence of the limits that bound the capabilities of the ablest men; nor have subsequent instances been wanting to shew that, notwithstanding the apparent similarity, a successful dramatist is not necessarily successful as a novelist. But it must, in addition, be added that Congreve's work is stated to have been produced at seventeen, though not published till some years after.

The success of "The Old Bachelor," which came out at Drury Lane in 1693, made him ample amends for this first failure. Its reception was very flattering, not only with the public, but the critics. Dryden, whom Congreve had previously propitiated by a strain of panegyric natural from a young author to a veteran, repaid it with interest, considering their relative standing, declared he had never seen such a first play, and, in conjunction with Southern and others, gave it the benefit of his experience in fitting it for representation. All the beauty and talent of Drury Lane combined to give *éclat* to the performance. Other rewards followed. Montagu, afterwards Lord Halifax, then of the Treasury Board, gave him a commissionership, and soon after another office in reversion.

Congreve followed up his triumph in the ensuing year with "The Double Dealer," which, though displaying maturer powers, did not give equal satisfaction. He received, however, what must have consoled him for his comparative failure, that epistle from Dryden, written in his finest manner, in which he not only recognised him as the rival of the old and the hope of the new drama, but as his own successor, to whom in most pathetic terms he intrusted the guardianship of his own fame. Such a delicious draught coming from such a quarter must have been almost intoxicating, not the less so that posterity has come to regard it as extravagant.

Drury Lane, being at this time without a rival, was managed in the spirit of all monopolies, so that Betterton and the other leading actors combined their exertions successfully in obtaining a patent for a new one in Lincoln's-Inn-Fields. Congreve cast in his lot with them, and the new concern was opened with his "Love for Love" in 1695. Once more he was rewarded with a brilliant success. The proprietors of the new house evinced their gratitude and satisfaction by offering him a share in the concern, on the terms of his producing them a play annually, with the very liberal proviso, making it subject to his health permitting. This most convenient clause was very fortunate, for his next performance did not make its appearance till 1697. This was his only tragic piece, "The Mourning Bride," the immense success of which was considered sufficient to cover his delinquency. It was not merely his greatest triumph, but placed him foremost among the tragic writers of the time, as he had previously been of those of comedy. Indeed, a passage in the beginning of it, describing the ruins of a temple, has been extolled by Johnson, who was no partial critic of Congreve generally, as finer than anything almost in the range of the drama; but in this case his praise, though just, is certainly overcharged.

As his productions seem to have been fated to alternately great triumphs and comparative failures, his next piece, "The Way of the World," which appeared in 1700, was his least successful effort, though deserving of a better fate; and this, combined with another circumstance which occurred at this time, induced him to relinquish dramatic pursuits in disgust. The event alluded to was the appearance of Collier's strictures on the stage two years previously. Having been already noticed in connexion with the other dramatic predecessors of Steele, it need not here be further referred to than to say, that Congreve's chagrin must have been greatly aggravated by his having made such a mistake as to take up the controversy, for which his talents were unfitted, and in which no talents could have made him successful, though a different treatment might have mitigated the measure of his defeat. As it was, even the voice of the green-room and the clubs was forced to yield the triumph to his opponent.

From a letter of Congreve's which is extant, it appears that he and Steele, who now took up the pen which the other had just laid down, though in a very different spirit, were at this time on very friendly terms. It was natural that such should have been the case. In addition to being a brother wit and dramatist, he was half his fellow-countryman; and though not a man of warm affections like Steele, he was very friendly in using the high social influence he possessed in favour of the brotherhood, and it was to him that Addison owed his introduction to the statesmen who so efficiently patronised him.

At the age of thirty, Congreve found himself, by the general voice of his contemporaries, foremost in two fields of literature, the successful cultivation of which is not often found united in the same person—a rare and giddy elevation. He afterwards interested himself in the theatre established by Vanbrugh and Betterton on the site of the Opera-house in the Haymarket; but only to the extent of writing some prologues and epilogues, and soon withdrew from the concern.

In 1710 he published his collected works. His miscellaneous pieces are of small account, though his "Doris," the description of a gay lady of quality, was immensely admired by his contemporaries. In a prose piece, he was the first to refer particularly to the humorous element as characteristic of the national literature. It is remarkable, and to be regretted, that he did not unite more with Steele and Addison in their periodical papers. At the suggestion of Swift, he contributed one paper to the spurious

Tatler, which the former aided in setting up for the benefit of his *protégé* Harrison.

In 1714, Congreve was made a Commissioner of Wine Licences, and shortly after, Secretary for Jamaica. In the same year Steele dedicated to him his " Poetic Miscellanies," where, after alluding to his literary eminence, he says, " I chose rather, as one who has passed many happy hours with you, to celebrate that easy condescension of mind and command of a pleasant imagination, which give you the uncommon praise of a man of wit,—always to please, and never to offend. No one, after a joyful evening, can reflect upon an expression of Mr Congreve's that dwells upon him with pain." After the death of Addison, Steele also appealed to him against the injustice of Tickell, as literary executor of his friend, in an epistle dedicatory to " The Drummer." Congreve also received the honour of Pope's dedication of his Homer, probably from uniting with his literary fame the respect and good-will of men of all parties. This good fortune, joined to the friendly offices of Swift, as well as Harley's appreciation of men of genius, preserved him from the loss of office during the Tory administration, though afflicted with a cataract which rendered him nearly blind.

The latter years of his life were passed in ease and retirement, solaced by an eminence of fame seldom so early won, or so little pursued, and the general laudation of his contemporaries. In the year following the appearance of " The Old Bachelor," he had received the tribute of praise from Addison in his verses on the English poets. Speaking of Dryden,

" Grown old in rhyme, but charming e'en in years,"

he adds—

> "How might we fear our English poetry,
> That long has flourish'd, should decay with thee,
> Did not the Muses' other hope appear,
> Harmonious Congreve, and forbid our fear;
> Congreve! whose fancy's unexhausted store
> Has given already much, and promised more:
> Congreve should still preserve thy fame alive,
> And Dryden's Muse shall in his friend survive."

From Dryden himself, as long as he lived, he received the most flattering eulogy, and Pope and Steele paid their contributions. Yet Congreve had the weakness, the ingratitude, to profess to hold lightly the fame which had procured him all this incense, and that in favour of the meaner consideration of social distinction. When Voltaire visited England he waited upon Congreve. With an ardent thirst of literary fame himself, the witty Frenchman paid the other many compliments on his writings, and to his amazement and disgust found them received in a way that to him was inconceivable. Congreve professed to consider them as trifles, and wished to be regarded merely as a gentleman who amused himself with writing. Voltaire's reply was, that if he had been so unfortunate as to have been merely a gentleman, he should never have been desirous of seeing him.* It was a just rebuke. With Congreve, the charming Mrs Bracegirdle, the celebrated actress, was the greatest among many favourites; and he, as well as Rowe, was said to have made love to her in the characters he wrote for her. She is understood to have reciprocated the feeling in more than an equal degree. But there was a grand lady who had an extravagant pas-

---

* See Voltaire's Letters on the English Nation.

sion for him—which can only be compared to that of Vanessa for Swift, with the difference that the one was married—that would have prevented the crowning of the hopes pretty Mrs Bracegirdle is believed to have entertained. The grand lady referred to was Henrietta, Duchess of Marlborough, and wife of Earl Godolphin, son of the Lord Treasurer. She was the heiress of the immense fortune of the duke, and by special licence permitted to bear the title in default of male issue.

Congreve had been a luxurious liver, and the infirmities of age came early upon him, though not to a degree to incapacitate him for the enjoyments of society, on which he was entirely thrown in his latter years, from the disease in his eyes having resulted in blindness. He was also troubled with the gout, and in the summer of 1728 resorted to the Bath waters as a remedy. From an internal injury he received at that time by the upsetting of his chariot, he suffered a gradual decay till the 19th of the ensuing January, when he expired at his house in Surrey Street.

Though there were some branches of his family not in affluent circumstances, to whom the L.10,000 of his saving would have been of the greatest service, and the same thing applied to Mrs Bracegirdle, who had claims upon him, yet he gratified his vanity by bequeathing it, where it was merely thrown away, to the Duchess Henrietta, in acknowledgment of her infatuated passion for him, and as a sequel to his comedy of "The Way of the World."

The duchess gave him a most magnificent funeral. The remains were laid in state in the Jerusalem chamber, and afterwards interred in the Abbey, where the ashes of many poets had previously been enshrined, though never perhaps before with such splendour. The Duke of Bridgewater, Lord Cobham, the Earl of Wilmington, General Churchill, and others of note, were the pall-bearers. A monument was also erected, with an inscription from her grace's own hand, recording his worth, and " the happiness and honour she enjoyed" in his friendship. The residue of the legacy was invested in a magnificent diamond necklace, which Dr Young, (of the " Night Thoughts,") after mentioning its having been shewn him, expresses his opinion that it would have been much better spent if it had gone to poor Mrs Bracegirdle, who only received some comparatively trifling bequest.

According to an absurd and perhaps fabulous story that has been preserved, the duchess testified her affection to the memory of her departed friend in more fantastic ways, and is said to have had an automaton model of him in ivory, which, like the original, was a constant guest at the table.

The fame of Congreve, notwithstanding the predictions of even such a judge as Dryden, has been evanescent, though the wit remains as bright as ever, but it is a wit aimless and objectless, and which ends in itself. The brilliancy dazzled his contemporaries and prevented them seeing clearly, as in the case of Swift with St John, whose fame in a different field was very much of the same order. The whole merit of Congreve lay in his dialogue. His plots are obscure and intricate to a degree, his characters uninteresting, except as brilliant talkers, but there the wit blazed and sparkled with a continuous brightness that has never been surpassed, and rarely equalled.

As the different volumes of the *Tatler* were inscribed to

some of the most eminent and accomplished men of the period, it may be desirable, before taking leave of the work, to glance at the subjects of these dedications, in accordance with the previously expressed aim of the present design, to include a group of sketches around the central figure. The first volume was addressed to Arthur Maynwaring, Esq., who was a leading member of the famous Kit-Cat Club, a distinguished political writer, and noted for his wit and elegant scholarship. In addition to these claims, there was another of a personal nature, which entitled him to this high honour of having his name first inscribed in the *Tatler*. In was to him that Steele probably owed his introduction to office, or, if not his appointment originally as the *Gazette* writer, at least its being made of any considerable value to him, by his interest with Harley, who raised the salary from L.60 to L.300 a year.

After assigning, with characteristic modesty, the original favourable acceptance of his labours with the public to the high pitch of reputation which Swift had given to Bickerstaff by the inimitable spirit and humour of the pieces he had written under his name, Steele goes on to add that the design had met with such success that there was scarcely the name of any one eminent for power, wit, wisdom, beauty, or valour but was included in the subscribers to it. In the collected form it was republished in volumes at a guinea.

Arthur Maynwaring, who was selected for a compliment which the highest in the land would have been proud to have received, was descended of an ancient Shropshire family, and was born at Ightfield in 1668. After receiving the rudiments of his education at the grammar-school of

Shrewsbury, he proceeded to Oxford, where he had the good fortune to be placed under the tuition of the eminent Dr Smalridge, afterwards Bishop of Bristol. On leaving Christ Church, after several years of study, he resided for some time at Vale Royal, in Cheshire, with an uncle, Mr Cholmondeley, a worthy gentleman, but whose Jacobite prejudices were such that he refused to take the oaths to King William. The nephew continued the cultivation of literary pursuits with assiduity, and having naturally imbibed the sentiments of his uncle, he gave expression to them in some satirical pieces—" Tarquin and Tullia,"* and " The King of Hearts"—aimed at the new government. This latter production was publicly imputed to Dryden by Tonson, but was disclaimed by him, at the same time that he mentioned the author favourably.

He soon after proceeded to London with the view of studying the law, where, having made the acquaintance of the Duke of Somerset, Lord Dorset, and other of the Whig leaders, he ultimately became a zealous convert to their political views. By the death of his father having come into a good estate, though heavily encumbered, he relinquished his legal studies and devoted himself to more congenial pursuits. On the conclusion of the treaty of Ryswick, he made a journey to France, and was fortunate enough to obtain an introduction to Boileau, at whose country seat he was hospitably entertained, and, among other guests, made the acquaintance of La Fontaine.

On his return he received the appointment of one of the Commissioners of Customs, in which office he displayed

* State Poems, vol. iii.

such zeal and probity, that, early in Queen Anne's reign, he received from the Lord Treasurer, Godolphin, the patent place of Auditor of Imprests, worth L.2000 a year. He was one of the poets of the Kit-Cat Club. He also carried on a regular correspondence with the Duchess of Marlborough, whose confidential secretary he called himself, and which has been recently published. In the Parliament of 1705 he was returned for Preston, in Lancashire.

His publications were various, both in verse and prose, which gained him much contemporary credit, but none of his writings have survived. He was the principal contributor to the *Medley*, which he started in opposition to the Tory paper the *Examiner*, and was occasionally assisted by Steele and Addison. He is also stated to have made several communications to the *Tatler*, and is supposed to have been the author of the letter of Prompter Downes, (which Steele expiated with the loss of his Gazetteership,) though his name is not generally given among the contributors. He died at St Albans, Nov. 13, 1712, and his life and posthumous writings were published in 1715, with a dedication to Sir R. Walpole.

The second volume was dedicated to Edward Wortley Montagu, Esq., second son of the Hon. Sidney and Lady Wortley Montagu, and grandson of Edward Montagu, the first Earl of Sandwich. His friendship was highly prized by Addison and Steele. The attainments of Mr W. Montagu were rather solid than brilliant. After completing his education, he had travelled in Germany, Switzerland, and Italy in 1702–3, where Addison and he met and corresponded, as they did ever after. The writer, after many compliments on his accomplishments, concludes—

"I know not how to say a more affectionate thing to you, than to wish that you may always be what you are; and that you may ever think as I know you now do, that you have a much larger fortune than you want."

There is a curious letter of his *apropos* of this subject, in reply to one from Addison under the date of July 21, 1711, containing a list of grievances and pecuniary losses, previously quoted,* which have puzzled his biographers. Addison writes:—

"Being very well pleased with this day's *Spectator*, (No. 123,) I cannot forbear sending you one of them, and desiring your opinion of the story in it. When you have a son, I shall be glad to be his Leontine, as my circumstances will probably be like his."

He adds, and it affords a proof of the opinion he had of his friend's judgment:—

"If you have any hints or subjects, pray send me a paper full. I long to talk an evening with you. I believe I shall not go for Ireland this summer, and perhaps would take a month with you if I knew where. Lady Bellasise is very much your humble servant. Dick Steele and I often remember you."

To the long catalogue of losses, Mr Montagu replies:—

"Notwithstanding your disappointments, I had much rather be in your circumstances than my own. The strength of your constitution would make you happier than all who are not equal to you in that; though it contributed nothing to those other advantages that place you in the first rank of men. Since my fortune fell to me, I had reason to fancy I should be reduced to a very small income. I immediately retrenched my expenses, and lived for six months on L.50 as pleasantly as ever I did in my life, and could have lived for less than half that sum. I often entertained myself with the speech of Ofellus in the second satire of the second book; and still think no man of understanding can be many days unhappy if he does not want health. . . . You were never in possession of anything you love but your places, and those you could not call your own."

Addison's arrangements not admitting of going on a visit which his friend had suggested, he proposed to take

* See notice of Addison, p. 169.

a house in Kensington, if Mr Montagu would join him, "not forgetting a cook and other particulars." To which Mr Montagu, assenting, after expressing his opinion that "the nation must be ruined by such a peace as is talked of," amusingly adds, "That we may bear up the better under misfortunes, I hope you will be nice in the choice of a cook and other particulars,"—shewing neither of the friends to be quite indifferent to creature comforts.

Mr Montagu made a very respectable figure in the House, where he was representative for Huntingdon in the fourth year of Queen Anne, and in every subsequent one, with the exception of two, till the end of her reign. He also represented at different periods the borough of Bossiney, and the cities of Westminster and Peterborough. He introduced various important and patriotic bills; among others, one "For the Naturalisation of Foreign Protestants," (Feb. 5, 1708;) "For Limiting the Number of Officers in the House of Commons, and for Securing the Freedom of Parliament," (Jan. 25, 1709;) and another the same year "For the Encouragement of Learning, and Securing the Property of Copies of Books to the right Owners thereof," (Dec. 21.) In his cousin, Charles Montagu, afterwards Lord Halifax, he found an effective patron.

In 1712, Mr Montagu, after a correspondence of about two years, was married privately, by special licence, to Lady Mary Pierrepont, eldest daughter of Evelyn, first Duke of Kingston, whose beauty and wit were the charm of the court in the succeeding reign, which soon after followed. As in the case of Addison, however, this celebrated beauty, with all her brilliant attainments, does not appear to have brought happiness to Mr Montagu. Their first married years were spent at Wharncliffe Lodge, near Sheffield, where their only son, called after his father, was born. Some of the sentiments in her letters before marriage may be worth quoting:—

"I am surprised at one of the *Tatlers* you send me. . . . Mr Bickerstaff has very wrong notions of our sex. I can say there are some of us that despise the charms of show, and all the pageantry of greatness, perhaps with more ease than any of the philosophers. In contemning the world they seem to take pains to contemn it; we despise it without taking the pains to read lessons of morality to make us do it. At least I know I have always looked upon it with contempt, without being at the expense of one serious reflection to oblige me to it. I carry the matter yet further: were I to choose of £2000 a year, or £20,000, the first would be my choice. There is something of an unavoidable *embarras* in making what is called a great figure in the world; it takes off from the happiness of life. I hate the noise and hurry inseparable from great estates or titles."

Very pretty sentiments, Lady Mary. But let us hear what she has to say after marriage and experience of the world. "Look upon this picture and upon this." In a letter of exhortation to her husband for his guidance in his parliamentary career she writes:—

"As the world is, and will be, it is a sort of duty to be rich, that it may be in one's power to do good,—riches being another name for power; towards the obtaining of which the first necessary qualification is impudence, and (as Demosthenes said of pronunciation (?) in oratory;) the second is impudence, and the third still impudence. No modest man ever did, or ever will, make his fortune. Your friend, Lord Halifax, R. Walpole, and all other remarkable instances of quick advancement, have been remarkably impudent. . . . Your modest man stands behind in the crowd, and is shoved about by everybody, his clothes torn, almost squeezed to death, and sees a thousand get in before him that don't make so good a figure as himself."

In order to appreciate this, it must be remembered that her husband was not a poor man, but, on the contrary, very wealthy. As Mr Montagu had been a vacillating lover, he appears to have been also a cool husband—but there may possibly have been reasons for both. Wit is very apt to possess the coldness and hardness of the diamond as well as its sparkle, and, when united to beauty and love of admiration, tends to destroy that womanly tenderness and devotion which constitute the charm and glory of domestic life. At all events, he seems to have left her in the country very much to herself. On the accession of George I., however, in 1714, when Lord Halifax rose to be First Lord of the Treasury, Mr Montagu was appointed one of that board, and Lady Mary quitted her retirement at Wharncliffe to grace that Court where her friends were in such favour. Her advent was hailed with a universal burst of admiration, in which the King and Prince of Wales joined. The triumph of her beauty was confirmed by the sparkling vivacity of her wit and conversation. At the same time she cultivated the society of all the notabilities of the period, Pope, Addison, Congreve, Young, Steele, and others, with several of whom she corresponded frequently. With Mrs Steele, we learn from a letter of Mr Montagu, she had been intimate before her marriage, probably from the contiguity of her residence to Hampton Court. Pope allowed the fervour of his admiration to transport him almost the length of a passionate lover. Independent of the impropriety, the absurdity of this from such a quarter led to a reception of his extravagance that terminated their friendship, and so mortified his vanity, that his subsequent conduct reflects indelible disgrace upon him. In his case, Congreve's line about the "fury of a woman scorned," appears to have been transferred to the other sex.

In 1716, the embassy to the Porte having become vacant, Mr Montagu gladly exchanged it for his Treasury appointment, and Lady Mary realised her ardent desire for travel—in which she was destined so much to distinguish herself both by her genius and philanthropy. War was then raging violently between the Turks and Imperialists, and, in accordance with the strong desire of the other Powers of Europe for a mediation, instructions were given to the new envoy and Sir R. Sutton, who removed from Constantinople to Vienna, for a plan of pacification.

Early in August, Mr Montagu and Lady Mary started on their journey, through Holland, Germany, and Hungary, receiving the greatest attention at all the Courts on the way, and making some stay at Vienna. From thence they returned, for some unexplained reason, to Hanover, where George I. was then staying, and only reached Adrianople on the 1st of April following. In that city, to which the Sultan had removed his Court, they remained two months. The tediousness of the journey was relieved, however, at least to Lady Mary, by the correspondence of her friends at home.*

The novel and luxurious life and scenes which presented themselves in this

"Clime of the East and land of the sun,"

---

* A few weeks after her departure, Pope writes :—" How desirous I must be of a correspondence with a person who has taught me, long ago, that it was possible to esteem at first sight as to love, and who has since ruined me for all the conversation of one sex, and almost all the friendship of the other. . . . How often have I been quietly going to take possession of that tranquillity and indolence I had long found in the country, when one evening of your conversation has spoiled me for a *solitaire* too! Books have lost their effect upon me; and I was convinced, since I saw you, that there is something more powerful than philosophy; and since I heard you, that there is one alone wiser than all the sages."

seem powerfully to have impressed her own mind, and the impression has been transferred to the pages of her correspondence, with a vividness and charming felicity that have never been surpassed, and recall "The Arabian Nights." She had been an early versifier, and her juvenile effusions remain; but, like Addison, her prose was destined to give a far higher notion of her poetical genius than her verse. During the excessive heat of the summer months, they retired, as was customary, either to the shores of the Bosphorus or the shades of the delicious forest scenery at Belgrade, about fourteen miles distant from Constantinople. There was a custom universally prevalent throughout the country to which she gave her early and earnest attention. This was what was there termed *grafting*, or inoculating for the small-pox, in which she felt the greater interest from having lost a brother, to whom she was much attached, by that malignant disease. Its ravages in these islands in former times were terrific, and only to be equalled by the more recent scourge of the cholera, while those whose lives were spared were generally cruelly marred for life. Of the efficacy of the simple remedy, Lady Mary soon became fully convinced, and proved her faith and courage by trying it on her own son, and her patriotism in resolving to extend the blessing to her own country.

At Mr Wortley's interview with the Sultan, who was then at Philipopoli, he made his public entry into that city as British ambassador, with a retinue of one hundred and fifty persons, besides the guards. After some time, finding the negotiations ineffectual, and his friends thinking he would better consult his own interests by his presence at Court, where he enjoyed the personal favour of the King, he received letters of recall under the Privy Seal, October 28, 1717, and a private one from his friend Addison, by whom they were countersigned, as Secretary of State, acquainting him with certain arrangements which had been made for his advantage. He did not complete his plans, however, for returning until the following June, when he began his voyage, through the Archipelago, taking with him some curious oriental MSS. (particularly those of "The Arabian Tales") which he had collected, and an inscribed marble from the shores of the Hellespont, which he presented to Trinity College, Cambridge. In the course of their voyage they landed at Tunis, from thence crossed the Mediterranean to Genoa, and proceeded home by way of Turin, Lyons, and Paris, arriving in England the latter end of October 1718, after an absence of two years.

On their return they were received with the most flattering attention at Court, where the regard in which Lady Mary was held for her beauty and wit was enhanced by the celebrity she had acquired in her travels. But she confesses in some of her letters that the great world did not satisfy her, and that her happy hours were dedicated to a few intimates. She renewed her intercourse with men of letters. Pope prevailed on Mr Montagu to take a house at Twickenham, and on Lady Mary to sit for her portrait to Kneller, to adorn his villa there. But all these interests and avocations did not divert her from the philanthropic object on which she was bent, of introducing inoculation, which she pursued, despite of incredible obloquy and opposition both from prejudice and interested motives, until she brought it to a successful result, by which she has earned the gratitude of her country. It is to be regretted that she did not confine her attention to such laudable objects, but about the same time was one of those led away by the mania for speculating in the nefarious South Sea bubble,—an infatuation almost universal at the time.

The date of her difference with Pope is uncertain, but there seems to have been a gradual coolness, from different causes, before the final rupture. In 1720 she mentions in one of her letters sometimes meeting Congreve, but Pope very seldom, at the same time she speaks of his subterranean grotto, which he had fitted up with looking-glasses, and its fine effect, as a thing she had heard of but not seen. She seemed to give him credit for selfishness in his proposed emendations of the "Town Eclogues," which she had written before going abroad, by disingenuously gaining the credit of having written them, or all that was best in them; and Pope became jealous of her partiality for the Countess of Bristol and her son, Lord Hervey, with whom she wrote joint verses. But, so late as 1727, there appears to have been no actual break between them, as she is mentioned in Gay's allegorical verses to Pope on the completion of his "Iliad" in that year, among the friends supposed to greet him. Her account of the final ground of quarrel was that he, when she least expected anything of the kind, having made some extravagant advances, her sense of the ludicrous, in spite of her efforts to look grave and angry, so overcame her that she gave way to an immoderate fit of laughter. Of the unmanly scurrility of his subsequent slanderous attacks upon her, it is only necessary to say, that the subterfuges to which he resorted to exonerate himself on that as on other similar occasions, so far as he was concerned, only aggravated the transaction.

Lady Mary's health in 1739 was in a declining state, and this was the plea of a step she now took which has always been regarded as a mysterious one,—her going to reside abroad alone. There had always been a great discrepancy between the disposition of Mr Montagu and Lady Mary, of which he seemed to dread the consequences even as a lover. If there was any difference between them, there was at least no open rupture, as she wrote him several letters in the course of her journey, and they afterwards corresponded. Her own account of the matter, (in a letter to Lady Pomfret from Venice, in the first year of her residence there,) was that she had long been persuading Mr Montagu to go abroad, which his public and parliamentary duties prevented his immediately doing; and, at length, tired of delay, she had, with his consent, started alone, he promising to follow her; but that till she knew whether or not to expect him, she could not meet her correspondent at Rome. Whether time went on insensibly without his being able to keep the engagement until separate residence became not difficult of reconcilement to both, or there was any other cause, of which this was merely the cover, it is fruitless to inquire. Certainly her inclination for foreign travel, at least, had been communicated to Mr Montagu before their marriage. After residing in Venice for better than a year, and forming many connexions with the noble families of that wonderful city, she made a short tour to Florence, Naples, and Rome. Spending the winter at Avignon and Chambery, she ultimately fixed her summer residence at Louvere, on the shores of Lake Isco, in the Venetian territory, with a view to the mineral waters of that place, from which she derived great benefit. In that secluded but beautiful place she took up her residence in a deserted palace, and gave herself up with the energy of her nature to the interests of a country life, planned her garden, superintended her vineyard and her silkworms, and by her kindness to the simple inhabitants, whom she instructed in various useful arts, became idolised among them. In that retirement, with books almost as her sole society,—but her correspondence evincing the deep interest she ever felt in her daughter, Lady Bute, and her family,— she spent many years of calm enjoyment, only interrupted by occasional visits to Genoa and Padua. She afterwards quitted her solitude and, in 1758, settled in Venice, where she remained till the death of Mr Wortley Montagu in 1761.

Writing to her husband from Venice, she says—"It is impossible to be better treated—I may even say, more courted,—than I am here. I am very glad of your good fortune in London. You may remember, I always told you it was in your power to make the first figure in the House of Commons."

She did not long survive Mr Montagu. At the instigation of Lady Bute, her daughter, she proceeded to England, where she arrived in October, after an absence of two and twenty years. But she bore with her a fatal malady, from which she had long suffered with the utmost fortitude. We are told that those who saw her after her return, "spoke with delight of the clearness, vivacity, and raciness of her conversation, and the youthful vigour that seemed to animate her mind. She did not appear displeased at the general curiosity to see her, nor void of curiosity herself concerning the new things and people that her native country presented to her view after so long an absence."* Her decease, which occurred August 21, 1762, was probably accelerated by the fatigue and excitement of her journey. Such was the comet-like career of this extraordinary woman, whose course was everywhere surrounded with a brilliant and luminous atmosphere, with courtiers, diplomatists, and poets in her train, attracted by her rare beauty and grace, and a wit yet more rare—sharp, pungent, and racy. If it did not make her enemies, with the love of mischief that accompanied it, she was fortunate indeed. The extraordinary resources and inherent energy of her mind were singularly displayed in her solitary foreign residence, where she surrounded herself with a paradise of delights in her bowers, her nightingales, her silkworms, her bees, and her vines, by the shores of Lake Isco. With the extraordinary tenacity of beauty to the remembrances of her youth, and a fear that haunted her, and breaks out in her letters even before her departure abroad—that of growing old, she had not consulted a mirror for the last eleven years of her life.

Of her family, her daughter, who she said from a child had been everything she could desire, was married to the Earl of Bute, and formed her chief interest in life. Her son, on the contrary, except that he monopolised the good looks of the family, was everything that she could have deprecated. He led an erratic and wandering life, beginning by running off to sea from school. He was possessed of

* Anecdotes by Lady Louisa Stuart—Lord Wharncliffe's edition of her works.

showy abilities, but joined to flightiness and duplicity. He wrote "Reflections on the Rise and Fall of the Ancient Republics," and for some time was representative for Bossiney in Cornwall. At length, wearied out with his conduct, and feeling him to be irreclaimable, Mr Montagu, by his will, cut him off from the succession to the family property, leaving him only a small allowance, but with a proviso that, if he left a legitimate heir, the property should return to him. Of this he endeavoured to take advantage by a Fleet marriage, but did not live long with his wife, and had no issue. He resided in the East for many years, where he cultivated rabbinical learning, and, it is said, professed Mohammedanism. After his father's death he returned to Europe; and in 1776 an advertisement appeared in one of the London papers,—which his family believed to have come from him,—offering marriage to a suitable lady who might have an heir ready to hand. It described the advertiser as "A gentleman who has filled two successive seats in Parliament, is nearly sixty years of age, lives in great splendour and hospitality, and from whom a considerable estate must pass away if he dies without issue." The requirements were "genteel birth and polite manners," &c. It was supposed that he had met with a person with the requisite qualifications, who was to meet him at Paris, but at Lyons, on his way thither, while eating of a beccafigue for supper, a bone stuck in his throat and caused his death.* Well might Lady Mary speak of the vanity of founding a family.

* Though the statement is repeated in Lord Wharncliffe's edition of Lady Montagu's works, a writer in Nichols' annotated edition of the *Tatler*, (vol. i. p. 42,) denies the advertisement, and professedly on the best authority, having any relation to Mr Montagu.

To return from what, if it appear too much of a digression, was too great a temptation to be resisted in a work professing to introduce as many of the notabilities of the time as possible. The third volume of the *Tatler* was inscribed to Earl, then Baron Cowper and Lord Chancellor. He was the most distinguished speaker in the Whig party, and Steele in celebrating his merits says,—

"The graceful manner, the apt gesture, and the assumed concern, are impotent helps to persuasion, in comparison of the honest countenance of him who utters what he really means. . . . It is this noble simplicity which makes you surpass mankind in the faculties wherein mankind are distinguished from other creatures,—reason and speech. . . . Had I any pretensions to a fame of this kind," the writer adds, with a subtle and graceful turn of compliment, "I should, above all other themes, attempt a panegyric upon my Lord Cowper; for the only sure way to a reputation for eloquence, in an age wherein that perfect orator lives, is to choose an argument upon which he himself must of necessity be silent."

The son of Sir William Cowper, Baronet, of Hertford, and educated to the bar, he had attained to all the honours of his profession at an almost unprecedentedly early age. Almost immediately on commencing practice he became Recorder of Colchester, and made a successful appearance in Parliament as representative for Hertford in 1695. In the following year he was one of the Crown counsel in the trial of Sir William Perkins for high treason in attempting the assassination of King William, and gave his support to the bill of attainder against Fenwick. In 1705 he succeeded Sir Nathan Wright as Lord Keeper of the Great Seal, the following year was created Baron Cowper of Wingham, as a reward of his services in promoting the legislative union with Scotland, and rose to be Lord High Chancellor in that succeeding. This dignity he retained till the resignation of the Whig ministry, when, though not a party man, he resigned the seals in September 1710, which the Queen reluctantly received. On the accession of George I., in 1714, he was again appointed Lord Chancellor, and, on resigning the Great Seal in 1718, was created Earl Cowper and Viscount Fordwich. As Chancellor he had dispensed with the customary new year's gifts of the members of the bar. His sagacity enabled him to foresee the destructive consequences of the South Sea bubble, which on principle he opposed; and as a proof of his incorruptibility to party influence, it is recorded that, though in habits of friendship with Marlborough, he resisted every attempt to induce him to put the Great Seal to a commission, making him generalissimo for life. Among his latest public acts were his opposition to the bill of pains and penalties against Atterbury, and an act for the imposing of a tax upon Roman Catholics. About the same time insinuations, reflecting on his political fidelity, were made by one Christopher Layer, who, in the course of his examination on a charge of high treason, endeavoured to implicate him with certain parties who were seeking the expulsion of the House of Brunswick. The charge was indignantly denied by Lord Cowper, who demanded an inquiry, but was assured by his brother peers that his character was unimpeachable. His decease occurred in 1723.

High professional and oratorical eminence was universally conceded to Lord Cowper. In the latter, Bolingbroke alone could be put in comparison with him; and if eloquence be the art of persuasion, Cowper would bear the palm. "He never spoke," says Chesterfield, "without universal applause. The ears and the eyes gave him up the hearts and understandings of the audience." A contemporary applied to him Ben Jonson's encomium on Bacon, and the notice of Swift towards a Whig, considering the quarter from which it comes, may be considered highly favourable. "As to other accomplishments," he says, "he was what we usually call a piece of a scholar and a good logical reasoner."

The fourth and last dedication of the *Tatler* volumes was to Charles, Lord Halifax, whom Steele addressed from "The Hovel at Hamptonwick," an elegant villa previously alluded to, saying that he "indulged a certain vanity in dating from this little covert, where he had frequently had the honour of his company, and had received from him many obligations." After telling him, in the usual complimentary strain of epistles dedicatory, that the bright images of the wits of past ages, and the noble plans of statesmen for the administration of affairs, were equally the familiar objects of his knowledge, he proceeds to add, as his crowning excellence—

"That wit and learning have, from your example, fallen into a new era. Your patronage has produced those arts, which before shunned the commerce of the world, into the service of life; and it is to you we owe that the man of wit has turned himself to be a man of business. The false delicacy of men of genius, and the objections which others were apt to insinuate against their abilities for entering into affairs, have equally vanished: and experience has shewn that men of letters are not only qualified with a greater capacity, but also a greater integrity, in the despatch of business."*

---

* Among the other instances to this effect, more remarkable at a period so incredibly corrupt than it would be at the present day, Addison refused a bank note of L.300, and afterwards a diamond ring, of the same value, from a Major Dunbar for some service, as appears by a letter of his published by Edward Curll.

Charles Montagu, Lord Halifax, to whom these high praises were not unjustly accorded, was grandson of an Earl of Manchester, but, being a younger son, was obliged to push his fortune. He was born at Horton, in Northamptonshire, April 16, 1661, and received the first part of his education at Westminster, from whence he proceeded to Cambridge. Some verses he wrote during his residence there on the death of Charles II. having attracted the notice of the Earl of Dorset, who was the great patron of men of letters at that time, that nobleman gave him an invitation to town, and made him acquainted with the leading wits. There, in 1687, he united with Prior—who as a youth had been entirely brought forward by Dorset—in the composition of "The City Mouse and Country Mouse," a satire on Dryden's "Hind and Panther," an encomium on Romanism, the result of the melancholy mercenary apostasy of his later years. In allusion to this popular travestie, when he was taken to Court by Lord Dorset he is said to have presented him to King William, saying, "Sire, I have brought a mouse to wait on your majesty"—to which the King is said to have replied, "You do well to put me in the way of making a man of him," and to have granted him a pension of L.500 a year. He was one of those who had signed the invitation to the Prince of Orange. Having married the Countess Dowager of Manchester, he relinquished his original design of taking orders, and obtained by purchase the Clerkship of the Council. Obtaining soon after a seat in Parliament, he soon distinguished himself by his energy, his eloquence and skill in debate, his business tact, and knowledge of constitutional questions, and rose to be the leader of the Whigs in the House. His promotion was rapid. He became successively a Lord of the Treasury, (1691-2,) Chancellor of the Exchequer, (1694,) and First Lord of the Treasury, (1698,) which office he again held on the accession of the House of Hanover. For his services in restoring public credit at a very critical financial crisis, and in effecting a new coinage, when at the head of the Exchequer, he received the thanks of the Commons, and was raised to the dignity of the peerage in 1700, under the title of Baron Halifax. It was during his administration that the Bank of England and East India Company were founded. During the Tory ascendency in Queen Anne's reign, articles of impeachment were twice presented against him by the Commons, to which he had given offence by supporting the measure in favour of a standing army. He was, however, effectually shielded by the peers. Party warfare is never very scrupulous, but at this period there was an intensity of malignity about it that seemed to discard all humanity. The individual who had rendered himself obnoxious was to be ruined hopelessly. In the same spirit they attempted to get up an impeachment of Lord Godolphin for corruption, although a minister of greater probity and ability never was at the head of the Treasury, nor was there a shadow of ground for any imputation of delinquency. Halifax had given unpardonable offence to Queen Anne by summoning the son of the Elector of Hanover as a peer of Parliament, under the title of the Duke of Cambridge, and she had in consequence, at the commencement of her reign, struck his name off the list of the Privy Council with her own hand. But he had not followed the example of his opponents by attempting to thwart the Government with factious opposition in consequence. On the accession of George I., he was again appointed First Lord of the Treasury, made a Knight of the Garter, and created Viscount Sunbury and Earl of Halifax. He did not long survive these honours, his death occurring the following year. His poems and speeches were published soon after. As a poet he probably never would have stood very high, but he is entitled to the praise of an enlightened politician, and a munificent patron of letters. The title of a Macænas has been justly accorded him. It was not merely to Steele that he was a warm friend, but with consistent munificence he patronised almost all those men of letters from whom the era has been termed Augustan. He made the fortunes of Addison and Congreve; and Prior, Locke, and Sir Isaac Newton were all promoted under his administration.

CHAPTER VI.

Letters of Steele during the publication of the *Tatler*—To his wife, to Mrs Manley, Dennis, and Swift—Steele appointed a Commissioner of Stamps—Notices of Steele in Swift's Journal to Stella—Notice of Public Events—Change of Ministry—Harley and St John—Steele's diversion in favour of his friends in *Tatler*—Loses his Gazetteership in consequence.

BEFORE following him in his new field of literary labour, let us bring up the arrears of Steele's correspondence left unnoticed during the continuance of the *Tatler*.

LETTER CXXV.   *To Mrs Steele.*
                                                April 19, 1709.

DEAR PRUE,—I have been with Tryon ;* he owns to some effects which will be of assistance to me. I call Heaven to witness, I value nothing but as you are partaker of it. Do not cast yourself down ; but depend upon it, that I shall bring you home what will make things have a cheerful aspect, and will do what may contribute to your satisfaction, which is all the ambition of yours eternally,   RICH. STEELE.

LETTER CXXVI.   *To Mrs Steele.*
                                                April 23, 1709.

DEAREST CREATURE,—This matter must be deferred till some hour in the evening, or some other day, for I cannot have money till after chapel. I am your faithful, tender husband,   RICH. STEELE.

LETTER CXXVII.   *To Mrs Steele, Berry Street.*
                                                May 5, 1709.

DEAR WIFE,—I desire you would pluck up a good spirit if possible, and come in a chair, the boy with you, who shall find me at the coffee-house

---

* " Who was in some way, as agent or otherwise, connected with his Barbadoes property."

under Scotland Yard gate, from whence we will go see a convenient place. Do not be dejected, if you value the life and happiness of your faithful

RICH. STEELE.

I enclose ten shillings.

LETTER CXXVIII.   *To Mrs Steele.*

May 5, 1709.

DEAR PRUE,—I desire you would go to the assignation between us at Westminster. Mr Montagu* has desired me to go with him to the Park; after I come from thence, I will come to you with good news.—Yours, ever, ever,   RICH. STEELE.

LETTER CXXIX.   *To Mrs Steele.*

May 5, 1709.

DEAR WIFE,—I cannot express to you the real sorrow the inequality of my behaviour gives me, when I reflect that I am in passion before the best of women. Dear Prue, forgive me; I will neglect nothing which may contribute to our ease together; and you shall always find me your affectionate, faithful, and tender husband,   RICH. STEELE.

LETTER CXXX.   *To Mrs Steele.*

May 5, 1709.

DEAR WIFE,—There is no doubt we shall be easy and happy in a few days. My dear life, nothing troubles me sorely, but the affront that *insufferable brute*† has put upon you, which I shall find ways to make her repent.—I am, my dear creature, entirely yours,   RICH. STEELE.

You shall hear from me in the morning.

LETTER CXXXI.   *To Mrs Steele.*

May 7, 1709.

DEAR PRUE,—I have been with Mr Compton, and have his orders to be at the office, with a request to keep it very secret that he does me this favour, for fear of his being importuned on the same account by others of the family.‡—I am your most affectionate and tender husband,

RICH. STEELE.

---

* Ed. Wortley Montagu, Esq.

† This probably refers, as Nichols seems to think, to the landlady of the house in Bury or Berry Street, as it is here spelt.

‡ "There is nothing known to throw any light upon this affair."

LETTER CXXXII.　　　To Mrs Steele.
　　　　　　　　　　　　　　　　　　May 7, 1709.
DEAR PRUE,—I am just drinking a pint of wine, and will come home forthwith. I am with Mr Elliott, settling things.—Yours ever, ever,
　　　　　　　　　　　　　　　　　　RICH. STEELE.

LETTER CXXXIII.　　　To Mrs Steele.
　　　　　　　　　　　　　Twelve o'clock, May 28, 1709.
DEAR PRUE,—I have received money, but cannot come home till about four o'clock, having appointed Mr Mills here at Moore's chambers at two o'clock.—Yours ever,　　　　　　　　　　RICH. STEELE.

LETTER CXXXIV.　　　To Mrs Steele.
　　　　　　　　　　　　　　　　　　June 9, 1709.
DEAR PRUE,—I put myself to the pain of absence from you at dinner by waiting to speak with Salkeild; therefore I hope you will forgive me for what I am punished in committing.

Dear Prue, I am unreservedly and faithfully yours,　　RICH. STEELE.

LETTER CXXXV.　　To Mrs Steele, last door but two, left hand, Berry Street,
　　　　　　　　　　　King's Head, Pall-Mall, Oct. 4, 1709.
DEAR PRUE,—I have done everything effectually which I went about. Mr Hopkins is coming to me hither, where we shall stay till a little after ten.—Yours faithfully,　　　　　　　　　RICH. STEELE.

LETTER CXXXVI.　　　To Mrs Steele.
　　　　　　　　　　　　　Savoy, Nutt's,* July 19, 1709.
DEAR PRUE,—I send this to let you know that I am come hither, and am obliged to despatch the main of the business† of this place to-night. As soon as I have done, I will come home to my dearest companion.—I am wholly yours,　　　　　　　　RICH. STEELE.

LETTER CXXXVII.　　To Mrs Steele, at Mr Sewell's, in King Street, near
　　　　　　　　　　　Whitehall Coffee-house.
　　　　　　　　　　　　　From Mr Nutt's, July 25, 1709.
DEAR PRUE,—I have finished the *Gazette* at the office; and am here ending the other business,‡ in order to have my evening with my wife

---

* The well-known printer.
† See *Tatler*, No. 44 and 45, vol. ii.
‡ See *Tatler*, No. 46, vol. ii.—*Auranzebe*.

Prue. Here is next door a fellow that makes old wigs new; therefore pray send both mine in the bed-chamber, by this boy, to your loving, devoted, obedient husband,   RICH. STEELE.

LETTER CXXXVIII.   *To Mrs Steele, at Mr Sewell's, King Street.*
July 28, 1709.
DEAR PRUE,—I enclose two guineas, and will come home exactly at seven.—Yours tenderly,   RICH. STEELE.

The following letter to a lady who was rather a voluminous author in her day, though not a person of much character, was occasioned by allusions in one or two *Tatler* papers written by Swift, who was subsequently the coadjutor of the complainant in writing for the Tory paper, the *Examiner*. She was afterwards reconciled to Steele, and in 1717 dedicated to him the tragedy of " Lucius," declaring at the same time that it was " only an act of justice, and to end a former misunderstanding between the author and him whom she here makes her patron," adding, that " she had not known a greater mortification than when she reflected on the severities which had flowed from her pen."

LETTER CXXXIX.   *To Mrs Manley.**
Sept. 6, 1709.
MADAM,—I have received a letter from you, wherein you tax me as if I were Bickerstaff, with falling upon you as author of " Atalantis," and the

---

* " This letter, which is printed here from Steele's autograph, has no date; but in the imperfect copy of it published by Mrs Manley, in her ' Memoirs of Europe towards the close of the eighth century,' dedicated to Isaac Bickerstaff, Esq., it is dated Sept. 6, 1709. Mrs Manley affirms that she transcribed the letter *verbatim ;* but it appears from comparing her transcript with the original, that she thought proper to omit the two paragraphs relative to what had happened between Steele and her, and his refusal of a certain sum of money which she had asked in loan, and also to change the emphatical word 'kindnesses' to 'services.' A note on the *New* TATLER, No. 65, to which the curious reader is referred, throws much light on this letter. See *New* TATLER, No. 63, p. 321. It is at present sufficient

person who honoured me with a character in that celebrated piece. What has happened formerly between us can be of no use to either to repeat. I solemnly assure you, you wrong me in this as much as you know you do in all else you have been pleased to say of me. I had not money when you did me the favour to ask a loan of a trifling sum of me. I had the greatest sense imaginable of the kind notice you gave me when I was going on to my ruin, and am so far from retaining an inclination to revenge the inhumanity with which you have treated me, that I give myself a satisfaction in that you have cancelled with injuries a friendship which I should never have been able to return. This will convince you how little I am an ingrate; for I believe you will allow, no one that is so mean as to be forgetful of kindnesses, ever fails in returning injuries. As for the verses you quote of mine,* they are still my opinion; and your sex, as well as your quality of a gentlewoman (a justice you would not do my birth and education) shall always preserve you against the pen of your provoked most humble servant, RICH. STEELE.

LETTER CXL.   *To Mrs Steele, at her lodging, over against the King's-head, Downing Street.*

Sept. 25, 1709.

DEAR PRUE,—I send this to put thy tenderness at rest; and acquaint you that Mr Margate had been so friendly as to take effectual care before he saw me.—I am, yours eternally, RICH. STEELE.

LETTER CXLI.   *To Dr Swift.*

Lord Sunderland's Office, Oct. 8, 1709.

DEAR SIR,—Mr Secretary Addison went this morning out of town, and left behind him an agreeable command for me, *viz.*, to forward the enclosed, which Lord Halifax sent him for you. I assure you, no man could

---

to mention that her friend Dr Swift was the real author of the *two most mighty Tatlers* to which Mrs Manley refers in the furious dedication of the book above mentioned. Steele disavows them with great truth, and with admirable magnanimity conceals the real writer to the last, though beyond measure provoked to the discovery of these and some other obnoxious papers, productions of the same pen."

* "The verses of Steele here alluded to, according to Mrs Manley's account of them, are as follows:—

"Against a woman's wit 'tis full as low,
Your malice as your bravery to show."

say more in praise of another than he did in your behalf, at that noble Lord's table on Wednesday last. I doubt not but you will find by the enclosed the effect it had upon him. No opportunity is omitted among powerful men to upbraid them with your stay in Ireland. The company that day at dinner were Lord Edward Russell, Lord Essex, Mr Maynwaring, Mr Addison, and myself. I have heard such things said of that same Bishop of Clogher* with you, that I have often said he must be entered *ad eundem* in our House of Lords. Mr Philips+ dined with me yesterday; he is still a shepherd, and walks very lonely through this unthinking crowd in London. I wonder you do not write sometimes to me.

The town is in great expectation from Bickerstaff; what passed at the election for his first table‡ being to be published this day se'en-night. I have not seen Ben Tooke § a great while, but long to usher you and yours into the world. Not that there can be anything added by me to your fame, but to walk bareheaded before you.—I am, Sir, your most obedient and most humble servant,   RICH. STEELE.

LETTER CXLII.   *To Mrs Steele.*

Nov. 20, 1709.

DEAR WIFE,—I have been in great pain of body and mind since I came out. You are extremely cruel to a generous nature, that has a tenderness for you that renders your least *dishumour* insupportably afflicting. After short starts of passion, not to be inclined to reconciliation, is what is against all rules of Christianity and justice. When I come, I beg to be kindly received, or this will have as ill an effect upon my fortune, as on my mind and body.   RICH. STEELE.

LETTER CXLIII.   *To Mrs Steele.*||

Tonson's, nine at night, [1709.]

DEAR PRUE,—I took Mr Clay with me to Tryon's, and we shall have justice done me as soon as possible, and immediate money.

There are new orders come hither from the Secretary's, which obliges me to wait for the proof.¶—Yours ever,   RICH. STEELE.

---

* Dr St George Ash.

+ Ambrose Philips, author of "The Distressed Mother," a tragedy, and some pastorals, &c.

‡ See *Tatler,* No. 81, and notes in new edition.

§ The bookseller.

|| "At Mr Sewell's house, in King Street, Westminster."

¶ Of the *Gazette.*

LETTER CXLIV.   To Mrs Steele.
[1709.]

Mr Tryon and Mr Water having desired to meet me at three o'clock, and the *Gazette* being not quite finished, though now near two, I have not time to dine. Therefore can only wish you a good stomach, and not come myself.

Dear Prue, you will find my service better than that of Binns, or anybody else.—Yours ever,
RICH. STEELE.

LETTER CXLV.   To Mrs Steele.
[1709.]

MY DEAR CREATURE,—I have received some money, and I will send you word in the morning of everything, and convince you of what you wish.—I am, thou best of women, thy friend, servant, and husband,
RICH. STEELE.

Be at rest, for all is well.

LETTER CXLVI.   To Mrs Steele.*
[*Tuesday, June* .... 1709.]

DEAR PRUE,—I send you this to tell you that I am going back again into the city, in order to dine with the gentleman who is to act between me and Tryon, and hope to bring things to so much reason as to be at ease in matters now pressing.

Dear Prue, I desire you to be careful of thy dear self. If thou goest to Binns, I will call for thee there.
RICH. STEELE.

From Mr Salkield's, one o'clock.

LETTER CXLVII.   To Mrs Steele.†
Oct. 1, [1709.]

DEAR WIFE,—I have been so much employed in settling some business to prevent being cheated by a set of shuffling fellows, that I could not get out of town. To-morrow I will write at large, if I cannot come, by a messenger on purpose on one of my horses. In the meantime, beg pardon for sending so small a sum.—I am your affectionate husband, and faithful humble servant,
RICH. STEELE.

---

* "At the third house, right hand, Berry Street, turning out of Germain Street."

† "At Hampton Court."

LETTER CXLVIII. To Mrs Steele.

Oct. 15, [1709.]

DEAR MADAM,—I have received a letter from you this day by your new man Jack, dated the 15th of last month.* I will wait upon you as soon as I can. I wonder at the question you sent me—for who should inter that gentleman but his executors? I am your most obedient husband,

RICH. STEELE.

LETTER CXLIX. To Mrs Steele.

Dec. 20, [1709.]

DEAR WIFE,—I beg of you to go to the Cockpit, and make my apology to my mother; and expect me as soon as I can possibly be disengaged from some company, where I am settling some matters I have already discoursed of to you.—Yours faithfully, RICH. STEELE.

LETTER CL. To Mrs Steele, at Mrs Binn's Lodgings, in Silver Street, near Golden Square.

Feb. 15, 1709–10.

DEAR WIFE,—I believe I am the first that ever rejoiced at the flight of one he loved. After I was done writing,† I went up to visit my sick wife, and found she was herself gone a visiting. I wish you had given me the pleasure of knowing you were so well, it would have given what I was writing a more lively turn.—I am your affectionate, tender, observant, and indulgent husband, RICH. STEELE.

LETTER CLI. To Mrs Steele.

April 7, 1710.

DEAR PRUE—I enclose you a receipt for the saucepan and spoon, and a note of £23 of Lewis's, which will make up the £50 I promised for your ensuing occasion.‡

I know no happiness in this life in any degree comparable to the pleasure I have in your person and society; I only beg of you to add to your other charms a fearfulness to see a man that loves you in pain and uneasiness, to make us happy as it is possible to be in this life. Rising a little in a morning, and being disposed to a cheerfulness, [*some words want-*

---

* Meaning, doubtless, by an oversight.
† *Tatler*, No. 134.
‡ The approaching confinement of her first child.

ing,] would not be amiss.—I am your most affectionate husband, and obedient servant, RICH. STEELE.

There are papers in the parlour window, dated from Hamburgh and other places, which I want.

LETTER CLII.　　　　To Mrs Steele.

May 3, 1710.

DEAR PRUE,—I shall stay at Tonson's till towards four o'clock; for having made up this day my account with Nutt,* I am doing the same here, being resolved to understand my affairs, and communicate them to you for your ease and convenience from this hour forward.—Yours eternally, RICH. STEELE.

LETTER CLIII.　　　　To Mrs Steele.

July 3, 1710.

DEAR PRUE,—I shall not dine with you, but will be with you before five, in order to take the air with you.—Yours ever, RICH. STEELE.

LETTER CLIV.　　　　From Mr Dennis.

July 28, 1710.

SIR,—I sent a letter on the 28th to your house, directed to Captain Steele, and desiring to see him that night, that I might ask his advice upon a business of importance, softly intimating at the same time that it was not in my power to wait upon him. But, having neither seen him, nor heard from him, I fancy that my old friend is departed, and that some gentleman has succeeded him in the old house, with the same name and the same martial title; a chance that happens oftener in the world than some people imagine. How should I have been surprised, in case I had gone myself, expecting from the similitude of name and title to have seen my old acquaintance! how should I have been surprised to have found a man with quite another mind, and quite another countenance! My old friend, as I thought at least, had civility, had humanity, had a good and engaging officiousness; and as I did not take him to want good nature, so he had what the French call a good countenance, that is, the countenance of one who is pleased with him who talks to him. But I suppose I should have found nothing of all this in the noble captain who succeeds him. You will say, perhaps, that you had no reason to make a visit to one whom you knew not, and are resolved not to know. But then, noble captain, you ought to have sent back my letter, and to have given me to under-

---

* Printer of the *Tatler*, as Tonson was the publisher.

stand that you are not the person I took you for; that you should have enough to do if you were obliged to own all the acquaintance of the captain your predecessor; that I am not the first man who has made this mistake, and shall not probably be the last. Had you done this, I had had no replication to make to so equitable an answer. I should only, perhaps, have advised you, in order to the preventing some troublesome visits, and some impertinent letters, to cause an advertisement to be inserted in Squire Bickerstaff's next *Lucubrations,* by which the world might be informed that the Captain Steele who lives now in Bury Street is not the captain of the same name who lived there two years ago; and that the acquaintance of the military person who inhabited there formerly may go look for their old friend even where they can find him.—I am yours, &c,

J. DENNIS.

LETTER CLV.   *To Mrs Steele.*
Half hour after eight, July 29, 1710.

DEAR WIFE,—I stay in town* to-night, very much against my inclination, having business of consequence with Mr Montagu, who goes out of town to-morrow, in order to take a voyage.—I am yours entirely,

RICH. STEELE.

LETTER CLVI. *To Mrs Steele, at Mrs Bradshaw's, at Sandyend.*
Cockpit, Secretary's Office, eight o'clock, Aug. 8, 1710.

MY DEAR,—When I was going out of town, I heard my Lord Treasurer† had this day resigned his staff, and was to [be succeeded] by my Lord Halifax. The resignation I find confirmed here, but others are said to succeed him. I stay in town to-night to see a friend who will be able to give me proper lights into the present affairs. Good night, dear Prue, and sleep pleased, for all will do well; for God will bless us.—Your faithful, affectionate husband,   RICH. STEELE.

LETTER CLVII. *To Mrs Steele, at Mrs Bradshaw's house, at Sandyend, over against the Bull Alehouse in Fulham Road.*
Berry Street, half hour after six, Wednesday, Aug. 9, 1710.

DEAR PRUE,—Thou art such a foolish tender thing that there is no living with thee.

---

* It appears from the next letter that they had moved to Sandyend, a hamlet near Fulham, where Addison also resided, the latter in the once residence of Nell Gwynne.

† Lord Godolphin. The office was put into commission August 10, and Earl Powlett at the head.—*Nichols.*

I broke my rest last night, because I knew you would be such a fool as not to sleep. Pray come home by this morning's coach, if you are impatient; but, if you are not here before noon, I will come down to you in the evening; but I must make visits this morning, to hear what is doing.—Yours ever, RICH. STEELE.

LETTER CLVIII.   To Mrs Steele.
Cockpit, Aug. 9, 1710.
DEAR PRUE,—I cannot possibly come, expecting orders here, which I must overlook, and having not half done my other business at the Savoy.*

Dear creature, come in the morning coach; and, if I can, I will return with you in the evening. Pray wrap yourself very warm.—Yours ever,
RICH. STEELE.

LETTER CLIX.   To Mrs Steele.
Bull Head, Clare Market, Aug. 24, 1710.
DEAR PRUE,—I beg of you to meet your brother Whig, Martyn,† and myself here. Ask for me.—Yours faithfully, RICH. STEELE.

LETTER CLX.   To Mrs Steele.
I am doing my business and cannot come home to dinner, but stay to come home more cheerfully.—Yours, RICH. STEELE.

LETTER CLXI.   To Mrs Steele.
Vere Street, Aug. 30, 1710.
MY DEAR PRUE,—If you can be so good as to forgive all that is passed, you shall [not] hereafter know any suffering from indiscretion or negligence. I have taken care of the matter mentioned in the letter you opened yesterday. Pray let me know how *Lugger* does. I am waiting here for a third person to go and receive money. Martyn sent an excuse yesterday that he was sick, and promises to come at ten to-day, but I shall not wait or depend on that, though I daresay he would do all he could.—Your affectionate and tender husband, RICH. STEELE.

Pray send linen, for I am to meet the parties before nine.

---

* See *Tatler*, No. 209, vol. v.
† Richard Martyn, Esq., one of Steele's colleagues, was a commisioner in the Stamp-Office.—*Nichols.*

LETTER CLXII.   *To Mrs Steele.*
                                        Aug. 31, 1710.

MY DEAR,—I have sent a message by Cave a little way off; as soon as he returns, I will come home. I have almost done one paper.*—Yours ever,   RICH. STEELE.

LETTER CLXIII.   *To Mrs Steele.*
                                        Sept. 29, [1710.]

DEAR PRUE,—Go to dinner. I have sent Cave to Martyn, and wait till he or his brother brings me the money.—Yours ever,   RICH. STEELE.

Upon second thoughts I will go and dine at the Gentleman-usher's table.

LETTER CLXIV.   *To Mrs Steele.*†
                                        [*Sept.* 30, 1710.]

DEAR PRUE,—I am very sleepy and tired, but could not think of closing my eyes till I had told you I am, dearest creature, your most affectionate and faithful husband,   RICH. STEELE.

From the press,‡ one in the morning.

LETTER CLXV.   *To Mrs Steele.*
                                        Oct. 2, 1710.

DEAR PRUE,—As soon as you have dined, if you please, come to Nutt's, where I am gone, for haste sake, to despatch my paper,§ and I will go from thence with you to see Dick ‖ at Lambeth.—Yours ever,
                                        RICH. STEELE.

LETTER CLXVI.   *To Mrs Steele.*
                                        Oct. 12, 1710.

DEAR PRUE,—I desire you to go to dinner. Be cheerful and beautiful, and I will come to you to your mother's between six and seven this evening.—Faithfully yours,   RICH. STEELE.

---

* See *Tatler*, No. 219, Sept. 2, 1710, vol. vi.
† "At her house at Hampton Court."
‡ "The *Gazette* printing office."
§ See *Tatler*, No. 232, vol. vi.
‖ Their first-born child, named *Richard*, who died in his infancy. See Let. CLI.

The intimacy of Steele with Swift has been previously noticed. He now made a memorable visit, arriving in London in the beginning of September 1710, with a commission to solicit from the Queen the remission of the first fruits and twentieth parts, payable to the Crown by the clergy of Ireland. There is reason to believe that he procured that commission with the view of pushing his own affairs at the present important crisis when the ministry was tottering. At all events he got so deeply involved in politics on his arrival that his stay was prolonged during the next two or three years. During that time he maintained a regular correspondence with Miss Esther Johnson, better known under the poetical name of Stella, in which he has celebrated her. This lady was the daughter of Sir William Temple's steward, (though some have professed to think her Temple's own,) and Swift's acquaintance with her had begun when he resided, many years previously, with that eminent man at Moor Park, as secretary and companion, where he had undertaken the superintendence of her studies. He had subsequently invited her and a female friend, Mrs Dingley, to Ireland, where they had then been for some years, ostensibly with a view to the greater cheapness of living, and the higher rate of interest for their money. The correspondence was maintained in the form of a journal or diary, and is very valuable as preserving a minute record of the events of those few eventful years. By bringing into one view the scattered notices of Steele that occur in it, we obtain glimpses of him and his affairs at this time more minute and interesting than are to be obtained from any other source.

Sept. 2, 1710.—Let all who write to me enclose to Richard Steele, Esq., at his office at the Cockpit, near Whitehall. 9. The *Tatler* [Steele] expects every day to be turned out of his employment. 10. I sat till ten in the evening with Addison and Steele. Steele will certainly lose his Gazetteer's place, all the world detesting his engaging in parties.* 18. Got home early, and began a letter to the *Tatler* (No. 230) about the corruption of style and writing, &c.

Oct. 7.—And now I am going in charity to send Steele a *Tatler*, who is very low. 10. I am now writing my poetical description of "A Shower in London," and will send it to the *Tatler*. 14. Your letter. . . . I doubt it has lain in Steele's office, and he forgot. Well, there's an end of that; he is turned out of his place. 22. I was this morning with Mr Lewis, the under-secretary to Lord Dartmouth, two hours talking politics and contriving to keep Steele in his office of stamped paper. He has lost his place of Gazetteer, L.300 a year, for writing a *Tatler* some months ago against Mr Harley,† who gave it him at first, and raised the salary from L.60 to L.300. This was devilish ungrateful; and Lewis was telling me the particulars: but I had a hint given me that I might save him in the other employment; and leave was given me to clear matters with Steele. Well, I . . . . went to sit with Mr Addison, and offer the matter at distance to him, as the discreeter person; but found party had so possessed him, that he talked as if he suspected me, and would not fall in with anything I said. So I stopped short in my overture, and we parted very dryly; and I will say nothing to Steele, and let them do as they will; but, if things stand as they are, he will certainly lose it, unless I save him; and therefore I will not speak to him that I may not report to his disadvantage. Is not this vexatious, and is there so much in the proverb of proffered services? When shall I grow wise? I endeavoured to act in the most exact points of honour and conscience, and my nearest friends will

---

* That is, in the *Tatler*, where two or three papers had recently appeared supposed to glance covertly at the new rumoured Tory ministry.

† When Steele received it during Harley's former Secretaryship, by the interest of Mr Maynwaring with him, he went to return his thanks, but Harley told him to thank Mr Maynwaring, who is actually surmised to have been the writer of the article in question, and who wrote and published at the time much more violent libels on Mr Harley. (See Nichol's "Annotated Edition of *Tatler*," vol. vi. p. 96, and Mr Forster's "Essay on Steele," p. 170 (note,) "Biographical Essays," third series.) It is to be remembered that the *Tatlers* described types of characters or classes under fictitious names, and it was only by inference that they could be applied to particular persons. With regard to Addison, "the discreeter person," as Swift calls him, it happens that, whether rightly or wrongly marked, one of the objectionable papers is attributed to him.

not understand it so. What must a man expect from his enemies?—this would vex me, but it shall not. 25. I dined to-day with Mr Addison and Steele, and a sister of Mr Addison's, who is married to one Mons. Sartre,* a Frenchman, prebendary of Westminster, who has a delicious house and garden; yet I thought it was a sort of monastic life in these cloisters, and I liked Larncor [his own vicarage] better. Addison's sister is a sort of a wit, very like him. I am not fond of her, &c.

Nov. 1.— . . . We have scurvy *Tatlers* of late, so pray do not suspect me. I have one or two hints I design to send him [Steele], and never any more; he does not deserve it. He is governed by his wife abominably, as bad as ——. I never saw her since I came; nor has he ever made me an invitation; either he dare not, or he is such a Tisdall fellow, that he never minds it. So what care I for his wit, for he is the worst company in the world till he has a bottle of wine in his head.

Dec. 2.—Steele, the rogue, has done the impudentest thing in the world; he said something in a *Tatler*, that we ought to use the word Great Britain, and not England, in common conversation, as the finest lady in Great Britain, &c. Upon this, Rowe, Prior, and I sent him a letter turning this into ridicule. He has to-day printed the letter, and signed it J. S., M. P., and N. R., the first letters of our names. Congreve told me to-day he smoked it immediately. 14. No, the *Tatler* of the shilling was not mine, more than the hint, and two or three general heads for it. I have much more important business on my hands: and besides the ministry hate to think I should help him, and have made reproaches on it; and I frankly told them I would do it no more.

Jan. 2, 1711.— . . . At six, went to Dartineuf's house to drink punch with him and Mr Addison. . . . Steele was to have been there, but came not, nor never did twice since I knew him to any appointment. . . . Steele's last *Tatler* came out to-day. You will see it before this comes to you, and how he takes leave of the world.† He never told so much as Mr Addison of it, who was as much surprised as I. . . . To my knowledge he had several good hints to go upon, but was so lazy and weary of the work that he would not improve them.

On the relinquishment of office by Harley and his party, as previously noticed, in 1708, the famous Robert Walpole

---

* "Mr Sartre died Sept. 30, 1713. His widow (afterwards married to Daniel Combes, Esq.,) died March 2, 1750."

† " I have nothing more to say to the world in the character of Isaac Bickerstaff. . . . I confess it has been a most exquisite pleasure to me to frame characters of domestic life," &c.

had commenced his long and memorable official career by succeeding St John as Secretary-at-War. Soon after, almost all the Whig leaders were pressed into the service, —Sir James Montagu, brother of Lord Halifax, as Attorney-General; Lord Somers, as President of the Council, on the death of the Prince-Consort; Lord Wharton, as Lord-Lieutenant of Ireland; and Lord Pembroke, as Lord High Admiral. To crown all, the campaign of that year was distinguished by the glorious victory of Oudenarde, which seemed to promise a speedy peace.

On the other hand, there were intrigues and cabals which tended to the weakness and division of the party; and when negotiations for peace were entered into at the Hague in the following year, they were finally broken off by indications that the French were only seeking to gain time and to create divisions among the allies. The war in consequence proceeded as before ; but, though the campaign was marked with the usual success and the memorable victory of Malplaquet, the comparative indifference with which the news of so decided a triumph was received afforded indication of the ardent desire for peace which had succeeded to former enthusiasm. At the same time the prospect of a pacific result, which might otherwise have followed, was deferred by the rumours which had reached the French Court of the decline of Marlborough's influence, and the critical state of the ministry, from the tone of public opinion and of the opposition in Parliament.

Harley, meantime, was not idle in his retirement, but busily engaged in his schemes and intrigues for compassing the plans so cunningly laid, but formerly so prematurely frustrated.

A variety of concurring causes—among which may be mentioned, the feeling occasioned by the pressure of the burden of the war, aggravated by a bad harvest and the reduction of wages among the artizans, imputed to the encouragement given by the Whigs to the naturalisation of the unfortunate Catalonian refugees, in addition, perhaps, to the love of change—all these had tended to create a strong reaction in public opinion in favour of the Tories. This feeling had been inflamed by the wide dissemination of Tory pamphlets through the length and breadth of the land; and the policy of the High Church party, who, on the ground that some of the Whig Government had been known as favourers of the Dissenters, let loose the war-cry of the Church in danger, which was taken up and re-echoed far and wide. Among those who contributed to swell the tide of popular fanaticism, one noisy and turbulent individual towered pre-eminent in giving a voice to the mutterings of the rising tempest, and inflated himself to

"Ride upon the whirlwind, and direct the storm."

This was Dr Sacheverell, rector of St Saviour's, Southwark, grandson of one of the Presbyterian ministers who had been ejected and silenced by the Act of Uniformity, for a subsequent infringement of which he had suffered a three years' imprisonment that caused his death. The zeal of the descendant of this martyr took a totally different direction. He had published several sermons, delivered on various public occasions, all more or less characterised by their violence and seditious tendency. But one which he preached at this important crisis exceeded in this respect all former precedent. On the 5th of November 1709, the anniversary of the Gunpowder Plot and the Revolution, he delivered a discourse in St Paul's, before the members of the corporation, full of the most extravagant political and theological violence, on the subject of *Perils from false brethren*. He denounced schism and schismatics, and those who would tolerate them; inveighed against the doctrine of resistance to authority, and covertly reflected on the memory of King William and the Revolution; dwelt on the treachery of ministers, the imminent danger of the Church, and the duty of standing forth in its defence. An audience favourably disposed goes a great way to make a successful orator, and he is said to have possessed in addition a good voice and address, and fluent declamation. The heat and violence of the style and manner, not less than the matter, excited the utmost enthusiasm among those for whom it was intended, though condemned by the reflecting and sober-minded. It was afterwards published with a dedication to the Lord Mayor, who had at first patronised him, but was inclined to draw back when it was too late. Its circulation was immense, and he became the general topic of discourse, either in praise or censure, in all companies. The Lord Treasurer was supposed to be reflected on under the title of *Volpone*.

In an evil hour, the ministers, in their resentment, decided on his impeachment. Lord Somers strongly opposed it, and urged an appeal to the ordinary legal tribunals, but his counsel was overruled. The proceedings were deferred till the latter end of the following February. It was like breaking a fly upon the wheel. The most elaborate arrangements were made, the stately hall of Westminster was arrayed in pomp for the reception of the Commons, resolved into a committee of the whole House, for attending the trial. But when we see the result for which this elaborate machinery was brought into play, and the public time wasted, it seems like a splendid introduction to nothing. The Government, unfortunately for themselves, instead of either treating his performance with the contempt it deserved, or giving it such notice as to prohibit such conduct with impunity, elevated him into the hero of the hour, by citing him before the highest tribunal in the State, while they became themselves the victims— for, though he was found guilty, yet the insignificance of the penalty (three years' suspension from preaching) after such a flourish of trumpets, was a striking example of the *Montes parturiunt, nascitur ridiculus mus.*

It is needless to enter into the particulars of the trial, in which the accused acted with the flippant self-sufficiency and arrogance that might have been anticipated. He was regularly escorted to and from Westminster Hall by an applauding crowd. Gathering confidence from impunity, and it was suspected not without the connivance of persons of position, they at length proceeded under cover of night to acts of the most atrocious violence and outrage, breaking into many of the most respectable Dissenting places of worship, and consigning their furniture to the flames ; nor was order restored but by the intervention of the military. After the trial, Sacheverell made a sort of triumphal procession through various parts of the country, and was received with the most extravagant honours.

The hopes that ministers entertained of a reaction in

their favour, by the discussion of constitutional principles and a vindication of the Revolution, were entirely disappointed. The reign of fanaticism was triumphant. Such popular demonstrations afforded the Queen the plea she wanted for following her inclinations in favour of her secret advisers. On the 5th of April, the Duchess of Marlborough had an audience of the Queen, which ended in a shew of reconciliation, which amounted to nothing. She gave unmistakable indications, by various acts, of a fixed design to mortify both the Duke and Godolphin, probably with the hope of inducing them to resign. In the absence of the Lord Treasurer at Newmarket, and without consulting him, the Queen, on the 13th of April, dismissed the Marquis of Kent as Lord Chamberlain, and placed the staff in the hands of the Duke of Shrewsbury, who, though making a fair show of friendship to ministers, had been intriguing with their enemies. Godolphin, instead of acting with becoming spirit and resigning the seals of office, induced his colleagues to temporise, persuading them, and perhaps himself, that he was submitting to the indignity for the sake of the public service. He had also the assurance of the Queen that no further changes were proposed, and that of Shrewsbury of his intention to act in unison with them. At the same time, promotions, to please the Court, were forced upon the Duke against his will. In the course of the summer (June 13th) the Duke's son-in-law, Sunderland, was dismissed from his office as Secretary of State. Still the Whigs were persuaded to submit. But on the 7th of August the Lord Treasurer himself was subjected to a similar fate, which was the signal for the resignation of all his colleagues, with the exception of Marlborough, who was still persuaded to act upon the weak policy that had been so derogatory to the party.

The long-threatened Tory Ministry was thus at length inaugurated, the principal members of which were the two traitors to the late Government—Harley and St John, the former as Chancellor of the Exchequer, and the other as Secretary of State. The Parliament was dissolved, and in the present temper of the nation, was succeeded by one in accordance with the views of the present occupants of office.

Godolphin died in 1712, in very poor circumstances, so much so, that it was supposed he would have to be under obligations to Marlborough—a proof that not much of the public money had stuck to him. He had brought the affairs of the Treasury into the most perfect order, and by his strict attention to business, the regularity of his arrangements, and the great confidence of the monied interest which he enjoyed, he had elevated the public credit to the highest pitch. But though entitled to the praise of the highest probity in the literal and vulgar sense of the term, the credit of a high-minded man otherwise can hardly be accorded him. The publication of the Stuart papers shews that he was tainted by a private correspondence with the exiled court, though possibly, as in the case of Marlborough, it may have been only the result of an unworthy timid precaution to keep himself well with them in any event.

With regard to Steele's personal affairs, we have seen that when he failed in his claims to succeed Addison in the Under-Secretaryship, (the north Briton, in whose favour it was given, having been Mr R. Pringle,) he was promised something else; and now, with greatly augmented reputation, he received, some time before the close of the *Tatler*, the tardy fulfilment of this pledge, by being appointed a Commissioner of Stamps. Unfortunately he lost, not long after, the previous appointment of Gazetteer, in consequence of some papers in the *Tatler*, in which he was supposed to have directed a masked battery at the heads of the new Tory Ministry in expectancy. Harley, on coming into power and taking his revenge in this manner, observed a sort of discriminating clemency in his punishment of Steele, taking from him only the office he had either given him formerly, or the value of which he had greatly enhanced.

With reference to the charge of ingratitude urged against him by Swift, though it might have been more judicious, (if people could always do what was wisest in moments of heat and excitement,) to have preserved the *Tatler* free from politics—it may be that Steele considered loyalty to his party paramount to considerations of personal obligation or interest. This view might be strengthened by remembering that the obligation was given as a favour to another and not to himself.* His forbearance he might also think the less called for, towards one who had himself attempted to supplant and undermine those friends whose power was now tottering, by the most underhand means, and with the basest ingratitude.

The obnoxious numbers were probably 190, 191, and 193. In the former he stated that he thought it the

* See note (†) p. 222.

shortest road to impartiality to declare himself at a time when the question was not one of names, but of things and causes. In the same number was a letter signed "Aminadab," written in the character of a Quaker, and attributed to Swift, in which he cautions the *Tatler* to reflect what a day might bring forth, to think of that as he took snuff. Unfortunately for himself, he was not guided by this friendly advice, but at least gave admission in immediately following numbers to two very satirical sketches of character (one professedly treating of stage affairs), which were generally applied—the *Examiner*, of course, said, contrary to the rules of resemblance,—to Mr Harley and some of his friends.

CHAPTER VII.

THE PERIODICAL ESSAYIST—SPECTATOR—1711, 1712.

Steele starts the *Spectator* on a similar plan with the *Tatler*, but with a new set of characters, in conjunction with Addison—Its unprecedented success—The *Spectator* Club—The De Coverley series of papers—Notice of the contributors, Philips, Budgell, Tickell, Hughes, Grove, &c.—The dedications, and the subjects of them—Close of the original series—An additional volume subsequently added, chiefly by Addison.

WHILST the friends and admirers of the *Tatler* were yet indulging their regret,* and its envious rivals, (for it had would-be rivals, as when has merit or success been without them?) their triumph at the literary suicide, its authors suddenly burst upon them in a new, and if not more brilliant, at least a yet more successful character—a literary metempsachosis. Its authors, far from betraying any sense of exhaustion, as some probably surmised, only two short months from the cessation of the former paper, emboldened by success, ventured on the experiment of a daily successor, with a confidence in their resources almost without a parallel in literary history.

On the 1st March 1711, the *Spectator* made its appear-

* "Steele's last *Tatler*," writes Swift to Stella, "comes out to-day. You will see it before this comes to you, and how he takes leave of the world. He never told so much as Addison of it, who was surprised as much as I. . . . To my knowledge he had several good hints to go upon, but he was so lazy and weary of the work, that he would not improve them."—*Journal, Jan.* 2, 1711.

ance. The introductory paper, in which the imaginary author gives an account of himself and his proposed lucubrations, was written by Addison in that style of quiet, elegant humour peculiar to himself. "I have observed," he says, "that a reader seldom peruses a book with pleasure till he knows whether the author of it be a black or a fair man, of a mild or choleric disposition, married or a bachelor, with other particulars of the like nature, which conduce very much to the right understanding of an author." The character of the *Spectator*, in which there are some touches not inapplicable to Addison himself, is very happily drawn. He is represented as a student and observer who has travelled and seen much of the world, and yet, from an insuperable natural diffidence (a quality that made it disagreeable to him to be talked to in mixed company, but especially to be stared at,) living in the world as a mere looker-on ; "by which means," he says, "I have made myself a speculative statesman, soldier, merchant, and artisan. . . . . I am very well versed in the theory of a husband or a father, and can discern the errors in the economy, business, and diversions of others better than those who are engaged in them, as by-standers discover blots which are apt to escape those who are in the game." He is also a great student, so that with so much observation of men, and skill in books, "I begin," he says, "to blame my own taciturnity ; and, since I have neither time nor inclination to communicate the fulness of my heart in speech, I am resolved to do it in writing, and to print myself out, if possible, before I die."

The sketch of the club, or *dramatis personæ*, in the second number, is by Steele. The adoption of the machinery of the club, which was referred to in the first number, added greatly to the dramatic interest of the paper; and, as the *Spectator* professed sympathy and interest in the concerns of all sorts and conditions of men, the members of the club carried out this view by personifying the various classes in society. First on the list, the immortal Sir Roger de Coverley, a Worcestershire baronet of ancient descent, whose great-grandfather is humorously represented as the inventor of the famous country dance of the name, stands as the ideal of the country gentleman, —not of the gross, swearing, illiterate, overbearing foxhunters of the time, and as they were to be found, at least partially, at a much later day,*—not such as the Squire Westerns, as found in the pages of Fielding, — sitting and drinking beer with their own footmen ; no stern, inexorable justice, but a refined, amiable gentleman, of most genial, and somewhat eccentric humour—a little way in the descent in the vale of years, but hearty, like one with whom time had dealt kindly. His eccentricities are represented as " arising from his good sense, and as contradictions to the manners of the world only as he thought the world in the wrong." But there was also a more sentimental cause, in a certain warp that his mind had received by his having, like a true knight, been crossed in love. A charming young widow, but, unhappily, as cruel as she was beautiful, had crossed his path. Previous to that event he had been what is called a fine gentleman, " had supped with Lord Rochester and Sir George Etherege, fought a duel, and kicked bully Dawson for calling him youngster."

* See Sidney Smith's account of the squire of his parish in Yorkshire.

This fatal beauty he had first met at the Assizes—where she attended on a question relative to her dower, and he as sheriff of his county, though only three-and-twenty—and there and then became incurably smitten. The following day he dined with her at a public table, and was helped from a dish by "the finest hand of any woman in the world." Not satisfied with the brave figure he made before his enslaver in all the "pride, pomp, and circumstance" of office, he ordered new liveries and fresh appointments with which to wait upon his charmer. The important day arrived, but though he was courteously received, the beauty almost annihilated him as much by her learning and mental attainments as by her personal charms. This was a fatal blow to a plain rustic squire, and though she gave him sufficient encouragement to lure him on, and evidently enjoyed the admiration she inspired, yet he found he could make no progress, which he partly attributed to a confidant she had. He soon discovered, however, that the beauty was an arrant coquette, and "removed from her slaves in town to those in the country according to the seasons of the year." So he desisted in his pursuit, but he mused upon her in secret, as he paced under the shade of his avenue, or carved her name upon the trees. Thus nursing his passion, though despairingly, he became very grave for a year and a half, resigned the splendours of his equipage, grew careless of himself, and never affected dress afterwards. But the sweetness of his disposition was such that it had not the effect of souring him; on the contrary, he became the friend and benefactor of all around him, by whom he was greatly beloved, and if he so much as coughed, or betrayed any unfavourable symptom suggestive of growing infirmity, his domestics looked grave and anxious. In contrast with Sir Roger, we are told of the squire of a neighbouring village who was on such ill terms with the parson that he used to pique him by not going to church, while the parson retaliated by preaching at the squire. To the passage in his life with the perverse widow are attributed certain inconsistencies and inequalities in his manner—and it is these little traits of eccentricity and quaintness, which some have considered as blemishes, though they are usually regarded as more or less common to all elderly single gentlemen, that give to this exquisite portrait its individuality and interest, as the gnarled and knotted oak receives strength and character from the parts which give to it an air somewhat fantastic and grotesque.

The account of the Coverley household is a homily to landlords and masters, illustrating by example how they would consult their own true happiness, by regarding the interests of tenants and dependents as their own, and by treating their domestics, as Swift expressed it, as humble friends. Yet there was one very usual mode of kindness to these latter of which the knight disapproved, that of masters giving their cast clothes to be worn by their valets, which he considered had an "ill effect upon little minds by creating a silly sense of equality between the parties. He was often pleasant on this occasion, describing a young gentleman abusing his man in that coat which, a month or two before, was the most pleasing distinction he was conscious of in himself."

There is naturally some slight discrepancy in the different parts of this fine portrait, owing to the different hands engaged upon it. The original conception was by Steele, who described the knight when first introduced to the reader as in his fifty-sixth year. But Addison, who early adopted the offspring of his friend, and developed with a careful hand its latent beauties, whether intentionally or not, evidently draws the knight as a man of more advanced age. So great was his affection for this character, that he was said to be jealous of any interference with it, and when the objectionable paper, No. 410, appeared, the sin of which is unsettled between Steele and Tickell, he determined to dismiss the fine old knight from the scene, lest, as he said, some one else should murder him. Suddenly we are informed of the decease of the good old man in a paper of consummate simplicity and pathos, No. 517, without any previous note of illness. The intelligence is communicated to the club in a letter from the faithful old butler at the hall, who says, "I am afraid he caught his death the last county sessions, where he would go to see justice done to a poor widow woman and her fatherless children; for you know, sir," the honest fellow adds, "my good master was always the poor man's friend." Hopes were at one time entertained of his master's recovery, he says, from the favourable symptoms that appeared on the receipt of a kind message from the widow lady, but this proved only a fallacious flickering in the socket.*

Of the thirty papers which comprise the Coverley series,

---

* The story of Addison vowing, with the solitary oath he is ever recorded to have uttered, to kill Sir Roger lest somebody else should murder him, in consequence of his indignation at the objectionable paper No. 410, rests on the authority of Budzell in one of the numbers of his *Bee*, at a time, as has been remarked, when the world was disposed to give him little credit. It may have been quite true, notwithstanding. The credit or discredit of the obnoxious paper rests

Addison wrote two-thirds and Steele the other third, with the exception of two or three papers by Budzell and Tickell. Addison usually gets the credit of the whole, though the original conception and first outline of the character, in addition to the considerable portion of the filling up already stated, belonged to Steele, including the most characteristic incident in the history—that of the good old knight's long and romantic attachment to the perverse widow, described particularly in No. 113.

The next member of the club referred to,—also a bachelor, as indeed they seem all to have been,—is the Templer, one of the honourable fraternity of briefless barristers. He is represented as having followed the law rather in obedience to the wishes of his father than his own inclination, which led him to the cultivation of letters, and especially of the drama. Though this is one of the few leading characters in the *Spectator* for which ingenuity does not seem to have busied itself in tracing an original, one might be disposed to think that Congreve was hinted at, as, in addition to his dramatic tendencies, the Templer is credited with "a great deal of wit."

As Sir Roger was the worthy representative of the landed interest, Sir Andrew Freeport is introduced in the same relation to that of commerce, respecting which he is represented as holding the most enlightened and liberal views. With that quiet humour and knowledge of the world which mingle in all these sketches, we are told that "as every rich man has usually some sly way of jesting,

between Steele and Tickell, and the preponderance of testimony or opinion is in favour of assigning it to the latter. It is singular that he should never have had his own papers authenticated, as he did those of his friend and patron Addison.

which would make no great figure were he not a rich man, he called the sea the British common." Not that he is represented by any means as dull; on the contrary, the pursuits of commerce have many compliments paid them in his person. In addition to indefatigable industry, strong reason, great experience, and enlarged views, the shrewdness and perspicuity of his discourse are said to give the same pleasure that wit would in other men.

The army, in like manner, is represented by Captain Sentry, next heir to Sir Roger, who, in addition to great courage and good understanding, is given a quality which is not always found in his profession, namely, invincible modesty. He quitted in consequence, we are told, a way of life in which merit was of little service in the way of promotion, without having something of the courtier as well; and though remarkably tolerant of what he suffered from, he could not always restrain the expression of his regret that it should be the fate of impudence to get the better of modesty. At other times he would frankly own that it was not unnatural it should be so, for, said he, "the great man who has a mind to help me has as many to break through to come at me as I have to come at him; therefore, he will conclude that the man who would make a figure, especially in a military way, must get over all false modesty, and assist his patron against the importunity of other pretenders, by a proper assurance in his own vindication."

Will Honeycomb represented the gay world, and was the repository of the fashionable gossip of a previous generation. "He is very ready," we are told, "at the sort of discourse with which men usually entertain women.

He can smile when one speaks to him, and laughs easily. He knows the history of every mode." Though thus the chronicler of distant times, he has taken such good care of himself that he maintains a green old age.

Lastly, religion is represented by a clergyman of grave, philosophic disposition. He is unattached, and is therefore, we are told, "among divines what a chamber counsel is among lawyers." He was only an occasional visitor, and, when he did attend, did not attempt to force the company upon serious topics; but the regard in which he was held by all the club induced them to draw him to speak on such subjects, which he did with a mingled modesty and authority, "as one who had no interests in this world, who is hastening to the object of all his wishes, and conceives hopes from his decays and infirmities."

Such is the Spectator Club. The sketches display great knowledge of the world, and of varied character and modes of life, drawn with a masterly and graceful hand. They gave assurance both of the practical design of the undertaking and of the eminent ability of the writers to impart to their lucubrations a lifelike and dramatic form, such as, in the words of Bacon, should "come home to men's business and bosoms." The aim of the writers, as expressed by Addison, was to effect by their papers something akin to what Socrates did in his day by his conversations—" to bring philosophy out of closets, and schools and colleges, to dwell in clubs and assemblies, at tea-tables and in coffee-houses."

The original series was brought to a close at the end of the seventh volume, forming 555 numbers.

Of the 635 papers in the eight volumes, 274 are attributed to Addison, and from 236 to 240 to Steele. To account for the numerical superiority of Addison over Steele, who was the responsible writer and conductor of the original paper, it must be remembered that the last was a supplementary volume, taken up by Addison after a considerable interval had elapsed from the cessation of the original work, and sustained almost entirely by his pen, or with only the aid of Budgell. Why the work should have been resumed after so long an interval is not distinctly known. It has been suggested that it may have been a speculation of Tonson's, with Budgell as editor, and Addison retained as a regular contributor. But this is mere speculation. Besides Addison and Steele, two other writers alone contributed to the original work to any considerable extent, namely, Budgell and Hughes. The first of these contributed, including the supplemental volume, thirty-seven papers, and the latter eleven. Several others, however, contributed to a small extent; and among these Pope has been named, though his papers, in common with Tickell's, have not been authoritatively traced. In the case of the leading writers, initial letters were added—Addison writing under the signature of one of the letters of the muse Clio,* and Steele under those of T. and R. Notwithstanding there is still considerable uncertainty in some cases.

Eustace Budgell, (1685-1737,) who, next to the two leading writers, was the most regular contributor to the *Spectator*, though on the most intimate terms with

---

* It has been ingeniously surmised that the letters were rather the result of chance, forming a curious coincidence, rather than anything intentional, the initial of each paper referring probably to the locality in which it was written—as C. Chelsea, L. London, I. Islington, O. Office. The suggestion is at least ingenious, and would remove any appearance of implied egotism.

Addison and Steele, presents a striking contrast either to the happily-tempered, calm serenity of the one, or the joyous vivacity, ardent temper, and deep tenderness of the other. He appears, though possessed of considerable ingenuity, to have been a person of ill-regulated mind, great vanity, and excessive irritability, which, with other passions, led to misfortunes which he attempted to repair by criminality and dishonour, and ended in the closing of his melancholy career by a catastrophe at which we stand breathless and aghast. He was the son of the Rev. Dr Gilbert Budgell, of St Thomas, near Exeter, and was born about the year 1685. His mother and Addison's were sisters, being daughters of Dr Gulston, bishop of Bristol. After studying at Christ Church, Oxford, he was entered of the Middle Temple. His inclination, however, added to the example of his distinguished kinsman, who was rapidly rising both in the world of letters and in public life, led him to the pursuit of polite literature. Addison acted the part of a kind friend to him, and was the means not only of introducing him to the literary circles of the metropolis, but when he went to Ireland as Chief Secretary, under Lord Wharton, in 1709, took Budgell with him as his private secretary, or in some similar capacity, and the two friends lived together on the most intimate terms. Addison's fortune proved a tide sufficient to float his relative into prosperity, and as long as he survived to counsel, and prosperity lasted, Budgell kept fair with the world. He contributed to the *Spectator* soon after the starting of that paper, and also to its successor, the *Guardian;* but though his name has been mentioned as a contributor to the *Tatler*, no communication of his has been traced.

What foundation there may have been for the traditional rumour, referred to by Dr Johnson,* that Addison wrote, or at least revised, his papers, so much as to make them almost his own, it is impossible now to say, though most probably only a piece of idle literary gossip. He also contributed one of the most successful of epilogues to Ambrose Phillips's "Distressed Mother," though of that also Addison got the credit, and apparently with more reason, from the more circumstantial manner in which it is mentioned; and, if it was so, it relieves Budgell of the imputation of gross egotism in his references to it. Such is the fate generally of being connected with superior reputation. By the death of his father, in 1711, Budgell's private circumstances were placed upon an easy footing, by the acquisition of an income of nearly a thousand a year, though encumbered to some extent. It is to the credit of Budgell that this acquisition of fortune had no effect in relaxing his exertions. Not only was he diligent in the discharge of his official duties, but, in addition to the contributions to the *Spectator*, he produced, in 1714, a translation of "The Characters of Theophrastus" from the Greek, of which it is enough to say that it received the praises of Addison in one of the numbers of the *Lover* In the latter part of the same year he became a member of the Irish parliament, having previously, on the accession of George I., been appointed Chief Secretary to the Lords Justices of Ireland and Deputy-Clerk of the Council of that kingdom. He was also, among other honours, elected an honorary bencher of the Inns of Court. Budgell was now in the prime of life, of engaging manners and prepossessing ex-

* Boswell's Life.

terior, with many accomplishments, good classical attainments, and an acquaintance with the languages of France and Italy. His fortune was easy, his reputation then unblemished, and his prospects as fair as a man with moderate wishes could desire. With a little discretion, less of vanity and passions more under control, he might have spent a happy and honoured life.

The following year (1715) added much to the responsibility and credit of his office. In consequence of the breaking out of the rebellion in favour of the Pretender, he had the charge of the embarkation of the troops from Ireland to Scotland, and his conduct displayed diligence, zeal, and disinterestedness in a remarkable degree. He declined any gratuity or fees for the commissions which passed through his office of the officers of militia then raised in Ireland; and when the Lord Justices were desirous that a handsome gratuity should be awarded him, to mark their sense of his zeal on this important occasion, he firmly declined to draw up a warrant for the purpose.

The reward, however, which he refused for the active discharge of his public duties, he soon after received in another form, through the friendship and partiality of Addison. In 1717, when he rose to be Secretary of State, he procured for Budgell the place of Accountant and Comptroller-General of the revenue in Ireland. From this culminating point of his fortune, an adverse wave in the following year flung him upon the strand.

The circumstance that deprived him at once of the accumulated honours and rewards of years of honourable exertion, arose from the appointment of the Duke of Bolton to the Viceroyalty in the year 1718. This nobleman had taken with him a Mr Webster, whom he nominated his chief secretary and a privy councillor. It appears that Budgell held this gentleman in no great regard, and could not conceal his mortification that the Duke, from whom he anticipated particular notice, should delight to honour one whom he held in such light esteem. Antipathy, even when not overt, is generally catching; and the subject of it in this case having the whip hand, was not long in making reprisals. Mr Webster had a friend and favourite for whom he wished to provide, and insisted on obtruding him upon the comptroller. Budgell vehemently resisted the intrusion, and was so carried away by the impetuosity of his indignation, as not merely to indulge in the most unbounded vituperation of his adversary—involving all his claims—but so far forgot himself as even to reflect upon the Lord-Lieutenant himself, though the affair has been exaggerated in some accounts, by being represented as a lampoon. The result, as may easily be imagined, was that, in due course, his services were dispensed with; and he immediately crossed the Channel, in order to escape from a disagreeable position, and to seek redress.

So exasperated was his mind, that he could not be prevailed on to submit in silence to his fate, and even the mild voice of Addison was without effect. He would aggravate his position by rushing into print with his wrongs. His statement was not without ability, which, with the interest excited by the circumstances of the case, caused it to circulate to the extraordinary extent, it is said, of eleven hundred copies in a single day. The effect, however, was only to embitter his enemies and widen the circle of them. Though vexed at his folly and extravagance, the amiable Addison did not forsake him, but exerted himself so successfully as to obtain from the Earl of Sunderland a promise in his favour; but the indiscretion of Budgell was once more fatal to his interest; for in the following year, having in a pamphlet attacked the Peerage Bill introduced by that nobleman, he naturally forfeited his claim upon his interest.

In the latter part of the same year, (1719,) he wisely sought by a change of scene to calm his ruffled feelings, and, after travelling through parts of France and Holland, proceeded to Hanover, and accompanied the royal suite to England. The result realised the truth of the remark of Horace—

"Cœlum, non animum mutant qui, trans mare currunt."

On his return, he seemed pertinaciously bent upon obtaining redress, by being reinstated in some official position; and only after repeated failures, and finding how determined was the opposition to him among his enemies, did he desist from the effort. His private fortune was considerable, and being without family, the object he sought was wholly unnecessary, and his eagerness not very dignified. Indeed, considering the moderate nature of his claims, and that no special honour could be derived from anything he was likely to obtain, a feverish thirst for revenge seems the only rational mode of accounting for his restless conduct. He might have remembered with advantage a Spanish proverb, referred to by Mr Maynwaring in one of his letters to the Duchess of Marlborough, in reference to the troubles and anxieties attendant on the highest offices— that they were at best but honourable slavery.

No sooner had he given up his official prospects in despair, than, perhaps to gratify a reckless excitement which the state of his feelings, if it did not create, must at least have greatly aggravated, he commenced gambling in the stocks. The South Sea mania was then at its height. Budgell threw himself into the vortex, and was soon victimised to the extent of L.20,000. At this crisis, far from being paralysed by the severity of the blow, he had almost realised his former desires by the talent, energy and fluency of speech he displayed in the concerns of the Company. Among the victims of the bubble scheme was the Duke of Portland, who had lost nearly the whole of his fortune in it. He had obtained the Governorship of Jamaica as a means of retrieving his affairs, and proposed to his fellow-sufferer, in consideration of those talents he noticed with admiration, to accompany him as his secretary, promising that he should be treated as a friend and brother. The offer was joyfully accepted; but whilst making his arrangements, the fates again cruelly interfered. So intense was the antipathy to him in official quarters, that it is said the Duke received an intimation from a Secretary of State that the Government would rather see any man in England patronised than Mr Budgell.

It was a cruel blow, and he must have been more than human not to have felt such persecution keenly. Again, returning to the struggle with hopeless energy, he strained every nerve to procure a seat in Parliament, and in these desperate efforts sunk the remainder of his fortune, to the extent of L.5000. In 1727 the Dowager Duchess of Marlborough, being strongly opposed to the existing ministry, and thinking that he had the making of a good opposition member, gave him L.1000 for a final effort, but with no better success.

He had now lost his

"Guide, philosopher, and friend,"

by the death of Addison; and his future career was from one downward step to another, till he reached the lowest abyss of infamy. Before descending to that point, however, he made some laudable efforts by the exercise of his talents. Had Budgell now taken up his pen in the spirit of his early days and early friends, he might have obtained for himself a creditable, though not a brilliant, reputation. But with the loss of his fortune, his principles seem also to have deserted him. As his prospects in this world darkened, so did his faith as regards the next, or even of good in this. He became a rancorous and unscrupulous pamphleteer; from that he descended to be a mercenary lampooner. He was the intimate associate of the leading deistical writers of the day, particularly Dr Tindal, in whose work, "Christianity as Old as the Creation," he is supposed to have been concerned.

Among the most unexceptionable of his publications were "Memoirs of the Life and Character of the late Earl of Orrery, and of the Boyle Family," which appeared in 1732, and the *Bee*, a weekly pamphlet or magazine, which he started in the latter end of the same year. This latter work met with considerable success, though principally taken from the papers, and extended to eight volumes or a hundred numbers. Its discontinuance was chiefly owing to his filling it with his private concerns, and to misunderstandings with the publisher.

He was also connected with the *Craftsman*, and wrote

numerous letters, pamphlets, and poems, chiefly on political and ephemeral topics, now of no interest.

At the death of Dr Tindal, which occurred before the close of the periodical work above referred to, a bequest to Budgell of upwards of L.2000, or nearly the whole of his property, was found in his will. Tindal, to aggravate the affair, had a favourite nephew in poor circumstances, and whom he had led to expect the bulk of his property. The result was that the validity of the will was contested, which ended in its being set aside. Among the attacks which the press showered upon him in consequence of the imputation of such an infamous transaction, were some very severe strictures in the *Grub-Street Journal*, which Budgell attributed, it is believed without any sufficient ground, to Pope, whom, in consequence, he attacked in the most scandalous manner in one of the numbers of the *Bee*. Pope took no notice of it at the time; but in the prologue to his "Satires," he jibbets Budgell among his libellers with his accustomed felicitous epigrammatic severity,—

"Let Budgell charge low Grub Street on my quill,
And write whate'er he please—*except my will.*"

With ruin and disgrace staring him on every hand, the wretched forger—for such he was considered—found existence no longer tolerable. Placing weights in his pockets, and taking a boat at Somerset Stairs, he threw himself over on reaching London Bridge. Such was the sad end of Eustace Budgell, May 4, 1737; and not the least extraordinary circumstance connected with it was the wretched-sophism with which he endeavoured to palliate the deed. On a slip of paper, which he left behind him, was written—

"What Cato did, and Addison approved, cannot be wrong."

To attempt seriously to shew the absurdity of inferring approval from a mere dramatic representation of what was not considered inconsistent with the principles of heathenism, would be merely to enter the lists with insanity, to which it is but charitable to suppose that the unhappy man was at least temporarily driven by the effects of misfortune, guilt, and remorse.

A memorandum, in the form of a will, written only a few days previously, was found among his papers, leaving all his personal estate to a natural daughter, Anne Budgell, then about eleven years of age. She subsequently went upon the stage, and died at Bath in the year 1755. She is said to have possessed considerable merit as an actress.

Of the papers of Budgell in the *Spectator*, it is unnecessary to speak particularly. They are distinguished by the letter X. They do not rise above mediocrity. Some of them are interesting, as forcibly inculcating principles from which the writer so sadly fell.

It is melancholy to contemplate the friend of Addison, and one whose early career had been so promising and irreproachable, led, by excessive vanity and ungovernable resentment and ambition, first to acts of rashness and indiscretion which blighted his prospects, and, in despair and recklessness, descending from one downward step to another, till he heaped upon his name every accumulation of infamy—infidel, gambler, forger, and suicide.

From the sad contemplation of powers misapplied, of a

life misspent and so awfully closed, it is gratifying to turn to one presenting a marked contrast, who, both as a man and a writer, was of greatly superior merit, who lived esteemed by the most eminent of his contemporaries, and died universally regretted. John Hughes, the intimate friend of Addison and Steele, was the son of a London citizen, but born at Marlborough in the year 1677. He received his education at the academy of Mr Rowe, a Dissenting minister, where he had the celebrated Dr Isaac Watts for a fellow-student, whose friendship he retained in after life.

In his nineteenth year he had planned a tragedy, and paraphrased one of the finest odes of Horace, and in 1697 made his poetical *début* on the "Peace of Ryswick." He early displayed great musical abilities likewise. His poetical pieces were therefore mostly of a lyrical kind, and some of them written for musical entertainments. Some of these had the good fortune to be set by Purcell, Pepusch, and Handel. The work on which his reputation chiefly rests is the "Siege of Damascus," a tragedy which, by a singular fate, was first performed, and that with success, on the night on which he died of a pulmonary complaint. Though it has occasionally been brought upon the stage since, it is rather a dramatic poem than an acting play. Having all his life been a valetudinarian, and incapable of violent exercises, he devoted his leisure to drawing, music, and poetry. He held a place in the office of Ordnance, and was secretary to several commissions connected with the naval dock at Chatham and Portsmouth.

He was not a great poet; yet Addison held his talents in such regard, that on Hughes urging him to put the finishing hand to "Cato," the author commissioned him to do so, which he was only prevented by finding soon after that Addison had himself made some progress in the fifth act.

His opera of "Calypso and Telemachus," represented in 1712, was received with marked favour. A few years later, he produced a masque called "Apollo and Daphne," of which, we learn from Dr Johnson, "the success was very earnestly promoted by Steele, who," he adds, "when the rage of party did not misguide him, seems to have been a man of boundless benevolence."

At a time when Steele was wholly engrossed with politics, Hughes proposed to Addison to start a new periodical, under the very prosaic name of the *Register;* but, though expressing himself favourably of the proposed plan, Addison excused himself, on the plea of requiring to take in fresh fuel,—but it is probable he felt that Steele was his real partner in such work, and preferred to wait the opportunity of renewing his engagement with him.

Hughes made various translations from the classics, with which he was intimately acquainted, including fragments of Anacreon, Pindar, Euripides, Horace, and Ovid, deserving, perhaps, of higher praise than his original compositions,—particularly his version of the "Pyramus and Thisbe" of the latter. He also made a translation of the tenth book of Lucan's "Pharsalia," which was intended as part of a complete version by various hands, projected by Tonson, but not executed.

As a prose writer he stood, perhaps, higher than as a poet, and produced, in addition to his contributions to the *Tatler, Spectator,* and *Guardian,* a variety of works both original and translated. Being acquainted with the languages both of France and Italy, he was induced to undertake a translation of Fontonelle's "Dialogues of the Dead," to which he added two of his own, taking for the interlocutors Lucius Junius Brutus and Augustus — Empedocles and Lucilio Vanini. This was published in 1708, (being dedicated to Lord Wharton,) and was succeeded in the following year by a version of the "Misanthrope" of Molière. A few years later he also produced translations of the Abbé Vertot's "History of the Revolution of Portugal," Fontonelle's "Discourse Concerning the Ancients and Moderns," and of the "Letters of Abelard and Heloise."

He wrote also two essays, one at the age of twenty-four, "On the Pleasure of Being Deceived," and the other at a later period, "On the Properties of Style;" a preface to a translation of "Boccalini;" a preface to "Kennet's History of England;" the "Lay Monastery," a periodical paper; a "Discourse on Allegorical Poetry;" and "Charon, or the Ferry Boat," a vision in imitation of Lucian.

He also performed the part of editor to Spenser's works, to which he added a "Life" of the author, a glossary, and a discourse on allegorical poetry,—but though he appeared well to understand and appreciate the genius of the poet, he seems to have been deficient in the requisite antiquarian lore. In all his writings he displays a clear, perspicuous, and graceful style, combined with judgment and erudition,—and they bear the impress of his amiable and benevolent disposition.

In his correspondence and remains, edited by his kinsman, Mr Duncombe, and accompanied with a biographical notice, are some sketches intended for the *Guardian*, but never sent. His contributions to that work were eleven complete papers, twelve letters, and part of No. 230. He also contributed several papers, as previously stated, to the *Tatler*, but only one paper of his in the *Guardian* has been traced.

Hughes at length received the reward due to his merit, by obtaining from Lord Cowper, on his resumption of the Chancellorship on the accession of George I., the valuable place of Secretary to the Commissioners of the Peace. It came too late, however, for him to reap any considerable advantage from it, as he did not long survive to enjoy it. His decease took place Feb. 17, 1719–20, the day, as previously stated, of the first representation of his " Siege of Damascus," which ten days previously he had dedicated to his patron, Lord Cowper.

Steele has left a high encomium on the talents of his amiable and accomplished friend. " Mr Hughes," he says, " could hardly ever be said to enjoy health, but was, in the very best of his days, a valetudinarian. If those who are sparing of giving praise to any virtue without extenuation of it, should say that his youth was chastised into the severity and preserved in the innocence for which he was conspicuous, from the infirmity of his constitution, they will be under new difficulty when they hear that he had none of those faults to which an ill state of health ordinarily subjects the rest of mankind. His incapacity for more frolic diversions never made him peevish or sour to those he saw in them ; but his humanity was such, that he could partake and share those pleasures he beheld others enjoy, without repining that he himself could not join in them. No ;

he made a true use of an ill constitution, and formed his mind to the living under it with as much satisfaction as it could admit of. His intervals of ease were employed in drawing, designing, or else in music or poetry; for he had not only a taste, but an ability of performance to a great excellence in those arts which entertain the mind within the rules of the severest morality, and the strictest dictates of religion. He did not seem to wish for more than he possessed, even as to his health, but seemed to contemn sensuality as a sober man does drunkenness; he was so far from envying, that he pitied the jollities that were enjoyed by a more happy constitution. He could converse with the most sprightly without peevishness; and sickness itself had no other effect upon him than to make him look upon all violent pleasures as evils he had escaped without the trouble of avoiding them. Peace be with thy remains, thou amiable spirit! but I talk in the language of our weakness. That is flown to the regions of day and immortality, and relieved from the aching engine and painful instrument of anguish and sorrow, in which, for a long and tedious few years, he panted with a lively hope for his present condition. We shall consign the trunk, in which he was so long imprisoned, to common earth, with all that is due to the merit of its late inhabitant."*

In the edition of the *Tatler*, published in 1797, a note on the humorous paper (No. 113) on the "Inventory of a Beau," furnished by Hughes, gives the following information, which is curious, both in a biographical point of view, and as an illustration of the fluctuations of fashion in costume. The Rev. Wm. John Duncombe, the only son of Mr Hughes's

* *The Theatre*, No. 15.

only sister, had a picture of Mr John Hughes, the author of this paper, when aged about twenty, in which he was represented in a full-trimmed blue suit, with scarlet stockings rolled above his knee, a large white peruke, and a flute half an ell long."

Mr Hughes was on the most intimate and friendly terms with all the leading wits of his time. He had taken great interest in Pope's translation of Homer, respecting which he furnished him with his advice in verse, including some very unnecessary prudential and financial considerations, and cautions him not to " trust to barren praise."

Pope has always been included among the occasional contributors to the *Spectator;* yet only one short paper (No. 527) has been positively assigned to him. Two others (Nos. 404 and 408) have, however, been surmised to be his with every probability, both from the finish of the style and the similarity of the tone of philosophic speculation with that which pervades his writings. His "Messiah," also, one of the loftiest of his compositions, first appeared in No. 378 of the *Spectator*. His contributions to the *Guardian* are, however, both more numerous and better defined.

The next most celebrated name among the contributors to the *Spectator* was Thomas Parnell, D.D., (1679-1718,) who, but for the greater amount furnished by others, and some personal considerations, would have been entitled to a prior notice. This amiable and accomplished man was born in Dublin in the year 1679. The family, which was of great respectability, had long been resident at Congleton, in Cheshire ; but the father of the poet, from his strong political feelings and dissatisfaction at the

Restoration retired to Ireland, where he purchased considerable estates, still retaining, however, the ancient family seat. Young Parnell had made such precocious progress in his studies, that at the early age of thirteen he was entered of the university of his native city. He took his degree of M.A. in 1700, and in the same year was ordained a deacon by Dr King, Bishop of Derry, a dispensation having been obtained from the primate in consequence of his being under age. Having entered priest's orders about three years after, on the 9th of February 1705 he was collated to the archdeaconry of Clogher by Dr Ashe, bishop of that diocese.

About the same time he consummated his domestic felicity by his marriage with Miss Anne Minchin, a lady of great beauty and amiability, to whom he had dedicated some of the earliest and sweetest effusions of his muse. Their union seems to have been peculiarly happy, though of his family two sons died young, and only one daughter survived, who was living in 1770.

Making annual visits to London, he soon became acquainted with the leading wits, particularly Swift, Gay, Pope, and Arbuthnot, to whom he was endeared by the amiability of his manners, as well as the charms of his conversation and the congeniality of his talents. In conjunction with them, he assisted in concerting the facetious Scriblerus Club, to the memoirs of which he contributed "An Essay concerning the Origin of Sciences."

A not unnatural result followed from this fascinating association, especially in the case of a man of easy nature. Parnell became weaned from the political principles of his early and hereditary sympathies. Such an event was but

R

too common at this period, when half the wits of the time had changed sides, and in two cases at least, those of Swift and Prior, displayed the proverbial zeal of converts; but with regard to Parnell, we may readily believe that there was little of self-seeking in the motive of the change, and that it was but the passive yielding to a stronger will rather than oppose it.

With the gifts of the poet, he had also the penalty, in the sensibility of the poetic temperament; and the early death of his wife, to whom he was deeply attached, so prostrated and preyed upon his spirits, never very equable, as unhappily to drive him to the resort of wine to excess as an anodyne to his grief. Swift, in his journal to Stella, under the date of August 1711, eulogises the deceased, and expresses his sympathy with his bereaved friend. It is melancholy to state that to the unhappy indulgence referred to, the premature death of this most amiable and highly gifted man has been assigned.

Swift tried to divert his mind and fix his interest on public events. In the following year he urged him to write a poem "On Queen Anne's Peace," with some compliments to Bolingbroke, which pleased the Secretary very much, and led to Parnell's introduction to him and the Lord Treasurer Harley. How Swift upheld the dignity of the literary order was strikingly shewn by a little incident in reference to Parnell. When he attended the levee with Swift, the minister requested that he might be introduced, spoke to him with great kindness, and invited him to his house. Swift adds,—"I value myself upon making the ministry desire to be acquainted with Parnell, and not Parnell with the ministry." Swift's opinion of Parnell's merit is shown by an expression in his journal, where, in speaking of the poem above referred to, he says, " and indeed he outdoes all our poets here a bar's length." He could hardly have meant to include his friend Pope in this criticism, though Hume has a remark giving him the preference, fifty to one, over one of the most brilliant and witty of poets, Cowley, which, on the same ground, might apply to Pope. " It is sufficient," he says, " to run over Cowley once; but Parnell, after the fiftieth reading, is as fresh as at the first."* Besides contributing to the facetious Scriblerus Club, which Pope had founded in conjunction with Gay, Arbuthnot, Swift, and others, his scholarship was of essential service to his friend in his translation of Homer, of which their correspondence affords abundant evidence. He also furnished an introductory essay on the " Life and Genius of Homer," and a " Life of Zoilus," the critic of the immortal bard, designed as a sharp and contemptuous satire on Dennis.

The playfulness of Parnell is said to have been exerted on one occasion in placing his friend in a ludicrous dilemma. He had been early noted for a remarkable retentiveness of memory, and being present when Pope was reading the first draft of the " Rape of the Lock " to Swift, he kept pacing out and in the room, not appearing to take any notice. He, however, noted the description of the toilet, which he translated into Latin verse, and some time after, when Pope was again reading it to some friends in his presence, accused him of having stolen the passage from an old monkish manuscript, and, in reply to his

---

* Essay on " Simplicity and Refinement."

protestations to the contrary, confounded the astonished author with the translation he had made.

The intimacy to which Swift had introduced him with Harley and Bolingbroke became very cordial, and as Parnell had made himself favourably known in the pulpits of the metropolis by his pulpit eloquence, in the course of his frequent visits from the year 1706, he would probably have reaped the benefit of it by some promotion, but for the breaking up of the Ministry on the Queen's death. Except as a matter of ambition, however, it was not necessary to him, as his private circumstances were very independent. Swift, possibly, may have felt some compunctions on the occasion in having linked his friend as well as himself to a hopeless party, and exerted his interest with Archbishop King on his behalf. Parnell consequently received a prebend's stall in 1713, and the vicarage of Finglass, which Goldsmith estimates, but there is reason to believe with great exaggeration, at L.400 a year. Johnson remarks on these promotions,—"Such notice from such a man inclines me to believe that the vice of which he has been accused was not gross or not notorious." The latter preferment he received in 1716, but did not long survive to enjoy it, having died prematurely at Chester on his way to Ireland, July 1718, in his 39th year. He was interred in Trinity Church in that city.

Parnell's poems were published by Pope, but without any account of the author, which he compensated in some measure by a very beautiful poetical dedication to Lord Oxford, in which he combined the eulogy of his departed friend with some high-flown and extravagant encomiums on the living peer, commencing—

> "Such were the notes thy once loved poet sung,
> Till death untimely stopp'd his tuneful tongue!
> Absent, or dead, still let a friend be dear;
> (A sigh the absent claims, the dead a tear!)
> Recall those nights that closed thy toilsome days;
> Still hear thy Parnell in his living lays."

The first personal notice of Parnell was the brief biographical sketch by Goldsmith, which, notwithstanding the meagreness of the materials, had the characteristic charm of his touch, and was the occasion of one of the handsome compliments of Dr Johnson, which he appeared to delight in paying to the author, whose sketch, he acknowledged, was his chief authority in his notice. The great drawback to Parnell, notwithstanding the simplicity and charm of his style, is the want of the popular element in his subjects, and the absence of anything of passion or enthusiasm in his manner. The periodical contributions of Parnell were in the style of visions and allegories, which Addison so successfully employed, without the coldness and tediousness which usually characterised them in other hands. Those of Parnell possess considerable merit, but none of his prose was equal to his verse.

The only other contributor to the *Spectator* whom it will be necessary to notice at large, from his intimate association with the writers, both literary and social, is THOMAS TICKELL, who holds a very high place among the minor poets. He was the son of the Rev. Richard Tickell, vicar of Bridekirk, in Cumberland, where he was born in 1686. In his 15th year he entered Queen's College, Oxford, where he took his degree of M.A. in 1708, and, two years after, was elected a fellow, obtaining a dispensation from the Crown for not complying with the statutes in taking orders.

A circumstance that occurred about this time, which influenced his future fortune in life, was his addressing some elegant complimentary verses to Addison on his opera of "Rosamond." This served as an introduction to the acquaintance of the author, which, from congeniality of tastes and manners, ripened into a warm and cordial friendship. He afterwards added another copy of verses on the publication of "Cato," and, the same year, (1713,) addressed his poem "On the Prospect of Peace," in reference to the pending negotiations, to the Lord Privy Seal, which, however sincere he might have been in the sentiments he expressed, could not have been very acceptable to Addison, with the views which he in common with all Whigs entertained of the Treaty of Utrecht. He was too liberal, however, and had too much regard for the writer to allow it to make any difference in their friendship, and even gave a favourable notice of the literary merits of the poem in the *Spectator*—expressing approval especially of its judicious rejection of the tedious pedantry of the classic mythology. But if the author expected promotion from making his court to the powers that be, he was disappointed. The poem had a very extensive circulation, running through six editions in rapid succession. However, he wisely took care to make himself strong on the other side, and in addition to the poem on "The Royal Progress," in the supplementary volume of the *Spectator*, intended to celebrate the arrival of George I. in his new dominions, he published in verse "An Epistle to a Gentleman at Avignon," where the Pretender then resided, in which, though written professedly in the character of a friend, he artfully ridicules the hopes of the party, and their dependence on imaginary means and ominous signs. This poem was also very successful, and stands high among those devoted to party interests. It was followed by an "Imitation of the Prophecy of Nereus," designed to throw derision on the plans of Mar and his associates, foretelling their discomfiture by Argyle.

Whether these laudations of the cause of the new dynasty would have availed in recommending him to favour at court may be questionable; but on Addison going to Ireland as secretary the second time, under Lord Sunderland, on the Hanoverian succession, he took Tickell with him as his private secretary. Sunderland did not long retain the viceroyalty, however, and Addison exchanged his office for that of a member of the Board of Committee of Privy Council for Trade.

It was in the course of the year 1715 that an event occurred in which Tickell was a principal, tending to widen the breach that, to the extent of some coolness, had previously existed between Pope and Addison. This was the publication of Tickell's poetical translation of "the First Book" of the Iliad. In the advertisement to the reader, it was stated that the translator had relinquished the design of proceeding further with the work on learning that it had been taken up by an abler hand—referring to Pope—and that his aim in publishing that specimen was to bespeak the favour of the public for a translation of the Odyssey, in which he stated he had made some progress. Addison had taken an opportunity of frankly excusing himself to Pope from looking at his work, as he had previously seen Tickell's. Pope then stated that he did not take it ill that Mr Tickell was going to publish his work, as he had as good a right to translate any author as himself, and it was entering on a fair field. He then requested that his second book might have the benefit of Addison's revision. It may be added that Tickell's publication did not appear until all Pope's arrangements had been made, so that he did not suffer in a pecuniary point of view. Yet he afterwards professed to have discovered a variety of concurring circumstances which induced him to suspect something underhand in the affair, and even the probability of Addison's being himself the translator.* Before he professed to have come to that conclusion, however, in a letter of his to Mr Craggs, there is the prose original of the famous sketch of Atticus. After alluding to " the Turk," and " the Little Senate of Cato," he says, " The new translator of Homer is the humblest slave he has ; that is to say, his first minister," and adds, " I fear no arbitrary highflying proceedings from the court faction at Button's." Spence, in his report of the concurring circumstances that made Pope suspect Addison as the writer, says, " Tickell himself, who is a very fair, worthy man, had since in a manner as good as owned it to him, (Pope.) When it was introduced into a conversation between Mr Tickell and Mr Pope, by a third person, Tickell did not deny it." If this was so, it must have been from following a habit of his friend Addison, mentioned by Swift, who, when he found any one incurably wedded to the wrong, humoured them, and sunk them still further in absurdity, or some other unaccountable reason. It may be added to Tickell's credit, that, he states, it having been his

* Watts, the printer of the work, declared that it was in Tickell's handwriting, but extensively altered and interlined by Addison. The MS., which is still preserved in the family, being recently examined by Miss Lucy Aikin, such was found to be the case.

intention originally to have dedicated the work to Lord Halifax, and he having died in the interim, he inscribed it, with a handsome eulogium, to his memory. This was a circumstance that did equal honour to both.

When Addison, two years after, (1717,) became one of the Secretaries of State, he gave the place of Under-Secretary to Mr Tickell. It is said that he communicated to Steele his intention in anticipation, and that he expressed decided objections in reference to certain attributed peculiarities of temper and other particulars. Addison probably on this occasion followed the common practice of asking an opinion when fully determined to follow his own. This, he not only did, but improperly allowed himself, if it be true as reported, to divulge the opinion expressed by Steele. The result was a serious animosity between Tickell and him during the remainder of their lives. It is to be hoped the affair may have admitted of some explanation which has not survived, as it is certainly not in keeping with the usual amiability of Addison's character.

On the death of Addison, which occurred soon after, (1719,) Tickell, as his literary executor, published his collected works, to which he added a biographical introduction and a beautiful "Elegy" to his memory, addressed to Lord Warwick, which has been very highly and generally admired. In the discharge of this office he indulged in some unwarrantable and depreciating inuendos reflecting on Steele, as if he had either not given Addison sufficient credit, or had been willing to take it to himself, which the latter warmly and justly repudiated.

Addison had recommended Tickell's interests to Mr Craggs, his successor, who did not long survive him, but

Tickell's prosperity did not cease with either. Some years after, he received the appointment of Secretary to the Lords Justices of Ireland, and in the following year, (1726,) vacated his Oxford Fellowship in consequence of having formed a matrimonial alliance at Dublin. The honourable official position last named he retained till his death, which occurred at Bath, April 23, 1740.

Though considered among the contributors to the *Spectator*, his papers have not been accurately traced, and of an attributed share still more considerable in the *Guardian*, its successor, one paper alone has been ascertained with certainty. Besides the poem of "The Royal Progress," previously referred to, he also contributed to the *Spectator* some eulogistic verses,* in which he says in reference to Steele and Addison—

> "Such gen'rous strifes Eugene and Marlb'rough try,
> And, as in glory, so in friendship, vie."

Tickell's most elaborate poem was entitled, "Kensington Garden." His felicity of versification was great, in that respect surpassing his friend Addison, though otherwise of course greatly his inferior. Personally, he is represented as of pleasing and amiable manners and lively conversation; of a gay and convivial temper, within the bounds of prudence, and in his domestic relations exemplary.

Of the other poetical contributors, besides Pope, pre-

* Considering the sentiments expressed in these verses, and the hope he expresses of his name surviving by their being enshrined in its pages, and his jealous care in republishing all the contributions of Addison, it appears remarkable that he should have taken so little trouble to claim or identify his own. Some have supposed those with the letter "T." to have been his, though it has usually been considered one of the initials adopted by Steele, and the objectionable paper of the Coverley series (No. 410) has been most generally assigned to him, though the question remains unsettled between him and Steele.

viously referred to, the celebrated Dr Isaac Watts communicated a paraphrase of the 114th Psalm; Dr Henry Bland, Head Master of Eton, and afterwards Dean of Durham, a Latin translation of Cato's soliloquy from Addison's tragedy; Gilbert Budgell, brother of Eustace previously noticed, some elegant amatory verses; Ambrose Philips, who comes more properly under notice in connexion with the *Guardian*, some peculiarly felicitous versions of some of the most exquisite poetical morsels of antiquity, including the " Hymn to Venus," and the fragment of the passionate love-song of Sappho, beginning,

" Blest as the immortal gods is he." *

---

* As it only falls within the scope of this work to notice at large the contributors who were either the personal associates of Steele and Addison, or of known literary reputation, the writers of casual communications may here be briefly enumerated. Of these the most considerable was the Rev. HENRY GROVE, a Dissenting divine of piety and learning, principal of the academy at Taunton, and author of some volumes of sermons, " An Essay on the Immateriality of the Soul," a " System of Moral Philosophy," &c., who contributed four papers of great merit to the eighth or supplementary volume, one of which Johnson considered among "the finest pieces in the English language;" Mr JOHN BYROM, a student of Trinity College, Cambridge, distinguished for his wit, learning, and piety, and author of the " System of Short-Hand " which bears his name, was the writer of two or three papers also in the eighth volume; Mr HENRY MARTYN, an excellent lawyer, scholar, and political economist, who is mentioned by Steele himself with high commendation as a contributor, but whose share has not been traced; Dr ZACHARY PEARCE, the afterwards eminent Bishop of Rochester, known by his writings and editions of the classics, the dedication of one of which (" Cicero de Oratore") to Lord Chief-Justice Parker, afterwards Earl Macclesfield, to whom he was quite unknown, was the immediate cause of his first promotion, wrote two admirable papers in the eighth volume, and one in the *Guardian*; Mr CAREY of New College, Oxford; Mr INCE of Gray's Inn, the latter spoken of very highly by Steele, but of whose respective productions nothing is known; the Rev. LAURENCE EUSDEN, who succeeded Rowe as poet-laureate; JOHN HENLEY, better known as orator Henley, who, though a graduate of Cambridge, distinguished by his early literary industry, and in orders, for the sake of metropolitan life relinquished a small country living, set up an oratory

A few words may be added, as in the case of the *Tatler*, respecting those eminent public characters to whom the different volumes of the *Spectator* were inscribed. The

in the vicinity of Clare Market, and sunk down to the character of a buffoon and mountebank; and having made known "his price" to Sir R. Walpole, with a hint if it were not accepted that "he wielded a pen," obtained L.100 a year, and started the *Hyp-doctor* in opposition to the *Craftsman*, which was the organ of Walpole's rival Pulteney. (The foregoing is not to be confounded with Anthony Henley, M.P., a man of talent and position, and the supposed author of the political article of the *Tatler* signed "Prompter Down.") A Mr GOLDING, of whom nothing is definitely known; Mr JAMES HEYWOOD, who had been a wholesale linen-draper in the city; Mr PHILIP YORKE, the afterwards Lord Chancellor Hardwicke, whose communication illustrates the difference between possessing the qualities that lead to eminence as a lawyer and minister and shining as an author; Mr PETER MOTTEUX, a Frenchman, who acquired the idiom of the language so well as successfully to translate "Don Quixote" and "Rabelais," and produce some popular plays, who held a place in the foreign post-office, and was the proprietor of an East India warehouse in the city; Mr JOHN WEAVER, a dancing-master; a Mr FRANCHAM, of Norwich, of whom nothing is definitely known; Mr ROBERT HARPER, an eminent conveyancer of Lincoln's Inn; Mr DUNLOP, Greek Professor at Glasgow, a vision or allegory, in conjunction with Mr MONTGOMERY, a merchant who traded with Sweden, which he is said to have left abruptly in consequence of something having reference to Queen Christina, which appears to have made a strong impression on his mind; Professor Simpson of Glasgow has also been named; the Rev. JOHN LLOYD, M.A.; the Rev. RICHARD PARKER, Steele's college friend, an eminent scholar, and Vicar of Embleton, in Northumberland, with whom, on his way to or from Scotland, Steele is said to have spent some time; a Mr WESTERN, of whom nothing particular is known; the Rev. Dr BROME, to whom the same remark applies; Dr FLEETWOOD, Bishop of Ely, eminent for his writings in history, antiquities, and theology; Miss SHEPHEARD and her sister, Mrs PERRY, descendants of Sir Fleetwood Shepheard, of facetious memory, the most noticeable result of the letter of the former lady being to draw from Addison the story of Theodosius and Constantia. These were mostly the writers of one paper, and a few of only a letter, the share of each of whom may be ascertained by a reference to any of the annotated editions, the statement of which could answer no useful purpose in this place. It was stated by Mr Murphy, in conversation with Johnson, that he remembered when there were several persons living in London who enjoyed a considerable reputation from having written only a single paper in the *Spectator*, and their names are here repeated to contribute to their continuing to enjoy their moiety of fame in connexion with the work, as well as to shew the variety of its contributors.

wonderful versatility of resource displayed in the volumes themselves, is scarcely more surprising than the variations of graceful compliment the author addresses to his patrons—touching with a dashing but delicate hand on the principal points of their public and private merits.

Those of the first of these distinguished persons on the present occasion were so various and transcendant, as might have exhausted the language of panegyric without doing more than justice to them. This was JOHN LORD SOMERS, the son of an attorney in extensive and respectable practice at Worcester, where he was born about the year 1650 or 1652. After passing through a course of instruction at the collegiate school of his native city, he proceeded to Oxford, where he merely took his bachelor's degree. At both places he is stated to have been more noted for the modest and retiring disposition which characterised him through life, than the display of the splendid abilities which marked his after career. Entering himself of the Middle Temple, he prosecuted his legal studies with an assiduity which, though from the profoundness of his attainments must have been great, he did carry the length of the narrowing process of permitting it wholly to absorb his attention or to exclude the claims of letters. Either at this time, or during the period of his college studies, he made translations of some parts of "Plutarch" and of "Ovid's Epistles," which were considered at least very respectable. After his call to the bar in 1676, he still continued his residence at the university, where his hereditary attachment to the principles of liberty was confirmed by his introduction, through his early friends the Earl of Shrewsbury and Sir Francis

Winnington, to some strenuous opponents of the arbitrary and unconstitutional proceedings of Charles and his infamous *cabal* ministers. By a series of tracts, which he commenced about this time (1681,) having reference to the subjects then agitating the public mind, he displayed his extensive and exact knowledge of constitutional history, and at a time when the cause of liberty was for a season struck down by the suppression of the Parliament, and the consequent assumption of absolute power by the King, commenced those exertions in its defence which, during his subsequent career, he never relaxed. One of these was a "History of the Succession," having reference to the proposed bill for the exclusion of the Duke of York, on the ground of his open profession of the principles of the Romish Church, and the clandestine correspondence he was discovered to have carried on with France, opposed to the religion and interests of his country. Another, entitled "A Just and Modest Vindication of the Two Last Parliaments," was produced in conjunction with Algernon Sidney and Sir Wm. Jones. A third, on an attempt being made to tamper with a grand jury in favour of the Court, was entitled "The Security of Englishmen's Lives, or the Trust, Power, and Duties of the Grand Juries of England explained."

Having removed to London in 1682, he rose rapidly in reputation at the bar, which was promoted by his being engaged the following year as junior counsel for the defence in a political prosecution of some importance relative to a riot at the election of sheriffs in the city. But the most striking evidence of the reputation he had established in his profession in a comparatively short time from his commencing practice, was his being retained, in 1688, among the counsel in defence of the Seven Bishops who had been committed to the Tower by the infamous Jeffreys, for modestly petitioning King James to be excused from reading in their pulpits the declaration of his *dispensing power* in matters of religion. His masterly argument in this cause, though too young in his profession to be a leading counsel, established his reputation. The issues of the cause were not inferior in importance to any ever tried within the walls of Westminster. His clients—the Seven Golden Candlesticks, as they were called—were acquitted. The Revolution rapidly succeeded, and James became a fugitive.

In all the great questions that followed Somers took an active part, or was the prime móver. He was one of those who concerted the invitation to the Prince of Orange. In the Convention Parliament, summoned by William on his arrival in 1689, he represented his native city of Worcester, and took a distinguished part as one of a committee appointed to confer with the Lords in the discussions which ensued relative to the word *abdicated,* in reference to James having left the kingdom. After the accession of William and Mary, he was a member of a committee for arranging the heads of such things as were necessary for securing the civil and religious liberties of the nation. This was the origin of the celebrated Declaration of Rights embodied in the report of this committee, which, having been accepted by the Crown and Parliament, became the groundwork of the constitution.

Soon after these events, Somers was appointed Solicitor-General, with the honour of knighthood. He was the staunch defender of the new settlement of the Crown and Government, to which he had so much contributed, against the insidious attacks of the Opposition, on the ground of the Convention not having been summoned by the King's writ, and spoke with an authority to which no one ventured to reply. Within a few years subsequently, Sir John Somers passed in rapid succession through the offices of Attorney-General, Lord-Keeper of the Great Seal, in which latter office he delivered his celebrated judgment in the case of the Bankers, and finally Lord Chancellor in 1697. He was at the same time elevated to the peerage as Lord Somers, Baron of Evesham.

This high office, however, was not destined to be long filled by one who so eminently adorned it. Before long he was sacrificed to the violence of faction. He was so much the stay and support of his own party, by his wisdom and moderation restraining its extravagance, and enjoyed so highly the confidence of the King, that the Opposition saw in his removal their only prospect of coming into power. By means of clamour, and the persevering agitation of a variety of frivolous and vexatious charges against the Chancellor, they had succeeded in retarding the public business, and wearing out the patience of the King. In the balanced state of parties at the period, he was induced to hope for relief from constant inquietude by listening to the insidious counsels of the Opposition leaders, promising a peaceful management of Parliament by the removal of Lord Somers. Eager for any prospect of peace, the King represented to the Chancellor the necessity of his resignation to the interests of his service; but at same time, out of personal consideration, was anxious that it might appear his own act. With this Lord Somers declined compliance, which might be construed into a dread of his enemies, or a tacit confession of fault in the discharge of his office, but on a formal demand of the seals, in consequence, they were immediately delivered.

The King probably anticipated that, by bribing the Opposition with power, he might depend on the Whigs, as his friends, not to thwart him. This was not a generous policy, and was expecting almost more than was reasonable from the disinterestedness of party. He soon found his hopes disappointed by the Tories, and that it was like attempting to pacify the wolf with the taste of blood to expect to appease their clamour with the spoils of office. No sooner did they find themselves in power than, not satisfied with the sacrifice of their enemy, they forthwith proceeded, on the most absurd and factious grounds, to impeach him of high crimes and misdemeanours. Yet, in reality, all the points of accusation had originated with the King, though of course, if they had been culpable in themselves, the ministers would have had to bear the blame, as the advisers of the sovereign.

One charge referred to an expedition which had been sent out, at the King's suggestion, against some pirates in the West Indies, of whose depredations complaints had been made. No fund existing to defray the expenses, the King had advanced a sum out of his private purse, and several noblemen connected with the Government had contributed towards it. The command having been given to a Captain Kidd, who proved unworthy of the trust by turning pirate himself, and was afterwards executed for his offences, an attempt was made to implicate the Chancellor

s

and the other subscribers as promoters of his criminal practices. Another charge referred to what were called the partition treaties, which the King had arranged when in Holland in 1698. Having received overtures on the subject from the French Government, which he entertained favourably, he wrote to the Chancellor requiring his opinion on the subject, and desiring a document in blank under the Great Seal for the appointment of commissioners to confer with those of the French Government. The Chancellor having consulted with other members of the Government, forwarded, along with the required commission, the result of this consultation, suggesting some objections to the proposed treaty. A third accusation was, his having obtained certain grants of crown lands. When the charges were first agitated in Parliament, Lord Somers entered into a calm and dignified statement of the facts. After various delays and differences between the two Houses, a day was at length fixed for hearing the impeachment, when the Commons not appearing to prosecute, the Peers acquitted Lord Somers, and dismissed the case. In his explanatory statement Lord Somers admitted the fact of the grants, but denied that they were the result of any solicitation on his part. At that time, the retiring pension which has since been considered an equitable compensation for the uncertainty of the office, and the relinquishment of private practice, a return to which is precluded, did not exist. It was as some equivalent that these grants had been made by the consideration and favour of the King.

The extravagance and malignity of these proceedings greatly disgusted the King, and caused him to repent of the step he had taken in withdrawing his favour from his tried friends and transferring it to their opponents, which he resolved never to repeat, and sought to remedy at the first opportunity. In the latter part of 1701, Lord Somers received a note from the King assuring him of the continuance of his friendship. Sometime subsequently steps were taken towards the formation of a Whig Ministry, but the completion of the arrangements were frustrated by the death of the King in the following spring.

Lord Somers in his retirement now devoted himself to the pursuits of science and letters, of which he had an exquisite relish, and was elected (1702) president of the Royal Society. His next public labours were devoted to rectify the defects in the administration of the law in the different courts ; and, in 1706, he introduced a bill into Parliament on that subject, by which he has earned the gratitude of posterity as a law reformer. In the same year he took a prominent part in devising and carrying out the legislative union with Scotland, which had been a favourite measure with King William.

The Whig interest in the Cabinet was once more in the ascendant, but Lord Somers was one of the old Whigs who, during the coalition period of the Ministry, maintained their independence, whilst giving a general support to the administration. Two years subsequently, (1708,) on the expulsion of Harley and his party, however, the Government becoming purely Whig, he accepted office as President of the Council. Their tenure of place might have been of longer date if his advice against the impeachment of Sacheverell had been followed, at the end of the next year, but his diffidence led him to yield too readily to counsels he disapproved. So far as he was concerned, however, the removal of the Whig Ministry in 1710 was probably felt as a relief, as he had been for some time suffering from bodily infirmity.

On the accession of George I., four years subsequently, he merely took his seat at the Council table, a paralytic attack, which impaired the vigour both of mind and body, rendering him disqualified for the active duties of office. He expressed his warm approval of the Septennial Bill as "the greatest possible support to the liberty of the country." Of the severities that followed the insurrection of 1715, he, who was the author of the settlement which conferred the crown upon the reigning family, entirely disapproved; and when informed that the King's advisers were against showing mercy in the case of Lord Derwentwater and the other prisoners, expressed much concern, and inquired, with tears, "whether they meant to revive the proscriptions of Marius and Sylla?" His decease occurred shortly after, in the year 1716.

The character of this eminent man formed a rare combination of great qualities. He united to genius a solid judgment, and to remarkable perspicacity of mind a masterly eloquence that made luminous the most obscure and intricate parts of his subject. Above all, in an age pre-eminent in perfidy, he displayed the most uniform consistency and singleness of mind, arising from the honesty of his heart. In his judicial capacity he was not only wholly incorrupt and impartial, but gentle and patient. As a legislator he brought to the consideration of public questions enlarged views of policy, profound constitutional lore, and a zeal for the service of his country that never relaxed in its patriotic efforts. In private he was noted for his extreme and uniform urbanity. In the dedication of Steele, after referring to his being master of the "arts and policies of ancient Greece and Rome, as well as the most exact knowledge of our own constitution in particular, and of the interests of Europe in general," he goes on to say,—

> "Your lordship appears as great in private life as in the most important public offices. . . . I would, therefore," he adds, "rather choose to speak of the pleasure you afford all who are admitted to your conversation, of your elegant taste in all the polite arts of learning, of your great humanity and complacency of manners, and of the surprising influence which is peculiar to you, in making every one who converses with your lordship prefer you to himself."

Besides this dedication, the portrait of Somers has been drawn by Addison in his "Freeholder," by Swift in his "Four Last Years of Queen Anne," in a tone that does him little credit, and by Horace Walpole, who justly ridicules that of Swift for its recognition of some of the mean and low reflections of his enemies. "Lord Somers," says Walpole, "was one of those divine men who, like a chapel in a palace, remain unprofaned when all the rest is tyranny, corruption, and folly."

To LORD HALIFAX, to whom the second volume was inscribed, it will be needless further to refer here, having previously been noticed as the subject of dedication to one of the *Tatler* volumes.

The RIGHT HON. HENRY BOYLE, youngest son of Charles, Lord Clifford, and afterwards elevated to the peerage as Lord Carleton, was the subject of dedication to the third volume. He was one of a family which, from the time of its founder, Richard the great Earl of Cork, who made an advantageous purchase of the property of Raleigh in Ireland, produced a remarkable number of persons of talent and merit. Mr Boyle had filled the office of Chancellor of the Exchequer at the close of King William's reign, which he retained from the year 1701 till, on the expulsion of Harley in 1708, he succeeded him as one of the Secretaries of State. He was the person employed by Lord Godolphin in his negociation with Addison relative to the celebration of the battle of Blenheim, at the suggestion of Lord Halifax. On the accession of George I. he was created Lord Carleton, and appointed President of the Council. He died in 1724, and his life was written by Budgell, Addison's relative.

The fourth dedication was to the Duke of Marlborough, then in retirement, and exposed to the unmitigated malignity of his enemies, who, finding that he was not to be won over, determined upon his ruin, so far as it was in their power to effect it. The intimacy of Steele with the great captain originated in a witticism at his expense, which being reported to him, was received with the good temper which so eminently characterized him. It was evident, therefore, that Steele was not blind to his weaknesses, but his ardent admiration of the great qualities of the hero were strengthened and confirmed by those amiable and engaging ones which he displayed in private, the gentleness and suavity of his manners and temper, in addition to his being a martyr as a Whig chief.

JOHN CHURCHILL, first Duke of Marlborough, son of Sir Winston Churchill of Wooton Basset, Wilts, was born in 1650. His father, who possessed some literary pretensions, having suffered in the royal cause, was at the Restoration favourably received at court, and this, his second son, at the age of twelve, appointed page to the Duke of York. His daughter Arabella, was at the same time one of the maids of honour to the Duchess, and afterwards filled a less reputable place, which was probably little regarded, however, in an age influenced by the example of a court of unprecedented corruption. The celebrated Fitz-James, Duke of Berwick, was her son. At the age of sixteen, young Churchill, by the favour of the Duke, was presented with an ensign's commission in a regiment of foot-guards. His first military service was at the Siege of Tangiers. In the war that followed that disgraceful and mercenary alliance formed by Charles with France against Holland (1672), he held the rank of captain in the auxiliary force under the Duke of Monmouth. The French army being commanded by Marshal Turenne, he had the good fortune to learn the practice of his profession under that great man, who called him his handsome Englishman, and to attract his favourable notice by his gallant conduct at the siege of Maestricht. For his service on this occasion, by which he saved the life of his own commander, he received the thanks of Louis at the head of the army, and was recommended for promotion. On his return in the following year, he was again attached to the household of the Duke of York. At a court such as that of Charles, with a noble figure, an eminently handsome countenance, and soft obliging manners, he would naturally be a favourite, and exposed to temptations. The notorious Duchess of Cleveland manifested her favour to him by a gift of L.5000, which he invested in a life annuity. In the year succeeding his return, he was promoted to a lieutenant-colonelcy. In 1679, he accompanied the Duke to the Netherlands, and the following year to Scotland. About the same time he received the command of a regiment of dragoons.

Two daughters of a Hertfordshire gentleman of the name of Jennings, who, like the Churchills, had suffered by his zeal in the royal cause, had been placed under the patronage of the Duchess of York. To one of these, Sarah Jennings, who had become the companion and favourite of the Princess Anne, and who was distinguished by her beauty and the vigour of her mind, Colonel Churchill became ardently attached, and their union was consummated about this time. She proved a valuable and suitable partner for such a man, with the single exception of an imperious temper,—with affection to confide in, judgment to counsel, zeal and ability to promote his interest and honour, and manners so exemplary as never to have incurred the breath of scandal. In 1682, he suffered shipwreck on a second voyage to Scotland with the Duke, and the same year was, by his interest, created a peer of that kingdom, as Baron Eymouth. On the accession of James, he was sent as ambassador to France, and on his return created a peer of England as Lord Churchill, Baron Sandridge, in Herts. In the same year he suppressed the rebellion in the west by the Duke of Monmouth. Though his loyalty and gratitude were proof against the offers made him by Monmouth, yet, if he was not a party to the invitation shortly after to the Prince of Orange, at least he joined him along with other officers immediately on his arrival. He did not, however, commit any breach of trust, and wrote a letter to the King, in which he represented himself as compelled by his religion and conscience to go against his inclination, his interest, and his duty to him. The plea would have been unimpeachable if Marlborough had shown himself a single-minded man; as it is, his motives are open to suspicion of deserting a falling cause.

On the accession of William and Mary, in 1689, his services were rewarded with the earldom of Marlborough, and the appointment of commander-in-chief of the forces serving in the Netherlands. The following year he served in Ireland, having declined to do so whilst James was present with the army, and distinguished himself by the reduction of Cork and other places. Soon after (1692) he was summarily dismissed from all his offices, and afterwards committed to the Tower on the charge of high treason. His accuser was an obscure prisoner, who forged treasonable letters in his name. They were well executed, but proved not to be genuine. But though the accusation fell to the ground, Marlborough had not innocence to console him; for, strange as it appears, the publication of the Stuart papers proves that a genuine correspondence of a similar kind did exist, and leaves a deep stain upon the honour of Marlborough, though many other leading politicians were open to the same imputation. The fact is difficult to account for. He has been represented as dissatisfied with the favour shewn by William to his Dutch followers, with his cold, repulsive demeanour, and his High Church zeal offended by his measures in favour of the Dissenters.

It was not till after the death of Queen Mary (1698) that a reconciliation ensued, when Marlborough was restored to the Privy Council, and appointed governor to the young Duke of Gloucester, son of the Princess Anne, and, after her, heir to the crown. Two years after, he was made commander-in-chief of the forces serving in Holland, and ambassador to the States.

On the accession of Queen Anne in 1702, the romantic friendship which had sprung up between her and her companion, the Countess of Marlborough, as well as the espousing of her cause by both in opposition to the Court, (one of the causes assigned for his temporary disgrace,) led to their having all the honours in the power of the crown heaped upon them. The countess was made Mistress of the Robes and Keeper of the Privy Purse ; he received the honour of the garter, was appointed Captain-General of all the forces at home and abroad, and sent plenipotentiary to the Hague, where his claims prevailed over those of all others to the command of the allied armies. He had been instrumental in inducing the Queen to confirm the alliance formed by her illustrious predecessor shortly before his decease, to restrain the exorbitant ambition of Louis XIV., which threatened the balance of power in Europe, and especially in reference to the usurpation of the Spanish Crown for his grandson, the Count Anjou. The history of Marlborough from that time belongs to that of Europe, in which he was among the principal actors, both in war and diplomacy, and can, therefore, only have the leading results briefly indicated. In the first campaign, though crippled by the timid policy of the civil deputies of the Dutch, attending the army, and their generals, and held back from attacking the enemy in a decisive engagement on several occasions when he was confident of victory, yet he drove them before him, and crossing the Meuse, reduced the line of strongholds which impeded the free navigation of that river, from Venloo to

Liege. For this important service, though greatly inferior to what he might have accomplished if his energies had not been paralysed by timid counsels, he was, on his return to England, elevated to the highest rank of the peerage, as Duke of Marlborough, was voted the thanks of both Houses of Parliament, and, by the express desire of the Queen, granted a pension of L.5000. The following year did little more than confirm and extend the previous acquisitions, owing to the supineness of the Dutch, and the want of unanimity in the counsels of the allies. It was, however, compensated by the splendour and brilliancy of the campaign of 1704. With the aid of their ally, the Elector of Bavaria, the French had achieved such successes in Germany as to reduce the affairs of the Emperor to the most critical position, fearing even to be besieged in his capital. Marlborough, therefore, formed the bold resolution to carry his arms into Germany to co-operate with Eugene and the imperial forces; but not daring to reveal his plans fully to the States, he merely obtained their sanction and that of the home Government, now that a small force was able to preserve the frontiers, to making the Moselle the centre of his next operations. His march confounded and perplexed the enemy. Reaching the Moselle, he thence directed his route with the utmost expedition to the Danube, where he attacked the enemy at Schellenberg, near Donawerth, where they were strongly posted. His success was complete,—their ammunition, tents, and baggage falling into his hands. The enemy shortly after, being reinforced with 30,000 men under Marshal Tallard, the combined French and Bavarian forces took up an elevated and very strong position at

Hockstadt, having on their right the village of Blenheim and the Danube, on their left a thick wood, and in front two rivulets, forming a morass. Marlborough having been joined by Prince Eugene with 20,000 men, the two armies were nearly equal, each numbering between fifty and sixty thousand men. The enemy had rather the advantage in numbers, and the strength of their position was such as would have rendered it imprudent to have attacked them, but for the imperious necessities of the campaign. After a sanguinary conflict, which lasted from one in the afternoon till sunset, a complete victory crowned the arms of the allies. Part of the enemy retreated under cover of the wood, but upwards of thirty squadrons were driven into the Danube, where a great part of them perished, and about ten thousand were made prisoners, of whom about twelve hundred were officers, including Marshal Tallard. The effects of this victory were incalculable. The electorate of Bavaria became the prize of the allies, the Emperor was relieved from a position of the most imminent peril, and, above all, the charm of invincibility attached to the French arms, both in their own eyes and those of others, by a long series of victorious aggressions, was dispelled, and European liberty relieved from the danger that threatened it. The remains of the vanquished army, recently so formidable, made good their retreat within the French frontiers. They were pursued across the Rhine by the allies, who entered Alsace and took the fortress of Landeau. Marlborough had meantime turned aside with expedition and garrisoned the city of Treves, and the stronghold of Traerbach on the Moselle, to the strategetical position of which he attached much importance.

Testimonies of national gratitude for so signal a service to the cause of European liberty, and so brilliant an addition to the glory of his country's arms, and in humiliation of its ambitious rival, were lavished without stint upon the victor. The gift of the royal manor of Woodstock was voted him, and on it erected the princely mansion of Blenheim, the architectural masterpiece of Vanbrugh. Medals were struck in honour of the event, which was also commemorated in song by Addison. The trophies of Blenheim were paraded from the Tower to Westminster. The Duke himself, besides receiving the thanks of both Houses of Parliament, was magnificently feted by the city authorities. But the most valuable of all the tributes conferred upon him was that of the Emperor, who created him a prince of the empire, no empty title, but endowed with the gift of the principality of Mindelheim.

Thus covered with honours, Marlborough did not suffer himself to repose upon his laurels, but, though thwarted and checked by the inactivity and timid policy of the Dutch deputies and generals, as well as the German allies, with the exception of his illustrious coadjutor, the Prince Eugene, continued through several successive years, during the continuance of his command, to add to them fresh and splendid accessions. These were—the victories of Ramillies (1706), taking its name from a small village ten or twelve miles north of the strongly-fortified city of Namur on the Meuse; Oudenarde, (1708); Malplaquet, (1709); and the reduction of numerous towns and fortresses, some of them deemed impregnable, including Ostend, Lille, Mons, Dendermond, Douay, Tournay, and many others. He broke through the lines which the ablest marshals of

France had constructed, after years of labour and immense expense, and boasted to be impregnable, as if they had been cobwebs.

On the retirement of the Whig Ministry with which he had been so long connected, in 1710,* by a mistaken policy he was persuaded by his party not to resign his command, and thereby exposed himself to great mortifications. That Ministry had at its head his wily antagonist, Harley, who

---

* In the same year Captain Steele (as he continued to be called for a considerable time after leaving the army) addressed to the Duke the following verses in imitation of Horace, Book i., Ode vi.:—

"Should Addison's immortal verse
Your fame in arms, great Prince, rehearse,
With Anna's lightning you'd appear,
And glitter o'er again in war,
Repeat the proud Bavarian's fall,
And in the Danube plunge the Gaul.
'Tis not for me your worth to show,
Or lead Achilles to the foe,
Describe stern Diomed in fight,
And put the wounded gods to flight;
I dare not, with unequal rage,
On such a mighty theme engage;
Nor sully in a verse like mine
Illustrious Anna's praise, and thine.
Let the laborious Epic lay,
In lofty lines, the chief display,
Who bears to distant realms his arms,
And strikes through Gallia dread alarms,
His courage and his conduct tell,
And on his various virtues dwell.
In trifling cares my humble muse
A less ambitious track pursues.
Instead of troops in battle mix'd,
And Gauls with British spears transfix'd,
She paints the soft distress and mien
Of dames expiring with the spleen,
From the gay noise, affected air,
And little follies of the fair,
A slender stock of fame I raise,
And draw from others' faults my praise."

had played him foul, and treated him with ingratitude in former years, and who now, finding he was not to be won over, at length complied with the desire of the more violent of his party by seeking his ruin. Even the severe and acrimonious Swift, who had gone over to the party in power, disapproved of the harshness shewn to him. " I question," he says, "whether ever any wise statesman laid aside a general who had been successful nine years together, whom the enemy so much dread, and his own soldiers cannot but believe must always conquer; and you know that in war opinion is nine parts in ten."* In the beginning of 1712 he was not only deprived of all his places, but vindictive proceedings commenced against him for imputed corruption in his office, the only foundation for which was his acceptance of perquisites which had been customary. He then retired in disgust to the scene of his former triumphs, and wherever he went, was received with the greatest honour. On the death of the Queen in 1714 he returned to England, and was soon after restored to his military rank as Captain-General and Master of the Ordinance by the new Government of George I., but did not again take any prominent part in public affairs. In 1716, he was attacked with paralysis, from the effects of which he recovered. The King would not accept his proffered resignation, out of consideration for his services. A fresh attack of his malady, which he suffered, ultimately reduced him to a state of second childhood, and proved fatal in 1722. Having no sons, his honours had been settled on his daughters and their heirs. His duchess survived him many years.

* Journal to Stella, Jan. 7, 1711.

Marlborough added to his unrivalled military renown the highest reputation as a skilful and able diplomatist. As a soldier, he was distinguished by his humanity to the conquered and his regard for those under his command. Apart from the besetting infirmity of avarice, his personal character displayed many virtues and amiable qualities, some of which have been previously alluded to, and which Steele celebrates in his dedication. After referring to the mild and gentle demeanour of him " who had carried fire and sword into the countries of all that had opposed the cause of liberty, and struck a terror into the armies of France," he adds—

"The Prince of Mindelheim may rejoice in a sovereignty which was the gift of him whose dominions he had preserved. Glory established upon the uninterrupted success of honourable designs and actions is not subject to diminution; nor can any attempts prevail against it, but in the proportion which the narrow circuit of rumour bears to the unlimited extent of fame."

The next to whom honour is done by the *Spectator* in the dedication of one of his volumes, is that remarkable person, in various ways, THOMAS, afterwards, Earl and Marquis of WHARTON, whose name has descended with rather an equivocal reputation. He was the son of Philip, sometimes entitled the *good*, Lord Wharton, distinguished by his opposition to the arbitrary measures of Charles I., and who was one of the Parliamentary commanders in the civil war. He opposed, however, the extreme measures which resulted in the death of Charles. His son, Thomas, who was born in 1647, inherited his attachment to civil and religious liberty, but soon discarded his Puritanism as incompatible with the partiality for pleasure which he early manifested. It has been said in extenuation of his indulgence in this respect, that he had been forced into a marriage which, though there was nothing objectionable to the lady, was not in accordance with his wishes. The plea, it must be admitted, is but an indifferent one. But the pursuits of the mere man of pleasure could fill but a limited space in the compass of a nature so various, and adorned with all the gifts of nature and art to shine in every sphere of life. He had such a superabundance of energy that he was able to throw as much into the greatest variety of pursuits as would in each have fully occupied any ordinary man. His vigour and versatility were indeed prodigious. Like Bolingbroke, though we are not told that he possessed his personal gifts, he seems to have taken Alcibiades as his model, and sought to combine the man of business and pleasure. He shone as a wit, was the dread of his opponents in the senate by his vigour, his audacity, his sarcasm; was foremost on the turf, and in his breed of dogs and horses; he cultivated the fine art, and in architecture and gardening particularly excelled; whilst in boroughmongering and electioneering his reputation was unique. One of the methods by which he extended his influence was by noticing and humouring any young man of promise on his first appearance. He opposed James as staunchly as his father had done the arbitrary measures of the first and second Charles. When the rebellion of Monmouth occurred, he was considered so suspicious a person that his house was searched for arms. He was one of the leading promoters of the invitation to the Prince of Orange, and among the first to join him on his landing, with a retinue and supply of arms. He had previously brought other arms to the aid of the cause, the

T

influence assigned to which some may now be inclined to smile at. The doggerel political ballad of "Lilli Burlero," which is sometimes said to have produced the Revolution, is attributed to him; of which it has been wittily said, that, if it did produce such an effect, there has been no such fortunate cackling since the saving of the capitol by the geese. But, without referring to that celebrated saying which attributes greater influence to popular ballads than to the laws themselves, see the effect produced in other cases—even in the face of reason itself—by apparently inadequate causes, as in the case of a foolish political sermon by Sacheverell, and the "Drapier's Letters" by Swift. But in this case it had reason on its side, and, as in the others, what seemed to produce the effect was only the applying of the match to a train ready to explode, and in this way it may have had some such result as that attributed to it.*

Wharton was a member of the Convention Parliament, called by William, and on the Revolution Settlement became Comptroller of the Household, Justice in Eyre, south of Trent, and Lord-lieutenant of Oxfordshire. On the accession of Anne in 1702, he was dismissed from his offices, and his name even erased from the Privy Council list by the Queen's own hand, as was that of Lord Halifax. But such energies as his were irrepressible, and when the prospects of the Whigs revived towards the close of 1706, not only was he restored to that honour, but he succeeded

* In an old Tory pamphlet this claim is attributed to an idle boast of the author:—"A late Viceroy (of Ireland,) who has so often boasted himself upon his talent for mischief, invention, lying, and for making a certain 'Lilli Burlero' song, with which, if you will believe himself, he sung a deluded prince out of three kingdoms."— *Wilkin's Political Ballads*, vol. i. p. 275.

in obtaining a step in the peerage, often as difficult as the first creation, as Viscount Winchendon and Earl of Wharton. A year or two later he was selected to fill the important office of Viceroy of Ireland, when he chose Addison as his secretary. It has been made a subject of remark expressive of surprise by Johnson, that Addison should be found acting with one of so opposite a character from his own. This was scarcely worthy of so sagacious and usually practical an observer of life. Though it might possibly have been more satisfactory, both to Addison and his admirers, if he had been associated with one more congenial in other respects than his political principles, yet men who have their way to make cannot always be choosers, and he was under political obligations to Wharton, having been brought into Parliament first by his influence. Neither are great qualities extinguished by being united with grave faults, though they may be depreciated. Swift, a Churchman, was not only on the most intimate terms with Bolingbroke, a notorious libertine and scoffer, but his great admirer. Johnson himself, too, had been the associate of one of the most indifferent character. Savage, in his early days, and, in his later, had a great regard for the accomplished but dissolute Beauclerc. With regard to Wharton, the decorous and pious Hughes, who declined to contribute to a volume of poetical miscellanies because it contained Pope's version of the "Wife of Bath," also dedicated one of his volumes to him. So that this hasty and inconsiderate remark was probably suggested by the traditional exaggerations of his enemies.

Lord Wharton contributed materially to the defeat of that intolerant measure, the bill against occasional conformity, the aim of which was to exclude Dissenters from office, and he adhered to the same policy in his administration in Ireland. On the accession of the House of Hanover in 1714, Lord Wharton filled the office of Lord Privy Seal, and at the close of that year was created Marquis of Wharton and Malmsbury in England, and Earl of Rathfarnham and Marquis of Catherlough in Ireland. On his decease in 1715, in consideration of his services, his son was raised to a dukedom. With something of his father's talents, by which he distinguished himself and might have pursued an honourable career, he possessed his faults in excess, and after rendering himself notorious by his intrigues, his levity, and his extravagance, by which he sunk his fortune, died in obscurity in Spain.

Though the dedications usually fell to Steele, one might suppose, from the acknowledgment of particular obligations and favours, that this one to Lord Wharton had been written by Addison. The writer adds—

> "We admire some for the dignity, others for the popularity of their behaviour; some for their clearness of judgment, others for their happiness of expression; some for the laying of schemes, and others for the putting of them in execution. It is your Lordship only who enjoys these several talents united, and that too in as great perfection as others possess them singly. Your enemies acknowledge this great extent in your Lordships' character, at the same time that they use their utmost industry and invention to derogate from it. But it is for your honour that those who are now your enemies were always so."

Pope has drawn his character in severe terms, yet with acknowledgment of the highest merit, in his first epistle :—

> "Wharton! the scorn and wonder of our days,
> Whose ruling passion was the lust of praise;
> Born with whate'er could win it from the wise,
> Women and fools must like him or he dies.

> Though wond'ring senates hung on all he spoke,
> The club must hail him master of the joke.
>
> . . . . .
>
> Ask you why Wharton broke through every rule?
> 'Twas all for fear the knaves should call him fool."

CHARLES SPENCER, Earl of Sunderland (1674-1722), was the person to whom the *Spectator* did honour in the next dedication. This nobleman, who succeeded to the title in 1702, had served an early apprenticeship to public life by having represented Tiverton from the attainment of his majority till called to the Upper House. By his talents and insinuating address, he succeeded in establishing and maintaining a remarkable influence at the courts of William and George I., to which his accomplishment as a linguist probably contributed, an advantage which may be estimated by the fact of Walpole having to maintain his intercourse with the latter sovereign in bad Latin. In 1700, he strengthened his political influence by taking, as his second wife, the Lady Anne Churchill, the Duke of Marlborough's second daughter. In 1705, he was engaged in a diplomatic capacity at the courts of Prussia, Austria, and Hanover, and was present when the Duke by invitation visited the emperor after the battle of Blenheim. Early in the following year he formed one of the commission appointed to arrange the legislative union with Scotland, and as the Whigs were then consolidating their interest in the Cabinet, in the ensuing September, he succeeded Sir Charles Hedges, as Secretary of State, against the wish of the Queen, who was with great reluctance prevailed on to part with his predecessor, and did not readily forgive this first Whig triumph over her. At this time Steele was officially connected with Sunderland by his appointment as Gazeteer, which he entered on the following May.

In 1710, when the Ministry was tottering through their folly in the impeachment of Sacheverell, the influence of the duchess gone, and Sunderland himself having displeased the Queen in a matter relating to the election of Scottish peers, he was one of the first victims. Though the duke employed all the force of his waning influence, and the duchess humbled herself in his favour, he was dismissed in the course of that eventful summer. The Queen broke his fall indeed by offering him a pension of L.3000, but, though by no means insensible to such considerations, his ruling passion appears to have been the love of power ; and resentment and disappointment having the mastery, he replied with dignity and spirit that " he was glad her Majesty was satisfied he had done his duty; but if he could not have the honour to serve his country, he would not plunder it."

On the accession of the House of Hanover, though disappointed in his expectations of being supreme in the new Cabinet, he was treated with much favour, and successively filled the offices of Lord-Lieutenant of Ireland, when Addison was a second time secretary there, Lord Privy Seal, Vice-Treasurer of Ireland ; and on the resignation of Walpole and Townshend, in 1717, to which he mainly contributed, those of Secretary of State, Lord President of the Council, Groom of the Stole, and finally First Lord of the Treasury. He had accompanied the King to Hanover in the year 1716, and on that occasion succeeded in increasing his influence over him to an extraordinary extent, a power which he retained to the end.

About the beginning of the year 1719, when he had for some time reigned in the Cabinet, occurred perhaps the most remarkable event of his political life. This was the introduction of the peerage bill intended to fix permanently the number of the members of the Upper House, and prevent any subsequent creations except to supply the place of those which had become extinct. The motives of the originator were as bad as the tendency of the bill would have been pernicious if it had unfortunately passed. A misunderstanding with the Prince of Wales, which left little prospect of reconciliation, made him anxious to consolidate his interest whilst he had time, and to curtail the power of the prince when he assumed the crown. The first he hoped to accomplish by the support of those whom he proposed to raise to the peerage before closing the door, and the latter by abridging the prerogative. It is doubtful if the King was aware of the design of the bill, but it is questionable if he had been, whether he would have much regarded it, as he had also quarrelled with his son, who appears to have been very hot-tempered, and had been ordered to leave the palace. This remarkable measure will be further referred to on a future occasion. It was passed by the Lords, but rejected by the Commons, chiefly through the strenuous exertions of Walpole. In this and the following year, Sunderland was one of the Lords Justices in the absence of the King in Hanover, and had the honour of the Garter conferred upon him. Walpole meantime had taken a position of such strength in opposition, that he found it necessary to admit him and his brother-in-law, Lord Townshend, to a participation of power.

The bursting of the notorious South Sea Bubble in 1721 proved fatal, not only to the political career, but the reputation of Sunderland, by his more than suspected participation in that first and most unexampled scheme of mercantile gambling; and though, in the inquiry that followed, while other members of the Government were expelled the House, and otherwise punished, he escaped by the Lords throwing their shield over him, and Walpole exerting his utmost ability in his behalf; yet public indignation was so strongly aroused upon the subject, that he found it necessary to retire. Though he clung to the possession of power with the utmost tenacity, he was forced with the greatest reluctance to relax his grasp. But he never forgave the man that saved him, because he also succeeded him. The short time that he survived was spent in desperate efforts in the restless hope of again attaining to power, or damaging and harassing those in possession of it, to which he was ready to sacrifice any and everything, intriguing with Tories and Jacobites to that end. His influence with the King, which he still retained, he exerted in a characteristic manner by an application, as if in the interest of his rival, that he might be made Postmaster-General for life, which, though a lucrative, was not then a ministerial or parliamentary place. The King's reply annihilated his hopes. After inquiring if the request was made at the instance of Walpole, and being answered in the negative, he desired that it might not be suggested to him. "I parted with him once," added the King, "against my inclination, and will never part with him again as long as he is willing to serve me."

The Earl of Sunderland appears to have been one of

those who owed his elevation to his position, joined to good management, an artful address, the prudent use of opportunities, and the skilful application of moderate abilities. He preserved a consistent, though not very single-minded reputation in prosperity, but how few can stand the test of adversity? Both in his political and speculative errors, he had abundance of examples to keep him in countenance in that age, and it is difficult to pass a severe judgment in such cases by the application of abstract principles. It seems remarkable that Walpole—whose name has descended with such a reputation for corruption, or at least the application of it to others, which is due rather to the traditional reputation he acquired by the attacks of a violent and interested opposition than strict justice—should, almost alone of that Ministry, have escaped the imputation of complicity by the collapse of the South Sea scheme. Of the others, in addition to Sunderland, the Chancellor of the Exchequor was expelled the House, and sent to the Tower, and two Secretaries of State, Craggs and Stanhope, were supposed to have died, (as one certainly did, and the other not without suspicion of violence), in consequence of the attacks made upon them relative to that disastrous affair.

With regard to Sunderland, he was personally an accomplished man, and the founder of the noble library at Althorpe.

The last of those public characters to whom the *Spectator* did honour was Sir PAUL METHUEN, (1671-1757), a lawyer, and displayed qualities not often combined with such a position. He was employed as ambassador at the Courts of Lisbon and Turin, where he earned the character of a skilful and able diplomatist—at the former, having arranged the celebrated commercial treaty which bears his name; and at the latter, in addition to his proper functions, distinguished himself in a military capacity, by sharing with the Duke of Savoy all the labours and perils of the day in which he recovered his capital. On his return he was honoured with the order of the Bath, and successively filled a variety of places, as a commissioner of the Admiralty and Treasury, Comptroller of the Household, and various others, between the year 1709 and 1732. He also represented the borough of Brackley about the same period in Parliament. Steele celebrates him in addition in his social character.

The eighth or supplementary volume of the *Spectator*, was dedicated, it is supposed by Budgell, to one of its own imaginary characters, Will Honeycomb, the original of which was supposed to be a Colonel Cleland. But with that volume, which, as previously mentioned, was taken up after an interval of some years, Steele was unconnected.

It may be proper to add a few words in reference to one or two points not previously alluded to. Of the origin of the work, or the nature of the arrangements respecting its publication, nothing is definitely known. It is probable that, as Swift surmised,* Addison and Steele clubbed in this respect, as well as in the production of the matter, and had share and share alike. Johnson states, we know not on what authority, that Addison received his share

* "Have you seen the *Spectator* yet, a paper that comes out every day? It is written by Mr Steele, who seems to have gathered a new fund of wit; it is in the same nature as his *Tatlers*, and they have all of them had something pretty. I believe Addison and he club. I never see them."—*Journal to Stella*, March 16, 1711.

"with avidity."* If so, it was the more remarkable as it was after he had entered on his official life, and, with his well regulated prudence, any great pecuniary difficulty must have ceased. In one respect he came to the task probably better prepared than Steele. There is reason to believe that he had a quantity of previously prepared matter on hand—including those various dissertations on the Imagination, (which Akenside afterwards made the foundation of his poem,) on Wit, and on Milton—so that what he said in his introductory paper, of printing himself out, was applicable to written as well as unwritten matter.

With regard to the success of the work it is difficult, amid the various conflicting statements, to arrive at a very precise result. It was at least altogether unprecedented, as that of the *Tatler* had previously been, at that period. But to form a just judgment with our modern ideas on the subject, the limited number of readers at the time must be borne in mind, for reading was not then the universal necessity that it now is. With regard to details, Addison states in No. 10, that 3000 copies were sold daily. After the imposition of the stamp in August 1712, it is stated by Steele, in his concluding paper, that the amount paid to the revenue averaged L.20 a week. On this statement Dr Johnson has calculated the circulation at 1680 copies daily. Some have thought that Steele's statement was a typographical error, and below the mark. But taking it and the calculation on it as accurate, it must be remembered that, though it doubled its price and survived the imposition of the tax, yet it is stated that its circulation fell to little more than half. On the other hand, Dr Fleet-

* "Lives of the Poets"—Addison.

wood, a suppressed article by whom had been published in it, states, in a letter to the Bishop of Salisbury, that the daily sale amounted to 14,000. At all events the average total circulation previous to the existence of the tax, must, on the most moderate estimate, have been thereabout, as Steele states in the paper above referred to, that the circulation when collected into volumes, at a guinea each, amounted to 9000. It is certainly remarkable that the circulation of the collected edition, and at such an advance in price, should have exceeded the current one. That was the first circulation, but numerous other editions followed subsequently.

Such is the result of all that can be arrived at respecting the original publication of this celebrated work—the first attempt at a popular literature in England—which may be regarded as the precursor not merely of the literary periodical press, but (what may be considered perhaps by some a more questionable merit) of the modern novel—in which respect Miss Aikin* thinks Steele may be taken as the representative of Richardson, and Addison of Fielding, so far at least as the possession of their respective characteristic qualities of the pathetic and the humorous.

* Life of Addison, vol. ii. p. 10.

CHAPTER VIII.

Correspondence during publication of *Spectator* — Reference to his mother's family—Poetical correspondence with Hughes and Pope—Anecdote of the *Censorium*, or private theatre of Steele—Criticism on Pope's Messiah—Addison disclaimsPopes' satire on Dennis—Pope's Dying Christian—Newcomb's encomium on Steele.

LETTER CLXVII.   *To Mr Keally.*

April 2, 1711.

SIR,—The bearer hereof, Mr John Bateman, is the nearest of blood to my uncle, Gascoigne, to whose bounty I owe a liberal education. He has a demand upon my Lord Longford, as administrator to my said uncle, together with some other debts which lie out in Ireland. I earnestly recommend his affairs to your favour and patronage, and desire you would stand by him, and appear for him, in order to his obtaining speedy justice. He is of himself an helpless, and your goodness herein will be the highest obligation to, Sir, your most obedient and most humble servant,

RICH. STEELE.

LETTER CLXVIII.   *To Mrs Steele.*

June 14, 1711.

DEAR PRUE,—I inclose you a guinea, and desire you to go before to Mrs Simpson's, if I am not ready to go with you, and call at your mother's at eight o'clock, for Mr Craggs and others do not come to us till late in the evening. Therefore pray be tractable to your enamoured husband and humble servant,   RICH. STEELE.

LETTER CLXIX.   *To Mrs Steele.*

[1711.]

PRUE,—Addison's money* you will have to-morrow noon. I have but

---

* "This was the loan which afterwards so unfortunately interrupted a long and early friendship. 'At the school of the Chartreux,' Dr Johnson observes, 'Mr Addison contracted that intimacy with Sir Richard Steele which their joint

18s., but have very many reasons to be in good humour, except you are angry with me.

If you can pay the woman for coals, you [may] have it from Ruth in the morning.—Your obedient husband, lover, servant, &c.

RICH. STEELE.

LETTER CLXX.   *To Mrs Steele.*

June 2, 1711.

DEAR PRUE,—I cannot come home to dinner. I dine with Tonson, at an ordinary near the Temple, with Mr Addison and another gentleman. A gentleman met me to-day, and acquainted me that John had been with him to be hired, so that you will be rid of him, and I will pay him when I come home. I would have you go out and divert yourself, and believe I love you better than life.—Yours,   RICH. STEELE.

I write from Mr Edward Lawrence's, whose sister would be glad of your company.

LETTER CLXXI.   *To Mrs Steele.*

June 14, 1711.

DEAR PRUE,—I am obliged to go with Mr Glanville to Sir Harry Furnasse's,† and cannot be home till nine at night. Thank God, all will now be done.—Your most obedient husband,   RICH. STEELE.

I will come to Berry Street at nine.

---

labours have so effectually recorded. Of this memorable friendship, the greater praise must be given to Steele. . . . Addison, who knew his own dignity, could not always forbear to show it, by playing a little upon his admirer; but he was in no danger of retort—his jests were endured without resistance or resentment. But the sneer of jocularity was not the worst. Steele, whose imprudence of generosity or vanity of profusion kept him always incurably necessitous, upon some pressing emergency, in an evil hour, borrowed L.100 from his friend; . . . but Addison, who seems to have had other notions of L.100, grew impatient of delay, and reclaimed his loan by an execution. Steele felt with great sensibility the obduracy of his creditor, but with emotions of sorrow rather than of any anger.' 'This fact,' Sir John Hawkins adds, 'was communicated to Johnson, in my hearing, by a person of unquestionable veracity, but whose name I am not at liberty to mention. He had it, as he told us, from Lady Primrose, to whom Steele related it with tears in his eyes. The late Dr Stinton confirmed it to me, by saying that he had heard it from Mr Hooke, author of the "Roman History," and he from Mr Pope.'"—See *Bee*.

* "This was Sir *Harry Furnese*, the rich alderman," of whom Swift says in the

LETTER CLXXII.   *To Mrs Steele.*
                                          June 21, 1711.
DEAR PRUE,—I am going about your commands, and will send word, or come home to dinner.—Yours ever,   RICH. STEELE.

LETTER CLXXIII.   *To Mrs Steele, last door Bromley Street,*
                         or Berry Street. †
                                          June 22, 1711.
DEAR PRUE,—Pray, on receipt of this, go to Nine Elms, and I will follow you within an hour.—Yours,   RICH. STEELE.

LETTER CLXXIV.   *To Mr Keally.*
                                          July 26, 1711.
SIR,—Happening to be now at Mr Addison's lodgings, and talking of you, (which we often do with affection), I recollected that I had not yet thanked you for your great kindness to Mr Batemen. The poor man acknowledges he should have made nothing of his journey without your assistance, for which you will ever have the blessings of his numerous family. You have laid an infinite obligation upon me in it.

My most humble service to Mr Thomas Vescy, who, I am sorry to hear, mistakes me.—I am, Sir, yours, &c.   RICH. STEELE.

LETTER CLXXV.   *To Mr Pope.*
                                          July 26, 1711.
SIR,—I wrote to you the other day, and hope you have received my letter. This is for the same end, to know whether you are at leisure to help Mr Clayton,‡ that is, me, to some words for music against winter.

Your answer to me at Will's will be a great favour to, Sir, your most obedient humble servant,   RICHARD STEELE.

Examiner, No. 40, "I know a citizen who adds or alters a letter in his name with every plumb he acquires; he now wants only the change of a vowel to be allied to a sovereign prince in Italy; and that, perhaps, he may contrive to be done by a slip of the graver on his tomb-stone." He died November 30, 1712.—*Nichols.*

* "The lodgings of her mother, Mrs Scurlock."

† "Their own residence."

‡ "In the *Spectator,* No. 258, December 26, 1711, is a letter, signed 'Thomas Clayton, Nicolino Haym, and Charles Dieupart,' announcing the plan of their intended concerts in York Buildings, and the terms of the subscription."

From this and the following letter to Mr Hughes, containing a musical criticism, it would seem as if Steele had a personal interest in these concerts :—

LETTER CLXXVI. To Mr Hughes.

April [1711.]

DEAR SIR,—Mr Clayton and I desire you as soon as you can conveniently to alter this poem* for music, preserving as many of Dryden's words and verses as you can. It is to be performed by a voice well skilled in recitative, but you understand all these matters much better than your affectionate humble servant, RICHARD STEELE.

LETTER CLXXVII. Mr Hughes to Steele.

April [1711.]

DEAR SIR,—Since you have asked my opinion about the music, I take it for granted you would have me give it you, and therefore I will shew you how faithfully I intend always to obey you, in doing it with a freedom which I would be loth to use to one for whom I had less friendship, and in whose candour and integrity I did not think myself safe.

I shall, therefore, without taking any hints from others, just give you some few observations which have occurred to me, as well as I could judge upon the first hearing.

That which seems to me to strike most are the prelude bases, some of which are very well fancied, but I am afraid they are in themselves too long, especially when repeated; for prelude-bases are only to begin the subject of the air, and do not shew any composition, (which consists in the union of parts), so that if they are not artfully worked afterwards with the voice part, they are no proof of skill, but only of invention.

The symphonies, in many places, seem to me perplexed, and not made to pursue any subject or point.

The last air of Sappho begins too cheerfully for the sense of the words. As well as I can guess, without seeing the score, it is in D sharp, from which it varies (in another movement of time) into B flat, 3d, and so ends, without returning to the same key, either flat or sharp. This being one continued air, (though in two movements of time), let some master be asked whether it is allowable (I am sure it is not usual) to begin an air in

---

* "Dryden's 'Alexander's Feast,' which Mr Hughes first adapted to music. It was afterwards set by Handel in 1736."

one key sharp, and end it in a different key flat ? For, though the passage is natural, the closing so is, I believe, always disallowed.

The overture of Alexander ought to be great and noble, instead of which I find only a hurry of the instruments, not proper (in my poor opinion), and without any design or fugue, and, I am afraid, perplexed and irregular in the composition, as far as I have any ideas or experience. Inquire this of better judgments.

The duet of Bacchus is cheerful, and has a good effect; but that beginning " Cupid, Phœbus," &c., I cannot think shews any art, and is, in effect, no more than a single air. Nothing shews both genius and learning more than this sort of composition, the chief beauty of which consists in giving each voice different points, and making those points work together, and interchange regularly and surprisingly, or one point following itself in both the voices, in a kind of canon, as it is called. These artfulnesses, when well executed, give infinite delight to the ear; but that which I have mentioned is not formed after those designs, but where the voices join, they move exactly together in plain counter-point, which shews little more than a single air.

I think the words in general naturally enough expressed, and, in some places, pathetically; but, because you seem to think this the whole mystery of setting, I take this opportunity to assure you that it is as possible to express words naturally and pathetically in very faulty composition as it is to hit a likeness in a bad picture. If the music in score, without the words, does not prove itself by the rules of composition which relates to the harmony and motion of different notes at the same time, the notes in the singing parts will not suffice, though they express the words ever so naturally. This is properly the art of composition, in which there is room to shew admirable skill, abstracted from the words; and in which the rules for the union of sounds are a kind of syntaxis, from which no one is allowed to err. I do not apply this last particular to anything, but only to give you a general idea of what is composition. Yet, upon the whole, as far as I am able to judge, the music of Sappho and Alexander, though in some places agreeable, will not please masters.

Having now given you my thoughts freely and impartially, (in which, perhaps, I may be mistaken), I will trust to your good sense for the use that may be made of this, and I beg it may not prejudice me with Mr Clayton or yourself, and that you will not let him know of this, but only inform yourself farther from others, on the hints here given.

I should not, you may be sure, give you or myself this trouble, but that I do not know how far it may concern your interest to be rightly informed, which is the only regard I have in shewing you this way how much I am, Sir, &c., JOHN HUGHES.

The mention of these concerts, and of the locality in which they were held, York Buildings, suggests a characteristic anecdote of Steele. He resided there for some time at a later period, and had fitted up in his house a handsome private theatre or hall, which he called the *Censorium*. As the work approached completion, wishing to judge of the important point as regards the conveying of sound, he requested the man who had the contract for the work to ascend the rostrum or platform at one end, and let him hear his voice. Having ascended, he stood for some time in a state of bewilderment, utterly at a loss what to say. Sir Richard, however, told him to say whatever came uppermost; when, elevating his voice to a pitch suited to his not very moderate notion of what was proper for an orator, he bawled out, " Sir Richard Steele, here has I, and these here men, been doing your work for three months, and never seen the colour of your money. When are you to pay us? I cannot pay my journeymen without money, and money I must have?" Sir Richard hastened to assure him that he was quite satisfied with the effect, that the sound was excellent, though the matter of his discourse was not quite to his mind.

LETTER CLXXVIII.   *To Mr Pope.*

Jan. 20, 1711-12.

DEAR SIR,—I have received your very kind letter. That part of it which is grounded upon your belief that I have much affection and friendship for you, I receive with great pleasure. That which acknowledges the honour done to your "Essay,"* I have no pretence to; it was written by one whom I will make you acquainted with, which is the best return I can make to you for your favour to, Sir, your most obliged humble servant,

RICH. STEELE.

---

* "This relates to the *Spectator*, No. CCLIII., which was written by Addison, and pays a handsome compliment to Pope's 'Essay on Criticism.'"

LETTER CLXXIX.   To Mrs Steele.
From Mr Ashurst's.*
Jan. 21, 1711-12.
DEAR PRUE,—I stay dinner here, but shall come as soon as I have dined. In the meantime, I desire you would order Michael to carry the enclosed to Mr Gibb's† lodgings, and bid him afterwards be in the way to wait for me.—Your obliged husband,   RICH. STEELE.

LETTER CLXXX.   To Mrs Steele.
Jan 22, 1711-12.
DEAR PRUE,—Give me till ten o'clock to-morrow without dunning for your payments; for Dizzle insists upon paying Butcher Gibbs, and settling two or three things before my domestic comes.—Yours,
RICH. STEELE.

LETTER CLXXXI.   To Mr Pope.
June 1, 1712.
SIR,—I am at a solitude,‡ an house between Hampstead and London, wherein Sir Charles Sedley died.§ This circumstance set me a thinking upon the employments in which men of wit exercise themselves. It was said of Sir Charles, who breathed his last in this room—

"Sedley has that prevailing gentle art,
Which can with a resistless charm impart
The loosest wishes to the chastest heart;
Raise such a conflict, kindle such a fire
Between declining virtue and desire,
Till the poor vanquish'd maid dissolves away
In dreams all night, in sighs and tears all day."

This was an happy talent to a man of the town; but, I dare say, without presuming to make uncharitable conjectures on the author's present condition, he would rather have had it said of him that he prayed

"Oh, thou my voice inspire,
Who touch'd Isaiah's hallow'd lips with fire!"

I have turned to every verse and chapter, and think you have preserved

---

* "Probably at Highgate."
† "A butcher. See next Letter."
‡ "It is to be feared there were too many pecuniary reasons for this temporary solitude."
§ "About eight or nine years before the date of this letter."

the sublime heavenly spirit throughout the whole, especially at—" Hark a glad voice"—and " The lamb with wolves shall graze." There is but one line which I think below the original:

"He wipes the tears for ever from our eyes."

You have expressed it with a good and pious, but not so exalted and poetical a spirit as the prophet, "The Lord God will wipe away tears from off all faces." If you agree with me in this, alter it by way of paraphrase or otherwise, that, when it comes into a volume, it may be amended. Your poem is already better than the Pollio.—I am, yours, &c.,

RICH. STEELE.

LETTER CLXXXII.   *From Mr Pope.*

June 18, 1712.

You have obliged me with a very kind letter, by which I find you shift the scene of your life from the town to the country, and enjoy that mixed state which wise men both delight in and are qualified for. Methinks the moralists and philosophers have generally run too much into extremes in commending entirely either solitude or public life. In the former, men for the most part grow useless by too much rest, and in the latter they are destroyed by too much precipitation; as waters lying still putrify, and are good for nothing, and running violently on do but the more mischief in their passage to others, and are swallowed up and lost the sooner themselves. Those, indeed, who can be useful to all states, should be like gentle streams, that not only glide through lonely valleys and forests amidst the flocks and the shepherds, but visit populous towns in their course, and are at once of ornament and service to them. But there are another sort of people who seem designed for solitude; such, I mean, as have more to hide than to shew. As for my own part, I am one of those of whom Seneca says, "Tam umbratiles sunt, ut putent in turbido esse quicquid in luce est." Some men, like some pictures, are fitter for a corner than a full light; and I believe such as have a natural bent to solitude (to carry on the former similitude) are like waters, which may be forced into fountains, and, exalted into a great height, may make a noble figure, and a louder noise; but, after all, they would run more smoothly, quietly, and plentifully in their own natural course upon the ground.* The consideration of this would make me very well content with the possession only of that quiet which Cowley calls the companion of obscurity.

---

* "The foregoing similitudes Mr Pope had put into verse some years before, and inserted in Mr Wycherly's poem on ' Mixed Life.' We find them in the versification very distinct from the rest of that poem. See his posthumous works."

But whoever has the muses too for his companions can never be idle enough to be uneasy. Thus, Sir, you see I would flatter myself into a good opinion of my own way of living. Plutarch just now told me that it is in human life as in a game at tables, where a man may wish for the highest cast, but if his chance be otherwise, he is e'en to play it as well as he can, and make the best of it.—I am, yours, &c. A. POPE.

LETTER CLXXXIII.　　　To Mrs Steele.
June 28, 1712.
DEAR PRUE,—I cannot come home till the evening. All is safe and well. My disappointment has produced a good of which you will be glad, to wit, a certainty of keeping my office * for resigning so great a prospect. —I am, dear thing, yours ever,　　　　　　　　　　RICH. STEELE.

LETTER CLXXXIV.　　　To Mrs Steele.
July 15, 1712.
DEAR PRUE,—I thank you for your kind billet. The nurse shall have money this week. I saw your son *Dick;* but he is a peevish chit. You cannot conceive how pleased I am that I shall have the prettiest house † to receive the prettiest woman, who is the darling of
RICH. STEELE.

LETTER CLXXXV.　　　From Mr Pope.
July 15, 1712.
You formerly observed to me that nothing made a more ridiculous figure in a man's life than the disparity we often find in him sick and well: thus one of an unfortunate constitution is perpetually exhibiting a miserable example of the weakness of his mind and of his body in their turns. I have had frequent opportunities of late to consider myself in these different views, and I hope have received some advantage by it, if what Waller says be true, that

"The soul's dark cottage, batter'd and decay'd,
　Lets in new light through chinks that time has made."

Then, surely, sickness, contributing no less than old age to the shaking down this scaffolding of the body, may discover the inward structure more plainly. Sickness is a sort of early old age; it teaches us a diffidence in

---

* " He was then a commissioner in the Stamp-office."
† " A house in Bloomsbury Square."

our earthly state, and inspires us with the thought of a future, better than a thousand volumes of philosophers and divines. It gives so warning a concussion to those props of our vanity, our strength, and youth, that we think of fortifying ourselves within, when there is so little dependence upon our outworks. Youth, at the very best, is but a betrayer of human life in a gentler and smoother manner than age: it is like a stream that nourishes a plant upon a bank, and causes it to flourish and blossom to the sight, but at the same time is undermining it at the root in secret. My youth has dealt more fairly and openly with me: it has afforded me several prospects of my danger, and has given me an advantage not very common to young men, that the attractions of the world have not dazzled me very much; and I begin, where most people end, with a full conviction of the emptiness of all sorts of ambition, and the unsatisfactory nature of all human pleasures. When a smart fit of sickness tells me this scurvy tenement of my body will fall in a little time, I am e'en as unconcerned as was that honest Hibernian, who, being in bed in the great storm some years ago, and told the house would tumble over his head, made answer, "What care I for the house, I am only a lodger!" I fancy it is the best time to die when one is in the best humour; and so excessive weak as I now am, I may say with conscience that I am not at all uneasy at the thought that many men whom I never had any esteem for, are likely to enjoy this world after me. When I reflect what an inconsiderable little atom every single man is, with respect to the whole creation, methinks it is a shame to be concerned at the removal of such a trivial animal as I am. The morning after my exit the sun will rise as bright as ever, the flowers smell as sweet, the plants spring as green, the world will proceed in its old course, people will laugh as heartily and marry as fast as they were used to do. "The memory of man," as it is elegantly expressed in the Book of Wisdom, "passeth away as the remembrance of a guest that tarrieth but one day." There are reasons enough in the fourth chapter of the same book to make any young man contented with the prospect of death. "For honourable age is not that which standeth in length of time, or is measured by number of years. But wisdom is the gray hair to men, and an unspotted life is old age. He was taken away speedily, lest wickedness should alter his understanding, or deceit beguile his soul," &c.—I am, yours, &c.,

A. POPE.

LETTER CLXXXVI.   *To Mrs Steele.*

July 24, 1712.

DEAR CREATURE,—All you desire shall be done. I beg of you to compose yourself, for nothing else can [make] happy one that doats on you so much that he cannot hide it, though he heartily wishes he could.—Yours unchangeably,   RICH. STEELE.

1712.] *Addison disclaims Pope's Satire on Dennis.* 311

LETTER CLXXXVII.   *To Mr Lintott.*

Aug. 4, 1712.

MR LINTOTT,—Mr Addison desired me to tell you that he wholly disapproves of the manner of treating Mr Dennis in a little pamphlet by way of Dr Norris's account.* When he thinks fit to take notice of Mr Dennis's objections to his writings,† he will do it in a way Mr Dennis shall have no just reason to complain of. But when the papers above-mentioned were offered to be communicated to him, he said he could not, either in honour or conscience, be privy to such treatment, and was sorry to hear of it.—I sir, your very humble servant,   RICH. STEELE.

LETTER CLXXXVIIL   *To Mrs Scurlock.*

Bloomsbury Square, Aug. 8, 1712.

DEAR MADAM,—Ever since I had the honour to be of your family, my heart has yearned to exert myself in a particular manner towards you, and to make your life easy and happy. The uneasinesses of my fortune have hitherto made it impracticable to me, and some little frowardnesses of Prue have also been a hindrance too. But, I thank God, matters are now settled after such a manner, and the renewal of my employments in my favour has enabled me to invite you hither, where you shall be attended with plenty, cheerfulness, and quiet. I shall wait on you to talk further on this subject; and, if you are averse to it, nothing shall be taken ill by, madam, your most obedient son and most humble servant,

RICH. STEELE.

LETTER CLXXXIX.   *To Mrs Steele.*

Aug. 21, 1712.

DEAR PRUE,—I beg pardon that I am to dine with Mr Montague.—Yours ever,   RICH. STEELE.

LETTER CXC.   *To Mrs Steele, at her house in Bloomsbury Square.*

Tuesday, Sept 2, 1712.

MY DEAR, DEAR WIFE,—I have sent my man to town to carry a letter of excuse to Mr Beranger, about going out of town with him. I hope this will find you and your family [well]; and I will be with you, God willing, to-morrow to dinner.—Your affectionate, faithful husband,

RICH. STEELE.

---

* " Of the frenzy of Mr John Dennis, a narrative written by Mr Pope. See his Letter to Mr Addison, of July 20, 1713."
† " Remarks on Cato."

LETTER CXCI.   To Mrs Steele.

Hampton Court, Thursday noon,
Sept. 17, 1712.

DEAREST WIFE,—The finest woman in nature should not detain me an hour from you; but you must sometimes suffer the rivalship of the wisest men. Lords Halifax and Somers leave this place after dinner; and I go to Watford to speak with the Solicitor-General,* and from thence come directly to Bloomsbury Square.—Yours faithfully,   RICH. STEELE.

LETTER CXCII.   To Mrs Scurlock.

Hampton Court, Sept. 27, 1712.

HONOURED MADAM,—The increase† of my family, and reflection upon what vast sums of money I have let slip through my hands, since I have had opportunities of mending my fortune in the world, have made me very anxious for the future. I understand there has been some discourse between my wife and yourself upon this subject; but, if there has anything passed too eager, I beseech you to attribute it to a laudable tenderness for a numerous family. All that I intend by it is, to know what foundation I may think I am upon with relation to posterity, which are your offspring as well as mine. I ask nothing of you; but, by the blessing of God, will add to the estate in the family as well as provide for my younger children, with as much haste as honour and integrity will permit. I only want to know, for the encouragement of my industry in so great a work, how all things stand now to a farthing. I am very much above any distastes to any one you may effect, but shall ever be ready to serve to my utmost any one that you are inclined to do for or favour. I send this before me, as a preface to a discourse of this kind when I have the honour to see you, and am, with the greatest truth, madam, your most obliged, and most humble servant,   RICH. STEELE.

LETTER CXCIII.   To Mrs Scurlock.

Bloomsbury Square, Oct. 25, 1712.

DEAR MOTHER,—I give you this, to lay before you in the humblest manner, what I think reasonable should be done in favour of me and mine.

---

* "Sir Robert Raymond, afterwards, in regular succession, Attorney-General, a sergeant-at-law, Chief-Justice of the King's Bench, and a Commissioner of the Great Seal."

† "Eugene, Steele's third child, was born in 1712."

You are well acquainted that I have had no fortune with your daughter; that I have struggled through great difficulties for our maintenance; that we live now in the handsomest manner, supported only by my industry. I say, madam, when you consider all this, and add to it, that my posterity is yours also, you will be, I doubt not, inclined that your estate should pass to them, I not having any view nor making the least request of any support from you during your life. The gentleman who brings this will inform you in what manner I desire this may be effected. He is a sensible and good man; and I hope you will be prevailed upon to do me the reasonable favour I ask you by his interposition between us. This provision made for my poor children, will make me meet all the changes and chances of this life with cheerfulness and alacrity; for want of which I have many melancholy reflections. The main of the estate is wholly in you; and that part which is my wife's I shall, I doubt not, find her ready to settle in the manner my friend will acquaint you.—I am, dear madam, your most obedient son and most humble servant,

RICH. STEELE.

LETTER CXCIV.   *To Mrs Scurlock.*
Oct. 31, 1712.

DEAR MOTHER,—As soon as I had left you this afternoon, I went to Mr Diggle, my friend, whom I sent to you in my behalf about the settlement. I find the whole is in you, and the part that depends to Prue is covered by assignments for debts you have paid, so that I have nothing to do but to prevail upon you. Please to put the anxiety of the father of a numerous family in your thoughts; and you will pardon my importunity to preserve them from want. When you have been thus kind to my poor children who descend from you, I can think of adding to their fortune with some alacrity; but to have the matter to do wholly myself, makes it so great a labour, that I am dispirited from beginning it. I do not desire any consideration of me myself; but I beseech God to put it into your heart to make a certainty for them.

I am in hopes, in your cool thoughts, you will approve of what I ask; which will ease the loaded heart of, madam, your most obliged son and most humble servant,   RICH. STEELE.

LETTER CXCV.   *From Mr Pope.*
Nov. 7, 1712.

I was the other day in company with five or six men of some learning, where, chancing to mention the famous verses which the Emperor Adrian spoke on his deathbed, they were all agreed that it was a piece of gaiety, unworthy of that prince in those circumstances. I could not but differ from this opinion: methinks it was by no means a gay, but a very serious soliloquy to his soul at the point of its departure; in which sense I naturally took the verses at my first reading them, when I was very young, and before I knew what interpretation the world generally put upon them.

> " Animula vagula, blandula,
> Hospes comesque corporis,
> Quæ nunc abibis in loca?
> Pallidula, rigida, nudula,
> Nec (ut soles) dabis joca?

"Alas, my soul! thou pleasing companion of this body, thou fleeting thing that art now deserting it! whither art thou flying? to what unknown scene? All trembling, fearful, and pensive! what now is become of thy former wit and humour? Thou shalt jest and be gay no more."

I confess I cannot apprehend where lies the trifling in all this: it is the most natural and obvious reflection imaginable to a dying man: and if we consider the emperor was a heathen, that doubt concerning the future fate of his soul will seem so far from being the effect of want of thought, that it was scarce reasonable he should think otherwise; not to mention that here is a plain confession included of his belief in its immortality. The diminutive epithets of *vagula*, *blandula*, and the rest, appear not to me as expressions of levity, but rather of endearment and concern, such as we find in Catullus, and the authors of the "Hendeca-syllabi" after him, where they are used to express the utmost love and tenderness for their mistresses. If you think me right in my notion of the last words of Adrian, be pleased to insert it in the *Spectator*,* if not, to suppress it.—I am, &c.

A. POPE.

Translated thus—

> "*Adriani morientis ad animum*," etc.
>
> "Ah, fleeting spirit! wandering fire,
> That long hast warm'd my tender breast,
> Must thou no more this frame inspire?
> No more a pleasing, cheerful guest?
>
> "Whither, ah whither art thou flying!
> To what dark, undiscover'd shore?
> Thou seem'st all trembling, shivering, dying,
> And wit and humour are no more!"†

---

* "See *Spectator* No. DXXXII., November 10, 1712."

† Byron also attempted the translation of these lines in his juvenile poems, and the reader may be gratified with comparing his lines with those of Pope:—

LETTER CXCVI.   *To Mr Pope.*
                                        Nov. 12, 1712.

I have read over your "'Temple of Fame" twice, and cannot find anything amiss, of weight enough to call a fault, but see in it a thousand beauties. Mr Addison shall see it to-morrow. After his perusal of it, I will let you know his thoughts. I desire you would let me know whether you are at leisure or not? I have a design,* which I shall open a month or two hence, with the assistance of the few like yourself. If your thoughts are unengaged, I shall explain myself further.—I am, yours, &c.
                                        RICH. STEELE.

LETTER CXCVII.   *From Mr Pope.*
                                        Nov. 16, 1712.

You oblige me by the indulgence you have shewn to the poem I sent you, but will oblige me much more by the kind severity I hope for from you. No errors are so trivial but they deserve to be mended. But since you say you see nothing that may be called a fault, can you but think it so, that I have confined the attendance of guardian spirits † to Heaven's favourites only? I could point you to several, but it is my business to be informed of those faults I do not know; and as for those I do, not to talk of them, but to correct them. You speak of that poem in a style I neither merit nor expect; but, I assure you, if you freely mark or dash out, I shall look upon your blots as its greatest beauties: I mean, if Mr Addison and yourself should like it in the whole; otherwise the trouble of correction is what I would not take, for I was really so diffident of it as to let it lie by me these two years,‡ just as you now see it. I am afraid of nothing so much as to impose anything on the world which is unworthy of its acceptance.

As to the last period of your letter, I shall be very ready and glad to contribute to any design that tends to the advantage of mankind, which I

> "Ah! gentle, fleeting, wav'ring sprite,
>   Friend and associate of this clay!
> To what unknown region borne,
>   Wilt thou, now, wing thy distant flight?
> No more with wonted humour gay,
>   But pallid, cheerless, and forlorn."

* "This was the *Guardian* in which Pope assisted."
† "This is not now to be found in the 'Temple of Fame.'"
‡ "Hence it appears this poem was written before the author was twenty-two years old."

am sure all yours do.* I wish I had but as much capacity as leisure, for I am perfectly idle, (a sign I have not much capacity.)

If you will entertain the best opinion of me, be pleased to think me your friend. Assure Mr Addison of my most faithful services; of every one's esteem he must be assured already.—I am, yours, &c.   A. POPE.

LETTER CXCVIII.   *To Mrs Steele.*

Nov. 18, 1712.

DEAR PRUE,—I am come from a committee where I have [been] chairman, and drank too much. I have the headache, and should be glad you would come to me in good-humour, which would always banish any uneasiness of temper from, dear Prue, your fond fool of a husband,

RICH. STEELE.

LETTER CXCIX.   *From Mr Pope.*

Nov. 29, 1712.

I am sorry you published that notion about Adrian's verses † as mine.

---

* "In a subsequent letter to Mr Addison, Pope says, 'As I hope, and would flatter myself, that you know me and my thoughts so entirely as never to be mistaken in either, so it is a pleasure to me that you have guessed so right in regard to the author of that *Guardian* you mentioned. But I am sorry to find it has taken air that I have some hand in those papers, because I write so few as neither to deserve the credit of such a report with some people, nor the disrepute of it with others. An honest Jacobite spoke to me the sense or nonsense of the weak part of his party very fairly, that the good people took it ill of me that I write with Steele, though upon never so indifferent subjects. This I know you will laugh at as well as I do; yet I doubt not but many little calumniators, and persons of sour dispositions, will take occasion thence to bespatter me. I confess, I scorn narrow souls of all parties, and, if I renounce my reason in religious matters, I will hardly do it in any other. I cannot imagine whence it comes to pass that the few *Guardians* I have written are so generally known for mine; that in particular which you mention I never discovered to any man but the publisher till very lately, yet almost everybody told me of it. As to his taking a more polite turn, I cannot in any way enter into that secret, nor have I been let into it any more than into the rest of his politics. Though it is said he will take into these papers also several subjects of the politer kind, as before; but I assure you, as to myself, I have quite done with them for the future. The little I have done, and the great respect I bear Mr Steele as a man of wit, has rendered me a suspected Whig to some of the violent; but (as old Dryden said before me) it is not the violent I design to please.'"

† In the *Spectator*, above referred to, [Nov. 10,] Steele says, "I claim to my-

Had I imagined you would have used my name, I should have expressed my sentiments with more modesty and diffidence. I only sent it to have your opinion, and not to publish my own, which I distrusted. But I think the supposition you draw, from the notion of Adrian's being addicted to magic, is a little uncharitable, (" that he might fear no sort of deity, good or bad,") since, in the third verse, he plainly testifies his apprehension of a future state, by being solicitous whither his soul was going. As to what you mention of his using gay and ludicrous expressions, I have owned my opinion to be that the expressions are not so, but that diminutives are as often in the Latin tongue used as marks of tenderness and concern.

Anima is no more than " my soul," *animula* has the force of " my dear soul." To say *virgo bella* is not half so endearing as to say *virguncula bellula;* and had Augustus only called Horace *lepidum hominem*, it had amounted to no more than that he thought him a " pleasant fellow :" it was the *homunciolum* that expressed the love and tenderness that great emperor had for him. And perhaps I should myself be much better pleased if I were told you called me " your little friend," than if you complimented me with the title of " a great genius," or " an eminent hand," as Jacob * does all his authors.—I am, yours, &c.   A. POPE.

LETTER CC.   *To Mr Pope.*

Dec. 4, 1712.

This is to desire of you that you would please to make an ode as of a cheerful dying spirit ; that is to say, the Emperor Adrian's " *Animula Vagula* " put into two or three stanzas for music. If you comply with this, and send me word so, you will very particularly oblige, yours, &c.

RICH. STEELE.

LETTER CCI.   *From Mr Pope.*

Dec. . . . . , 1712.

I do not send you word I will do, but have already done, the thing you

---

self the merit of having extorted excellent productions from a person of the greatest ability, who would not have let them appeared by any other means; to have animated a few young gentlemen into worthy pursuits, who will be a glory to our age ; and at all times, and by all possible means in my power, undermined the interests of ignorance, vice, and folly, and attempted to substitute in their stead, learning, piety, and good sense. It is from this honest heart that I find myself honoured as a gentleman-usher to the arts and sciences. Mr Tickell and Mr Pope have, it seems, this idea of me. The former has written me an excellent paper of verses in praise, forsooth, of myself; and the other enclosed for my perusal an admirable poem, which I hope shall shortly see the light."

* " Jacob Tonson."

desire of me. You have it (as Cowley calls it) just warm from the brain. It came to me the first moment I awaked this morning: yet you will see it was not so absolutely inspiration,* but that I had in my head not only the verses of Adrian, but the fine fragment of Sappho, &c. :—

THE DYING CHRISTIAN TO HIS SOUL. ODE.

Vital spark of heavenly flame,
Quit, oh, quit this mortal frame:
Trembling, hoping, lingering, flying,
Oh, the pain, the bliss of dying!
Cease, fond nature, cease thy strife,
And let me languish into life.

Hark, they whisper; angels say,
Sister spirit, come away!
What is this absorbs me quite,
Steals my senses, shuts my sight,
Drowns my spirits, draws my breath!
Tell me, my soul, can this be death?

The world recedes; it disappears!
Heaven opens on my eyes! my ears
  With sounds seraphic ring!
Lend, lend your wings! I mount! I fly!
O grave! where is thy victory?
O death! where is thy sting?

Among the "excellent productions" which Steele justly claimed to himself the merit of having extorted" from persons of ability, this beautiful ode is not the least.

In a poetical satire, published this year (1712) by a Mr Newcomb, entitled "Bibliotheca; a Poem, occasioned by the sight of a Modern Library," the writer, after tracing the progress of oblivion in a style similar to that afterwards adopted by Pope in the "Dunciad," passes a high encomium on Steele and his labours, which may be worth quoting.

* "It has been suggested that some part of what is here ascribed to inspiration, and said to have come warm from Pope's heart, dropt originally from the pen of Flatman."

"Still to proceed the Goddess try'd,
Till STEELE's immortal works espy'd ;
Trembling her dreaded foe to view,
She sunk, and silently withdrew ;
While Sarum's * labours, round her spread,
Sustain and prop her drowsy head.
 Hail, mighty name ! of all thy pen
Has dropt, to charm both gods and men,
Time nor oblivion ne'er shall boast
One line or single period lost !
Improving youth, and hoary age,
Are better'd by thy matchless page ;
And what no mortal could devise,
Women by reading thee grow wise ;
Divines had taught, and husband's rav'd,
Now threat'ned, then as poorly crav'd,
But, spite of all, the stubborn dame
Remain'd our curse, and still the same ;
Modish and flippant as before,
The smoothing paint and patch are wore ;
Two hours each morning spent to dress,
And not one ounce of tea the less :
While the provoking idiot vows
Her lover fairer much than spouse.
 Great Socrates but vainly try'd
To sooth the passions of his bride ;
Her female empire still she holds,
And as he preaches peace, she scolds :
In vain he talks, in vain he writes ;
One kissing while the other bites ;
Precepts with her, and moral rules,
Are only gins to hamper fools ;
And, preach and dictate what he will,
Madam persists, Xantippe still.
But wedlock by thy art is got
To be a soft and easy knot ;
Which smiling spouse and kinder bride
Now seldom wish should be unty'd ;
Think parting now the greatest sin,
And strive more close to draw the ginn :

---

* Bishop Burnet.

Taught by those rules thy pen instills,
Nobly to conquer human ills;
The female sufferer now sustains
Each mournful loss with lessen'd pains;
A week is now enough to pine,
When puking lap-dog cannot dine;
While grief as real swells her eyes
When spouse, as when her parrot, dies.
The fop no longer shall believe
Sense ty'd to every modish sleeve,
Nor, conscious of his wants, presume
To measure merit by perfume;
That courage in Pulvilio dwells,
The boldest he who strongest smells;
To prove his sense no longer bring
The doughty proofs of box and ring;
Strongly professing ne'er to know
An ass conceal'd beneath a beau;
Each taught by thee, shall hence confess
Virtue has no regard for dress;
That the bright nymph as often dwells
In homely bays as rural cells;
And in a ruff as fairly shin'd,
As now to modern peak confin'd;
Blushing, thus half-expos'd to view,
Both for herself and mistress too.
 The widow, pining for her dear,
Shall curse no more the tedious year;
In sighs consume each pensive day,
Nor think it long from June to May.
See how the pensive relict lies,
Oppress'd with spouse's fate, and dies;
That Betty with her drops in vain
Recalls her flying soul again;
No colour now so fair appears,
As is the sable vest she wears,
To her the only garment vow'd,
Till death exchange it for a shroud,
And her cold ashes kindly place
Once more within her lord's embrace.
 The ladies, pleased with thee to dwell,
Aspire to write correct, and spell:
We scarce behold, though writ in haste,

> Five letters in a score misplaced;
> Marshall'd in rank they all appear,
> With no front vowels in the rear,
> Nor any, out of shame or dread,
> Skulking behind that should have led;
> In every line they now demur,
> 'Tis now no longer, Wurthee Surr;
> With half our usual sweat and pain,
> We both unravel and explain,
> Nor call in foreign aid to find,
> In mystic terms, the fair one's mind.
>   Maintain, great sage, thy deathless name,
> Thou canst no wider stretch thy fame,
> Till, gliding from her native skies,
> Virtue once more delighted flies;
> By each adoring patriot own'd,
> And boasts herself by thee enthroned!"*

It may be here mentioned as a subject of regret that we should have no letters to or from one who had expressed a desire for Steele's correspondence,—Lady M. W. Montagu. Lady Mary had been acquainted with Mrs Steele before her marriage, and with himself after, and from his great intimacy with her husband, she says in one of her letters to the latter, "I wish you would learn Mr Steele to write to your wife."

* Nichol's Select Collection.

CHAPTER IX.

THE PERIODICAL ESSAYIST AND DELINEATOR OF CHARACTER—
1713.

Steele starts the *Guardian* as a sequel to the *Spectator*—Its plan—Nestor Ironside, guardian to the Lizard family—Its members—Notice of the contributors, Bishop Berkeley, Pope, Gay, Addison, &c.—Subjects of dedications—Controversy with the *Examiner*—It diverges into politics, and is discontinued.

WHATEVER may have been the particular motives that influenced Steele in laying down the *Spectator* at a time when it had attained to such celebrity, and there appeared so much inducement to continue it, we cannot regret the dropping of the different papers and resuming his labours under a new title. It has contributed greatly to their variety, and each successive effort stimulated his invention to fresh sketches of character and clubs, and developed in new social combinations his wonderful knowledge of human nature and of life. In the collected form in which they were to descend it may have been justly felt that it was an advantage to break their continuity. At all events, that it was from no feeling of exhaustion that they were discontinued is very evident. Perhaps an irksome sense of the monotonous effect of maintaining the same characters for an indefinite length of time may have had some influence. But whatever may have been the cause of his literary suicide, he seemed, like the Phœnix, to gather new life from the ashes of his former existence. At no former period did he appear to bring to his task greater resources, though it can scarcely be said that his characters were quite so felicitous. As in the case of the *Tatler*, he wrote a large number of papers consecutively with only casual assistance.

The *Spectator* had been brought to a close December 6th, 1712, (though a supplementary volume was afterwards added by Addison in 1714,) and, on the 12th March 1713, the first number of the *Guardian* was issued, and, like the *Spectator*, of which it was indeed but the sequel under another title, continued daily. From the letter to Pope, under the date of Nov. 12, 1712, previously given, we have seen that he contemplated the new paper before laying down the old one; and recognising the eminent merit of the rising young poet, he endeavours to enlist his services along with others, and to infuse fresh blood into the undertaking. Of the new pens that came to his aid, the most considerable, both in point of ability and extent, was that of the celebrated Dr Berkeley; while Gay, Ambrose, Philips, Tickell, Rowe, and others, by their casual communications, completed his literary brigade, and served as skirmishers and light cavalry.

The platform was certainly somewhat more contracted than that of its predecessor. The author assumes the name of *Nestor Ironside*, an elderly gentleman, and guardian to the Lizard family, a group of figures whose portraits he sketches so vividly, that they stand out from the canvas. The circle consists of the venerable and devout dowager of Sir Ambrose Lizard, the college companion of Mr Ironside, and the friend of his youth; the widow of Sir Marmaduke, in the prime of life, a lady of fine understanding and a noble spirit, who is sometimes spoken of by her Christian name of Aspasia; and her four sons and five charming daughters, whose characters are touched with nice discrimination. Lady Lizard herself, though past the shining period of the bloom of youth, is in that rich autumnal season of life when, with an ample fortune, (other cares being superseded,) the gratifications which it brings—those of state and equipage, of being much esteemed, visited, and generally admired—are, Mr Ironside thinks, generally more pursued than in earlier years. He was not prepared to say that she had not a certain vanity in being still a fine woman, and neglecting those addresses she might even then have affected. Of the young ladies her daughters, —Jane, Annabella, Cornelia, Betty, and Mary,—the first is a notable manager in household affairs, added to good sense and piety, but has not escaped the snares of the tender passion withal; the second, under an affable, frank exterior, is artful, cunning, and observing, but joined with sense, good looks, wit, and other of the most agreeable qualities; the third is a student, Mr Ironside fears, of romances, which he took occasion to rail at, in which she professed to join,—but the giddy part of her sex rallied her on her retired habits, being occasioned by the absence of the particular company she wished; the fourth pretends to be very knowing in matters of fashion and the gossip of the day; the youngest, whom Mr Ironside had called the *Sparkler,* and the others rally, as Mrs Ironside, from their mutual partiality, was eminently good-natured and generous; and indeed Old Nestor thought if all the good qualities that adorn human life became feminine, they might be supposed to blossom in his youthful ward. The sons are, Sir Harry, Thomas, William, and John. The young baronet, in his six-and-twentieth year, with a good unencumbered estate in Northampton, possesses a solid understanding rather than shining abilities, and displays those qualities fitted to render him respected as a country gentleman, as well as some promise, Mr Ironside thinks, of those which might make him useful in the Senate; the second possesses general accomplishments, an easy demeanour, great suavity and blandness of mind and manner, which fit him eminently for the life of a courtier, to which he aspires; the third, who, on the contrary, is sharp and inquiring, is a Templer; the youngest, a fellow of college, is of a serene cheerfulness, tinctured with a noble vein of poetry and ardour of mind, which give Mr Ironside great hopes of his eminence in the sacred calling to which he was destined.

In such a family circle Mr Ironside thought that passages that occurred could not fail to afford his readers entertaining and possibly useful notices for their guidance in life. But in addition to their tea-table, and the genial matter to be drawn from that intercourse, the venerable Nestor tells us that, having got "his wards pretty well off his hands," the care of whose interests he took to be too narrow a scene to pass his whole life in, he was enabled to extend the sphere of his operations, and sought to apply the energies and the zeal he had devoted to the welfare of a few, and the experience he had acquired thereby, to the general good.

Mr Ironside had expressly intimated his design of steering clear of politics in the very outset of his labours, where, after stating the aim of his paper as "no less than to make the pulpit, the bar, and the stage all act in concert in the care of piety, justice, and virtue," he adds, " I am past all the regards of this life, and have nothing to manage with *any person* or *party*, but to deliver myself as an old man with one foot in the grave."

It would have been well, equally for his own peace and the interests of literature, if Mr Ironside had kept this wise resolve steadily before him, and acted on it consistently; but, alas for human resolutions, even of ancient gentlemen with one foot in the grave, he had reached but his fortieth number when he broke through it by a violent altercation of a political character with the *Examiner*, the result of which was an open breach with Swift. In No. 41, under date of April 28, in stigmatizing a scurrilous article in which the writer of the Tory paper had not scrupled to drag in the name of a young lady, the daughter of a nobleman who had rendered himself obnoxious by leaving their party, and one of the ladies of the court, Steele made use of some very severe remarks unmistakably pointing to Swift as " an estranged friend," and open to suspicion from his connexion with the paper. The unfortunate consequences of this step will be seen in the subsequent correspondence between the parties. Nor was this a solitary instance of his departure from the principle of neutrality with which he had set out. He returned to the subject in No. 53, and in No. 128, (Aug. 7, 1713,) after having in the previous June resigned all his public employments and emoluments, he again, by the publication of the famous paper on the demolition of Dunkirk, exposed himself to a malignity and scurrility scarcely to be paralleled even in the unscrupulous warfare of party.

The exciting character of the times acting on his ardent temperament made him desirous of meeting his antagonists on equal terms, not by the equally unscrupulous use of personal abuse, for in that respect he maintained an honourable distinction, but by the possession of an organ which, without excluding literary matter, would be professedly devoted to political disquisitions. Under these circumstances, we need scarcely be surprised by the sudden termination of a paper professing to be exclusively literary in its character, an event which occurred Oct. 1, 1713, after the issue of 175 numbers. The immediate cause being a quarrel with Tonson, the publisher, as reported by Pope, may admit of doubt. Steele would appear to have entered upon it without any communication with his distinguished friend, then engaged in bringing his "Cato" upon the stage, and to have prosecuted it with great personal energy for many successive weeks with little assistance, although the contributions of his literary friends and of the letter-box* were as abundant ultimately as he had previously experienced them. In the second volume, Addison furnished a large number in succession. On the whole, though it cannot justly be regarded as equally felicitous in design with its predecessor, the papers are in themselves exceedingly good, though perhaps with too great a preponderance of gravity; and the abrupt discontinuance of the *Guardian* was a source of disappointment both to the public and its

* The following notice of the Lion's Head Letter-Box, which Steele mentions as having carried with him when he gave up the *Guardian* for the *Englishman*, appeared in the London papers :—" The beautiful carved and gilt Lion's Head Letter-Box, which was formerly at Button's Coffee-house, was, on Wednesday, November the 7th, 1804, knocked down at the Shakespeare Tavern, Covent Garden; to Mr Richardson for £17, 10s. The Antiquarian Society offered Mr Campbell 100 guineas for this piece of curiosity not twelve months since."

contributors. Steele's papers are eighty-two in number, of which it is enough to say that they quite equal his *Spectators*. With the exception of one paper, (No. 67,) Addison did not give his valuable assistance till the appearance of No. 97, when he contributed twenty-seven in succession, and in all fifty-one, of his accustomed excellence.

After Steele and Addison, the most considerable contributor to the *Guardian* was Dr GEORGE BERKELEY, the celebrated metaphysician, afterwards Bishop of Cloyne, a man not only of extraordinary endowments, natural and acquired, but of singular amiability and simplicity of character. This eminent man was born at Kilcrin, near Thomastown, County Kilkenny, in the year 1684, and like many of his distinguished countrymen, received his early education at the Kilkenny Grammar School. After studying at the University of Dublin, he became a Fellow of that college in 1707, and the same year published his first production, a small mathematical treatise. Two years after appeared his "Theory of Vision," in which he was the first to lay down certain principles which subsequently became an acknowledged part of the science of optics, particularly that the relation between sight and touch was the effect of habit. New light was thereby thrown on some of the phenomena of the science previously regarded as inexplicable. But it was in "Principles of Human Knowledge," which appeared in 1710, and his "Dialogues" three years later, that he gave to the world his famous metaphysical theory. In these works he contends that the existence of matter is incapable of demonstration; that what we call material objects are merely impressions of the mind, stamped thereon by the Supreme Being, according to certain laws of nature from which He never deviates ; and that the invariable adherence to these rules forms the only reality of the external material world, and so effectually lays the line between the impressions of sense and the mere ideas of the mind, that there is no more possibility of confounding them on this theory than on that of the ordinary one of the assumed existence of matter. Though these ideas about ideas savour strongly of having been imbibed from the visionary speculations of his favourite Plato, yet they were in reality only carrying out the reasoning of a variety of philosophers from the time of Aristotle, and including Descartes, Leibnitz, and Locke. With the latter, whose writings at this time had excited much inquiry on subjects connected with the philosophy of the mind, Berkeley differed on the question of abstract ideas, the existence of which he denied as original qualities of the mind, assigning satisfactory reasons for that opinion.

On the first appearance of Berkeley's work he had sent copies to Whiston and Clarke. The former, who had succeeded Newton in the mathematical chair at Cambridge, which he had recently lost on account of his opinions, professed to know nothing of the matter, but wished Dr Clarke to answer it. When he went over to London a few years after to publish the sequel in the form of " Dialogues," Addison brought them together ; but, as is usually the case, without any satisfactory result, and Berkeley is said to have complained that his opponent, though unable to reply, would not acknowledge himself convinced. But his system had the same advantage to a disputant with the Socratic method, that, whether true or not, it was very puzzling to an antagonist. Steele and Swift at this time equally exerted their utmost influence in his favour by introducing him to those who might be serviceable to him, and the former took the opportunity of securing his co-operation in the *Guardian*, which he had then recently started. By Swift he was introduced, among others, to Lord Berkeley of Stratton as one of his clan, and to the Earl of Peterborough, who being shortly after appointed ambassador to Sicily and the other Italian States, availed himself of the services and company of one of such distinguished attainments, by offering him the post of his chaplain and secretary. On his return, in the latter part of the following year, (1714,) owing to the death of the Queen and the consequent change of Ministry, his hopes of preferment through his present interest being gone, he some time after, on recovering from a fever with which he had been seized, accompanied Mr Ashe, son of the Bishop of Clogher, on the tour of Europe, as companion and tutor. In addition to what was usually included in the grand tour, they visited Apulia, Calabria, and in a particular manner the whole of the beautiful island of Sicily. Of this latter country Mr Berkeley had collected materials for a natural history, which were unfortunately lost on the passage to Naples. At Lyons he wrote a tract, "De Motu," which he had printed shortly after his return, and of which, meantime, he presented a copy to the Royal Academy at Paris. During his stay in the latter city he had taken the opportunity to visit the celebrated Malebranche, which is said to have had a very unfortunate result. The philosopher was then suffering from a pulmonary attack, and Berkeley had found him engaged in cooking something intended as a remedy for his complaint. Turning the conversation on the subject of his visitor's metaphysical system with which he was acquainted, through the medium of a translation, in the ardour of discussion forgetting his ailment, he is said to have over-exerted himself so much as never to have recovered the effects.

After an absence of better than four years, Berkeley returned to London in 1721, shortly subsequent to the crisis occasioned by the bursting of the South Sea Bubble, and the general distress which he witnessed, amounting to a national calamity, strongly excited his sympathy, and led him to publish in the course of the same year " An Essay towards preventing the ruin of Great Britain." Through the friendship of Pope, with whom he had been made acquainted by Steele, Berkeley was at this time introduced to Lord Burlington, whose esteem for him was enhanced by congeniality of taste in acquaintance with architecture. This led to his recommendation to the Duke of Grafton, who was proceeding to Ireland as Lord-Lieutenant, and shortly after made Berkeley the offer to accompany him as chaplain. He had previously been elected, in 1717, senior fellow of his college; and now, at the close of 1721, took his degree of Bachelor and Doctor of Divinity.

In the following year Dr Berkeley had a very remarkable and unlooked-for accession of fortune. Some time after his first arrival in London he had been introduced casually to Mrs (as it was then customary to call single ladies) Esther Vanhomrigh, whom Swift has celebrated under the name of *Vanessa*, but had not seen her since, and now she had bequeathed him half of her property, amounting to L.4000, and named him one of her executors.

Swift had made the acquaintance of this lady also after he went to London in the latter part of 1710, and her mother and sister being then alive, had become very intimate in the family. He had undertaken the superintendence of her studies, and the result was a very ardent attachment which she did not conceal. On making the discovery, he wrote one of the finest and most elaborate of his poems, entitled "Cadenus and Vanessa," in the form of a mythological allegory, in which he rallied her on her choice of a grave parson of forty to fifty, but though expressing himself flattered, evaded any conclusive answer. After his return to Ireland, on the death of her mother and sister, she purchased a property at Celbridge, a pleasant village near Dublin, and in the bowers that she planted there nursed her hopeless passion. Her ardour placed Swift in a very awkward predicament, for at the time he made and cultivated her acquaintance, he was making love, as far as such a man could do, to her he celebrated as *Stella* in that journal or diary he forwarded her, all the time of his stay in London, to Dublin, where she then resided. He subsequently submitted tardily and reluctantly to a private marriage, which was a mere mockery, as they never lived together. The knowledge of this coming to Vanessa, in addition to the feelings produced by his cruel severity to her, and the sense of injury she felt in his having, if not encouraged, at least not taken the means to prevent the first growth of her attachment, whilst he had himself a prior one, induced her to alter the will she had made in his favour, and divide her property equally between her legal agent, a Mr Marshall, and Dr Berkeley. The correspondence which had passed between Swift and the deceased he, as an executor, out of consideration probably to both, thought proper to suppress.

In the year 1724 Dr Berkeley was promoted to the Deanery of Derry, estimated at from L.1100 to L.1500 a year, and at the same time resigned his fellowship. He had not long enjoyed this perferment when he determined on carrying out a project which had for some time occupied his attention, and with this view issued in the following year "Proposals for the Conversion of the American Savages to Christianity." His plan was by means of a college to be established in the Bermudas or Summer Islands; and, having communicated his project to Government, he offered to resign his own ample preferment, stipulating only for L.100 a year, and dedicate his life to the instruction of the American aborigines. His proposal being acceded to by the Government, he sailed for Newport, Rhode Island, on the mainland, in 1728, accompanied by the lady he had recently married, the daughter of John Forster, Esq., Speaker of the Irish Parliament, and three junior fellows of Trinity College, Dublin, Messrs Thompson, Rogers, and King, on whom his self-denying example had such influence that they were prepared to share his fortune on a salary of L.40 a year. At Rhode Island he purchased property for the proposed college in anticipation of the promised funds, and during his residence there contributed materially to the advancement of learning. Either during this period or previously his sanguine sentiments found vent in some verses, probably the only flight of his muse, in prophetic anticipation of the future greatness of this western hemisphere :—

> " The muse, disgusted at an age and clime
>   Barren of every glorious theme,
>   In distant lands now waits a better time,
>   Producing subjects worthy fame :
>
> " In happy climes, where, from the genial sun
>   And virgin earth such scenes ensue,
>   The force of art by nature seems outdone
>   And fancied beauties by the true :
>
> " In happy climes, the seat of innocence,
>   Where nature guides and virtue rules ;
>   Where men shall not impose for truth and sense
>   The pedantry of courts and schools :
>
> " There shall be sung another golden age,
>   The rise of empire and of arts ;
>   The good and great inspiring epic rage,
>   The wisest heads and noblest hearts.
>
> " Not such as Europe breeds in her decay,
>   Such as she bred when fresh and young,
>   When heavenly flame did animate her day,
>   By future poets shall be sung.
>
> " Westward the course of empire takes its way :
>   The four first acts already past,
>   A fifth shall close the drama with the day :
>   Time's noblest offspring is the last."

Shortly after his return from America in 1732, Dr Berkeley made public the fruits of his learned leisure there, in a series of dialogues after the manner of Plato —with whose genius his bore considerable affinity—under the title of " Alciphron ; or, The Minute Philosopher." It was an elaborate and learned refutation of the freethinkers of the age in their various forms, in which some of the arguments and illustrations were drawn from his peculiar views and applied with great ingeniousness. It is scarcely matter of surprise if his metaphysical theory—calling in question the existence of matter, at least in the ordinarily-received sense, and the almost equally inconceivable disinterestedness of his Bermuda scheme to those incapable of appreciating it—should have subjected him to reflection as a visionary. On the publication of this work it was presented to Queen Caroline by Dr Sherlock, who left it to her Majesty to decide whether the author was open to such an imputation. Dr Berkeley had previously been presented by his friend Mr Molyneux, the mathematician and correspondent of Locke, to this princess, who entertained a very high opinion of him, previous to her coming to the throne. He was in consequence nominated, at her instance, to the deanery of Down, in Ireland; but owing to its having been previously promised, or some informality, it was not carried out. The queen then declared that, since they would not allow Dr Berkeley to be a dean in Ireland, he should be a bishop. He was consequently nominated Bishop of Cloyne, on a vacancy occurring early in 1734.

Shortly after this event, a considerable agitation was created in the scientific world by the publication of his next work, "The Analyst," addressed to an infidel mathematician, by whom Dr Halley was understood to be referred to. Its design was to shew that mathematicians, who so much deprecated mysteries in religion, were guilty of admitting much greater mysteries and even falsehood in science, in proof of which he adduced the doctrine of fluxions as a glaring example. In the following year he displayed his patriotism by publishing "Queries" for the good of Ireland. It may be mentioned that one of his early correspondents was Mr Prior, to whose public spirit the formation of the Society of Arts in Dublin was chiefly owing. Bishop

Berkeley's subsequent publications were chiefly of a temporary nature, to which it is unnecessary particularly to refer.

In the exemplary discharge of the duties of this see, in the spirit of primitive times, the good bishop continued nearly twenty years—declining the temptations offered him of exchange for a richer preferment. But, about his sixtieth year, finding his health failing, and having suffered for some time from a nervous cholic, he became desirous of a change of scene, and duties less responsible and onerous. With this view, he had attempted to exchange his office for a canonry or headship at Oxford, being further influenced in his choice by the motive of superintending the education of a younger son who had recently entered as a student of Christ-church College. Failing in this, he wrote to the Secretary of State requesting permission to resign, and stating his reasons for so singular a request. The king, no doubt from personal consideration, as well as that of the loss to the Church of such an ornament, refused the application, saying that he should die a bishop in spite of himself, but granted him full permission to reside where he pleased.

This royal pleasantry was not long in being realised. He had removed with his family to Oxford in midsummer 1752, where he had earned the high respect of the learned members of the university among whom he resided. On a Sunday evening, however, in the middle of the following January, just after having been commenting with his accustomed mental vigour on a passage read by Mrs Berkeley, his daughter, on presenting him a cup of tea, found him quite dead in his chair. He had been seized with paralysis of the heart, and had passed away as in a quiet sleep. He was in his sixty-ninth year. In addition to the qualities of a fine writer, Dr Berkeley had the reputation of one of the most universal scholars of his age. Nor was his knowledge confined to what was merely scholastic; he possessed an extensive acquaintance with every useful and liberal art. Neither was the range of his virtues less comprehensive; and his character was happily summed up by Bishop Atterbury after making his acquaintance:—"So much understanding, so much knowledge, so much innocence, I did not think had been the portion of any but angels, until I saw this gentleman."

The contributions of Dr Berkeley to the *Guardian* were fourteen papers in all, of which eleven are occupied in the defence of revealed religion against the free-thinkers of the age. These present in a clear and lucid manner arguments and illustrations relative to the various evidences and pleas for the reasonableness of revelation. Of the three on other topics, one is on the discovery of the pineal gland, with a humorous and satirical account of a supposed residence in those of philosophers, poets, beaux, mathematicians, belles, and politicians; another on natural and artificial pleasures, and the importance of cultivating a taste for the former; and the third on the character and writings of Fénelon. As the only fact of the kind recorded, it may be mentioned, that for each of these papers Berkeley is stated, on the authority of Dr Hoadly, to have received a guinea and a dinner with Steele.

The next most considerable contributor to the *Guardian* was Pope, who was at this time rising to the poetical supremacy he ultimately attained, and soon after removed to that beautiful locality with the shining Thames winding its way in front, Richmond Hill in the distance, and Ham's embowering shades opposite,—scenes which he has identified with his labours and his life. ALEXANDER POPE was born in London in 1688. His father having realised a fortune, variously stated at from ten to twenty thousand pounds, as a wholesale linen-draper—a circumstance of which, though with no reason to be ashamed of it, the poet, with characteristic vanity, preserved a mysterious silence—retired to Windsor. In a small villa, with a few acres of land which he purchased at Binfield, in the outskirts of the forest, he resided for many years with his family, and being a Roman Catholic, and attached to the exiled family, preferred living frugally on his capital, to investing it in public securities. In that retirement the early years of the poet were spent. Being remarkably delicate, his education was very desultory, with the additional disadvantage of frequent change of masters. He taught himself to write by copying printed books, which he did with great neatness. At different times he was under the tuition of two or three priests, went to a Catholic school at Twyford, near Winchester, and again to one at Hyde Park Corner. Books were his earliest companions, and the first of these to fall into his hands included Ogilby's wretched metrical version of "Homer" and Sandy's Ovid's "Metamorphoses." These first served to direct his taste to poetry; and at the school where he was last placed, occasional opportunities he enjoyed of visiting the theatre induced him to attempt the construction of a sort of drama, consisting of scenes from the former, the passages being connected together with verses of his own, which was performed by

his school-fellows. At the age of twelve he returned to Binfield to his parents, and there devoted himself to a course of poetical studies, being at the same time under the private tuition of another priest. Waller, Spenser, and Dryden were his great favourites. The intense veneration he had for the literary chiefs led him about this time to obtain a sight of the last of these at his club at Wills's Coffee-house, which must have been very shortly before the decease of the grand old man, and which he recorded in the words "Virgilium tantum vidi." He afterwards made his poetry the subject of his especial study as a model of harmony, which, though he never attained to the richness or the sonorous and majestic swell of his master, contributed, along with others, to his carrying English verse to the utmost mechanical perfection and melody. About this time he had composed some fragments of an epic poem entitled "Alcander," and imitations of all the great masters. He had also added so much French and Italian to his "little Latin and less Greek," as enabled him to extend his reading to those languages.

His first published poem, the "Ode to Solitude," was the production of this period, and gave no extraordinary promise beyond the attainment of neatness and skill in versification. His translation of the "Thebais" of Statius and of "Sappho to Phaon," are said to belong to his fourteenth year, and, if not subsequently recast, must be considered remarkable for that age. Two years later he commenced his "Pastorals," which, however, were not published till some years after, but being handed about in MS., they gained him the acquaintance of several distinguished persons. Among these were Sir William Trumbul, a retired statesman in his neighbourhood; Wycherley, Walsh, a poet and man of fashion; Somers, Garth, and others. The result of his intimacy with Wycherley has been previously noticed; but that of Walsh, whom Dryden had called the greatest critic of his day, proved a valuable acquisition in directing his studies to the attainment of accuracy and melody of versification. Among other early acquaintances was Mr Cromwell, a pedant and beau, to the imitation of whom may probably be attributed the poet's pert and flippant style of gallantry to the fair sex. Jervas the painter, and also the translator of "Don Quixotte," whose art he at one time thought of cultivating, was likewise one of his early friends.

At sixteen, (1704,) besides his "Pastorals," he put the first hand to his "Windsor Forest," and in the same year in which he published the former, (1709,) he wrote his "Essay on Criticism," which has received the praise of Johnson, to which, especially if the age of the writer be considered, it is justly entitled. Some allusions which he made in that poem reflecting on Dennis the critic called forth a savage retort on his part, and was the commencement of a life-long enmity between them. Meantime, he was pluming his wing for higher flights, and produced shortly after his "Ode to St Cecilia's Day," and his "Choruses," and in 1711 produced his "Elegy to an Unfortunate Lady," the most pathetic and among the most finished of his compositions. The latter is said to have had a personal origin, though involved in some obscurity. It is stated that there was an attachment between the subject of it and himself. She was deformed like himself, but was above him in fortune and social position; and, refusing to comply with the wishes of a cruel guardian in her choice, she was forced into a convent, where she was treated with great strictness, and at last put an end to her existence. Another piece of a somewhat kindred nature, among the most vivid and impressive of his productions, the "Epistle of Eloise to Abelard," though of uncertain date, was probably the production of some years later.

The "Messiah," which was largely indebted to the imagery of
"Wrapt Isaiah's wild seraphic fire;"
and some passages of which were altered at the suggestion of Steele, appeared originally in the *Spectator* in 1712. In the same year, he reached what has been regarded as his highest point as a poet in the "Rape of the Lock," a mock-heroic poem which originally appeared in two cantos, and in that state was eulogised as *merum sal* by Addison, who endeavoured to dissuade him from the risk of injuring it by the addition of the sylphs. He fortunately persisted in his plan, and the two cantos were expanded into five. But no one in whose mind the idea was not as perfect as in his own could have anticipated the exquisitely felicitous adaptation of the Roscicrucian machinery which he effected. Yet Pope professed to have then first made the discovery of Addison's jealous and envious disposition, whilst in the following year he endeavoured to dissuade Addison from risking "Cato" on the stage, where it was so great a success, no doubt owing to adventitious causes. This affords a tolerable test of the justness of Pope's waspish suspicions of Addison, to which Mr Thackeray, contrary, as we think, to the evidence, has given his sanction. But, to return to the poem, it originated in a liberty taken by Lord Petre

with Mrs Arabella Fermor, in applying the scissors to one of her ringlets, which produced a feud between the two families. The poet sought to reconcile them, and succeeded. But the brilliant production was a double triumph, for it silenced those critics who so ingeniously manipulated a definition as to call in question the claims of Pope to the title of a poet, because the nature of his general subjects did not indicate the possession of invention and imagination. The felicitous conception distances every competitor of the comic epic. In the course of the same year appeared his " Temple of Fame," founded on Chaucer, which, like most of the others, had undergone a two years' probation from its production. Though, as a whole, not among his most popular productions, there are passages in it which in descriptive felicity he has scarcely surpassed.

The year 1713 was an eventful one to Pope. In it appeared his " Windsor Forest," with a dedication to Lord Lansdowne, the first part of which, as previously stated, was produced in his sixteenth year, and not only bears the marks of juvenility, but is deficient in individuality. The second part, however, which is historical, ranks among his happiest efforts. Addison's " Cato" being brought upon the stage this year, he contributed to it a noble prologue; and when a severe critique was written upon the play by Dennis, Pope retorted upon him by a humorous piece of scurrility, which, as Addison not only disapproved of, but probably saw in this volunteered service only an opportunity sought to avenge his own quarrel, which he had provoked with the critic, he felt called upon to disclaim any participation in it. This was probably the foundation of the coolness between Pope and Addison. He was enlisted at this time by Steele as a contributor to the *Guardian*, and this year he also issued proposals for his translation of Homer, from which he derived his chief emolument. He had now secured the friendship and admiration of the most distinguished men of all parties, including Lords Halifax, Somers, Bolingbroke, Oxford, and Peterborough ; Congreve, Garth, Atterbury, Arbuthnot, Swift, and others, most, if not all of whom, promoted the subscription. Swift was particularly zealous in his behalf. He used such diligence, that his first volume, containing four books of the " Iliad," was ready in 1715, and appeared in quarto, with a dedication to Congreve. It has been made a subject of surprise that he should have conferred an honour which dukes and ministers would have been proud to receive on one so little able to patronise him. But, in addition to his great literary reputation and high social position, he possessed the advantage of being a sort of neutral man who was respected and stood well with all. The reception of so brilliant a production (although to be regarded only as an exquisitely polished and harmonious paraphrase of the original) was such as might naturally be expected, and placed him in circumstances that enabled him to remove from Windsor to a situation more convenient to his friends and the town. Accordingly, having induced his father to part with the property at Binfield, he purchased a villa on the Thames at Twickenham, and five acres of ground, which his taste converted, with its grotto and its miniature groves, into a little fairy retreat, which his genius has consecrated.* His father did not long survive, but his mother was spared him

---

* Perhaps it would be difficult to name a case of greater Gothic barbarism than that of which Pope's villa has been the victim. It has fallen beneath a Cockney

many years to call forth his heart's best trait in his exemplary filial piety.

The year 1718 witnessed the completion of his Homeric task, which Gay celebrated in a picturesque poem entitled a "Welcome on his Safe Return from Troy," and representing his friends as congregated on the shore to greet him with an ovation on his arrival. It was no unprofitable voyage that. It realised him upwards of L.5000, whilst he had not previously made as many hundreds by his own writings, and even the smaller sum would probably have rejoiced the heart of Homer himself. Of the rival translation of Tickell, mention has already been made, and it is unnecessary that it should be further alluded to. He soon after undertook the sequel of the task by commencing the translation of the Odyssey, in which he associated with him the pens of Broome and Fenton. Pope himself only executed twelve books—the half—but his coadjutors performed their part so well under his general supervision that there was no apparent discrepancy. The publication was completed in 1725, and though not so remunerative as the former in a pecuniary point of view, added considerably to his finances, realising L.3000, after paying his assistants L.800. He had Dennis, as usual, dogging him. "The trumpet of Homer," he said, "with its loud and various notes, dwindled in Pope's lips to a Jew's trump."

He had previously published a collected edition of his works in 1717, and four years subsequently undertook the editorship of Shakespeare, for which, as the event proved,

invasion, instead of being religiously preserved; some wealthy tea merchant from the city, probably, having erected in its stead a Chinese temple—a desecration enough to disturb the irritable little bard in his grave.

he was but indifferently qualified. The consequence was a severe, though not altogether unmerited, criticism by Theobald, which Pope subsequently retorted by making him the hero of the "Dunciad," until a later offender, Colley Cibber, was elevated to his place. He himself tells us in lines which may be considered to embody the history of the "Dunciad"—

> "Whoe'er offends, at some unlucky time,
> Slides into verse, and hitches in a rhyme."
> —*Sat.* 1, b. ii.

It was rather before this period that his principal intercourse with Lady M. W. Montagu occurred, to whom he had written in the most extravagantly complimentary style, which she quietly put aside or turned off with a smile, whose portrait he had got painted, whose husband he had induced to reside in his vicinity, but which ended in the bitterest enmity, and in a manner little to the credit of the poet. This has, however, been previously sufficiently dwelt upon in the notice of Lady Mary. Another lady, Miss Martha Blount, the daughter of a Roman Catholic gentleman at Reading, whose acquaintance he had made many years before leaving Windsor, and his conduct to whom is almost as mysterious as that of Swift to Stella, continued through life his confidential friend, and was painted at full length along with himself.

His next publication was the "Miscellanies," in prose and verse, which appeared in 1727 in four volumes. They were written in conjunction with Swift and Arbuthnot, and included the celebrated "Memoirs of the Scriblerus Club," and the "Treatise on Bathos, or the Art of Sinking in Poetry." This latter drew him into trouble, for, appended to the specimens he gave were initial letters and blanks, as he said, scattered at random,—a statement not likely to receive much credence from those to whom they applied. The consequence was that he was assailed with galling and long-sustained abuse in the newspapers by the writers attacked. This and other previous attacks induced him to undertake that elaborate retort, in which he stormed his enemies with a blasting fire of ridicule and wit—overwhelmed them in a promiscuous deluge of scorn and contempt, but which has done his memory or the cause of literature little service.*

About this time Pope had a narrow escape from drowning, having been thrown into the water by the overturning of Lord Bolingbroke's carriage, in which he was proceeding home. Horses and carriage were precipitated over a bridge, and the windows being closed and stiff, he was only released by the glass being broken, which cut two of his fingers so severely as to deprive him of the use of them.

The success of that personal satire upon Addison made Atterbury recommend to Pope that as he had found out where his strength lay, he should employ it in a similar manner. He now produced the fruits of that advice by the publication of his elaborate mock-heroic poem of the "Dunciad," which appeared first in Ireland, probably by an arrangement with Swift, who had given the aid of his caustic irony, and possibly with the view of its being attri-

* "Pope, I fear," says Mr Thackeray, " contributed more than any man who ever lived to depreciate the literary calling [by establishing that Grub Street tradition]. It was not an unprosperous one before that time ; at least, there were great prizes in the profession, which had made Addison a minister, and Prior an ambassador, and Steele a commissioner, and Swift all but a bishop. The profession of letters was ruined by that libel of the 'Dunciad.'"—*Humorists*, Lect. iv.

buted to him. In the following year (1728) it appeared in an improved edition in London. The diction is in his most finished style, but the subject is of no general interest, except for that love of mischief and personality [which finds but too many admirers, without reference to the cruelty, illiberality, and injustice of which others are the victims. Even this interest has ceased. Not to speak of his having been the aggressor in very many instances, he has carried his revenge to unwarrantable lengths, and vilified many ingenious and worthy persons who had given no ground of offence.* Mr Thackeray has eulogised his triumphant efforts by comparing them with the victories of Bonaparte and other conquerors. If others read the accounts of aggression, slaughter, and plunder with the same sickening sense of choking indignation that we do, they would have fewer admirers, and, if the parallel hold good, the same applies to the pen as to the sword :

" 'Tis good to have a giant's strength,
But not to use it like a giant."

The true honour of the possessor of high powers is in using them for high purposes ; and the application of them to mean, unworthy, or selfish ends is only their disgrace. The poem was, we learn on the authority of Pope himself, pre-

* In the correspondence with Aaron Hill relative to the "Bathos" treatise and "Dunciad," Pope had made very modest professions, of which it is easy to estimate the value, of never having valued himself very highly for his poetry, and took his stand on his moral character. In his reply, Hill quietly but effectually took that ground from under him. " Neither would it appear to your own reason," he says, " at a cooler juncture, over-consistent with the morality you are so sure of, to scatter the letters of the whole alphabet, annexed at random, to characters of a light and ridiculous cast, confusedly, with intent to provoke jealous writers into resentment, that you might take occasion, from that resentment, to expose and depreciate their characters." There is indeed reason to believe that the "Dunciad" was written *before* the "Bathos."

sented to the King and Queen by Sir Robert Walpole, who, on this or some other occasion, made him the offer of a pension, which he declined, as he had previously done to Halifax. He seemed to regard it as a snare to deprive him of his independence.

At the suggestion of Bolingbroke, he now (1729) turned his attention to ethical topics, and with him for his

" Guide, philosopher, and friend,"

sketched out the plan of his philosophical essay. Whilst engaged upon it he also commenced his "Ethic Epistles," which appeared at intervals in the course of 1731 and the following year. By the first of these, which now stands as the fourth, he was again drawn into trouble by his incurable love of personal satire. Having severely ridiculed the house, furniture, gardens, and entertainments of a person of great wealth and little taste, under the title of Timon, he was generally believed to have satirised the Duke of Chandos, who, whatever his errors in taste and love of display, was not only a man of great general beneficence, but one to whom Pope was under obligations. His disclaimer received but little credence with the public, though accepted by the duke with great magnanimity, at the same time evidently not believing in its validity.

In the latter year above referred to (1732) appeared anonymously the first part of his "Essay on Man," addressed to Bolingbroke, which was completed in the course of the two following years, and acknowledged at the conclusion. As a not unnatural result of having sat at the feet of St John for his philosophy, the principles of the essay were attacked for their imputed theism and fatalism. The poet himself was probably little aware of the tendency of what he was inculcating, nor perhaps very particular on the subject, so that he gave to his polished verse an air of philosophic plausibility. Indeed the general reader was perhaps equally obtuse and indifferent on the subject of its abstract philosophy, and sufficiently delighted with the beauty of its pictures and illustrations, and its terse and compact diction. His "Imitations of Horace" followed, which were also suggested by Bolingbroke, and commenced in 1733. Among the subjects of his satire, in the prosecution of which he had now fairly embarked, and which occupied him for several succeeding years, were Lord Hervey, the Vice-Chamberlain, and Lady Montagu, whom he had drawn under the titles of Lord Fanny and Sappho. They combined to meet him with his own weapons, and his hatred and resentment to the latter having carried him the length of perpetrating a couplet of the grossest description, devoid of all decency, he was again driven to the most miserable wriggling and shuffling by being called to account. When *he* could think even personal infirmity a just ground of reflection, and point his satire with it, as he had done with Lord Hervey,[*] any ignoble topic of retort need scarcely surprise us. They attacked him on the ground of his birth, and his vanity so far got the better of every other consideration that he replied by making out a pedigree for himself, which never received any corroboration either from those connected with his own family or that with which he claimed kindred. In this genealogy he traced his family to the Earls of Downe. To such wretched shifts

---

[*] "What? that thing of silk,
Sporus, that mere white curd of asses' milk?"

was he reduced by exerting what he considered his strength on the weakness of others. Of the pain that he inflicted on himself an example is related by his friend Richardson the painter, who found him on one occasion reading a pamphlet written as a retort against him by Colley Cibber. "These things," said he, with a sickly smile, throwing it down, "are my diversion," whilst, said Richardson, every muscle was quivering with agony.

In 1737 Pope published a collection of his correspondence in quarto. The ostensible excuse for this was the recent appearance of a surreptitious collection. The investigation of this mysterious affair led to the inference that the writer himself was at the bottom of it. The story is too long to be more than very generally referred to. Curll, the publisher, had announced his intention of bringing out a life of Pope, and advertised for materials. Soon after he had an anonymous communication merely signed "P. T," offering him a collection of the poet's letters ready printed, on moderate terms. The writer expressed his opinion that these would probably be found to contain his whole history, and Curll ultimately purchased and published the work. Pope then took proceedings against him, and published his own genuine edition by subscription, on the plea of self-defence. Besides a variety of other suspicious circumstances, Pope publishes some of the letters in his edition erroneously—that is, two or more letters fused together, just as they occur in the spurious edition, and not after the originals. But above all, the anonymous correspondent communicates the pedigree previously referred to, but never heard of from any other quarter than the poet himself. All this finessing and mystification were to save the imputation on his vanity to which he might have been exposed. The correspondence of literary men, especially in their lifetime, was then something new. It was not the popular element in our literature which it has since deservedly become. Pope's collection—which includes those of his friends—is certainly interesting, though his own letters are too studied, artificial, and affected. He was surpassed in his own time in this class of composition by Lady Montagu, and subsequently by Cowper and Gray.

For some time previously the state of his health had led him to make frequent visits to Bath, where he made the acquaintance of Mr Allen of Prior Park in that neighbourhood, the original of his "Man of Ross," and of Fielding's "Squire Alworthy." By introducing to this excellent man another recent acquaintance, Warburton, he unconsciously tended very materially to promote the interest of one who had performed for him a signal literary service, and helped to pave his way to the episcopal bench.

Another literary friendship, made some time previously, in which he indirectly helped to promote the interests of the subject of it, may be here referred to. This was the Rev. Joseph Spence, author of the "Polymetis," and professor of poetry at Oxford. An "Essay on the Odyssey," which he had published in 1726, about the time Pope was engaged on the same work, led to their acquaintance. He became the intimate friend of Pope, and his "Anecdotes" of him were indeed the first approximation in our literature to the biographical minuteness of Boswell, though without his colloquial and dramatic interest. But, holding the pen for Pope, his authority is not always to be implicitly relied upon.*

Pope had long suffered from a chronic headache, in addition to general debility, and to these were latterly added symptoms of dropsy in the chest. This, accompanied with asthma, proved fatal in 1744, whilst he was engaged in preparing a complete edition of his works. His remains were interred at Twickenham in the same vault with his parents, to whom in life he had been so affectionate and devoted. What he had failed to accomplish himself was executed by Warburton, to whom he had bequeathed his writings, by an elaborate edition of his works in 1757.†

Mr Thackeray has stated, with reference to Pope's correspondence, that "his closest friends were among the delights and ornaments of the polished society of that age." His acquaintance certainly included many that were so, as was natural in such a case. But of his special friends, with

---

* The anecdotes of Spence long lay in the library of the Duke of Newcastle in MS., under an impression that the reputation of individuals or families might suffer by its publication. Malone had the use of it for his " Life of Dryden," and Dr Johnson in writing that of Pope in his " Poets," which he did with unusual minuteness. It was first published in 1819 by Mr Singer.

† Among the portions of the edition of his works he was preparing, found to have been printed off, were his "Epistles and Satires," the severest and most exaggerated of which, that on the characters of women, contained a satire on the Duchess of Marlborough, then surviving in her 84th year, under the title of "Atossa." These lines he had read both to her and the Duchess of Buckingham, telling each they were designed for the other. "The Buckingham," says Walpole, "believed him : the Marlborough had more sense, and knew herself, and gave him L.1000 to suppress it, and yet he left the copy behind." Warton gives his sanction to the story, and Warburton partially. Bolingbroke, on inquiry, confirmed it, and expresses censure. Of course neither party was likely to make an absolute bargain, but that doesn't alter the fact, except in a legal point of view. She is said to have made him understand that she knew who was meant, and if she gave him the L.1000 afterward, the object could not be mistaken, and the acceptance of it was a tacit sanction of the compact.

some exceptions, (particularly Arbuthnot, who would indeed have been a man among men in any age, and Gay, one of the most amiable, simple, and single-minded of mortals,) we cannot help thinking that there was a remarkable predominance among them of vanity and selfishness, if not duplicity, realising the foregathering of birds of like feather. We have the perfidious Oxford; the selfish, overbearing, acrimonious Swift, who, like Pope, thought himself at liberty to vilify his species, as if he had himself been an unexceptionable model; Atterbury, whom Swift, in a notice of him to Stella, artfully insinuates was very cunning, and who, with all his accomplishments, bore the reputation of an insincere man. Though he professed the greatest friendship for Pope, and presented him with his Bible whilst in the Tower in 1722, previous to his banishment for treason, yet he could not refrain from the expression of his private opinion by the phrase of "crooked mind and crooked body." And lastly, we have Bolingbroke, after a theatrical display of his grief at the death of the poet, and exclaiming "O God, what was man?" five years later, when he could no longer defend himself, abusing him and permitting others employed by him to abuse him, in the coarsest terms in (probably pretended) indignation at the discovery of his treachery in relation to his "Patriot King."*

* He had given Pope a commission, as being more conversant with printers, to procure a few copies of his "Patriot King" for his private distribution. Instead of executing this faithfully, it appeared at his decease that he had not only ordered an edition of 1500 copies to be kept by the printer, but had taken some liberties with the MS. However unjustifiable this might have been, as the motive was certainly not mercenary, and was probably intended to promote the fame of his friend by insuring the publication of the work, Bolingbroke might at least have restrained Mallet, whom he afterwards employed to edit it, from re

It is certainly invidious in general to dwell upon the errors and weaknesses of those who have conferred either benefit or high pleasure on the world, except in such cases as Pope and Swift, where they have shown no mercy to those of others, but used their strength to crush those weaker than themselves, and made their revenge as lasting as their fame.

Pope's share in the *Guardian* was eight excellent papers, which, as they may be easily referred to, need not be particularly dwelt upon, with one or two exceptions, those of Nos. 46 and 91. A series of six papers had been introduced by Steele, commencing with No. 15, and the remainder between Nos. 22 and 32, giving a review of ancient and modern pastoral poetry; and the latter, after an allegorical account of Arcadia, concludes by representing Philips, for whom he had a particular friendship, as the lineal descendant of those who bore sway in those regions—Theocritus, Virgil, and Spenser. As Pope had four years previously commenced his poetical career with his pastorals, this decision, in which posterity, so far as it regards this class of poetry, has pretty much coincided, was too much for his patience. He therefore, with that finesse of which he has proved himself so great a master, sent this paper anonymously to the *Guardian*, in which he institutes a comparison directly between his pastorals and those of Philips', and in which the final decision appears the same as that of the *Guardian*. This was done with so

flecting coarsely on the memory of his deceased friend. It has been suggested that the real ground of complaint with Bolingbroke was Pope's having put his writings out of his control, and that in employing Mallet he was conciliating one then supposed to be engaged on the life of Marlborough; but who was satisfied with receiving the L.1000, and left the work undone.

much plausibility, apparent seriousness, and delicate irony, as is said even to have deceived Steele. He selected Philips' worst passages and placed them in juxtaposition with the best of his own. Though he professed to award him the palm as an Arcadian, it was evident, by a comparison so made, with whom the poetical superiority at least rested. The murder was soon out, and the wrath of Philips was fierce. He is said to have hung up a rod at Button's to be applied to his rival, and it is stated that Pope, thinking discretion the better part of valour, refrained from that resort. But if we may credit his own statement, in a letter to Mr Craggs, he went as usual and never had any outrage offered him.

Notwithstanding the naturally extreme sensitiveness of Pope, with his temperament, in reference to his figure, he has himself, in Nos. 91 and 92, indulged in some very humorous sallies, and sketched some portraits evidently suggested by it, in his account of the club of little men :—

" Dick Distich, by name, we have elected president, not only as he is the shortest of us all, but because he has entertained so just a sense of his stature as to go generally in black, that he may appear yet less. Nay, to that perfection is he arrived that he stoops as he walks. The figure of the man is odd enough ; he is a lively little creature, with long arms and legs ; a spider is no ill emblem of him. He has been taken at a distance for a small windmill ; but, indeed, what principally moved us in his favour was his talent in poetry, for he hath promised to undertake a long work, in short verse, to celebrate the heroes of our size. He has entertained so great a respect for Statius on the score of that line—
> Major in exiguo regnabat corpore virtus.
> ' A larger portion of heroic fire
> Did his small limbs and little breast inspire,'

that he once designed to translate the whole ' Thebaid ' for the sake of little Tydeus."

It may be added that, though noted for the economy of

his habits, he was not incapable of generosity; and, in addition to his liberality to Savage, of whom, however, Johnson says he exacted some dirty work, he also assisted Dodsley when he commenced bookseller with L.100.

Another contributor to the *Guardian*, who was also one of the most genial and interesting of the Twickenham literary circle, was JOHN GAY, (1688-1732,) born like Pope in the revolution year, at Barnstable, or, according to other accounts, at Exeter. Though of a good Devonshire family, yet being in reduced circumstances, he had been apprenticed to a silk-mercer in London. He very soon manifested such a decided antipathy to his intended calling, however, that he was released from his indentures. He then devoted himself to poetical pursuits, and produced the first fruits of his muse in 1711, under the title of " Rural Sports," with a dedication to Pope, which led to a very cordial life-friendship. After having felt the effects of his thoughtless improvidence in the low state of his finances, his spirits rose proportionably the following year by his good fortune in being appointed secretary to the Duchess of Monmouth, which quite accorded with the easy, luxurious disposition of Gay. His " Trivia," or art of walking the streets, a very happy production of the mock-heroic kind, followed shortly after. Having failed in his first efforts to participate in dramatic honours and rewards about the same time by the production of a comedy and farce upon the stage, entitled " The Mohocks," and " The Wife of Bath," in the following year he was engaged by Pope as an ally in his quarrel with Philips. With this view, he produced his "Shepherd's Week," so called from consisting of six pastorals, in which he followed the rural simplicity of Philips, which Pope was

censured for contemning. Though the design was entered upon with something of a burlesque view, yet it was executed with so much felicity and spirit, that he was considered to have surpassed both his ally and opponent. The work was inscribed to Lord Bolingbroke, and on its appearance in 1714 was highly successful. The result of this was his appointment as secretary to the Earl of Clarendon, ambassador at the court of Hanover. Scarcely, however, had he been a fortnight in the scene of his official duties, when his hopes were blighted by the death of the Queen. His present position, indeed, served as an introduction to the royal family who were to succeed, but it had also the unhappy effect of keeping him dangling about a court in the vain hope of some substantial preferment which he was never destined to receive. That dedication to Bolingbroke probably stood in his way. Swift called it his original sin. By the advice of Pope, however, he paid his compliments " in the poetical way" to the Princess of Wales on her arrival in England, and was favourably received at court. This raised his spirits—always easily elevated and easily depressed—and he soon after brought upon the stage his pleasant trifle, the "What d'ye call it," "a tragi-comic pastoral farce," as he expresses it, which on the author's third night was honoured by the presence of their Royal Highnesses. It was regarded as a satire on the high buskin style of tragedy, and provoked those concerned. It contains that charming ballad—

" 'Twas when the seas were roaring."

The profits of the piece were considerable. The simplicity, sweetness, and sincerity of his nature, in addition to his poetical reputation, made him deservedly a favourite with all who knew him, and he was indulged with jaunts, in which he delighted, by his great friends. One of these he made in 1716 by the favour of Lord Burlington to his native county, and commemorated in some verses, as he also did an excursion in the following year, in which he accompanied Mr Pulteney, afterwards Earl of Bath, to Aix.

Shortly after his return from this latter trip, he brought upon the stage his comedy of " Three Hours after Marriage," in the production of which he had been assisted by Pope and Arbuthnot; but, notwithstanding the aid of such valuable allies, and the principal characters being recommended by the art of the two best comedians of the day, Johnson and Mrs Oldfield, its reception was decidedly unfavourable on the very first night. Among a variety of other satire, that on Dennis as "Sir Tremendous, the greatest critic of our age," was no doubt contributed by Pope. An incident connected with this piece originated his long hostility to Colley Cibber. Two of the characters had been introduced as a mummy and crocodile, in satirical allusion to the pursuits of Dr Woodward as an antiquarian and naturalist, which, after some previous flat humour, drew forth hisses. In performing the character of " Bayes," in " the Rehearsal," some time after, when Pope happened to be present, Cibber made some extempore remarks, as were usual in this character, in which he alluded to his having been anticipated in a similar design, which fell in with the humour of the house, and was received with a burst of applause. Pope went behind the scenes livid with rage, and abused Cibber, as he described it, till he almost foamed; and he declared—and indeed there was very little of venom about him—that this was all the provocation he was conscious of to provoke his lasting vindictiveness and enmity.

In the following year (1718), Gay spent a part of the summer at an old romantic seat of Lord Harcourt in Oxfordshire, where he commemorated the fate of two rustic lovers who were struck dead together by a flash of lightning while seeking shelter from a thunder-storm in a hayfield. This so fell in with Pope's sentimentalism that he despatched it to Lady Montagu,[*] in a letter, without acknowledgment, and afterwards to Martha Blount.

There is little reason to believe that with his thoughtless habits he had saved anything out of the current receipts of his writings. But, by the advice of his friends, he brought out a collected edition of his works in 1720, and having such an extensive acquaintance among the affluent, it was

[*] Lady Mary returned from Constantinople at the close of this year, and two years later Gay received some of the most beautiful and passionate lines Pope ever wrote, in reply to his congratulation on the completion of Pope's house and grounds—showing that, if evanescent, his passion for Lady Montagu had been very ardent; but the open confession of such a passion for a married woman is not a little remarkable, and by one so little like a lover, (though it was not till somewhat later that his infirmity became so extreme that he required to be laced in buckram and the constant attendance of a nurse):—

> "Ah, friend, 'tis true—this truth you lovers know—
> In vain my structures rise, my gardens grow;
> In vain fair Thames reflects the double scenes
> Of hanging mountains, and of sloping greens:
> Joy lives not here; to happier seats it flies,
> And only dwells where Wortley casts her eyes.

> "What are the gay parterre, the chequer'd shade,
> The morning bower, the evening colonade,
> But soft recesses of uneasy minds,
> To sigh unheard in to the passing winds?
> So the struck deer, in some sequester'd part,
> Lies down to die, the arrow at his heart,
> There, stretch'd unseen in coverts hid from day,
> Bleeds drop by drop, and pants his life away."

so successful that he realised a thousand pounds by it. Such a sum in hand seemed a fortune to a poet, and he consulted all his friends how he should dispose of it. Various advice was given, of which he took none, but, seized with the prevailing infatuation of the time, invested in the South-Sea Company, of which Secretary Craggs had presented him some stock. At one time he believed himself worth twenty thousand pounds, and lived accordingly, but awoke from the dream to find the original capital and the delusive profits gone together. The effect of such a reverse to one so easily depressed was very serious. He was attacked with a violent colic, which, but for the care and assiduity of Arbuthnot, would, it was thought, have proved fatal. When he had sufficiently recovered his health and spirits, he set to work on a tragedy he had planned, entitled "The Captives," which, after having been previously read by invitation before the Princess of Wales, was performed at Drury Lane in 1723, when their Royal Highnesses favoured it with their attendance. The Princess also encouraged him to write some fables in verse for the use of the Duke of Cumberland, subsequently the victor of Culloden, then only a child, which, contrary to the advice of Pope, he undertook, and the "Fables," which rank among the best in the language, and the most finished of his works, were published in 1726. But the prediction of his monitor was realised in the result.

On the accession of George II. the following year, to his great disappointment he was offered the place of gentleman-usher to the Princess Louisa, then quite a child, which he not only declined but resented as an indignity. Swift suggests that in the "Fables" he was thought to be somewhat too bold with the court. It was whilst Gay was in this mood that he worked up a suggestion made him by Swift, that a Newgate pastoral would make a pretty odd sort of thing. He inclined more to the experiment of a comedy, and tried his hand at it, though Swift did not like the plan so well. His friends all helped him, but, contrary to the traditional account, Pope states that the assistance was confined to hints and verbal criticisms. They were all dubious of it. Congreve foretold that it would either be a great success or a great failure. Such was the history of the famous "Beggars' Opera." It made its appearance at the close of 1727, and its success exceeded any previous example. The good feeling of the house, which his friends were anxiously awaiting, increased at every act, and ended in a clamour of applause. The satire had a double application, being directed equally against the Italian Opera and the court. It was humorously said of the manager and author that it had made "Gay *rich*, and Rich *gay*." Besides being performed in the metropolis sixty-three successive nights, and renewed the following season with no diminution of favour, it made its way to all parts of the provinces, and in some of the large towns had almost an equal run. The ladies had fans with its favourite songs, and house-screens were furnished from it. Miss Fenton, who performed Polly, became so great a public favourite that her likeness was engraven and her life written, letters and verses to her published, as well as pamphlets reporting her *bon mots*, and she herself finally became Duchess of Bolton. As a burlesque, the "Beggars' Opera" is among the best in the language, and not only banished for a couple of years the Italian Opera, against which its satire was in part directed, but originated the English Ballad Opera.

The immense success of this piece induced Gay to attempt a sequel under the title of "Polly," which, like most second parts, was a failure. The chamberlain also, judging of it perhaps by the former, or to punish his previous political allusions, refused to sanction its performance. This was the best thing that could have happened for the interest of the author, especially considering the essential flatness of the piece; for his friends and the public resenting this exercise of authority, the former exerted themselves so effectually in its behalf, that when he published it, he realised about L.1200 by it,—a sum very much more considerable than he had reaped from the representation of the earlier and more meritorious part. Nor was this all, for the Duke and Duchess of Queensberry expressed their sense of his treatment by the court so warmly that they threw up their respective places, and carried the poet with them in their retirement to share their heart and home during the brief remaining years of his life. With them he varied the scene from one of their seats to another, now at Richmond, then at a delightful retreat at Amesbury, on Salisbury Plain, near Stonehenge, and again in Scotland, where he made the acquaintance of another dramatic Arcadian, Allan Ramsay. His accession of popularity induced him to hope that he might successfully recast his rejected "Wife of Bath," and he had it brought again upon the stage in 1730. But he was fated to disappointment, and his unequal spirits sunk into despondency. His natural love of ease had increased upon him, and, like Pope, his indulgence in the pleasures of the table in excess, at least for his constitution, aggravated his complaint, and he became plethoric. A gloom overspread his mind, which neither the brotherly tenderness of the duke, nor the sweet smiles of the charming duchess, could chase away He had been able however, at intervals, to complete his opera of "Achilles." But, coming up to town for the winter, he was seized with an inflammatory fever, which led to mortification of the stomach, that terminated fatally in three days, December 1732. He was interred in Westminster Abbey, and a handsome monument erected to his memory by the noble friends who had loved him so well in life, with the well-known inscription by Pope. By the kindness of the duke in taking charge of his pecuniary affairs, for which he was so much better qualified than one who was

"In wit a man—simplicity a child"—

he left L.3000 behind him. This, with the profits of his new opera, which was very well received, went to two widowed sisters of the poet. His loss was mourned with an affecting tenderness by Pope and Swift.

The contributions of Gay to the *Guardian* were a letter of a humorous character on the cures performed by flattery, and one paper on dress, a subject that would appear to have been worn out in the previous lucubrations of Steele and Addison, but by an ingenious comparison of his subject with poetry, he succeeded in treating it with originality, wit, and fancy, not untinged with satire.

The only other contributors to the *Guardian* whom it will be necessary to notice particularly were Philips and Rowe, the dramatists. The former of these, AMBROSE

PHILIPS, of an old family in Leicestershire, after studying at St John's College, Cambridge, repaired to the metropolis, and frequented Button's Coffeehouse, where the wits then resorted. He seems to have formed a particular friendship with Addison and Steele. Previous to his leaving college, he had become an assiduous student and cultivator of poetry, and about 1708 had published his six pastorals. That was the year preceding the appearance of those of Pope, and the result of the rivalry occasioned by this simultaneous appearance, and the friendly criticisms of Philips in the *Spectator* and *Guardian*, has been previously referred to. Though Pope took a very ingenious method of appealing from that criticism, yet the judgment of posterity has sanctioned the justice of awarding to Philips the palm of superiority in the characteristic simplicity of his pastorals, as well as greater originality in discarding the trite classical mythology and the substitution of one highly picturesque, fresher, and more racy of the soil. One of the earliest and best of Philips' productions was a "Poetical Epistle" from Copenhagen in 1709, and addressed to the Duke of Dorset. It appeared in an early number of the *Tatler*. This is a winter piece of great merit, which Steele compares to a painting by some of the best masters. Its excellence, indeed, was such that even Pope, who satirised Philips under the character of *Macer*—

> "'Twas all the ambition his high soul could feel,
> To wear red stockings, and to dine with Steele,"

and constantly endeavoured to depreciate him, had the candour to speak of it in one of his letters as the production of a man who could write very nobly. From all the notices we have of Philips, he would appear to have been a favourite with Steele and Addison. The former, writing to Swift in October 1709, says, "Mr Philips dined with me yesterday. He is still a shepherd, and walks very lonely through this unthinking crowd in London." Swift, writing to Stella in the latter part of 1711, says, " I met Pastoral Philips and Mr Addison on the Mall to-day, and took a turn with them, but they looked terribly dry and cold. A curse on party."

It was in the latter year that Philips produced his first dramatic piece, " The Distressed Mother," founded on the Andomaque of Racine, when his friends used their utmost exertions to promote its success—packing a house for him, and Addison carried Sir Roger de Coverley to witness the performance. He even contrived to do a service at the same time to his friend Budgell by re-writing an epilogue he had produced, and giving him the credit of it, at a time when he was making interest for a public employment. This proved to be the most successful production of the kind that had ever appeared, and added considerably to the credit and success of the play, being recited twice on the first three nights by the celebrated Mrs Oldfield. This was he whom Pope described as

" So obliging that he ne'er obliged."

Philips afterwards (1721) produced two other tragedies, entitled, " The Briton," and " Humphrey, Duke of Gloucester," the latter indebted to the second part of Shakespeare's Henry VI. These, though not without considerable merit, have not retained possession of the stage. In the latter part of the reign of Queen Anne, Philips was secretary to the Hanover Club, which was of much the same nature as the Kit-Cat. In this capacity Pope charged him with having treated him unhandsomely in relation to the Homer subscriptions, and with having represented him as an enemy to the Government, and as being concerned in the *Examiner* paper. After all the absurd things that he attributed to Addison in relation to himself, we need not attach much importance to these. As a contributor to the *Spectator*, he has been previously referred to. Shortly after the accession of George I. (1717), he was placed in the commission of the peace, and appointed a commissioner of the lottery.

In the following year he started " The Freethinker," a periodical paper by which he not only gained reputation, but valuable friends, and which led to promotion much greater than he was destined to receive, though probably anticipated, in consideration of his political zeal. Among other coadjutors in this publication were Dr Boulter, the afterwards eminent Archbishop of Armagh, then only the humble minister of a church in the borough, and the Right Hon. Richard West, afterwards Lord Chancellor of Ireland. On Dr Boulter's promotion to the primacy in Ireland, he took Philips with him as his secretary, and procured him a seat in Parliament there. In 1726, he became secretary to the Lord Chancellor, and subsequently (1733) Judge of the Prerogative Court.

In 1748, being then at an advanced age, and wishing for retirement, he purchased an annuity of L.400. Having shortly after visited London, he brought out a new edition of his poetical works, but only survived till the following year, when an attack of paralysis proved fatal in his 78th year.

Little is known personally of Philips, but the inference, from his great intimacy with Addison and Steele, as well as the subsequent friends he made, and their zeal in promoting his interest, is highly in his favour. One of the few particulars that may be gathered respecting him was a certain unusual solemnity of manner. His quarrel with Pope was the cause of his literary character being unduly depreciated, and the soubriquet of *Namby Pamby* was given him by Henry Carey, who burlesqued some of his pieces in short lines so humorously that the credit of them was given to Pope and Swift, who did join in the ridicule, though they did not originate it. The name of Pastoral was given him, not only as is frequently done from a first work, but probably also to distinguish him from John Philips, the author of the famous mock-heroic poem of the "Splendid Shilling," and the rival of Addison in celebrating the victory of Blenheim. Though the general poetry of Philips is not of a very high order, the winter piece from Copenhagen, and some of his translations from the Greek, are of first-rate excellence. The only known contribution of Philips to the *Guardian* is an elegant and ingenious paper (No. 16) on a subject that had not been previously touched upon, that of song-writing, which makes it a matter of regret that he should not have pursued it more fully and in all its branches.

The last whom it will be necessary to notice particularly was another dramatist of greater reputation, NICHOLAS ROWE, (1673–1718,) the son of a sergeant-at-law, and educated at Westminster School, being chosen one of the King's scholars there about his twelfth year. Under the famous Dr Busby he continued his studies until he was sixteen, and besides attaining proficiency in the classical languages, had made considerable progress in Hebrew. He gave early indication of a bent to poetry, and displayed great facility in versification, not merely in English, but in the classical languages. Being destined for the same profession as his father, he was entered as a student of the Middle Temple, and far from proving himself

> "A clerk fore-doomed his father's soul to cross,
> Who pens a stanza when he should engross,"

devoted himself assiduously to the study in its most enlarged and liberal view, and not merely as a collection of dry precedents and statutes. Being called to the bar, from the progress he had made and the connexions he possessed, he might have pursued the profession with every prospect of success, but being left in independent circumstances by the death of his father about the same time, he did not hesitate in his choice of a pursuit. Before his passion for poetry and the *belles lettres* every other ambition vanished, and seemed as nothing in the comparison. In this resolution he was confirmed by the success of his first performance, "The Ambitious Stepmother," a tragedy, written in his twenty-fifth year. Though not free from the faults of first productions, it exceeded in fire and elevation any of his subsequent writings. It was succeeded by a numerous series of tragedies appearing at tolerably regular intervals up to the year 1715—of which the principal were "The Fair Penitent," (1703,) "Jane Shore," (1714,) and "Lady Jane Grey," his last. Some of his dramas still retain possession of the stage, and they are generally interesting and striking in the fable and conduct, and characterised by great elegance and harmony of versification. In 1706 he also made an unsuccessful attempt at comedy, under the title of "The Biter," and at the representation is said to have appeared highly delighted with what he considered the hits in it, whilst the audience looked grave. Indeed, he is said to have laughed everywhere except in his tragedies, though noted for decorum both in his writings and conversation.

In 1709, he edited an edition of Shakespeare, accompanied with a life, which, though not devoid of merit, is not equal in research to some editions which have since appeared. But it contributed to make the great dramatist better known at a time when his merits had ceased to be popularly appreciated, or even known, to a degree now scarcely credible.

When the Duke of Queensberry (father of Gay's patron) was Secretary of State, he appointed Rowe Under-Secretary, an office which he held for three years until the death of his principal. After this, a curious story is told of him by Spence, on the authority of Pope. It is said he went one day to pay his court to the Earl of Oxford, then Lord High Treasurer, who asked him if he understood Spanish. Rowe replied in the negative; but thinking that the minister might intend to employ him on some political mission, he added that in a little time he did not doubt of making himself master of it. Accordingly, after taking his leave, he made his arrangements for retiring to a farm-house, where he might pursue his studies without distraction. After a few months' application, he again waited on the minister, and acquainted him with the result, on which he broke out with the remark, "How happy are you, Mr Rowe, that can enjoy the pleasure of reading and understanding Don Quixote in the original." This anecdote has been told by Johnson in such a way as to require the explanation he adds, that Pope did not believe the minister intended any injustice to Rowe, and attributed it to his odd way. And indeed such a supposition is only fair to Oxford, who was noted for his regard for men of letters; and even if he had not, cannot be conceived, whatever his political faults, capable, as a gentleman, of committing so gross and wanton an insult. Everything depends on the way of telling a story. If Rowe merely went to pay his respects to the minister in the hope of something resulting from it, which is the natural supposition, then Pope's inference was only a reasonable one; but it would cease to be so if, as Dr Johnson says, Rowe had directly asked for an appointment, and such a question had been put to him afterwards.

On the accession of George I., however, Rowe met with considerable favour, being soon after appointed Poet-Laureate, and one of the Land Surveyors of the Customs. The Prince of Wales also gave him the place of Clerk of his Council; and Lord Chancellor Parker, on receiving the seals, unsolicited, made him Secretary of the Presentations. But this accumulation of good fortune he did not long survive to enjoy, his decease occurring at the early age of forty-five, nearly the same as Addison.

His translation of the "Pharsalia" of Lucan, some portions of which had appeared in the Miscellanies, was published posthumously, and is considered by Johnson one of the greatest productions of English poetry.

It is remarkable that, notwithstanding his talents, and the character given of him for amiability, good nature, and freedom from envy or malice, that there appears to have been some coolness between Addison and him. On Addison's appointment as Secretary, some one told him how pleased Rowe had been at his good fortune; to which he is said to have replied that his levity of heart was such that he would have been the same if he had heard that he was hanged.*

Rowe's connexion with the labours of Steele and Addison was very slight. He had joined with Prior and Swift in a letter of raillery to the *Tatler* on some remarks Steele had made on the subject of Scotland being designated North Britain since the Union. The only communication of Rowe to the *Guardian* which makes the subject of it the more surprising, is a witty letter in No. 118, (in reference to the gilt lion's-head letter-box at Button's,) soliciting the establishment of an outriding lion, or a jackal or two, for the benefit of those at a distance.

Among those previously noticed who contributed one or two papers each, were Parnell, Tickell, Hughes, and Budgell; Dr Pearce, the afterwards eminent Bishop of Rochester; the Rev. Laurence Eusden, who afterwards rendered both himself and the office contemptible by succeeding Rowe as Poet-Laureate; the learned Dr William Wotton; the Rev. Deane Bartelett, a fellow-collegian with Steele at Merton; Dr Thomas Birch, Chancellor at Worcester; Henry Martyn, the political economist; Henry Carey of New College, Oxford; Richard Ince of Gray's Inn, conveyancer; were also contributors. A paper has also been attributed to Dr Edward Young of the "Night Thoughts," but is not authenticated.

The first volume of the *Guardian* was inscribed to

* *Addisoniana.*

GENERAL, afterwards EARL, CADOGAN, one of Marlborough's most skilful and able officers, to whom he intrusted the encampment in all his campaigns. He was Plenipotentiary to the Spanish Netherlands in 1706; in 1716, Governor of the Isle of Wight and Ambassador to Holland, and created Earl Cadogan in 1718. On the death of Marlborough, he became Master-General of the Ordnance, which he retained till his decease in 1726. Steele, in complimenting him on his eminent zeal and ability in his profession, says :—
"Your country knows how eminently you excel in the several parts of military skill, whether in assigning the encampment, accommodating the troops, leading to the charge, or pursuing the enemy, the retreat being the only part of the profession which has not fallen within the experience of those who learned their warfare under the Duke of Marlborough."

The second was dedicated to WILLIAM PULTENEY, afterwards Earl of Bath, (1652-1764,) the political opponent of Sir Robert Walpole. He was descended of an ancient family, studied at Christ Church, Oxford, and after some time spent in travel, entered Parliament. He became a strenuous opponent of the Ministry of the latter years of Queen Anne. On the accession of the House of Hanover in 1714, he became Secretary at War, but a difference with Walpole drove him into the ranks of opposition. He then joined with Bolingbroke in an anti-ministerial journal called *The Craftsman*. In 1731, a duel with Lord Hervey, the Vice-Chamberlain, gave such offence to the King, that, with his own hand, he struck his name out of the Privy Council, and ordered his removal from the Commission of the Peace. The animosity of the court only tended to inflame the ardour of his opposition, and to increase his popularity. He contributed materially to driving Walpole from office in 1741, when, with Lord Carteret, he united with the other members of the Ministry; and he was raised to the peerage as Earl of Bath, but his popularity immediately vanished. By the death of his only son the title became extinct.

CHAPTER X.

Correspondence during the publication of the *Guardian*—Steele's quarrel with Swift—His letter to Addison complaining of Steele, in reference to the *Guardian*—Steele's reply—Swift's farewell letter, and partial reconciliation—His confession of Whiggism—Notice of the Dean—Steele resigns his Commissionership, and enters Parliament.

LETTER CCII.   *To Mrs Steele.*
March 28, 1713.

DEAR PRUE,—I will do everything you desire your own way.—Yours ever,   RICH. STEELE.

LETTER CCIII.   *To Mrs Steele.*
April 22, 1713.

DEAR PRUE,—I have met with Doggett,* and we shall fall into a discourse which will turn to account. I shall dine with him at some eating-house. If you will be exactly at five at Button's,† we will go together to the Park,

---

* "Thomas Doggett, an author and actor, who had, not long before the date of this letter, thrown up in disgust his office of joint manager of Drury Lane Theatre, which he had sometime held with Wilks and Cibber. By his frugality, he secured a sufficient competence to retire from the hurry of business whilst in the height of his reputation. In political principles, to use the words of Steele, he was ' a Whig up to the head and ears;' and so strictly was he attached to the interests of the House of Hanover, that he never let slip any occasion that presented itself of demonstrating his sentiments in that respect. The year after George I. came to the throne, Doggett gave a waterman's coat and silver badge, to be rowed for by six watermen on the 1st of August, being the anniversary of the accession, and at his death bequeathed a certain sum of money, the interest of which was to be appropriated annually for ever to the purchase of a like coat and badge to be rowed for in honour of the day. The ceremony continues to be annually performed, the claimants setting out on a signal given at that time of the tide when the current is strongest against them, and rowing from the Old Swan, near London bridge, to the White Swan at Chelsea."

† " A famous coffee-house in Covent Garden, frequented at that time by all the wits."

or elsewhere, and be with you all night, if you condescend to take me out of my truckle-bed.—Yours faithfully, RICH. STEELE.

LETTER CCIV.   To Mrs Steele.
Nine in the morning, May 5, 1713.

DEAR PRUE,—I have sent Will to get a place in the coach for your new maid, and am going out to visit the company I invited to Hampton Court, to know their resolution. Your maid may be always with the children. If the appointment holds, I will send Will also this afternoon with further directions. I value a person you are fond of too much to ride late in the evening; therefore shall set out myself early in the morning to-morrow.— Your obedient husband, RICH. STEELE.

Swift, in a letter to Addison, dated May 13, 1713, complains of Steele's treatment of him in charging him with being the writer of the violent Tory paper, the *Examiner*:—

"I was told yesterday," he says, "by several persons, that Mr Steele had reflected upon me in his *Guardian*, which I could hardly believe until sending for the paper of the day. I found he had, in several parts of it, insinuated with the utmost malice that I was author of the *Examiner*,* and abused me in the grossest manner he could possibly invent, and set his name to what he had written. Now, Sir, if I am not the author of the *Examiner*, how will Mr Steele be able to defend himself from the imputation of the highest degree of baseness, ingratitude, and injustice? Is he so ignorant of my temper and of my style? Has he never heard that the author of the *Examiner* (to whom I am altogether a stranger†) did, a month or two ago, vindicate me from having any concern in it? Should not Mr Steele have first expostulated with me as a friend? Have I deserved this usage from Mr Steele, who knows very well that my Lord

---

* "In the *Guardian*, No. LIII., Mr Steele says,— . . . 'I have carried my point, and it is nothing to me whether the *Examiner* writes in the character of an *estranged friend* or an *exasperated mistress*.' By the first of these appellations, Dr Swift is to be understood; by the latter, Mrs Manley, authoress of the Atlantis, who likewise, in conjunction with Oldisworth, wrote in the *Examiner*, often under the direction, and with the assistance of Swift, but oftener without leading-strings."

† "The reader will please to recollect the received opinion that Dr Swift never wrote any *Examiner* after June 7, 1711. The curious may see an accurate and satisfactory account of the *Examiner*, and of this circumstance particularly, in the new edition of the *Tatler*, with notes, vol. v., No. 210, p. 307, note."

Treasurer* has kept him in his employment upon my entreaty and intercession ?† My Lord Chancellor ‡ and Lord Bolingbroke will be witnesses how I was reproached by my Lord Treasurer, upon the ill returns Mr Steele made to his Lordship's indulgence," &c.

---

* " Robert Harley, Earl of Oxford."

† " I sat till ten in the evening with Addison and Steele. Steele will certainly lose his Gazetteer's place, all the world detesting his engaging in parties."—Swift, *Journal to Stella*, Sept. 10, 1710.

" I was this morning with Mr Lewis, the Under-Secretary to Lord Dartmouth, two hours talking politics, and contriving to keep Steele in his office of stampt paper. He has lost his place of Gazetteer, £300 a year, for writing a *Tatler* some months ago against Mr Harley, who gave it him at first, and raised the salary from £60 to £300. This was devilish ungrateful, and Lewis was telling me the particulars; but I had a hint given me that I might save him in the other employment, and leave was given me to clear matters with Steele. Well, I dined with Sir Matthew Dudley, and in the evening went to sit with Mr Addison, and offer the matter at distance to him as the discreeter person, but found party had so possessed him, that he talked as if he suspected me, and would not fall in with anything I said. So I stopt short in my overture, and we parted very dryly; and I shall say nothing to Steele, and let do as they will; but if things stand as they are, he will certainly lose it unless I save him; and therefore I will not speak to him that I may not report to his disadvantage. Is not this vexatious? and is there so much in the proverb of proffered services? When shall I grow wise? I endeavour to act in the most exact points of honour and conscience, and my nearest friends will not understand it so. What must a man expect from his enemies? This would vex me, but it shall not; and so I bid you good night, &c."—*Ibid.*, Oct. 22.

" Lewis told me a pure thing. I had been hankering with Mr Harley to save Steele his other employment, and have a little mercy on him, and I had been saying the same thing to Lewis, who is Mr Harley's chief favourite. Lewis tells Mr Harley how kindly I should take it if he would be reconciled to Steele, &c. Mr Harley on my account falls in with it, and appoints Steele a time to let him attend him; which Steele accepts with great submission, but never comes nor sends any excuse. Whether it was blundering, sullenness, insolence, or rancour of party, I cannot tell, but I shall trouble myself no more about him. I believe Addison hindered him out of mere spite, being grated to the very soul to think he should ever want my help to save his friend; yet now he is soliciting me to make another of his friends Queen's Secretary at Geneva: it is poor Pastoral Philips."—*Ibid.*, Dec. 16.

" One story," says Nichols, " is good till another is heard. See a very different account of the whole transaction pointed out in a note on the new edition of the *Tatler, ut supra*, vol. vi., No. 228, p. 95 *et seq.*"

‡ Lord Harcourt.

The contents of this letter having been communicated by Addison to Steele, he wrote as follows to Swift in reply:—

LETTER CCV.   *To Dr Swift.*

May 19, 1713.

SIR,—Mr Addison showed me your letter, wherein you mention me. They laugh at you, if they make you believe your interposition has kept me thus long in my office. If you have spoken in my behalf at any time, I am glad I have always treated you with respect, though I believe you an accomplice of the *Examiner*. In the letter you are angry at, you see I have no reason for being so merciful to him, but out of regard to the imputation you lie under. You do not in direct terms say you are not concerned with him, but make it an argument of your innocence, that the *Examiner* has declared you have nothing to do with him. I believe I could prevail on the *Guardian* to say there was a mistake in putting my name in his paper; but the English would laugh at us, should we argue in so Irish a manner. I am heartily glad of your being made Dean of St Patrick's.—I am, sir, your most obedient, humble servant,

RICHARD STEELE.

LETTER CCVI.   *From Dr Swift.*

SIR,—   .   .   .   .   .   .   *

I may probably know better, when they are disposed. .   .   .
The case was this:—I did, with the utmost application, and desiring to lay all my credit upon it, desire Mr Harley (as he then was called) to show you mercy. He said " he would, and wholly upon my account, that he would appoint you a day to see him; that he would not expect you should quit any friend or principle." Some days after, he told me, "he had appointed you a day, and you had not kept it;" upon which he reproached me as engaging for more than I could answer, and advised me to more caution another time. I told him, and desired my Lord Chancellor and Lord Bolingbroke to be witnesses, that I would never speak for or against you

---

* " It has unluckily happened that two or three lines have been torn by accident from the beginning of this letter; and, by the same accident, two or three lines are missing towards the latter part, which were written on the back part of the paper which was torn off. But what remains of this letter will, I presume, be very satisfactory to the intelligent reader upon many accounts."—So says Deane Swift, Esq., the biographer of his eminent relative.

as long as I lived; only I would, and that it was still my opinion, you should have mercy till you gave further provocations. This is the history of what you think fit to call, in the spirit of insulting, " their laughing at me ;" and you may do it securely, for, by the most inhuman dealings, you have wholly put it out of my power, as a Christian, to do you the least ill office. Next, I desire to know, whether the greatest services ever done by one man to another may not have the same turn as properly applied to them ? And, once more, suppose they did laugh at me, I ask whether my inclinations to serve you merit to be rewarded by the vilest treatment, whether they succeeded or no ? If your interpretation were true, I was laughed at only for your sake, which, I think, is going pretty far to serve a friend. As to the letter I complain of, I appeal to your most partial friends, whether you ought not either to have asked or written to me, or desired to have been informed by a third hand, whether I were any way concerned in writing the *Examiner ?* And, if I had shuffled, or answered indirectly, or affirmed, or said, I would not give you satisfaction, you might then have wreaked your revenge with some colour of justice. I have several times assured Mr Addison, and fifty others, " that I had not the least hand in writing any of those papers, and that I had never exchanged one syllable with the supposed author* in my life that I can remember, nor even seen him above twice, and that in mixed company, in a place where he came to pay his attendance." One thing more I must observe to you, that, a year or two ago, when some printers used to bring me their papers in manuscript, I absolutely forbid them to give any hints against Mr Addison and you, and some others, and have frequently struck out reflections upon you in particular; and should (I believe) have done it still, if I had not wholly left off troubling myself about those kind of things.

I protest I never saw anything more liable to exception than every part is of the letter you were pleased to write me. You plead "that I do not, in mine to Mr Addison, in direct terms say I am not concerned with the *Examiner.*" And is that an excuse for the most savage injuries in the world a week before ? How far you can prevail with the *Guardian,* I shall not trouble myself to inquire; and am more concerned how you will clear your own honour and conscience than my reputation. I shall hardly lose one friend by what you† . . . I know not any . . . laugh at me for any . . . absurdity of yours. There are solecisms in morals as well as in languages ; and to which of the virtues you will re-

---

* " It is clear that Swift all along alludes to Oldisworth as the author of the *Examiner.* Steele, on the contrary, sets out on the supposition that those papers were still the production of Swift and Mrs Manley."

† Manuscript here torn again as previously noticed.

concile your conduct to me, is past my imagination. Be pleased to put these questions: "If Dr Swift be entirely innocent of what I accuse him, how shall I be able to make him satisfaction? and how do I know but he may be entirely innocent? If he was laughed at only because he solicited for me, is that sufficient reason for me to say the vilest things of him in print, under my hand, without any provocation? and how do I know but he may be in the right, when he says I was kept in my employment at his interposition? If he never once reflected on me the least in any paper, and hath hindered many others from doing it, how can I justify myself for endeavouring in mine to ruin his credit as a Christian and a clergyman?"—I am, sir, your most obedient humble servant,

JON. SWIFT.

LETTER CCVII.   *To Dr Swift.*

Bloomsbury Square, May 26, 1713.

SIR,—I have received yours, and find it is impossible for a man to judge in his own case. For an allusion to you, as one under the imputation of helping the *Examiner*,* and owning I was restrained out of respect to you, you tell Addison, under your hand, "you think me the vilest of mankind," and bid him tell me so. I am obliged to you for any kind things said in my behalf to the treasurer; and I assure you, when you were in Ireland, you were the constant subject of my talk to men in power at that time. As to the vilest of mankind, it would be a glorious world if I were: for I would not conceal my thoughts in favour of an injured man, though all the powers on earth gainsaid it, to be made the first man in the nation. This position, I know, will ever obstruct my way in the world; and I have conquered my desires accordingly. I have resolved to content myself with what I can get by my own industry, and the improvement of a small estate, without being anxious whether I am ever in a court again or not. I do assure you, I do not speak thus calmly, after the ill usage in your letter to Addison, out of terror of your wit or my Lord Treasurer's power, but pure kindness to the agreeable qualities I once so

---

* "When the curious reader has considered what is forcibly alleged in the notes on the new edition of the *Tatler ut supra,* he will probably be convinced of three things: 1. That Steele's *estranged friend* was really an accomplice of the *Examiner,* and an actual writer in that paper long after the time commonly supposed; 2. That Steele was not guilty of that ingratitude to Mr Harley of which he was accused; and 3. That the disagreement between two such men as Swift and Steele is a melancholy proof of the lengths to which party madness will carry even the best of men."

passionately delighted in in you. You know, I know nobody but one that talked after you, could tell " Addison had bridled me in point of party." This was ill-hinted, both with relation to him, and, sir, your most obedient humble servant, RICH. STEELE.

I know no party ; but the truth of the question is what I will support as well as I can, when any man I honour is attacked.

LETTER CCVIII. *From Dr Swift.*

May 27, 1713.

SIR,—The reason I give you the trouble of this reply to your letter is, because I am going in a very few days to Ireland : and, although I intended to return towards winter, yet it may happen, from the common accidents of life, that I may never see you again.

In your yesterday's letter, you are pleased to take the complaining side, and think it hard I should write to Mr Addison as I did, only for an allusion. This allusion was only calling a clergyman of some little distinction an infidel ; a clergyman who was your friend, who always loved you, who had endeavoured at least to serve you, and who, whenever he did write anything, made it sacred to himself never to fling out the least hint against you.

One thing you are pleased to fix on me, as what you are sure of ; that the *Examiner* had talked after me, when he said, " Mr Addison had bridled you in point of party." I do not read one in six of those papers, nor ever knew he had such a passage ; and I am so ignorant of this, that I cannot tell what it means : whether, that Mr Addison kept you close to a party, or that he hindered you from writing about party. I never talked or writ to that author in my life ; so that he could not have learned it from me. And, in short, I solemnly affirm that, with relation to every friend I have, I am as innocent as it is possible for a human creature to be. And, whether you believe me or not, I think, with submission, you ought to act as if you believed me till you have demonstration to the contrary. I have all the ministry to be my witnesses, that there is hardly a man of wit of the adverse party whom I have not been so bold as to recommend often and with earnestness to them ; for, I think, principles at present are quite out of the question, and that we dispute wholly about persons.* In these last you and I differ ; but in the other I think we agree : for I have in print professed myself in politics to be what we formerly called a Whig.

---

* "Steele says, ' I thought it was the shortest way to impartiality to put myself beyond farther hopes or fears, by declaring myself at a time when the dispute is not about *persons* and parties, but things and causes.' "—*Tatler*, No. 193.

As to the great man * whose defence you undertake, though I do not think so well of him as you do, yet I have been the cause of preventing five hundred hard things being said of him.

I am sensible I have talked too much when myself is the subject: therefore I conclude with sincere wishes for your health and prosperity, and am, sir, yours, &c., JON. SWIFT.

P.S.—You cannot but remember that in the only thing I ever published with my name, I took care to celebrate you as much as I could, and in as handsome a manner as I could,† though it was in a letter to the present Lord Treasurer. J. S.

Painful as it is to find two such men as Steele and Swift discarding the amenities of letters and of friendship, and indulging in party bickerings which ought to be left to inferior spirits, it is pleasant at least to find in both, after abusing each other in good set terms, a more generous flow of feeling and a return to something almost of tenderness. It can hardly be denied that, after the first burst of asperity of temper, there is something almost touching in the calm remonstrance of Swift and his self-vindication, which gains our sympathy, and that it is difficult to acquit Steele of characteristic warmth and hastiness, and of being for once wanting in his characteristic good nature. To appearance, at least, Swift certainly comes out the clearer of the two. All that can be said as regards Steele (if he was mistaken) is that it was a misconception acted on in a moment of irritation. What private information he may

* " The Duke of Marlborough."

† " In his 'Proposal for Correcting the English Tongue,' Swift says, 'I would willingly avoid repetition, having about a year ago communicated to the public much of what I had to offer upon this subject, by the hands of an ingenious gentleman, who for a long time did thrice a week divert or instruct the kingdom by his papers; and is supposed to pursue the same design at present under the title of *Spectator*. This author, who hath tried the force and compass of our language with so much success, agrees entirely with me in most of my sentiments relating to it; so do the greatest part of the men of wit and learning whom I have had the happiness to converse with.' "

have had that may have led him to believe his friend to have been acting with duplicity, we cannot now tell. At all events, he was naturally greatly irritated at the scurrilous abuse of the *Examiner*, and may not unreasonably have thought that even supposing Swift did not write personally, that with his interest with the party and the paper, others would not have attacked him if he had not given it his countenance; and we see he still calmly expresses the opinion that he was an accomplice. There are also two or three other suspicious circumstances. The cautious wording of his reply is rather remarkable, and though the not denying a charge point blank in the first instance, especially in a man of so proud a nature as Swift, is not necessarily to be construed into an argument of guilt, yet if it be strengthened by other circumstances of a suspicious tendency, some importance may reasonably be attached to it. Swift's last acknowledged contribution to the *Examiner* was No. 45 of the original edition, dated June 7, 1711, but we now know that in his communications to Mrs Johnson (Stella) he acknowledges having written the first part of No. 46, and his continuing to dictate and to give hints occasionally,* yet in his letters to Addison and Steele on this occasion he affects to be wholly unconnected with it. Then he makes confession here of never having ceased to be a Whig, and singularly enough seems to calculate upon Steele's sympathy on that ground, while he was notoriously allying himself with the opposite party, and among the most violent and energetic of its leaders.

* " I have got an underspur-leather to write an *Examiner* again; *and the Secretary and I will now and then send hints;* but we would have it a little upon the Grub Street, to be a match for their writers."—*Journal to Stella*, Dec. 5, 1711.

In fact, everything with him, including literature, was obviously and, with regard to the latter, confessedly merely an instrument of self-aggrandisement; and though the world professes to make some convenient distinction between party morality and personal honour, yet it is difficult to say where the distinction is to end or to what it may lead—nor is it easy to avoid feeling the ground uncertain in dealing with those who deliberately make choice of that equivocal position. Taking these circumstances into consideration, it is difficult to feel much sympathy in the first vehement fury of Swift, which the subsequent terrible calmness in one of such an intensely irritable temperament, in the latter part of his remonstrance, might lead us to accord. Nor can we, without indignation, remember the intense malignity with which he subsequently pursued Steele,* though professing on this occasion to part with a feeling, or an appearance of partial reconciliation and good will.

As Swift is now about to disappear from the scene, some notice of him, which was deferred for the sake of convenience at the time he was connected with Steele as one of his earliest coadjutors in the *Tatler*, may not here be out of place. But a life involving so many topics of discussion, can only be comparatively slightly touched upon. It is a story which has been often told, with variations according to the sympathies of the narrator, and theories more or less absurd, attempting to solve the mysterious

---

* "If," says Mr Thackeray, "undeterred by his great reputation, you had met him like a man, he would have gone home, and, years after, written a foul epigram about you, watched for you in a sewer, and come out to assail you with a coward's blow and a dirty bludgeon."—*Humourists*, Lect. 1.

problems involved in it by other mysteries, some extravagant, others not fit to be repeated, and all save one inadequate. Some have resorted to the extreme hypothesis, as the only key to the whole, of his comparative insanity all through life ; whilst others, including eminent medical authorities,* have denied that he ever was insane in the popular and or- dinary sense of the term. JONATHAN SWIFT (1667-1745) was the posthumous son of an attorney in Dublin, who held the office of Steward of the Inns of Court.† His family was con- nected with that of Dryden, his father being second cousin to the poet. To the kindness of his uncle, Godwin Swift, a barrister, he was indebted for his education. His early experience of dependence was keenly felt, and probably first tended to embitter his spirit, being aggravated by supposing his relative in better circumstances than he was. After a preparatory education at the famous Grammar School of Kilkenny, in his fourteenth or fifteenth year he entered the University of Dublin. To whatever cause it may be attributed, he is numbered among those of whom Goldsmith, Sheridan, and Scott are remarkable examples,

* " The Closing Years of Swift's Life," by Dr Wilde of Dublin, in which an interesting volume was founded on the original design of a merely medical in- quiry, suggested by another eminent medical man, into the nature of Swift's disease, at a time (1835) when his remains being exhumed owing to repairs in the cathedral of St Patrick's, gave additional interest to the subject.

† His family were of Yorkshire and clerical; and Spence reports Pope (pro- bably by mistake) as making him by his own statement born at his mother's native place, Leicester, and being the son of a clergyman. Writing to Pope in reference to his published letters, he expresses himself, and others who highly valued him, as grieved that he should make no distinction in speaking of Ireland, between the people inhabiting what was formerly called the Pale, and the native or Celtic population. Of the former, he expresses the opinion that they " are much more civilised than many counties in England, and speak better English, and are much better bred." Pope, however, professed to trace his own family to Ireland.

whose imputed dulness in youth has been succeeded by the most shining abilities in after life. He took his bachelor's degree, but only *speciali gratia*. This mortification had the effect of making him study eight hours a day for the next seven years. In the Revolution year he lost his uncle, when about one and twenty, and went to pay a visit to his mother, who, in the interim, had removed to her native place of Leicester. By her advice, he went to pay his respects to Sir William Temple, to whose lady she was distantly related, and whose father, Sir John Temple, when Master of the Rolls in Ireland, had been the friend of Godwin Swift. The retired diplomatist, who was then living at Sheen or Richmond, and soon after removed to Moor Park, in Surrey, received him kindly, took him under his protection, and defrayed his expenses for two years at Oxford, in order to take his master's degree. Afterwards he went to reside with Sir William as companion and secretary. This accomplished man, in addition to his reputation as a statesman, was one of the first models of English prose, which he wrote with a consummate ease and negligent elegance, previously unexampled, of which it is enough to say that it appears to have been studied with as much care by Addison, as the verse of Dryden by Pope. Swift's position gave him many advantages, in the conversation and experience of Sir William, and his access to the library at Moor Park. He had also an opportunity of coming under the notice of the illustrious William, who had known Temple in his diplomatic capacity in Holland, and when he was suffering from gout would sometimes visit Moor Park to consult him. Swift was present at their conversations, and used to tell how the King had taught him, perhaps as Sir William was showing him his garden, and being wheeled round in his chair, the way of cutting asparagus in the Dutch mode. He also offered him the command of a troop of horse, which Swift declined on the ground of his inclination being towards the Church. Notwithstanding all these advantages, however, Swift became dissatisfied. Sir William was naturally kind and amiable, but with a courtly and stately fastidiousness, and being advanced in life and suffering from the gout, this second scene of dependence could not have been without its trials to one of his temper. He blamed Temple with neglecting his interests in order to retain his services. He remonstrated, and at length (1694) left in resentment and returned to Dublin. Sir William offered him a small appointment in the Rolls Court there, worth L.100 a year, on which he said, a scruple he had of entering the Church for a support being removed, as he had now an opportunity of living without it, he designed to take orders. This looks very like an early specimen of his irony and a reflection on such a handsome provision. Having carried out his intention, in the following year he received, through the interest of Sir William with Lord Deputy Capel, the prebend of Kilroot, in the north of Ireland, worth L.100 a year.

A little experience probably wearied him of this solitude, and led him to regret the advantages he had relinquished. An urgent entreaty of Sir William for his return, with the prospect of future preferment in England, was gladly complied with, and he resigned his prebend in favour of a poor curate acquaintance. He was cordially welcomed on his return to Moor Park, and he lived in the utmost harmony with Sir William till his death in 1699, when he left him L.100 and the care of his works. In fulfilment of this trust, Swift soon after published Temple's writings with a dedication to the King. He had not unreasonably indulged hopes of promotion through Temple's interest with the King, and the latter is even said to have given him encouragement. William's notions, however, were all military, and, whether owing to displeasure at the rejection of his first offer, or from oversight, Swift failed to realise his expectations. He had previously tried the powers of poetical flattery in vain, having written bad Pindaric odes both to the King and Sir William. Dryden, on seeing these, had incurred his everlasting enmity by saying, "Cousin Jonathan, you will never be a poet." After ineffectual dallying about the court for some little time, another patron turned up. The Earl of Berkeley made him the offer to accompany him to Ireland, on becoming one of the Lords Justices there, in the joint capacity of secretary and chaplain. Again he was fated to receive but indifferent treatment, an interested party having persuaded Lord Berkeley that the former appointment was unsuited for a clergyman, or he making the plea to get rid of his engagement. Some other equivalent, however, was probably promised. The rich deanery of Derry, then vacant, was in the gift of his patron, and Swift appears to have had some prospect of it, but fortune jilted him once more. In addition to many other reasons, the Bishop of Derry, whilst acknowledging his talents, requested that it might be given to an older and graver person. So he was obliged to put up with the smaller livings of Agher and the vicarages of Laracor and Rathbeggin, near Dublin, the united incomes of which did not much exceed a third of the value of the deanery.* Of these he took possession before the close of 1700, and in a manner highly characteristic. Entering the curate's house at Laracor, he introduced himself as "his master." This humour of going rough-shod through the world was possibly adopted as an indemnification of the bitter sense of his early dependence, and to sound the dispositions of those with whom he came in contact. If they took it well he usually made it up to them in after kindness. His discharge of his clerical duties was exemplary, and he even undertook a voluntary addition to them, by having prayers twice on week days, though he could not restrain his humour, however ill-timed or indecorous.†

Previous to this Swift appears to have seriously contemplated matrimony. He had made the acquaintance of a sister of one of his college companions, named Waryng, a lady of some considerable fortune, with whom he exchanged vows. In 1696, probably holding, not unreasonably, that the connubial state was designed for adversity, and tended to facilitate better fortune which it commonly comes only to share, he appears to have met the reasons of the lady against delay with an ardour of passion and asseveration almost astounding considering his subsequent conduct towards the sex. Though with so little of romance

* Johnson says half. Lord Jeffrey, in his essay on Swift, calls it L.400 a year, which he estimates, considering the difference in the value of money, as equal to L.1200 at the present time.

† His congregation, probably small at most, and possibly distant, do not seem immediately to have appreciated the week-day innovation, and on the first occasion there was no one but himself and the clerk. Swift, with the utmost gravity, commenced, "Dearly-beloved Roger, the Scripture moveth you and me in sundry places," and so proceeded to the end.

about him, he had a fancy for romantic names, and he called this fair one *Varina*, to whom he writes: "Surely, Varina, you have but a very mean opinion of the joys that accompany a true, honourable, unlimited love; yet either nature and our ancestors have highly deceived us, or else all other sublunary things are dross in comparison." Varina, however, persisted in being in no hurry to wed, but the engagement was not broken off. Now, however, when in a position to marry according to the received opinions of the world, he writes her in a tone cold, dry, and hard, depreciating the value of his livings, giving a dismal picture of the locality, reminding her of former impediments she had interposed, with oblique innuendoes reflecting on her fortune and person, a catalogue of exactions to his humours, and other particulars, little short of insulting. The letter was taken, as it was no doubt intended, as a termination of the correspondence. The secret may perhaps be found in an accession he had made to his society shortly after his settlement at Laracor. It was no doubt at his suggestion that the charming Esther Johnson, better known by the name of Stella, under which he has celebrated her, went at this time, along with Mrs Dingley, a distant relative of the Temple family, to reside in Dublin. The ostensible reason was the cheapness of living and the higher interest to be obtained for money. Stella was then in her eighteenth year, her companion about fifteen years her senior. The younger lady had been a resident at the same time as Swift in the household of Sir William Temple, to whom her mother was housekeeper. Mrs Johnson, the elder, was the widow, according to her own account, of a decayed merchant, afterwards master of a vessel trading to Holland. She had several children, of whom the youngest was this interesting, elegant, and intellectual girl.* Swift had undertaken her education, and a strong mutual regard between pupil and master ensued. From the time of her residence in Ireland she and her companion would reside at the vicarage in his absence, but he was at least exemplary in his strict attention to avoiding any ground of scandal by never allowing himself to be in her company without the presence of a third person. But to one who had meant to realise the hopes which any woman would naturally entertain who had left her country and friends for the society of one man, and at his suggestion, such

* Rumour, ever busy, has represented her as the daughter of Temple. Dr Wilde has revived it in an article in the *Gentleman's Magazine* for 1757, which he admits that Sheridan and others of Swift's biographers have slighted, and which appeared some time after the publication of Lord Orrery's work on Swift. The writer of the communication, after referring to Mrs Johnson as a handsome and highly intellectual woman, and alluding to the other members of her family, says of Esther, that she "only of all her children was permitted to reside with her at Moor Park, where she was educated. . . . But had dress shown no distinction between her and the rest of her mother's children, nature had already distinguished her sufficiently. Her mother and brother were both fair, her sister is said to have been the same. The boy, . . . said to be like his father . . . was fair to an uncommon degree; yet Esther's eyes and hair were of a most beautiful black. . . . And could the striking likeness have been overlooked, Sir William's uncommon regard for her, and his attention to her education, must have convinced every unprejudiced person," &c. See "Closing Years of Swift's Life," pp. 108-110. Whatever the truth of the matter may be, it is certainly remarkable, if such were the case, that mother and daughter should reside in his house and his wife living, unless indeed they only arrived during Swift's second residence there. With regard to Sir William's care of her education, as referred to, it is known that though she would have done credit to the best education, yet, notwithstanding her mental accomplishments, her early education had been so greatly neglected that the few years after she was in her teens that she had the benefit of Swift's instruction could not make up for it, and left her still greatly deficient in very elementary matters, as may be seen by references in Swift's Journal to her.

exact precautions would have been unnecessary, and for their fulfilment a miserable substitute. There will be occasion to refer to the subject again.

Swift had adopted the political principles of his early patron, Temple, and, shortly after his settlement at Laracor, drew his pen in support of the last Whig Ministry of King William, against the violent and factious proceedings of the Commons. This first essay as a political pamphleteer was published in 1701, under the title of " A Discourse on the Contests between the Nobles and Commons in Athens and Rome." At the ripe age of thirty-four did he for the first time endeavour to attract the attention of those in authority by showing his power to serve them, and thus draw himself out of the obscurity of the life of a country parson. The monotony of his seclusion at Laracor was broken by occasionally leaving his willows and his canal for the society of the wits in the great metropolis, among whom he asserted for himself a foremost place by the publication, though anonymously, in 1704, of his famous "Tale of a Tub," designed to satirise the disputes between the various theological parties. This remarkable work he is said to have written or planned in his nineteenth year, previous to his leaving Dublin, and to have forborne to publish during that long interval. It displayed unrivalled powers of satirical humour. Its literary merit is quite peculiar among his writings, nor did he ever equal it in fluency and vivacity of style. But though it gained him the highest reputation as a wit, it had the practical effect of barring his promotion in the Church, though it eulogised it in its own fashion. The levity of some portions even raised suspicions of infidelity, an imputation which, though generally acquitted of it by posterity, appears to be impliedly revived against him by Mr Thackeray. During these visits he frequented the St James's Coffeehouse, which was the great resort of the Whig wits. Congreve he had previously met at the table of Sir William Temple, and probably through his means added Addison, Steele, and Pope to his acquaintance. Addison, who had recently returned from his travels, which he had published, in the following year presented him with a copy of his book, and a complimentary inscription as "the greatest genius of his age."

It was four years later before he again attracted public notice by his pen, when he compensated for his silence by the variety of his publications, theological and literary. The former included his "Sentiments of a Church-of-England Man," and an ironical "Argument against Abolishing Christianity;" the latter, "Predictions for the Year 1708," in ridicule of Partridge the almanac-maker and astrological impostor. This subject being followed up by himself and others of the wits who joined in the joke, the town was kept in convulsions of laughter, and, to add to it, Partridge had the absurdity to attempt a reply. By this means the pseudonym of Isaac Bickerstaff, which he employed on that occasion, became so popular, that when Steele started the *Tatler* in the following year he adopted it and carried on the astrological jest. To that paper Swift was one of the earliest contributors. In the same year he also published "A Project for the Advancement of Religion," addressed to Lady Berkeley.

Shortly after his return to Ireland at that time, an explosion of High-Church fanaticism occurred, which had been sedulously fostered as a convenient cover for party purposes; and the foolish sermon of a foolish parson, Sacheverell, and the scarcely less foolish importance into which it was elevated by the notice of the Government, proved the straw thrown up which showed how the wind blew. The political elements were all in confusion, and Swift having got himself appointed to a commission for obtaining the remission of the first fruits and certain other dues payable by the Irish clergy to the Crown, hastened, with so good a pretext, to the scene of action, to see if anything was to be picked up out of the wreck. His politics had previously been exposed to some severe trials. In the previous year (1709) he had applied to Lord Halifax for his interest in the reversion of Dr South's prebend at Westminster : " Pray, my lord," said he, " desire Dr South to die about the fall of the leaf." Finding that Dr South was obdurate enough to live on, towards the close of the same year he put in his claim for the anticipated vacancy in the see of Cork, but it was given to the Provost of Trinity College. Swift then became a dissatisfied Whig. The hand in the barometer of his politics began to oscillate towards "change." He arrived in London in the beginning of September 1710, and immediately waited upon Lord Godolphin, " who," he says, "received me with a great deal of coldness, which has enraged me so, I am almost vowing revenge."* What that was we see by an entry a few weeks later: " I have almost finished my lampoon, and will print it for revenge on a certain great person." And, again, October 4 : "I gave my lampoon to be printed. I have more mischief in my heart ; and I think I shall go

* " Journal to Stella," Sept. 9, 1710.

round with them all as this hits, and I can find hints." On the same day he was presented to Harley the new Minister, (the whole of the Whigs having resigned on the 20th of the previous month,) "who," he says, "received me with the greatest respect and kindness imaginable." In an entry a few days previously, he says, "I am already represented to Harley as a discontented person, that was ill-used for not being Whig enough, and I hope for good usuage from him." His being so well aware of it looks very like having had a hand in it. These passages require no comment. They sufficiently indicate the ready convert, and the kind of work he was prepared to begin with to prove his zeal. It has been supposed that when he paid his visit to Lord Godolphin he made him an offer of his pen. This was probably before he thought the prospects of the party desperate, for on the total retirement of the Ministers on declining to coalesce with the newly-appointed ones, he says, "I am almost shocked at it, though I did not care if they were all hanged." If this was so, it was probably the rejection of his offer that made him, after "talking treason for an hour and a half against the Whigs," return home, "rolling resentment in his mind, and framing schemes of revenge." As to mere coldness, Godolphin was characteristically a cold-mannered man, and the treatment he had received was not likely to improve him in that respect.

The flattering attentions of the new Minister had the effect desired by both parties. He dined frequently with Harley, but regularly on Saturdays, when only a select party of the Ministry, including Mr Secretary St John, Lord Keeper Harcourt, and Lord Rivers, another Whig convert, were admitted at first, but afterwards enlarged to sixteen. This was almost equivalent to admitting him as an un-official member of the Cabinet. Such treatment must have inspired him with hope as well as gratified his revenge. The change once made without much coyness on his part, he threw himself into the struggle with all the fierce energy of his nature. He was not squeamish in his work. He libelled his former friends "all round," as he had proposed. He wrote up the administration in pamphlets, squibs, and street ballads. The *Examiner* paper, which was started in the beginning of August 1710, and to which Prior, who had also recently gone over to the party, St John, Atterbury, Dr Friend, and others contributed, was in want of such a vigorous and steady hand, and he took it up and conducted it for eight months. His recognised contributions were thirty-three in number, commencing with No. 14 of the original edition, which, however, has been made but No. 13 in the after editions, the original No. 13 having been omitted in the republication, being a defence of passive obedience. The reason he assigned for giving it up was, that his style had become known, and that he had made enemies in an inverse proportion to friends by it. To restrain the impetuosity of the more violent of the party, and to prepare the public mind for a peace with which the permanence and interests of the Ministry were considered to be identified, were two of the great tasks which had to be accomplished, and Swift undertook them both,—the first in a "Letter to the October Club," in 1711, though probably in his private opinion not differing much from them; and the other at the close of the same year, in his pamphlet on "The Conduct of the Allies." The latter was an immense success, having gone through several editions, amounting to 11,000 copies in two months. Appearing just before the meeting of Parliament, it formed a text book for the speeches of ministerial members, and turned the tide of popular opinion against the war. This, in the next year, he followed up with "Reflections on the Barrier Treaty."

But in the midst of all this work and excitement he had been able to give his attention to a purely literary matter, and addressed a letter to Lord Oxford with a "Proposal for Correcting, Improving, and Ascertaining the English Tongue," which was exceptional among Swift's writings in several points. It was the only one to which he put his name, and it was one of the least accurate of his productions. He proposed the institution of an academy with this view, similar to that of Paris. Remarks have been made as to the inadequacy of Swift's philological attainments which are very little to the purpose, for if he had contemplated the task himself he would not have proposed an academy. But, whatever the merits of the project, the Ministry had more urgent work on hand, and it was permitted to drop.

Whether Swift was compromised, and to what extent, in the intrigues of the Cabinet, or of some of its members, has been questioned. But there is a very remarkable passage in his journal at the time of the crisis which led to the creation of the twelve new peers, which appears hardly compatible with conscious innocence. The ground seemed to be giving way under them, and Swift was seized with a panic. We do not remember to have seen the passage referred to: "I was this morning with Mr Secretary; we are both of opinion that the Queen is false. I have desired him to engage Lord Treasurer that, as soon as the change is resolved on, he will send me abroad somewhere or other, where I may remain until the new Ministry recall me; and then I will be sick for five or six months till the storm have spent itself. I hope he will grant me this, for I should hardly trust myself to the mercy of my enemies while their anger is fresh."* Certainly he was conscious of having rendered himself so obnoxious to the personal resentment of his opponents that it may admit of some explanation on that ground alone.

Another subject that has been variously alluded to was the tone of something more than equality, of bravado, which he assumed with the Ministers, which may perhaps have been aggravated by their tardiness in doing him any substantial service. As to resentment at the offer of a L.50 note, it was what a much less man than Swift might naturally feel at such a reward of his services (even considering it as only an instalment) by one who had the whole patronage of the Government in his hands, and was estimating him as an ordinary hireling. At his levee, when Lord Oxford asked him to introduce Dr Parnell, he said, to a man like Parnell, the first advances should come from him, and he very good naturedly went about from room to room, with his treasurer's staff in his hand, inquiring for Dr Parnell. Swift justified this on the ground that a man of genius was a greater character than a Minister. This may be perfectly true, but the more genuine the pretension, the less need of parading it, or

* "Journal to Stella," Dec. 9, 1711.

failing in respect for others or in an observance of time and place. If respect is not to be paid to office, on the same grounds the Crown itself might come into contempt. "If we let these great Ministers pretend to too much," he says, "there will be no governing them." And, again, "I use the Ministry like dogs, because I expect they will use me so. I never knew a Ministry do anything for those whom they made the companions of their pleasures ; but I care not." Was this so? We shall see. Meantime it gave him greater warrant for his cavalier treatment of the Ministers. On one occasion he made the Lord Treasurer the bearer of a message to the First Secretary that he would not dine with him if he dined late. But the stories may sound very odd with the mere facts, which in the occurrence were very different. Swift at the time was suffering with headache.

At length, in 1712, he was tantalised with the vision of a mitre, which there can be little doubt he had always had in his eye as the goal of his ambition. A vacancy occurred in the see of Hereford, which he applied for, and it has been thought the Ministers were not disinclined to reward his services on the occasion, but that their intentions were frustrated by Sharpe, Archbishop of York, and the Duchess of Somerset. The former, whom he represents as the tool of others' malice, produced against him the "Tale of a Tub," as objectionable on the ground of its levity, if not rendering his principles doubtful. To the resentment of the latter he had exposed himself by having lampooned her. The archbishop, according to his statement, appears to have made some subsequent amends, but in the meantime he stopped his advancement. In the following year, when the health of the Queen made the duration of the Cabinet extremely uncertain, he not unnaturally resented decidedly the lukewarmness of friends for whom he had made such sacrifices and performed such services, and turned restive. He states in the journal that having seen the warrants for three deaneries without his name being included, he went to the Lord Treasurer and told him, "he could not with any reputation stay longer unless something honourable were given him." He showed such determination to carry out his resolution, saying he would not see them again if something were not done, that the warrants were stopped, and he received the deanery of St Patrick's, Dublin, to which his name has given a world-wide celebrity. Such a tardy and almost compulsory acknowledgment of a debt is certainly a reflection on the liberality and gratitude of the Ministers. After going to take possession, in a few weeks he was obliged to return to attempt a reconciliation between Oxford and Bolingbroke, whose dissensions had now reached an extreme point, and threatened the dissolution of the Ministry. This year he is supposed to have begun his "History of the Last Four Years of Queen Anne," which Bolingbroke characterised as "a seasonable pamphlet for the Administration, but a dishonour to just history." It was only published posthumously, and not with any credit to his reputation.

Early in the following year (1714) appeared his pamphlet entitled "The Public Spirit of the Whigs," in reply to Steele's "Crisis," which, among other effects, by its rough handling, sent the Scottish peers in a body to the Queen, praying that a proclamation might be issued against their libeller. L.300 was in consequence offered for the discovery of the author, but, by some diversion in his favour, he was enabled to evade it. Finding his task of mediation hopeless, he retired at midsummer to a cottage in Berkshire, where he took lodgings. In this retreat he produced his "Free Thoughts on the Present State of Affairs," in which he alludes to the causes of the divisions in the Cabinet, and recommends the adoption of such rigorous measures against Dissenters, Whigs, and Low Churchmen, as should for ever disqualify them from holding any office of authority whatever in all time to come, and such an extension of the prerogative as would have made the sovereign virtually absolute. Even Bolingbroke thought it too strong; and his most distinguished biographer, Scott, though connected with the same party, considered it as "counsel most likely, if followed, to have led to a civil war." He himself admits it could only have been compassed by remodelling the army. Of course it was very natural that he should never want to see the Whigs in power again, for he had gone too far to retrace his steps in their direction. But it shows how desperate must have been the crisis to require such remedies—as desperate indeed as the case of the poor dying Queen with whose life the fate of the Ministry was identified. In another month she was no more—her two rival Ministers having ended their quarrel, in the meantime, by Bolingbroke, with the aid of Lady Masham, succeeding in ejecting his chief with ignominy, only to be involved in a common proscription.

Swift then retired in sullen despair to the duties of his cathedral, and had so exasperated the now triumphant

Whigs that he probably owed his impunity to his cloth. He appears, however, to have been very unpopular on his first arrival, and to have been exposed even to insult in the streets as a Jacobite. He was exemplary in the discharge of his duties; and not only succeeded in overcoming the opposition he at first received, but introduced some salutary reforms in the regulation of his chapter. Gradually, he made his way to social favour by his receptions once or twice a week, and ultimately found himself surrounded by the learned and fashionable of either sex.

During his four years' residence in London, he maintained the practice of keeping a regular diary or journal, which being made up of personal particulars and allusions to public events and characters, is very interesting. This interest is enhanced from the character of the person, Stella, to whom it was regularly transmitted in Ireland.[*] It affords traces of two circumstances which affected his after life. One of these was the return of attacks of vertigo, and deafness on one side, from which he had suffered at Moor Park, and attributed, the first to a surfeit of golden pippins, and the other to imprudent exposure in a garden seat. The other circumstance was the acquaintance he then formed with the family of Mrs Vanhomrigh, the widow of a Dutch merchant, who had accompanied King William, and had held a lucrative appointment during the campaign in Ireland as Quartermaster of Stores. The family then resided in London, where they visited well,

---

[*] She had been so long resident there, and had acquired such a partiality for the people and the country, that she displayed her humour by retorting Swift's direction of his letters to her of "Dublin, Ireland," by directing hers "London, England."

and Swift soon became very intimate in the house. The elder of two daughters, Esther, was lively, susceptible, and fond of reading; and Swift undertook to direct her studies. From that time the tone of the journal to the other Esther becomes gradually colder. The ascendancy of his mind, for it could scarcely have been his person, looking out of those clear azure eyes, became again apparent. Whether originally dazzled by his reputation, and actuated by the vanity of sharing it, or that there was something really attractive even to the young and fair, as well as to men, in the gentler side of that rugged nature, the pupil soon manifested a warmer feeling than his lessons were calculated to inspire. On that discovery, the mentor describes himself as having

> Felt within him rise
> Shame, disappointment, guilt, surprise.

He pretended at first not to understand, and afterwards tried the power of raillery. In the poem of "Cadenus and Vanessa," one of the most elaborate of his metrical pieces, which he wrote on the occasion, he affects to make light of the capricious choice by which

> "Vanessa, not in years a score,
> Dreams of a gown of forty-four."

In the form of a mythological fable, he represents Venus and the Graces as having showered their favours on the infant Vanessa; and Pallas being induced, by a stratagem of the former, to bestow upon her, in addition, masculine judgment and wit. A young lady of twenty would be free indeed from vanity if she failed to be elated with such flattery from one of the very foremost wits of his age. But Vanessa, notwithstanding, would have liked a more definite answer, which he evaded. In this state matters remained until he retired to Ireland, when, with the feeling of the earlier, and perhaps in some respects superior claims he had upon him there, in order to save him probably from the trouble of any further complication, he endeavoured to disengage himself more distinctly from any tie, and offered her only the most distant friendship. But it was too late.

For several following years he gave himself up to study and retirement, of which that former tie was the chief solace. On what understanding, implied or expressed, Stella first went to Ireland, it is impossible to say ; though the mere fact of a young lady of eighteen giving up her family and country for the society of one individual, would of itself imply something ulterior. In the journal, however, which he forwarded her from the latter part of 1710, we have the means of judging in some degree at a later period. He associates her in all his plans of life, and there is an implied union of interests : " I would make M.D. and me easy, and I never desired more,"—M.D. being a cipher which, for some reason, he used for Stella. In the early part he protests that he had never had a happy day since he left her ; that nothing would rejoice him so much as when he returned, and that " he loved her more than his life, a thousand, thousand times." Dr Wilde is of opinion that, but for his prolonged residence in London, and had there been no impediment to their union, " he would probably have married Stella,"*—that is, we suppose, in the ordinary sense. But at the time of his going to London she had been nine or ten years in Ireland. Swift was turned of

---

* " Closing Years of Swift's Life," p. 114.

thirty when she first arrived, and was in quite sufficiently good circumstances to have married—certainly very much better than when, some years previously, he was so urgent with Miss Waryng (Varina) to carry out their engagement. At length, a clergyman of the name of Tisdall made proposals to Stella, which she referred to Swift, and which he got rid of by imposing unreasonable or impossible conditions. But this evidently riveted her claims upon him. Indeed, except to bring his own affair to an issue, such a reference from a woman of mature age was wholly uncalled for. She might have consulted him as a friend herself, but to give him the power of a veto, was evidently an appeal to his generosity, or rather his sense of justice. He denied to others the happiness he had not the heart to enjoy himself. But this, we may suppose, in addition to her suspicion of a rival in Vanessa, induced him to resort to a miserable compromise, which deprived her of the prospect of a happy home in any other quarter, and without the hope of sharing his, without any position in the eyes of the world but one of the most equivocal appearance towards himself. He consented to a private marriage in the year 1716, of which the ceremony is said to have been performed in the deanery garden, without witnesses, by Dr St George Ashe, formerly his college tutor, then bishop of Clogher.* Such an un-

* Of this, however, there is no positive evidence, though the fact is sufficiently confirmed by the tacit admission of his intimate friends, Drs Delany and Sheridan, and various other circumstances. It was first made public in the work of Lord Orrery on Swift, some years after his death. Of the various reasons assigned for his not acknowledging it, Lord Orrery attributed it to pride. He could not, in his opinion, endure the thought of acknowledging the daughter of Sir W. Temple's servant. But this was a mistake, though her mother did afterwards marry a Mr Moss, not a menial servant, but who had held the respectable situation of steward to Temple. It is said he had himself stated his having long

natural position could not of course accord with the reasonable expectations of any woman, and by any one of spirit such an equivocal position must have been keenly felt. Stella appears to have pined away, and her health, spirits, and beauty to have been greatly impaired. Swift was her laureate; and in his birthday verses to her for 1720 he says—

> "Now, this is Stella's case, in fact,
> An angel's face a little crack'd;
> Could poets or could painters fix
> How angels look at thirty-six."

In the year following his private marriage with Stella, Vanessa, who, in the meantime, had lost her mother and all her family but one invalid sister, who died soon after, went to Ireland. After some time, she took up her residence at Marley Abbey, her property, near Celbridge, a village a few miles from Dublin. She renewed her advances to him. Swift endeavoured to persuade her to leave Ire-

resolved not to marry until he had a certain income, nor after an age when he would have a prospect of seeing a family provided for. Lastly, the article revived by Dr Wilde, and previously referred to, not merely makes Stella Temple's daughter, which might have been the case, but endeavours to complicate the affair, and to account for Swift's conduct by giving him the same relationship, which is utterly incredible. The magazine writer says, "When she thought proper to communicate to her friends the Dean's proposal, and her approbation of it, it then became absolutely necessary for that person, who alone knew the secret history of the parties concerned, to reveal what might otherwise have been buried in oblivion."—(*Closing Years of Swift*, p. 113.) The person referred to we may suppose to have been her companion, Mrs Dingley. It was evidently not consistent with a secret and merely ceremonial marriage that she should have openly announced it to her friends, nor the making known of the secret history with the dissatisfaction she felt at it not being acknowledged. If the person who was in possession of this secret history, whoever it may have been, told it *before* the marriage, it would have *prevented* it; if *after*, then it does not explain the fact of the marriage having been merely ceremonial. This ingeniously concocted piece of gossip, then, completely fails (even if true) as an exculpation of Swift.

land. He also tried the experiment of inducing her to fix her affections elsewhere. She resisted him in both. Notwithstanding his sternness to her at times, he could not resist the pathetic and passionate ardour of her appeals to him, and visited her occasionally in her retirement; an event which she is said to have always marked by planting a laurel with her own hand. Of course to one so interested, the fact of Swift's intimacy with her rival was not likely to remain long a secret. Unable longer to endure suspense, and resolved to know the cause of his cruelty to her, she at length wrote to Stella to know the nature of her relations with the Dean. Indignant that he should have given any one the right to interrogate her on the subject, Stella inclosed the note to Swift, and without seeing him, went on a visit to the house of a friend in the country. On receipt of the fatal document, Swift rode out to Celbridge, and entering the room where Vanessa was sitting, with that terrible look which he assumed when angry, flung down a packet on the table, and strode out without uttering a word. The poor creature, as soon as she had sufficiently recovered her composure, opened the packet, and found it only to contain her own note to Stella. It was her death-warrant. Her perturbation of mind brought on a fever, of which she died a few weeks after, in the autumn of 1723. She had previously altered a will formerly made in Swift's favour, leaving her property, amounting to L.8000, to strangers, and directing the publication of the poem in which he had celebrated her merits. The event and the publication together gave a great shock to both Swift and Stella. He suddenly left town, and made a journey southwards, nor was he heard of for two months. Whilst the poem, which was one of the most considerable from the pen of Swift, was a general topic of conversation, some visitors casually came to the house where she was stopping, and without knowing her, remarked in her presence, " What a wonderful woman Vanessa must have been to have inspired the Dean to write so in her praise!" " She was not so sure of that," was her reply, " since we know that the Dean has written very finely on a broomstick."

Swift, after having long refrained from interference in public matters, in the year 1720 published a " Proposal for the Universal Use of Irish Manufactures," which harmless, if not laudable, as it seems, the English manufacturers had so much influence with the Government as to cause the printer to be prosecuted. The notoriety of this, of course, caused a great accession of popularity to the writer. Four years after, an opportunity occurred for striking a memorable blow at the administration. The occasion of this was a patent granted by a former ministry to one Wood for a copper coinage for Ireland, the deficiency in the existing one being a source of inconvenience. This called forth the celebrated " Drapier's Letters" by Swift, " those brazen monuments of his fame," as Lord Orrery styles them, so called from the fictitious signature assumed. The writer, by denouncing the coin as base metal, which it was ruinous to receive, and the patent as a scandalous job, was so successful in raising a general opposition to the new currency, that it was ultimately withdrawn. Considered as an extraordinary triumph of wit, it was complete. But though even Johnson, no doubt from the want of accurate information, appears to give his applause, and his representation is almost invariably taken for granted in every notice of

Swift, a candid consideration of the subject can only lead to the conclusion of his factious motives, and the sophistry of his reasoning, even if his facts were correct, which they were not.* What should we say to a crusade against the Bank of England or Ireland on the ground that their notes were of no intrinsic value? In copper coin especially the intrinsic value can be a matter of the least possible moment so long as it is a legal tender. But in a country which found so few friends and champions, motives were not to be narrowly scanned, and it was the prelude to the statement of more important and real grievances. Above all, he taught the people to know their own strength, and their gratitude was unbounded. From that time he may be said to have possessed almost the power of a dictator. A reward of L.300 had been offered without success by the Government for the discovery of the author. A characteristic anecdote is related in reference to it. His butler alone, who transcribed the MS., was in the secret. Soon after the appearance of the proclamation, he had remained out all night, and there was reason to fear that he had been tempted to claim the reward. On his return the Dean ordered him to strip off his livery and leave the house, saying that he thought he was in his power, and would submit to his misconduct. The man very humbly made confession of his fault, and intreated that he might not be exposed to such a temptation. But the Dean was inexorable. When the term of the proclamation was expired, he returned, and Swift, calling in the other servants, told them they were no longer to call the butler by

* See notice of Walpole, vol. ii., p. 251.

his Christian name as formerly, but Mr Blakeney, verger of St Patrick's.

Two years after, (1726,) with the prestige of his recent political triumph, and carrying with him the matter of his greatest literary one, in the manuscript of Gulliver, Swift paid a visit to England, the first since the death of Queen Anne. The greater part of that summer he spent with Pope. On this occasion of revisiting the scenes of his former political triumphs and final discomfiture, something of hope and ambition seems to have revived. He waited on Sir R. Walpole, ostensibly with the view of representing to him, in an impartial manner, the affairs of Ireland, but without any result; and he was favourably received at Leicester House, where the Prince and Princess of Wales held their court. But the news of the alarming illness of Stella hastened his return to Ireland, where, on his arrival, he had the satisfaction of finding her much improved. On the 1st of November appeared, anonymously as usual, the "Travels of Gulliver," the reception of which was such that the impression was exhausted in a week. Gay, who singularly enough does not appear to have been in the secret, though evidently with strong suspicions of the authorship, wrote him that it was universally read from the Cabinet Council to the nursery. Arbuthnot, who was in the secret, told him it was likely to have as great a run as John Bunyan, and mentioned a story of a master of a vessel who said he knew Gulliver well, but that he lived at Wapping, and not at Rotherhithe, as stated. No other production of Swift's pen has contributed so much to his fame with posterity. It is at once a book for children and philosophers; but its wonderful imagination and wit, especially in the latter part, are tainted with the writer's misanthropic views; and a satire carried so far as to amount to a libel upon human nature, equally discreditable to him as a man and an author.

In the following spring, (1727,) Stella's improved health appearing to warrant his absence, he again crossed the channel. With still heightened reputation, and in the flush of his greatest literary triumph, the welcomes and congratulations of his friends and all circles he frequented were showered upon him, and he was received in a very flattering manner at Leicester House by the Princess of Wales. He once more indulged hopes of English preferment; and these were increased by the anticipated dismissal of the minister on the death of the King, in consequence of the misunderstanding in which he had been involved with the Prince by the quarrel between the father and son. But Walpole found means to confirm his power, and the anticipated result failed. Three days after the accession of the Prince of Wales and Princess Caroline, Swift attended court and kissed hands. He had meantime employed his prolonged visit, again extending to several months, in conjunction with Pope, with whom he resided, as previously, to such good effect, that the result appeared in three volumes of joint "Miscellanies" in prose and verse, which were published in the course of the summer and the following spring. As Pope had the management of the publication, some of his contributions, particularly the "Treatise of the Bathos," with the notes appended to it, which drew on him the attacks of the lesser poets and writers, were probably inserted without the knowledge or against the judgment of Swift. He had previously written him, disapproving on policy of such provocations, with which Pope appeared at the time to agree. He also included his satire of Atticus (on Addison) which Swift is said to have been displeased with him for writing.

In the autumn he made a pretext of business to change to London, having had an attack of his giddiness, and thinking two sick friends too much in one house. After about a month spent there he was again hurried back to Ireland by intelligence of the relapse of Stella. She survived, however, two or three months, but died at the close of the following January. Swift, who was still unwell himself, was not present. "He would not," he said, "for the universe be present at such a trial as seeing her depart." And writing to a friend of the probability of his own recovery, he asks to what advantage? after "the loss of that person for whose sake only life was worth preserving." In his character of her, written immediately after her decease, he says, "She was sickly from her childhood till about the age of fifteen, but then grew into perfect health, and was looked upon as one of the most beautiful, graceful, and agreeable young women in London, only a little too fat. Her hair was blacker than a raven, and every feature in perfection. She had a gracefulness somewhat more than human in every motion, word, and action."

A very interesting anecdote referring to the close of her life has been differently related, if indeed the different versions refer to exactly the same time; but even the variations show how the concealment of her marriage preyed upon her mind. The first version is given by Swift's biographer, Sheridan, on the authority of his father, Dr Sheridan, who was the intimate friend of Swift, and one of Stella's executors. It represents Swift, in reply to her earnest appeal that their marriage might be acknowledged, "in order to put it out of the power of slander to be busy with her fame after death," as sullenly walking out of the room without reply. This, it is added, "threw Mrs Johnson into unspeakable agonies, and for a time she sank under so cruel a disappointment. But, soon after, roused by indignation, she inveighed against his cruelty in the bitterest terms." The other version rests on the authority of Mrs Whiteway, an intimate friend, as reported by Mr Theophilus Swift; and one would gladly hope may be the more accurate account. Towards the close of her life, when in a very weakly state, she had gone in a chair to the deanery. Becoming very faint, she had lain down. The dean had prepared some mulled wine, and sitting beside her holding her hand, addressed her in the most affectionate terms. After a little time Mrs Whiteway, out of politeness, retired to the adjoining room, leaving the door partially open for the air, while Swift and the invalid conversed in a low tone. Though above indulging any idle curiosity, she could not avoid overhearing the dean say, in reply to some remark by Stella, "Well, my dear, if you wish it, it shall be owned." To which the latter answered with a sigh, "It is too late." The subject to which these remarks referred, though not mentioned, can admit of little doubt.*

By the death of Stella, Swift was bereft of his chief solace in life. He felt the want of company, but his deafness increasing, disqualified him for it; whilst the growing

---

* Scott's "Memoirs of Swift," p. 354.

asperity of his temper, and his parsimonious disposition, drove away his friends. To aggravate his position, his eyesight began to fail, and with his usual inflexibility he adhered to a resolution which, for some unaccountable reason, he had formed against the use of glasses. Thus his last remaining resource of reading was cut off. Exercise alone was left him; and this he carried to excess, as he had always done contrary to advice, and consequently greatly reduced his system. Yet in the following year, he appears to have seriously contemplated a return to politics as a diversion of his discontent and want of excitement. His friend, Bolingbroke, notwithstanding the favour shown him in withdrawing the proceedings against him, and afterwards restoring his property, had joined in the most violent and factious opposition to the Minister who had conferred those favours, though at first professing to devote himself in retirement to philosophy and agriculture. In a remarkable letter which Swift wrote him in the year 1729, after dwelling with censure on the politics of the day, he says, " I will come in person to England, if I am provoked, and send for the dictator from the plough." He then expresses the wish that he should receive such a commission, and "not die here in a rage like a poisoned rat in a hole." He acknowledges that, in default of this, he "loves *la bagatelle* better than ever ;" and adds the startling confession, "I am forced to play at small game, to set the beasts here a-madding, merely for want of better game." What a commentary on his boasted patriotism, and how uncharitable it would have seemed if such a reflection had come from any pen but his own!

His feelings at this period are strikingly indicated by the

productions of his pen, and by allusions in his correspondence. In a letter to Pope, in June 1731, he complains of his lowness of spirits, and adds, "I am growing less patient with solitude, and harder to be pleased with company, which I could formerly better digest when I could be easier without it than at present." The close of the same year produced those remarkable verses on his own death, which, notwithstanding the satire, if they were not written with suffused eyes, are well calculated to produce them in a thoughtful reader. The "Legion Club," a tremendous satire on the Irish Parliament, in like manner displays the excessive irritability and violence of his temper. In 1736, whilst engaged in writing it, he was seized with one of his attacks of the head, of so severe a nature as obliged him to refrain from any serious or prolonged mental exertion in future. Yet in the following year he inflicted that merciless satire on Bettesworth, a sergeant-at-law, whose offence was that he had taken part in Parliament in favour of some measure which tended to cut down the fees of the clergy. Swift, with a two-edged weapon, wreaked his vengeance at once on the Dissenters and the lawyer for equally daring to have an opinion of their own. Speaking of the presumption of the former in considering themselves as brother Protestants and fellow-Christians, he says,—

> "Thus at the bar the booby Bettesworth,
> Though half a crown o'erpays his sweat's-worth,
> Who knows of law, nor text, nor margent,
> Calls Singleton his brother sergeant."

The lawyer, who was a pompous sort of man, was naturally furious, and made somewhat inflated vows of vengeance on the Dean. He went and called upon him, and, being shown up, introduced himself, saying, "Mr Dean, I am Sergeant Bettesworth." "Indeed," said the Dean, "of what regiment, pray?" He got rid of acknowledging the authorship by pleading the advice of eminent lawyers whom he had known in his youth, not to do so in such cases. But he confessed that his victim showed more wit than he had given him credit for, by comparing him to one of his own Yahoos who bespattered all mankind from a position of security. In the same year, he wrote to Dr Sheridan, "My friends have all forsaken me, except Mrs Whiteway, who preserves some pity for my condition, and a few others, who love wine that costs them nothing."

In this state, suffering much from despondency, he continued for the next few years; and feeling the burden of life so much that he would take leave of a friend after a day pleasantly spent without any disagreeable occurrence, saying, "Well, God bless you, good night; and I hope I shall never see you again." On one occasion, a heavy pier-glass fell on the spot where he had been the moment previously, and on being congratulated on his narrow escape, said, "I am sorry for it." In the year 1740 he settled his affairs, and put the last hand to his will. His memory was much impaired. Writing to Mrs Whiteway, he says, "I hardly understand one word I write. I am sure my days will be very few; few and miserable they must be. If I do not blunder, it is Saturday, July 26, 1740. If I live till Monday, I shall hope to see you, perhaps for the last time."

From this time the bright luminary of his reason suffered an eclipse, and set in darkness and gloom. In the following year, being incapable of managing his affairs, it was found necessary to have guardians appointed for the purpose. The last person he knew was Mrs Whiteway, as appears from a letter of hers, dated November 1742. He continued to walk ten hours a day. His food, which was served up to him cut, he would not touch if the servant remained in the room, and would leave perhaps for an hour. At one time his left eye swelled to the size of an egg, and mortification of the lid was feared. The pain was so intense that five attendants for a week had difficulty in restraining him from tearing it out. At the same time large boils appeared upon his arms and body. He remained for a long period in a lethargic condition. He had, however, intervals of returning consciousness, and sometimes made great efforts to speak; but being unable to find words, appeared greatly distressed, would sigh heavily, shrug his shoulders, and shake his head. After he had remained silent a whole year, his housekeeper going in to tell him it was his birthday, (November 30) and that the populace were preparing bonfires and illuminations, as usual, to celebrate it, he said, "It is all folly! they had better let it alone." Sometimes he would call his servant by name, and once after much uneasiness at not finding words to express himself, said, impatiently, "I'm a fool." But it is remarked by his relative and biographer, Mr Deane Swift, that *he never*, that he heard of, *talked nonsense*, or *said a foolish thing*. During one of his intervals of consciousness, he was taken out for an airing in the park, and observing a building that was new to him, asked what it was. Being informed that it was an ammunition magazine. "Oh," he said, "let me make a note of that," producing his pocket-book—"my tablets, as Hamlet says." He then put down in pencil the last lines he ever wrote :—

> "Behold a proof of Irish sense—
> Here Irish wit is seen!
> With nothing left that's worth defence,
> We build a magazine."

After a prolonged continuance in this melancholy state, he was released from his sufferings at the close of 1745, in the 78th year of his age, leaving the bulk of his property, amounting to ten or twelve thousand pounds, to endow the hospital for diseases of the mind which bears his name. According to Dr Wilde, his disease originated in *cerebral congestion*, popularly termed fulness of blood to the head. On a *post-mortem* examination, the skull was found to be charged with water, arising from softening of the brain. A member of his chapter had suspected this, and proposed his being trepanned.

Having so far exceeded our proposed limits, we cannot dwell on the personal or literary character of Swift. Of the former—which appears a mass of contradictions—it may be stated on the bright side, that in the period of his political influence he exerted himself in the most active manner in recommending all persons of literary merit to those in authority, without reference to their politics—and that, though, in a letter to Mr Pulteney in 1737, he expressed his detestation of a philanthropus as being "now a creature (taking a vast majority) that I hate more than a toad, a viper, a wasp, a stork, a fox, or any other that you will please to add"—yet he gave regularly a fixed proportion of his income in charity, and kept several hundred pounds floating in small loans to poor tradesmen and basket women.

It seems that what Steele had said to Swift relative to retiring from public employment was no mere bravado, as appears from the following letter, written little more than a week after, in which he gave in his resignation as a Commissioner of Stamps :—

LETTER CCIX.   *To the Right Honourable the [Earl of Oxford,]*
Lord High Treasurer of Great Britain.

Bloomsbury Square, June 4, 1713.

MY LORD,—I presume to give your Lordship this trouble to acquaint you that, having an ambition to serve in the ensuing Parliament, I humbly desire your Lordship will please to accept of my resignation of my office as Commissioner of the Stamp Revenue.

I should have done this sooner, but that I heard the commission was passing without my name in it, and I would not be guilty of the arrogance of resigning what I could not hold. But having heard this since contradicted, I am obliged to give it up, as with great humility I do by this present writing. Give me leave on this occasion to say something as to my late conduct with relation to the late men in power, and to assure you, whatever I have done, said, or written, has proceeded from no other motive but the love of what I think truth. For, merely as to my own affairs, I could not wish any man in the administration, rather than yourself, who favour those that become your dependants with a greater liberality of heart than any man I have ever before observed. When I had the honour of a short conversation with you, you were pleased not only to signify to me that I should remain in this office, but to add, that if I would name to you one of more value, which would be more commodious to me, you would favour me in it. I am going out of any particular dependence on your Lordship; and will tell you, with the freedom of an indifferent man, that it is impossible for any man who thinks, and has any public spirit, not to tremble at seeing his country, in its present circumstances, in the hands of so daring a genius as yours. If incidents should arise that should place your own safety, and what ambitious men call greatness, in a balance against the general good, our all depends upon your choice under such a temptation. You have my hearty and fervent prayers to Heaven to avert all such dangers from you. I thank your Lordship for the regard and distinction which you have at sundry times showed me; and

1713.] *Resignation of Commissionership.* 419

wish you, with your country's safety, all happiness and prosperity. Share, my Lord, your good fortune with whom you will. While it lasts, you will want no friends ; but if any adverse day happens to you, and I live to see it, you will find I think myself obliged to be your friend and advocate. This is talking in a strange dialect from a private man to the first of a nation ; but to desire only a little exalts a man's condition to a level with those who want a great deal. But I beg your Lordship's pardon ; and am, with great respect, my Lord, your Lordship's most obedient and most humble servant, RICHARD STEELE.

There can be no mistake in this bold and manly letter as an indication of something in the wind, either prophetically anticipated by Steele or founded on rumour. With regard to his resignation, Swift, in a pamphlet in which he entered the lists against him (though anonymously) and with no sparing hand, remarks,—" 1. A new commission was every day expected for the stampt-paper, and he knew his name would be left out, and therefore his resignation would have an appearance of virtue cheaply bought. 2. He dreaded the violence of creditors, against which his employments were no manner of security. 3. Being a person of great sagacity, he hath some foresight of a change from the usual age of a ministry which is now almost expired ; from the little misunderstandings that have been reported sometimes to happen among the men in power ; from the Bill of Commerce being rejected,"* &c.

LETTER CCX.   *To Mrs Steele.*

Tonson's, June 6, 1713.

DEAR PRUE,—I shall not come home to dinner ; but, if you will call here at six o'clock, we will take the air together.—Yours more than you can imagine or I express, RICH. STEELE.

---

* " Importance of the *Guardian* considered," &c.

LETTER CCXI. *To Mrs Steele.*

June 10, 1713.

DEAR PRUE,—I send herewith the copy of the settlement, which lay at Frodan's, but cannot find my deed among his papers, which relates to Barbadoes. He himself is light-headed.—Your affectionate obedient,

RICH. STEELE.

LETTER CCXII. *To Mrs Steele.*

June 20, 1713.

DEAR PRUE,—To keep things in order from that quarter, I am gone to Highgate to dinner; have been pretty successful this morning. Send for *Queer-ones* to keep you company. At night we will talk over all.—Your faithful, affectionate husband, RICH. STEELE.

Since the above, I have received a message from Mr Addison, who put off the meeting with Mr Ashurst, and has engaged me to meet some Whig lords. In the evening at six you shall know where I am.

LETTER CCXIII. *To Mrs Steele.*

July 1, 1713.

DEAR PRUE,—If you please to be in readiness about one o'clock, I will send you word where I shall be, and go with you to Mr Hoole's* to see the entry.† I have discharged Hugh, and have his receipt.—Your most affectionate, faithful husband, RICH. STEELE.

I have given his black cloaths,‡ for I will never strip a servant.

---

* A stationer next door to Ludgate Church, as we learn from a subsequent note.

† "This was the public entry of the Duke D'Aumont, the French Ambassador, who came this day in state from Greenwich to the Tower by water, and afterwards paraded, in a style of great splendour, through the city to Somerset House, where he was magnificently entertained till the day of his public audience, the 4th of July, when he proceeded to St James's in the same form as was observed at his entry. A full and curious account of the whole solemnity may be seen in the *Political State* for 1713, vol. vi., p. 34."

‡ "The mourning probably for his mother."

LETTER CCXIV.   *To Mrs Steele.*

July 2, 1713.

DEAR PRUE,—I wish you a good journey; take care of yourself, and expect to find me at home to receive you to-morrow evening.—Your most humble servant,   RICH. STEELE.

LETTER CCXV.   *To Mrs Steele.*

July 10, 1713.

DEAR PRUE,—This is only to acquaint you that I have almost finished my vexations; and I shall, from to-morrow, be in a regular and methodical way.

You are my pride, my pleasure, my ambition, and all that is agreeble to your affectionate and faithful husband,   RICH. STEELE.

LETTER CCXVI.   *To Mrs Steele.*

July 13, 1713.

DEAR TYRANT,—I have seen Carpenter this morning, and he says it is all one to him, we may keep the woman in the house; so that what you have to do, is only to get linen, &c., bundled up against evening. You shall hear from me again about five o'clock. I beg of you to govern me as gently as you can, for you have full power over your affectionate, constant, obedient husband,   RICH. STEELE.

LETTER CCXVII.   *To Mrs Steele.*

July 22, 1713.

I write because I hear you give yourself up to lamentation.* You have, indeed, no cause for it; and I beseech you to repose the confidence in me which is deserved from you by your affectionate and tender husband,

RICH. STEELE.

---

* " Within a month after the date of this letter he was elected member for Stockbridge; and, strange to tell, the election of *poor Dick* was followed up by a petition against it on the score of bribery!—See 'Journals of the House of Commons,' March 3, 1713-14. As Steele was expelled the 17th on another business, the petition was of course withdrawn April 17, 1714."

LETTER CCXVIII.   *To Mrs Steele.*
                                       July 27, 1713.
DEAR WIFE,—If you please to call at Button's,* we will go together to Brompton.—Yours ever,   RICH. STEELE.

LETTER CCXIX.   *To Mrs Steele.*
                                       July 30, 1713.
DEAR PRUE,—If you have not secured Morgan Davies at dinner, I would dine in Paul's Churchyard, in order to go to Tryon after change.—Yours ever,   RICH. STEELE.

I will be at home at five, therefore do not send for me here except Davies is with you.

LETTER CCXX.   *To Mrs Steele.*
                                       Sept. 29, 1713.
DEAR PRUE,—I have settled all things to great satisfaction, and desire you would stay at home, but send the coach for me to come to you, to take the air and talk farther.—Yours,   RICH. STEELE.

LETTER CCXXI.   *To Mrs Steele.*
                       Bloomsbury Square, Dec. 24, 1713.
DEAR PRUE,—I dine with Lord Halifax, and shall be at home half hour after six.

For thee I die, for thee I languish.   RICH. STEELE.

---

* "Button, who had been a servant in the Countess of Warwick's family, kept a coffeehouse on the south side of Russell Street, about two doors from Covent Garden, and was under the patronage of Addison. Here it was that the wits of the time used to assemble. It is said, when Addison had suffered any vexation from the countess, he withdrew the company from Button's house.—*Johnson's 'Lives of the Poets.'*"

END OF VOL. I.

BALLANTYNE, ROBERTS, AND CO., PRINTERS, PAUL'S WORK, EDINBURGH.

www.ingramcontent.com/pod-product-compliance
Lightning Source LLC
Chambersburg PA
CBHW032007300426
44117CB00008B/927